ALSO BY JUANITA TISCHENDORF

Who Says I'm Small
Til Death Do Us Part?
The Madman The Marathoner

Juanita Tischendorf

An UnFair Advantage
(A Murder In Oklahoma)

An UnFair Advantage
(A Murder In Oklahoma)

By Juanita Tischendorf

THIS IS A J. TISCHENDORF BOOK
PUBLISHED BY J TISCHENDORF SERVICES

www.lulu.com

Library of Congress Cataloging in-Publication Data
Tischendorf, Juanita, [date]
An Unfair Advantage / Juanita Tischendorf – 1st ed.
p.   cm.

NonFiction

Published in the United States of America

ISBN: 978-1-928613-85-5

Dedication

This book is dedicated to Erik Saxton, my son who I will miss every day of my life. An UnFair Advantage is the story of an unnecessary murder that took place in Oklahoma in 2010 and the Oklahoma criminal justice system that acted quickly and effectively in solving the crime and imposing a just penalty.

TABLE OF CONTENTS

ACKNOWLEDGEMENT

I would like to express my gratitude to the many people who saw me through this book; to all those who provided support, talked things over, read, wrote, offered comments, and assisted in the editing, proofreading and design.

I would like to thank God for enabling me to have the strength to know that though I will never recover from the loss of my son, I can learn to accept and go on.

I am heartily thankful to my husband, Mark Tischendorf, whose encouragement, guidance and support from the initial to the final level enabled me to complete this book.

Thanks to my family, who always understand and know what I need to hear.

Thanks to my friends and to those of Erik's who helped by offering their love and providing precious stories of times they had shared with my son.

Thanks to Detective Lyndell Easley of the OCPD, Homicide Unit who was always available to answer questions or point me in the right direction.

Thanks to Jennifer Austin of the Cleveland County, Oklahoma City Assistant District Attorney office for not only her excellent defense of my son, Erik Saxton, but for her understanding of my need to stay involved.

Thanks to Kerrin Jones of the DA office in Oklahoma, for giving of her time to explain details of the court system and to provide the website addresses that kept me up to date on the case.

A special thanks to Jane Glenn Cannon of News OK in Oklahoma who not only published information on the case, but who was so willing to share personal information that helped form a bond between us.

Finally for the news media who did personal interviews and presented tasteful details on their stations. Thank you Alexa

Arnold of 13 WHAM-TV, Berkeley Beam of WHEC-TV, YNN News in Rochester NY, and News 9; Oklahoma's Own.

Last and not least: I beg forgiveness of all those who have been with me over the course of the years and whose names I have failed to mention.

INTRODUCTION

I want to tell you a story about hope and despair, about wants and needs and about love and death. Over the course of my life I recorded what was wonderful and I recorded what was hard to overcome because writing was what it took to help my mind accept what it had to accept and prepare for what might happen later.

You may think that I have primed myself to be strong and accept what would come to pass, but in reality, no amount of preparation can keep you from being knocked off your feet at that last moment. No matter how strong, no matter how much support there is, it can never be enough because it will take you by surprise and feel like someone punched you in the stomach without giving you prior warning. Yet, slowly, and I mean slowly, time does heal all wounds and life goes on, not as planned, but bearable.

PREFACE

Over the past years this country has watched its share of criminal trials and the intense public interest only continues year after year as more dramatized cases catch the interest of the media and the public.

I am going to tell you about a murder that made mention in a few papers, a few local television coverages in Rochester, New York, Oklahoma City, Oklahoma and a splash of coverage on the internet.

This story has all the ingredients for sensationalizing. There is a victim who is black, a dwarf and is partially paralyzed. There is a murderer who is almost 6 feet, female and white. Then there is the need to understand all the underlying pieces that lead to this outcome. So why was this life altering story passed over.

There is one reason that this crime did not become a news sensation. Though not a headliner, this story involved outstanding police work. It is a great example of how diligence and proper procedures lead to a conviction in short order. It shows how having open channels can result in the right outcome for all concerned.

Admittedly I am not an authority on criminal investigations, but I became learned on this case from beginning to end as the mother of Erik and later as the parent who needed to tell his story.

Throughout the case it was always evident that the matter was being handled judiciously and once I obtained the files and interview films I could see for myself the talent of all those involved at the beginning, middle and end of the case.

This case was not a headliner, but this book has given me a new respect for the law and those who uphold it. I admit at first I was afraid that there would not be justice for Erik, and I wanted this to play out in the media so that it wouldn't get swept under the carpet. But I needn't have worried.

I need to write this book to have closure because it is what I have always done. But I also need to write this book to show that for all the unscrupulous publicity police forces across the country have manifested, there are some police forces that do their job by the book no matter what color the victim may be.

I am Erik Saxton's mother and I miss him every day. I miss knowing I can pick up the phone and talk to him or plan a trip to visit him in Oklahoma City. For me this was not only personal, but a very important case to warrant coverage.

As an author I was supplied with the case files which included the 911 call, officer reports that covered what they were dispatched to do, what they found, and the investigation that followed. It took some time before I was able to look through those files and watch the recorded interviews, but once I did I knew that I was lucky to have Oklahoma City representing my son.

So why didn't this case catch the fancy of the media? Simply because the case was handled with the best investigation, capture of the guilty party and respect for the murdered victim. That does not draw media attention.

CHAPTER 1: THE 911 CALL

(SEPTEMBER 16, 2010)

Alexander Graham Bell once stated that "before anything else, preparation is the key to success." In times of an emergency, preparation can be the difference between a minor problem and a major fiasco and that stresses the importance of the 911 call. The number "911" is the universal emergency number and such calls provide invaluable clues to investigators because the caller, in fact, may have committed the crime. Homicide calls to 911 are unique. They originate from distressed callers confronted with urgent life-and-death situations. These initial contacts can contain the most valuable statements since they are the least contaminated by outside influence. Later the suspect attempts to conceal the truth, attorneys' will advise them to remain silent, and investigators' will present them with leading questions. Fortunately, 911 calls are recorded. Therefore, investigators have access to the transcript and the actual call which contain important evidence. They can examine both the words and the tone of voice and later an analysis of the calls can provide investigators with immediate insight and interviewing strategies to help solve homicide cases.

###

On September 16, 2010 at around 9:30 a.m. the following call comes into the 911 Dispatch.

Operator: 911, what is your emergency

Caller: Yeah I need an ambulance.

Operator: Let me connect you, Hold on.

Caller: Okay. (Phone is ringing)

Operator: What is the address of the emergency?

Caller: Ah, it's 3042 SW 89th

Operator: 3042 SW 89th

Caller: Yes, it's the Hunt Apartments.

Operator: Give me just a moment. My ticket didn't go over to the cab.

Caller: I'm sorry,

Operator: No that's okay; it's not your fault. Give me a moment to get it to the radio. Do I need to take NW or SW?

Caller: Ma'am, I'm sorry, its SW 89th I believe it is 3042

Operator: Since you are on a cell phone please repeat the whole address so I can make sure I have it correct.

Caller: 3042 SW 89th

Operator: And is this an apartment

Caller: Yes, it's letter E

Operator: What is the name of the apartment?

Caller: The Hunt Apartments

Operator: Do we need a building number?

Caller: Its letter E. It's the first apartment when you come into the complex

Operator: Is the address the building number, 3042?

Caller: I don't know Ma'am. I'm a friend, I am living with a disabled man and he is on the floor and I don't know if he is breathing.

Operator: Okay what is the cell phone number you are calling from?

Caller: (Caller gives the cell number.0

Operator: We do have help on the way. You are with him now?

Caller: Yes I am.

Operator: How old is he?

Caller: I don't know, about my age 38, 39

Operator: Is he awake?

Caller: No, (she starts calling out to him)

Operator: How is he laying; is he on his back?

Caller: No, he's on his stomach

Operator: Roll him over on his back and then check to see if he is breathing.

Caller: Erik get on your back.

Operator: If he's not responding you will need to roll him over. Is he breathing? (pause) You need to get him on his back.

Caller: He's not.

Operator: He's not breathing?

Caller: He's not responding. He's drunk. He was drinking last night. I took the bottle away from him.

Operator: Do you have him on his back?

Caller: Yes,

Operator: Okay put one hand on his forehead and the other under his neck, tilt his head back; put your ear next to his mouth. Can you hear any breathing?

Caller: He's heavy he's dead weight. (Calls out his name.) I can't ma'am. (Caller starts crying.)

Operator: You can't?

Caller: No

Operator: Okay, so you just found him this way.

Caller: Yes, after I woke up.

Operator: Okay, Is there a defibrillator available?

Caller: A defibrillator, what's that.

Operator: Okay, we have help on the way. You've got him on his back?

Caller: Yes

Operator: No pillows under his head?

Caller: No pillows?

Operator: No pillows.

Caller: No, he's flat.

Operator: Okay. Look in his mouth for food or vomit; is there anything in his mouth?

Caller: (Slight pause) No

Operator: Okay and you already put your hand on his forehead and the other under his neck and tilted his head back correct?

Caller: Yes

Operator: Okay and you still are not feeling any breathing.

Caller: I don't know. Let me put the phone down okay. (Sounds of her motion to put the phone down.)

Operator: Listen carefully. I'm going to tell you how to do chest compressions. Listen to me before we start.

Caller: I'm going to put you on speaker phone.

Operator: Okay. (Slight pause) Put the heel of your hand on his breastbone in the center of his chest right between his nipples. Put your other hand on top of that. Do you understand me so far?

Caller: Yes

Operator: Okay, Listen carefully. You will push down firmly, two inches, with the heel of your hand touching his chest.

The call last three minutes, fifty-eight seconds and ends abruptly.

During the 9-1-1 call that was made by Clara Blocker on the day after the murder, the missing element of the call is how calm and collected she begins the report and how frantic she becomes by the end.

CHAPTER 2: INVESTIGATING THE SCENE

(SEPTEMBER 16, 2010)

The crime scene investigator returns the microphone to its clip and begins the drive to the latest assignment. His investigation begins at that point because usually the radio dispatch message is brief and seldom reveals the full nature of the incident. Most often this is done to avoid attracting on-lookers and the media who may be monitoring the dispatch frequency. As the CSI turns onto the street, his first instincts kick in as he "turns on" his powers of observation. He may make a mental note of what he sees, hears and smells-or better still-records them on a digital voice recorder. His first reaction to the scene must be, "Does anything look out of place? What odors may be noticeable and are there unusual sounds

###

On Thursday, September 16, 2010 at 9:47 a.m. The investigation at the Crime Scene begins.

Sergeant Jay A. Coffey, becomes the primary officer and scene security who receives a call to perform a welfare check on a subject at 3042 SW, 89th Street, Apt. E. Unlike with searches, he does not have to obtain a warrant to do a welfare check, also called a wellness check. He knows that most welfare checks are done when someone calls and ask that a family member or friend be checked on because they have not heard from the person or believe that they may be in need of assistance.

When Sergeant Jay Coffey arrives at 9:50 a.m. he makes contact with the first responders that include Paramedic, Joanne Dornbof, and Emergency Medical Technician (EMT) Chris Lyons who have been at the scene since 9:47 a.m.[1] The EMSA -

---

[1] EMT is short for EMT-Basic, or EMT-B, and refers to a technician who has less training than an EMT-Paramedic, often simply referred to as a paramedic. EMTs and Paramedics both provide care for patients.

Oklahoma City office is located at 1111 Classen Drive, approximately 15 minutes away from the scene. The call comes into their office shortly after 9:30 a.m.

Arriving at 9:49 a.m. are first responders Brett Sutterfield, Tony Sussa, Bill Boyd and Lance Jones of the Oklahoma Fire Department located at 201 N Broadway, approximately 16 minutes from the crime scene. They inform Sergeant Jay Coffey they have checked the premises and ensure him the scene is safe.

Sergeant Jay Coffey surveys the area. He then turns his attention to the first responders who are checking the victim's airway. The victim appears to be unconscious.

"Do you have a name?" he asks

"Yes, Erik Saxton."

"How did you find the victim?" Sergeant Jay Coffey asks.

"We found him barely breathing. We checked to see if there was any visible airway blockage but found none so began CPR. We tried to get a history from the person who made the 911 call but she didn't know much about the victim. She said he was in his late 30s, didn't know if he was a diabetic or had a heart condition. She said that he did have epilepsy and took medication for that. We started an IV and we checked his pulse, blood pressure, temperature and respiratory rate. He's been unconscious since our arrival so we were unable to get an account of what happened to him."

Sergeant Jay Coffey asks, "Anything else?"

"Yes, take a look at these cuts and bruises on his body. The caller says that he falls all the time, but this looks like more than just falling. Looks more like he was beaten up. His left eye is so swollen shut that we couldn't even force it open."

Sergeant Jay Coffey leans over for a closer look, trying not to get in the way of the first responders.

The EMT says, "His pulse is weak and we can't do any more here so we are going to transport him to the Southwest Medical Center."

"You mentioned the 911 caller. Is she still here?" Sergeant Jay Coffey asks.

"Yes, I think so. She was sitting outside."

Sergeant Jay Coffey goes outside to speak to the reporting person.

Sergeant Jay Coffey walks up to the person he sees sitting outside. He introduces himself and then asks if she is the one who made the 9-1-1 call. The woman says, "Yes".

He next asks her name and she says, "Clara Blocker".

"How do you know the victim?"

"I've known Erik for about a year, but I have been living with him on and off for about a month."

Sergeant Jay Coffey ignores the fact that she hasn't answered the question and moves on.

"Tell me what happened that made you call 911."

Her answer is more thorough as she shares with Sergeant Jay Coffey that on Wednesday, September 15, at around noon, one of Erik's friends, known as Chase, had brought over a bottle of Tvarscki Vodka. Ms. Blocker says that Chase did not stay long, but that Erik began to drink the vodka. She adds that he drank all the time so it was not a big deal. She stayed in the apartment with him until around 6:30 p.m. when she left with her friend David who took her to the Cricket Store to put more minutes on her cell phone.

She has stopped talking so Sergeant Jay Coffey's asks, "So what do you think happened to him. Was he alone or with this man Chase when you left the apartment?"

Clara thinks a moment and then says, "No one was in the apartment with Erik. He was alone. I don't know what happened to him. He was like that when I returned a little after 7:30 p.m."

"Where was Erik when you returned."

"He was alone in the apartment and was standing in his bedroom leaning against the side of his bed. I saw that his eye was swollen and asked him what had happened. Erik said, 'Nothing'.

Clara adds that he was real quiet for the rest of the evening.

Sergeant Jay Coffey has listened closely to what she has said and decides to prompt her a little by saying, "The EMT thinks that Erik has been beaten. What do you think?"

Clara considers this and says, "Erik always stumbles and falls when he drinks so I think he fell and hurt himself."

"So did you stay at the apartment the rest of the evening," he asks.

Clara replies, "We stayed at the apartment until around midnight and then Erik and I walked to the 7-Eleven to get him a coke."

"Is that the 7-Eleven on S May Ave and SW 89th St"

"Yes, that's the one."

"What happened next?"

"We got the coke and walked back to the apartment and once we got back, Erik passed out."

"Where did he pass out?"

"In the living room on the floor."

"What did you do then?"

"I figured he needed to sleep it off so I left him there on the floor."

"So you left him sleeping on the floor. So why did you call 911."

"The next morning when I got up, Erik was still sleeping on the floor so I tried to wake him up but couldn't so I called 911".

That is her story. Sergeant Jay Coffey listens to what Clara has said but is not totally buying it. Now he looks at his notes, thinking about what the EMT said. The EMT's assessment is that the victim appears to have been beaten up. Sergeant Jay Coffey makes his next move. He takes out his cell and dials the OCPD located at 701 Colcord Drive, thirteen minutes away.

CHAPTER 3: A MATTER OF ASSAULT AND BATTERY (SEPTEMBER 16, 2010)

Assault and Battery are two separate offenses against a person. When they are used in one expression they are defined as unlawful and unpermitted touching of another. The main distinction between the two offenses is the existence or nonexistence of a touching or contact. While contact is an essential element of battery, there must be an absence of contact for assault.

The CSI should be expeditious and methodical and after arrival, should assess the scene and treat the incident as a crime scene. The initial responding officer should approach and enter the crime scene while remaining observant of any persons, vehicles, events, potential evidence, and environmental conditions.

In Oklahoma, assault and battery are two separate crimes but they can be charged as the single crime of "assault and battery." A wrongdoer is guilty of "assault and battery" when the act of assault culminates in a battery. This crime can be a misdemeanor or a felony in Oklahoma. Assault occurs when a person threatens or attempts to cause physical harm to another person. The threat must involve physical action like drawing a fist or charging toward a victim. Words alone are not enough. A battery is the intentional use of force against another person, causing harm or offense to the victim. Striking a person with a fist and spitting on another, both are acts that constitute battery.

###

Sergeant Jay Coffey talks with Lieutenant Shubert, filling him in on the incident and tells him that the Oklahoma Fire Department and EMSA personnel said that to them it looks like Erik has been beaten up by someone. Sergeant Jay Coffey asks him to come to the crime scene as they are getting ready to transport the victim. When he hangs up, Sergeant Jay Coffey re-enters Apartment E. Since the arrival of the first responders and Sergeant Jay Coffey, this area has been considered to be a crime scene and nothing has been disturb inside or outside the apartment.

Lieutenant Shubert arrives at 3042 SW. 89th Street, Apartment #E. at 10:00 a.m. the first responders are in the process of transporting the victim. Lieutenant Shubert goes over and takes a quick look at Erik, noting the bruises and the black eye. He moves back and watches as the first responders carefully lift Erik up and settle him on the gurney.

While Lieutenant Shubert goes over to speak to Sergeant Jay Coffey, the first responders are engrossed in readying Erik for transport. Once on the gurney, they cover him with a sheet. Carefully they wheel the gurney out of the apartment. By 10:10 a.m. they are leaving the premises.

Lieutenant Shubert, serving as the primary scene supervisor now, is in agreement with Sergeant Jay Coffey and decides to assign this to the Assaults division. He places the call.

When the Assaults division is reached, Lieutenant Shubert explains the details that have been so far disclosed on the case. At 11:13 a.m. the Assaults Division agrees with their suspicions and informs them they will take the case. They will send Lieutenant Greg Johnston.

Continuing his job as scene security while the detectives conducted their investigation, Sergeant Jay Coffey kept up the crime scene log. He also made a point of going to the management office for the Hunt Apartments. Here he asked if there were any emergency contact names and numbers on the lease. There was. The individuals listed are Juanita Tischendorf, Erik's mother, and Marilyn Goodban, a family friend. On his way back to Apartment #E, Sergeant Jay Coffey gives the names and numbers to the detectives, letting them know that the emergency contacts have not been contacted at this time.

CHAPTER 4: A HOMICIDE

(SEPTEMBER 16, 2010)

The term Homicide is the causing of death of another human being and can be classified as unintentional or intentional homicide. This is the first determination that must be made in a homicide case.

There are many different types of homicides and because they are treated differently the type needs to be determined. Such types of homicide can include murder and manslaughter. Murder is usually an intentional crime. Manslaughter is seen as voluntary when it involves hitting someone with intent to kill them, whereas involuntary manslaughter is unintentionally causing their death. In many cases, homicide may lead to life in prison or capital punishment, but if the defendant in a capital case is determined to be mentally disabled in the United States he or she cannot be executed.

###

On September 16, 2010 at 10:45 a.m. while still at the scene, Sergeant Jay Coffey receives a call from the Integris Southwest Medical Center where the first responders have taken the victim. The caller informs the Sergeant that at 10:42 a.m. Erik Saxton was pronounced dead.

The course of the investigation now takes another turn. Sergeant Jay Coffey ends the call from the medical center and immediately dials the OCPD, Homicide Division. He reaches Detective Lyndell Easley and informs him of a possible homicide at the address of 3042 SW 89th Street, Apartment E. Detective Lyndell Easley tells Sergeant Jay Coffey he is on his way.

Detective Lyndell Easley's partner, Inspector Whitebird is already investigating another case so he leaves the precinct alone and arrives at the scene at 11:10 a.m.

On his arrival Detective Lyndell Easley places a call to his partner, Inspector Whitebird and lets him know he is at the homicide scene at 3042 SW 89th Street, Apartment #E. They agree that Inspector Whitebird should go to the OCPD Homicide office while he assist CSI with the scene. This way, Inspector Whitebird will be able to conduct any interviews if needed, at the precinct. That taken care of, Detective Lyndell Easley begins his walkthrough and makes notes on the layout and contents of the crime scene.

"The location of 3042 SW 89th Street is a component of the apartment complex known as The Hunt and this property is marked with a sign on the north side that reads E-H. There is an additional sign that reads Building 42 on the south side of it. The complex is on the south side of SW 89th Street in the 3000 block. The building, 3042, is the first building on the west side of the drive into the complex and Apartment E is a one bedroom, first floor apartment, located on the NE corner of the building."

"The entry door to the apartment is constructed of steel, and is hinged on the west side. This door has the letter E affixed to it in a silver character that is approximately two inches in height and located at eye level to the average height adult. A glass storm door is installed on the door frame and this hinges on the east side. "

"On the west side of the entry door to the apartment is a small concrete patio, which is furnished with a folding chair and folding table. On the top of the table is an empty Marlboro cigarette package, a ceramic coffee cup, and a small amount of medical debris."

With the outside area description around Apartment #E completed, Detective Lyndell Easley enters the residence.

"There is a nylon duffle bag in the foyer, and a vodka bottle on the hearth in front of the fireplace. The foyer leads into the living room which is furnished with a black leather couch on the south wall, a computer table with a computer on top on the east. An end table along with a kitchen-chair and electric fan are on the east wall. The fireplace is on the west wall of the living room and there it is revealed a substance that appears to be smeared blood located on the wall to the south of the fireplace."

"There is medical debris on the floor of the living room, as well as what appears to be blood stains and fecal matter on the carpet."

"To the west of the couch, and south of the electric fan, lying on the floor is an electronic device that is a DVD player, and also a Motorola handheld radio similar to those issued to officers by OCPD."

Detective Lyndell Easley pauses the recording and then goes to talk with Sergeant Jay Coffey. He asks that he try and locate the owner of the radio.

Sergeant Jay Coffey makes some calls and catching up with Detective Lyndell Easley informs him that the radio is the property of EMSA and one of their representatives is on his way to the scene to recover this property. Detective Lyndell Easley stops to thank him.

"The living room is also furnished with a small bookcase. A black nylon backpack is sitting on the desk chair. Directly to the south of the living room and sharing an adjoining wall is the kitchen which is furnished with a stove, dishwasher, refrigerator, double sink, and microwave oven."

"The dining area is west of the kitchen and has a folding table on the south wall along with a folding ladder on the east wall."

"Down a very short hallway is the bathroom on the south side and the bedroom on the north side. In the bathroom is a clothes hamper that holds two towels, stained with what looks like blood, as well as a pink, salmon colored shirt that is wet to the touch."

"The bedroom is furnished with a queen-sized bed in the northwest corner, and a television set resting atop a wooden chest on the east wall. Two cardboard boxes containing miscellaneous items are on the south wall."

"There are little shards of glass covering the floor on the south and the east side of the bed and looking closer I can see there are shards of the same type of glass clinging to the vertical surface of the foot of the bed."

"A green throw rug is lying on the floor at the foot of the bed and on closer observation I can see a small amount of what appears to be blood staining the threshold of the bedroom door."

Detective Lyndell Easley carefully looks inside the backpack on the desk chair in the living room and finds two letters addressed to Erik Saxton at this address. One of the letters is postmarked September 7, 2010 and the other is postmarked September 13, 2010. Both letters have the return address of Teresa Stanfield who resided at 201 N. Shartel, Oklahoma City. The letter postmarked 9/07/2010 was signed, Your wife Teresa. The final line in this letter reads, "Tell E I said hi and thanx 4 takin care of my girl." The second letter has a postscript that reads, "I've been calling 886-7076." This is the telephone number that Clara provided as her own number when interviewed about this incident. It is apparent that Stanfield addressed this letter to Erik, but intended the contents to be for Clara. The letters are subsequently booked into the OCPD.

That concludes Detective Lyndell Easley's walk through.

###

There are now several personnel onsite. Along with Sergeant Jay Coffey and Lieutenant Shubert, Detective Pena arrives at 10:43 a.m., Lieutenant Greg Johnston of the Homicide Division arrives at 11:13 a.m., Detective Rob Benavides arrives at 11;17 a.m., and Detective Gary Damron arrives at 11:17 a.m.

###

Detective Lyndell Easley is aware of the crime scene progression. He knows that the incident originated as a sick call, with the reporting person, Clara Blocker. She is still at the scene when he arrives and now he turns his attention to her.

Detective Lyndell Easley makes his way outside where the suspect has been standing off to the side of the crime scene. She has a bandana tied tightly against her scalp and is wearing cut offs, a T-shirt and sandals. She is quite tall, he estimates her height at around 5' 10" or more. He knows Clara has told her story over and over again and now as he approaches, it is easy to tell she is agitated. He tries what he hopes is a different tactic.

Slowly he approaches and says, "Hello, my name is Detective Lyndell Easley. I know you have been very cooperative, but I hope you can answer just a few more questions."

Clara says, "Okay."

AN UNFAIR ADVANTAGE   BY: JUANITA TISCHENDORF

"What is your full name?"

"Clara Ann Blocker."

"And the victim; do you know his name?"

"Yes, it's Erik Saxton."

"I know you have been asked this before, but can you tell me what happened here?"

Detective Lyndell Easley has been filled in by others at the scene as to what Clara has told them. Clara changes her story. She says that Erik was drinking, quite heavily yesterday. Detective Lyndell Easley interrupts her to verify she is talking about Wednesday, September 15. She says she is and then she continues.

Clara now says that instead of him falling and hurting himself, that he was apparently assaulted and that it had to happen between 6:30 p.m. and 7:30 p.m. on Wednesday. This was the time when she was away from the apartment.

Detective Lyndell Easley knows that she has originally told Sergeant Jay Coffey that the victim had fallen, but he doesn't mention this.

"Clara, how do you know Erik?"

"I've been staying with him for almost a month now." She adds, "Can I go in and get some clothing and some of my personal items."

"Not at this moment. This is a crime scene and everything needs to remain here for now."

It is best, he feels to continue while her mind is fresh and while she is still unaware that Erik has died. Knowing this, who knows how she will respond and she might change her story. This information may stop her from answering any further questions.

Already he has obtained some pertinent information. Clara has said she is living in the apartment. Aware that she is living on the premises he asks if she would be willing to sign a search waiver to give consent for them to process the scene. He informs her that she doesn't have to consent. It is up to her.

Clara, obviously wanting to get this over with says, "Yes, go ahead".

Detective Lyndell Easley reaches into his folder and presents Clara with the search waiver paperwork and offers her a pen.

26

While she looks it over he excuses himself. Standing a little distance from her Detective Lyndell Easley places a call to Sergeant Jeffrey and ask that he come to this location to serve as a witness for the signing of the search waiver. He adds that he will also need him to transport the suspect to the OCPD headquarters.

He then goes over to assist Clara in filling out the form. He makes sure she completes the areas requiring her name. Then, Detective Lyndell Easley fills in the information required by him as issuing the search waiver.

The completed document states. :"I, Clara A Blocker, after having been advised of my right not to have a search made of the premises herein after mentioned without a search warrant, and of my right to refuse to consent to such a search, thereby authorize Oklahoma City Police and Detective Lyndell Easley, officers of the Oklahoma City Police Department, to conduct a complete search of my premises located at 3042 SW 89th St. #E, Oklahoma City, Oklahoma. These officers are authorized by me to take from my premises any letters papers, materials, or property which they may desire. This written permission is being given by me to the above named officers voluntarily and without any threats or promises of any kind."

A few minutes later, Sergeant Jeffrey joins them and watches as Clara signs the form with her complete name. Under the Witnesses section, Sergeant Jeffrey signs his name and badge number. The form is then dated as 9/16/10.

Sergeant Jeffrey hands the form to Detective Lyndell Easley and he reviews the information to make sure it is complete, then puts it in with the other paperwork he has obtained.

###

Detective Lyndell Easley has listened to what Clara has to say. While he listens he has studied her body language and facial expressions. He is not convinced that she is telling him the truth. Those who have committed a crime sometimes call police very early to cover their bases and that seems to be the case here. That and the fact that to him Clara's emotions don't fit. Her demeanor is just too calm. Plus she is giving too many details and they have been changing from each telling. At this point he believes that

Clara is attempting to convince him of something happening to Erik while she was away from the apartment. She doesn't seem to show any sign, though, that they are looking at her as a suspect and that will play in their favor.

"Clara, we need to take your statement. Do you mind going with Sergeant Jeffrey to the precinct?"

Clara again is cooperative and says, "Sure," and willingly goes with the Sergeant.

###

As soon as Sergeant Jeffrey leaves with Clara, Detective Lyndell Easley makes a call to OCPD. He contacts his partner, Inspector Whitebird to alert him that the suspect is on her way. He tells him what he has gleaned from Clara and what the other officers have also learned. He gives him a general picture of the crime scene and the possible evidence items he has noted. Finally he tells Inspector Whitebird that he has a search waiver signed by the suspect and they will be doing a thorough search of the area. Any new details he will call in.

Inspector Whitebird tells Detective Lyndell Easley that he will begin the interview as soon as the suspect arrives and will keep him abreast of any new information he gets from her.

Lieutenant Shubert completes his job at 3042 SW 89th St. #E and leaves the crime scene at 11:30 a.m.

It is 12:30 p.m. when Clara arrives at the Oklahoma City Police Department. She is immediately ushered into the building and taken to an unoccupied interview room. Sergeant Jeffrey then goes to tell Inspector Ken Whitebird that Clara Blocker has arrived.

###

At 3042 SW 89th St. #E the real job begins. Hopefully the first responders haven't caused too much disruption to any potential physical evidence. Before even stepping inside the structure, the entrance and exit are controlled. Sentries are now stationed at all possible ingresses. The CSIs establish the boundaries of the crime scene and out comes the crime scene tape.

Sergeant Jay Coffey continues to serve as primary officer and scene security. With the classification of the case as Homicide,

Lieutenant Greg Johnston will serve as the Homicide Supervisor and Detective Lyndell Easley, Detective Pena, Lieutenant Greg Johnston, Detective Rob Benavides, and Detective Gary Damron will serve as crime scene investigators. They will get statements from witnesses and survivors as well as give pertinent information to the scene processors.

It is now around 11:30 a.m. on September 16. At this point Detective Lyndell Easley leaves Apartment #E to conduct a canvass of the area. He is assisted by Officer Rob Benavides and Officer Gary Damron.

###

On September 16, 2010 at approximately 11:45 a.m. Inspector Chris Miller, along with Inspector Lord leave the Hunt Apartments at 3016 SW 89th, in Oklahoma City, and head west on SW 89th St toward S Drexel Ave. They turn right to merge onto I-44 E and exit to merge onto I-240 heading toward Ft Smith. They go a little over two miles and exit on S Western Ave. Six miles and eleven minutes later they arrive at Integris Southwest Medical Center at 4401 South Western Avenue, in Oklahoma City.

While Inspector Ken Whitebird and Detective Lyndell Easley are working the homicide. Inspector Miller and Inspector Lord pull into the Emergency Department entrance on the west side of the building and they enter. They pass through security and ask at the desk if there are any family members of Erik Saxton present. They next check to see if there are any potential witnesses at the emergency room.

They are finally able to speak with Master Sergeant (MSergeant) Dennis Bueno who has been at the hospital for some time and he tells them there have been no relatives or potential witnesses at the hospital to see or speak with Erik.

MSergeant Dennis Bueno fills them in, saying that he went to Southwest Medical Center, Examination Room #1 and has maintained security of the body of the victim who died at 10:42 a.m. He informs them that Erik has been examined by Dr. Chad Borin who is the Emergency Room Physician and that according to the hospital staff, Erik was already dead when he arrived at the Emergency Room. Later Dr. Borin saw Erik in Exam Room #2 and pointed out evidence of trauma to Erik's left eye area that had a large bruise and also told him that Erik's head appeared to be swollen. Relieved by Inspector Miller and Inspector Lord. MSergeant Dennis Bueno leaves Integris Southwest Medical Center.

With the information obtained from MSergeant Dennis Bueno. Inspector Chris Miller places a call. They will need to have the victim photographed.

###

While processing another scene CSU, Lieutenant L Withrow receives a call from Inspector Chris Miller and informs Sergeant Everett Baxter of a homicide that took place at 3042 SW 89th Street, #E and that the victim is at the Integris Southwest Medical Center at 4401 South Western Avenue, in Oklahoma City. Sergeant Everett Baxter, along with Sergeant Curtis Ferguson head immediately to the Southwest Medical Center and arrive there at approximately 12:15 p.m.

Sergeant Everett Baxter begins taking overall, mid-range and close-up photographs of the body. He then photographs the injuries both with and without a scale. He works diligently making sure he doesn't miss anything.

###

The photographs completed, Sergeant Everett Baxter leaves Integris Southwest Medical Center. Inspector Lord and Miller stay with the body until the Medical Examiner transport arrives

At this point Inspector Lord places a call to the Office of Chief Medical Examiner. Every death that is due to or might reasonably have been due to a violent or traumatic injury or accident is to be investigated by the medical examiner. Inspector Lord and Miller obtain a copy of the report completed by Dr. Chad Borin and another one will go with the body to the Office of the Chief Medical Examiner. Inspector Lord and Miller will fill them in on the details of the crime scene and Dr. Chad Borin will give details concerning the death of Erik Saxton.

Once contacted the Medical Examiner's Office sends a transport vehicle and the body is released by the Southwest Medical Center.

The Medical examiner, will play an important part in this case as their findings may be called upon in court to help the court understand physical evidence and how it relates to the cause of death, time of death, etc. in a criminal trial. In order to determine the cause and manner of death, an autopsy will tell what happened, and sometimes just as importantly, what didn't happen. If this is indeed a murder, the autopsy will generate a legal document that can be used in court.

Erik Saxton's body and belongings collected by the Medical Center are taken to 901 N. Stonewall where the Medical Examiner, Chai S. Choi will take custody of his body. The items that will be collected at the morgue into evidence are one pair of black and gray underwear briefs, one pair of grey Hanes shorts with draw string, one pair of gray and white Nike shoes, one 7-11 receipt and an Oklahoma SDL, $1.21 cash, right and bag, left hand bag, right hand fingernails, left hand fingernails, pubic hair, scalp hair, DNA Blood card and morgue prints.

Detective Pena leaves the Hunt Apartments at 12:30 p.m.

Sergeant Everett Baxter with Sergeant Curtis Ferguson then proceed to the crime scene at 3042 SW 89th Street, #E and arrive there at approximately 12:45 p.m. Their job will be to find, evaluate and collect the physical evidence.

At 1:40 p.m. Lieutenant Greg Johnston leaves the Hunt Apartments.

###

The first step for the CSI in processing the scene is to obtain a diagram of the Hunt Apartment complex layout. Normally a rough sketch would have to be made, but when it comes to apartment complexes, the diagrams are readily available. As he makes his way to the complex office, Sergeant Curtis Ferguson keeps his eyes open, searching for anything that might be evidence in this case. When he reaches the office, the manager is very cooperative and supplies Sergeant Curtis Ferguson with the sketches he needs. For starters, the diagram of the complex will serve to verify the location of 3042, SW 89th St. #E within the complex. For the diagram of the layout of the apartment with each room labeled he asks for several copies. He will need to add to these. One will show where the furniture and fixtures are situated in the apartment. Another will be marked to show where each piece of evidence is found.

With the diagrams in hand, Sergeant Curtis Ferguson makes his way back to Apartment #E, again looking around for any possible evidence.

Once back at the scene of the crime, Sergeant Curtis Ferguson begins by moving through the rooms of the apartment and drawing in the furniture located in each room. When this is done, he assigns Sergeant Everett Baxter the duty of scene photographer. Sergeant Everett Baxter has already begun taking pictures of the Hunt Apartment area outside of Apartment #E. As he enters the apartment he begins taking overall, mid-range and close-up photographs of the scene. He takes photos of the rooms just as they appear so he can make a visual comprehensive view of the scene. Next he narrows the scope to include specific areas of the room and it's furnishings that are part of the evidence discovered. These shots are close up so that each item and area are clearly depicting the evidence. The photos will include a close up of the spot found on the box spring under the mattress. Another of a Financial Information form that is addressed to Clara Blocker and a Community Sentencing Probation Plan from the District Court in the State of Oklahoma , also carrying the name of Clara A. Blocker is found and photographed.

On the fireplace hearth a close up is taken of the Vodka bottle, Styrofoam cup, yellow coffee cup and an ashtray. In the next there is a close up of what appears to be a blood stain on the carpet in the living room and another of what appears to be a blood stain on the side of the dining room chair. Each area is pointed out as he makes his way through the crime scene area. From the walls, to the clothes hampers, to the laundry basket Sergeant Everett Baxter continues to take the photos, making sure to not miss one area of evidence.

Once the area of the rooms are complete, Sergeant Everett Baxter is next directed to the back pack. With assistance he photographs the contents which belongs to Clara. There are bags of prescription medications, three letters with their envelopes, and other personal female items.

Sergeant Curtis Ferguson and Everett Baxter work together knowing that there is an inability of a single photo to show an entire crime scene, so several shots will be needed.

The layout diagrams, being prepared by Sergeant Curtis Ferguson will be used in conjunction with the photographs, to provide a clear, complete and accurate view of the crime scene.

Along with providing the notes he prepared during his walk through, Detective Lyndell Easley would receive a call from Detective Ken Whitebird that would shed light on some pieces of glass they found and a DVD player. These could be the weapons used in the crime.

Just as important Sergeant Curtis Ferguson and Everett Baxter report any items that might help in Detective Ken Whitebird's interview.

Sergeant Curtis Ferguson will begin recording the details of Detective Lyndell Easley's findings on a final Apartment #E . He will number the locations of the discovery of what appears to be evidence for the case on another of Apartment #E diagram and on yet another Apartment #E diagram copy he will include the full dimensional size of the apartment, and furniture located in the rooms.

Diagramed and photographed as evidence is a Sungate model DVD Player, numerous pieces of broken glass and possible hair fibers, one bottle of Tvarscki 100 proof vodka, one green bathroom rug, one red S/S Structure shirt, size S, one white bath towel, one blueish green hand towel, one white bed sheet, one green Cherokee T-Shirt (bloody), seven sets of wet swabs from red stains believed to be blood found on floors, and walls throughout the apartment.

Once the photographs and the diagrams are complete the evidence can be collected. It is crucial that this be done properly. The CSI choose the proper size and material for the evidence and package each piece of evidence separately and then properly label, seal, and document it. They use packing tape to seal bags and boxes.

For basic collection, they use an assortment of clean, new paper and new Ziploc bags. The paper is used for items that need to breathe so the fingerprint evidence, towels and pieces of clothing go in paper, even if wet. To keep from losing them, any small items are attached to an evidence sheet and then packaged.

The hair found on the site is collected with tweezers and placed in a clean pharmaceutical paper being put in a glassine[2] envelope, which is folded and sealed shut.

The large DVD player is collected, and documented with a property tag.

At the scenes they collect DNA evidence using swabs. They have tagged blood, saliva, and urine stains which they let air dry at the scene. When they're dry, they package each in a separate swab box.

On each piece of evidence that is 'bagged' it is recorded who found the evidence, the date it was found, where at the crime scene it was found, and a full description of what the evidence is.

The evidence log book is steadily growing. The full evidence list would include a total count of 28 pieces of evidence, with a full explanation of where the evidence was found, who found the evidence, and a full description of the item. This list included items on Erik's person, and the items on Clara Blocker.

Sergeant Everett Baxter assist in identifying, marking and collecting the evidence. Finally on September 16, at 3:10 p.m. the scene processing is complete. All evidence collected is given to Sergeant Curtis Ferguson to take with him and shortly after 3:10 p.m. both Sergeant Curtis Ferguson and Sergeant Everett Baxter leave the crime scene and return to the CSU office where Sergeant Everett Baxter will download two hundred twenty five digital images into the CSU computer for archiving.

---

[2] Glassine is a smooth and glossy paper that is air, water and grease resistant. It is impervious to Oil, Grease and Water.

While the diagramming, photographing and evidence collection is going on, Detective Lyndell Easley begins conducting a canvass of the area at around 11:30 a.m. assisted by Officer Rob Benavides and Officer Gary Damron.

Once the scene investigation is complete, Detective Lyndell Easley is notified and he intern notifies the manager of the apartment complex, Johanna Powell. Upon learning that the investigation of the apartment is complete, Johanna goes to secure the premises. The lock for the apartment door is equipped with a lock that requires a key to activate, and Detective Lyndell Easley is informed that the office has a duplicate copy of the key.

Detective Lyndell Easley at this point lets Johanna know that he will attempt to contact the next of kin for Erik and will provide them with the necessary information in order that they can retrieve Erik's personal possessions and handle any issues that require attention.

CHAPTER 5: KNOCKING ON DOORS

(SEPTEMBER 16, 2010)

Crime scene investigators must ask the right questions quickly to gather information about a crime before memories begin to change. Whether the crime scene involves murder, assault, or burglary the crime scene investigator has a very small window of opportunity to interview witnesses on the spot. The more efficient the crime scene investigator works in gathering vital information right away, the faster and more effectively he can get to the rest of the investigation process.

###

At the site of the Hunt Apartments on Thursday, September 16, a neighborhood canvass is taking place. Before they begin, the management supplies them with a list of names of the apartment residence.

Detective Rob Benavides starts at 11:20 a.m. he knocks on Apartment #G where Robert Blanchard lives but no one is home. He then walks behind the building and comes in contact with Cynthia Lena in the parking lot.

Cynthia asks, "What is going on."

Detective Rob Benavides says, "We are conducting an investigation into the murder of Erik Saxton who lived in Apartment #E. Do you know him?"

Cynthia says, "Yes, he was murdered? I pick up trash for the apartments and saw Erik the day before."

Detective Rob Benavides verifies that. "You saw him on Wednesday, September 15.?

"Yes, that's right."

"How did Erik appear?"

Cynthia replies, "He appeared normal."

"Do you know what happened Wednesday evening at his apartment?"

"No, I don't know anything about that."

"Well, thank you Cynthia. If we need anything further we will get in touch."

Detective Gary Damron begins his apartment canvass at 11:20 a.m. on September 16 as well. He leaves his card to have the resident call him when he finds no one a home in Apt. F where Amanda McDonald lives.

At Apartment D, he speaks with Joshua Adams at 12:00, on September 16, 2010.

"Are you Joshua Adams?"

"Yes, I am."

"Do you know Erik Saxton who lived in Apartment E?"

"No, why?"

"He was murdered last night."

"I and my wife just moved into the apartment only two weeks ago and we don't know any of our neighbors."

"Did you hear or see any type of disturbance on Wednesday?"

"I heard a siren around 9:30 p.m. but didn't know what it was about. With the hospital next door there are ambulances going there often. But, no, I'm not aware of anything occurring in the building."

"Well, thank you for your help Mr. Adams. If you remember anything more, give me a call."

No one his home when he knocks on Apartment C which is the residence of Thu Tran so he leaves his card to have them call.

At 11:53 a.m. Detective Gary Damron and Detective Ron Benavides leave the Hunt Apartments.

Detective Lyndell Easley was still at the scene of 3042 SW. 89th Street, Apartment E, when at 1:30 p.m., on Thursday, September 16, 2010 Amber McDonald who lives in Apartment F, located right next door Apartment E and on the ground floor, walked up to the scene.

"What happened?" she asked

Detective Lyndell Easley introduced himself and told her that there had been a murder.

"There was a lot of activity at that apartment last night," Amber replied.

"What kind of activity," Detective Lyndell Easley asked.

Amber explained that she and her sister, Mandy arrived at the Hunt Apartment complex around 7:00 p.m. on the evening of Wednesday, September 15. They parked on the south side of Mandy's building. This building is west of the scene of the incident and shares a common interior wall.

Amber observed a white female subject walking to the south on the sidewalk between the two buildings and talking on a cell phone.

Detective Lyndell Easley asked her to describe the woman and Amber says that she wore blue Capri pants, a white tank top, and a bandana on her shaved head.

This is a perfect description of Clara Blocker. Amber said that her first impression was that the female was a cancer patient and obviously seemed to have mental issues. As Amber and Mandy walked north on the sidewalk to Mandy's apartment, the female followed them, causing Amber to feel uneasy.

They reached Mandy's apartment and entered, at which time Mandy called their mother who was coming to the apartment to watch a movie with her daughters. She wanted to warn her of the female outside and instructed her to call when she arrived so Mandy could go out and walk her inside.

The mother arrived at quarter to eight o'clock and Mandy walked to the parking lot to accompany her mother. Amber stated she ignored the female as they walked to Mandy's apartment and the female said to her as she walked by, "hey baby girl". Amber could hear her talking on a cell phone, saying something about $100. Amber stated she presumed the female was attempting to purchase illegal narcotics and was sure of this when she and her sister were trying to fix the light in front of her apartment and the female was walking around in front of the apartments still talking on her phone.

At that time she heard her telling the person on the phone that she had a $100 and asked if they were cooking. After the female got off the phone Amber heard the female talking to the person inside the apartment telling him to let her into the apartment, but she could not hear this reply.

Amber said she could see a black male through the window of Apartment E, but she had not seen him outside at any time. After Amber and her mother returned to the apartment, Amber stated she could still hear the female outside pacing back and forth for a period of about an hour. When Amber left the apartment sometime around nine, nine-thirty p.m., the female was no longer outside.

With contact cards left at empty apartments, that was all they could do for the day. At 3:10 p.m. Detective Lyndell Easley, Sergeant Jay Coffey, Sergeant Everett Baxter, and Sergeant Curtis Ferguson left the Hunt Apartment property.

Later when we visit the premises, we receive a different story from the office manager concerning Erik and the other residents.

CHAPTER 6: OKLAHOMA CITY PRECINCT

(SEPTEMBER 16, 2010)

Obtaining information that an individual does not want to provide constitutes the sole purpose of an Interview. A successful Interview results in a guilty confession or admitting participation in an illegal activity. However, interrogators frequently do not acquire information that is critical to successful case resolution. Often, guilty suspects leave the Interview room without making the smallest admission.

Many murderers do things in predictable and secretive ways to cover their tracks. They leave town and flee the scene, trying to not draw attention. Not in this case. The suspect not only made the 9-1-1 call, but stays on the premises even after the police arrive on the scene.

###

On Thursday, September 16, 2010, at around 12:40 p.m. Clara waits in the interview room at the Oklahoma Police Department. She sits fidgeting as she anticipates the arrival of someone to join her. She looks around the small enclosure that has a desk, a black plastic chair with metal legs and no arms. She has been directed to sit in this chair by the officer who showed her into the room. There is a similar chair off to the left side of the room and another chair in front of the small table. This table is hooked to the wall.

She looks down at the phone she holds in her lap, and then releases one hand, bends her arm at the elbow and lays her head against the palm of that hand.

The interview room holds no decorations. There are no pictures on the grey walls or anything beyond a box of Kleenex and a Styrofoam white cup on the table to focus her attention on while she waits.

Clara wears a bandana around her head, black frame glasses, a black sleeveless t-shirt, and a pair of baggy low slung grey jeans.

She rubs her neck, looks at her elbow and then wraps her arms in close to her body as she leans back against the wall, waiting.

She takes a look at her phone. Four minutes and ten seconds have passed when finally there is the sound of the door to the interview room being unlocked and a person enters. It's Inspector Ken Whitebird.

"Hello," he says, "How are you?"

Clara replies, "Tired!"

Inspector Whitefield responds, "Makes two of us. It's been a long week."

Inspector Whitebird introduces himself then informs Clara that his partner, Detective Lyndell Easley, spoke to her at the scene. He adds that he assumes Detective Lyndell Easley told her that they would be working this homicide…he pauses and adds, or whatever it is right now.

Clara says, "I'm here for whatever you all need. My friend has seizures and all and he was drunk last night. I called 911 because he was not breathing."

"I am totally confused. She says, "I've been sitting here waiting and I l look up and sees it says 'Homicide' above me."

Inspector Whitebird tells her that a death has occurred and it's an unexplained death so they called homicide in because they don't know what happened.

It takes a bit before it sinks in and then Clara, in shock, says, "Erik's dead?" She seems shaken, but then recovers quickly.

Inspector Whitebird asks, "Did you not go to the hospital with him?" Clara responds that she could have but had police all around. She tells Inspector Whitebird that she did call her pastor.

Inspector Whitebird moves on and asks her address. Clara gives him Erik's address. He asks her the name of the apartment and she adds, the Hunt Apartments. He pauses to write it down. You can hear Clara as she whispers, 'What the hell'.

Inspector Whitebird asks if she is employed and she says she is not, adding she is on probation and is in the Firststep rehab program. He asked about her probation and she tells him it is for distribution in Oklahoma County and possession in Garvin County.

"How did you meet Erik," Inspector Whitebird asks.

"I met Erik almost a year ago at his apartment." She adds that she met him through someone living with him, a man named Charles and they call him C. It was back when she was using so that's why she can't remember too much about it. She says that Erik had bad people around him and they were taking advantage of him and that's why she moved in. When asked how long ago was that. She added she has been living with him for about a month.

Inspector Whitebird asks about her relationship with Erik and she says they are just friends adding that she is gay and that she has a girlfriend.

She says she doesn't know much about his personal live so she couldn't answer the questions she has been asked about this. She knows he was married, but didn't know much else about him other than that. Detective Whitebird mentions that she had said he had seizures and Clara responds that she did know this and also that he was taking Topamax for his seizures.

While Inspector Whitebird writes some information down in his notebook, Clara says she can't understand how he could be dead because he was beat up a little bit, but that was all.

Inspector Whitebird asks if she had a fight with him and she says 'no', adding that he's a midget; a little man.

When asked how he was beat up she says that his one eye was black and he had a cut on his lip is all.

Inspector Whitebird then asked her starting from last night to tell him what happened.

Clara says she slept by the door because Erik was drunk and she didn't want him to get out. Inspector Whitebird interrupts and asks exactly when they started drinking and Clara says she hadn't been drinking but Erik started drinking around noon. She says a few minutes later that she drank a little bit, but wasn't drunk, she doesn't do that, and then she whispers, 'I'm on probation".

When asks to continue, Clara says she left after Chase came over with the vodka, a friend of Erik's, and adds to this announcement, "A real preppy Indian guy". Clara states she got up in just enough time to go to the Cricket Store with David.

Detective Whitebird asks, "Does Chase have a last name?" Clara replies she doesn't know his last name.

Detective Whitebird tells her to continue.

She says Chase came over with the vodka around noon, but Inspector Whitebird again interrupts to ask Clara how many bottles they had.

Clara says there was a one fifth size bottle of Tvarscki Vodka and she drank half of the fifth and she didn't know how much Erik drank.

She continues saying that she then laid down and when she got up it was around 6:30 p.m. She had to leave and when she left Erik was only a little beat up and that was all.

Inspector Whitebird asks, "Where was Chase."

"Chase left before I left".

Inspector Whitebird asks why would Chase bring the bottle and not drink with him. Clara said she didn't know why.

Inspector Whitebird asks if Erik had a cell phone and Clara replies that he only has a land line. Inspector Whitebird comments, "Then how did Chase know to bring a bottle?"

"I don't know. People just showed up".

Inspector Whitebird asks Clara. "When Chase came over was Erik beat up?"

"No, he wasn't until I came back with David."

So many contradictions, so many illogical statements seemed to be coming from Clara. Inspector Whitebird does not point this out, yet, but continues the interview.

Inspector Whitebird asks, "Does David have a last name?"

Clara says, "Elkins".

"Do you have a phone number for David Elkins?"

Clara looks at her phone and says she has a couple. She gives him both of the numbers and Inspector Whitebird writes them down.

Inspector Whitebird next asks, "When you called David, did you see Erik before you left?"

Clara doesn't answer right away. She hemmed and hawed a bit and then says, "I saw him, but I was a little tipsy then."

"What time did you return and noticed Erik had been beaten up?"

"It was around 7:30 p.m. when we returned and it was then that I noticed Erik had been beaten up."

"What were you doing at Cricket?" Inspector Whitebird asks and Clara states she was putting minutes on her phone.

He next asks, "Was anyone at the house when you left?"

Clara responds, "No", Erik was drunk and he left the apartment unlocked."

Now she adds one more point to her story. It is obvious that even she knows that her story is not making sense so she again changes the facts.

"To be honest I think that Erik was drunk and I don't think he was beaten up but instead I think that he fell."

It is at this point Inspector Whitebird decides to press Clara with the contradictions in her story. He says to her that she has told him that Erik had been beaten up and the only other person at the residence was her. Now she says that Erik fell. Showing frustration, Inspector Whitebird says to Clara she needs to tell him what happened.

Clara is silent, obviously knowing her story is falling apart.

Inspector Whitebird asks Clara if Erik fell before and she says, 'Yes'. Next he asked what happened when she got back.

Clara says Erik was still drinking. She said to him, "Let's go to 7-11".

Inspector Whitebird asks, "What time was that?"

Clara adds that it was around midnight when they went to the 7-11 on the corner of 89th Street. Erik went with her and she got him a cherry Pepsi and she got herself some more cigarettes. Clara then tells Inspector Whitebird the cashier asked her if Erik was all right as he had blood on the corner of his mouth.

That's all she says on the matter, brushing over this statement and not adding if she responded to the cashier or if anything more was said. She goes on and says that when they got back to the apartment she lay down on a pallet she made in front of the door so Erik wouldn't go out and she stayed there by the door all night.

"So nothing happened while I was with him."

Inspector Whitebird asked Clara to stand up and pull up the legs of her shorts. Clara obeys. Inspector Whitebird looked closely and says she has bruises on her knees and that they look like carpet burns.

Not missing a step, Clara says that she had sex with a friend of hers. Detective Ken Whitebird asked when that was. Clara replies, "It was a couple days ago".

Detective Ken Whitebird looks again and says, "They are fresh burns and could have happened in a fight".

Not giving her a chance to respond and trying to force the truth, he adds, "If something occurred in the apartment, maybe Erik assaulted you and you hit him back. If something occurred between the two of you, you need to tell me now. I don't want to put words in your mouth, but you need to come clean because I don't want to have to go to the DA and tell the DA you lied".

Clara doesn't seem shaken by Inspector Whitebird's statement. She says, "Erik and I have never gotten into an altercation. I don't know anything about him getting hit in the head These bruises are from different incidents".

He can feel the tension in the room as he adds to his notes.

Inspector Whitebird ask, "Was there frequent visitors at Erik's".

Clara says, "No. No one comes over and gets violent with Erik."

Clara pauses then adds, " I don't believe this is happening. It just doesn't make sense."

Again she pauses and says, "I have not been able to call anyone and I don't believe that Erik is dead. I don't believe that this is a homicide".

Inspector Whitebird replies, "Erik is dead and this is most probably a homicide."

Clara responds with, "I don't understand any of this".

Now Clara takes another pose. The irritation she is feeling is apparent in her voice. "You don't know Erik. Erik is a loving person and not the type someone would hurt. He is disabled and he wants to get a job. He is a good person and people don't come in and hurt him".

Ken Whitebird gives her a moment to calm herself and then asks, "How old is Chase?"

"I think he is in his 30s".

Detective Ken Whitebird changes the direction of the conversation again. "How long have you been staying with Erik?"

"I have stayed with him off and on over the year I've known him and this is the longest time I have stayed with him."

"How long is that?"

"About 30 days", she replies.

Now it is her turn to change the subject. "Pastor Urey Kenoles has been to Erik's apartment. The apartment is nice. The pastor helps Erik get around."

"Do you have a phone number for this pastor?"

Clara says, "I have his card in here." She fumbles through her wallet and finally finds what she is looking for. She hands Inspector Whitebird the pastor's card.

Inspector Whitebird who has not been at the crime scene next asks, "Is Erik black?" and Clara says, "Yes".

Detective Ken Whitebird turns his attention to the card that Clara has given him and begins writing the information from the card down on his pad. He gives Clara the card back. At that instance, Clara's phone rings. She looks to see who is calling and then disconnects the call.

Clara now says off handedly. "I am to go back to the Firstep program tomorrow and this was like a going away party."

Detective Ken Whitebird knows about the Firstep Recovery Programs for Women. It provides an opportunity for those with alcohol and chemical dependencies to become clean and sober and reclaim the productive lives they once had. Firstep is a long-term, residential, work-recovery program.

"Clara, so when was the last time you saw Erik alive?"

"At 8:00 a.m. this morning. Erik was alive and breathing."

This time it is Detective Ken Whitebird's phone ringing. He looks to see who is calling and then he disconnects the call.

Inspector Whitebird looks at his notes and asks, "What type of seizures did Erik have?"

"I don't know." Clara pauses and adds. "Erik told me that he hasn't been seeing his neurologist at all. He has a disability check but he doesn't have insurance." As an explanation or a way to cast attention in another direction, she explains that she thought that info might help.

There is silence then Clara again says, "This just doesn't make sense."

Inspector Whitebird tells Clara to take a moment and get her thoughts together. With that said, he stands up, collecting his notepad and phone and leaves the room, locking the door behind him.

Alone again, Clara looks down at her lap, belches and rocks slowly side to side. She leans back and crosses her arms and then grabs a Kleenex out of the tissue box on the table and blows her nose. She doubles it up and lays it on the table next to her phone. She crosses her arms again and stares down into her lap. She sits still without moving for almost two minutes and then straightens her clothes and twist sideways on the chair, crossing her legs.

She picks up her phone and looks at it, obviously noting the time. She has been in the interview room for thirty-one minutes and it begins to show as she starts fidgeting. She puts her chin on her left hand with her other arm remaining across her waist. She is still, as if she is sleeping. She shifts again, wrapping both hands across her waist. After a bit she leans forward and them resumes her previous position, arms crossed, head down. She makes slight movements now and then as if trying to keep awake or find a comfortable position in the hard plastic black chair with the metal legs and no armrest.

Clara has now been in the interview room for over thirty-eight minutes. She picks up her cell phone and begins to dial a number. She puts the phone to her ear and then checks it as if unsure she has dialed right. Someone finally answers:

She first asks the caller if they are still out of town. She says, "Erik is dead". There are a lot of yeses, ahuh, and finally she says, "I don't know, I don't know" followed by "I'm wondering if something happens while I was gone. Because when I came back he was a little beat up David, but that doesn't' add up David, him being dead".

She pauses and then adds, "I started at nine this morning dealing with detectives and all. My pastors have been out and I can't reach them".

Clara adds, "I don't know, so. Yeah....yeah well". Clara listens and stretches her arms up and around before another series of "yeah, all right, and right". This is followed by, "down at the headquarters on Concord in a little room."

Clara tells David that her phone is about to go dead and that the detectives said they will give her a ride back to the apartment but she doesn't know where she will stay. Her pastor hasn't called and she doesn't want to go to Firstep. She has no cash and had wanted to get a hotel room but she is short on cash and she is really freaked out. This is followed by another series of yesses.

Clara stands and moves about. David says something to her.

"I'll ask them. Are you going to go home tonight. I'll call you back because my phone is about to go dead, and my pastors won't be able to call me".

Clara tells David that she has given them both of his numbers and that she feels they are trying to turn this back on her, saying that when people drink and all. Clara says she doesn't know what happened. She continues to say that something is not adding up right. She knows he hasn't been seeing his neurologist and tells David she showed the paramedics his pill bottle.

Clara adds, "So you will be going out of town tonight?" David responds and Clara says she doesn't know where she will be tonight. She thanks David, telling him she appreciates him and that she will call him when she finds out if they are going to help her or what is going on. The conversation is ended.

She walks around with her hands in her pocket and bobs back and forth like a fighter would do. Finally she sits back down again. Clara crosses her arms and puts her head down. She belches and lets air out. She has now been in the room almost forty-nine minutes according to her phone. It is then that the sound of the door being unlocked attracts her attention.

The door opens and Inspector Whitebird enters and takes the seat across from her.

Clara moves her chair closer to the wall and leans her head against it as she waits for Inspector Whitebird to say something.

"Did you render aid to Erik this morning when he was bleeding?"

Clara seems to not understand what he is asking so Inspector Whitebird says that there were bloody towels in the hamper.

Clara finally says, "Yes, I did. He had blood on his mouth."

"What did you do with the towels?"

"I put the towels in the bathroom."

Next Inspector Whitebird, without mentioning where the information came from, asks Clara, "What did you mean when you told David that Erik might not let you back in the house?"

Clara doesn't seem surprised by his question. "Because Erik was drunk."

"You were drunk too."

Again she doesn't react to his statement. "I told Erik not to leave the door unlocked and we have argued about him leaving the door unlocked before."

Not letting up, Inspector Whitebird says, "Could it have been because you got into an altercation."

Clara says, "No." Then adds, "The door was unlocked when I came back."

Inspector Whitebird shows his irritation as he says her story is not matching up. At the scene she told detectives someone came and beat Erik up, but, Inspector Whitebird, adds the only person at the apartment was her. He continues saying that she has recent injuries.

"Show me your hands," Inspector Whitebird says. Clara complies.

Inspector Whitebird says to Clara that Erik was beaten up and that two people were drinking and people act different when they have been drinking. He again says that if she and Erik got into an altercation and she didn't mean to hurt him she needs to tell him now.

Clara says, "He was beaten up when I got back". Repeatedly she says drunk or not she did not put her hands on him.

"It happened while I was gone and when I asked Erik what happened he wouldn't tell me. People have come in the apartment and hurt him before. People have gone into the apartment and stole things from him."

Inspector Whitebird asks, "What people."

"A black dude named C."

Inspector Whitebird says, "You haven't told me everything and I knows you are hiding something"

Not missing a beat, Clara says, "That is what I've been hiding".

"Were you there when it happened?" Inspector Whitebird asks

Clara says, "No".

"How do you know it was C."

"The door was unlocked and there was a Black dude in the apartment when I woke. I asked Erik if my money was still in the apartment and that was when I saw C."

Inspector Whitebird needs clarification so he asks Clara if she is saying that when she got up, she saw C, a big black dude, but Erik wasn't beat up then.

Clara tries to make the story make sense as she says, "C was f--king with me, trying to get my money out of my bra. Erik either let him in or the door was unlocked. I chased him out of the apartment. I said what the f--ck are you doing in here".

Inspector Whitebird asks, "How does Erik know C?"

"C use to be a roommate of Erik's".

Inspector Whitebird asks, "Did C come back or not?"

"I locked the apartment but when I came back Erik's eye was puffy and his lip was cut. I don't know if C came back or not."

Now she changes her tactic. "It wasn't that big a deal. Erik was drunk is all and he had a seizure so I thought I better call 911. I did not put my hands on him."

Inspector Whitebird, regarding her last statement says, "Maybe if you were sober, but when people are drinking it is different".

He tells Clara that there is a difference between, premeditated murder and accidental murder. He tells her he knows she is not telling the truth. She says she is telling the truth and that she is not afraid to go to prison because she's been there before.

This is not news to Inspector Whitebird who in preparing for the interview with Clara has received information back on her from his request to N-DEx. This is the law enforcement national data exchange and law enforcement records The N-DEx is a national system designed to search, link, analyze, and share criminal justice information that includes incident and case reports found in various information systems and recorded in a number of formats across the country.

Inspector Whitebird sidesteps and says, "If this is an accident tell me now".

Clara goes into a rendition of Erik being her friend and she doesn't know what Inspector Whitebird wants her to say.

The conversation is heated as Inspector Whitebird says, "I want the truth, that's what I want you to tell me." He pauses. "Do you want to be put in custody? Do you want me to take this to the next level? I am giving you the opportunity to tell me the truth."

Inspector Whitebird carries it a step further. "I know you are lying to me. I'm not stupid. I just want the truth so that I can tell the DA you told me the truth."

Inspector Whitebird ends his accusations saying that he is going to give her a couple of minutes to think about it. Inspector Whitebird then gets up, takes his pad and phone and goes to the door of the interview room. He opens the door, steps through and then locks the door of the room, leaving Clara alone.

Alone again, Clara checks her phone then puts it back on the table again. She has been in the interview room for over one hour now. After a bit she picks up her phone and turns it on and makes a call.   On Clara's side the phone call is with several individuals and it goes like this.

"Yeah you all called. Who, Farue, well I don't know what is going on with me, Erik is dead. Yeah I had to call 9-1-1 this morning. Call....Who.....Farue? I don't know what is going on with me I am talking with the Detectives."

Clara then tells the person on the other end what she has been told. She tells him that she tried to bring Erik back and that she has been dealing with detectives since 9:00 a.m. and does not understand how Erik died.

Clara says, "I am not playing a game here this is serious. Erik is dead, Laurie, I tried to bring him back, but I couldn't. I may be arrested. They may put me in jail, I don't know. Will you all come and get me. I have nowhere to go and nothing.   I don't know....You are my friends, aren't you? You know.   Fight or no fight it doesn't add up."

"Hey, Vaugh, Erik was drunk and tripping all night. What happens is he was a little beat up and I didn't put my hands on him? We drank a little more and I called 9-1-1 because he wasn't breathing, and I thought....this morning....Vaugh. I don't get it. I don't understand. The detective thinks I did it, you know that Interview thing, and wants me to say I did it.

"I don't' know. What do you think....Yeah you and me both. I will call you all when I know what's up. I was going to the hospital to see him but he didn't make it. I just thought he was going into a seizure and all. I didn't think it was that serious.   I don't think this makes any sense."

"Wants to know who came over and I don't want to get you people involved. I will call you all. I just want to let you all know what is going on......yeah.....yeah, I know.....Yeah, yeah he is dead Vaugh. ..You know what I mean....ahuh.....wow. I have been in this room forever. They said they would drive me back to the apartment. I am freezing......let me call you back, my phone is about to go dead. I love you all...I love you all."

Clara sits down crosses her arms, head leaning against the wall and waits, repositioning her legs now and then. Her phone rings. Clara picks it up and looks to see who is calling. She can hear someone at the door and disconnects the call without answering.

Inspector Whitebird unlocks the door and enters the Interview room. He looks at Clara and says they are going to get some photos of her injuries. Clara says nothing.

Receiving a call from Inspector Whitebird, the following transpires.

On September 16, 2010 at approximately 1:00 pm, Officer Chris Click receives a phone call from Sergeant Everett Baxter advising him that he is currently working a homicide scene at 3042 SW 89th Street, Apartment E. Sergeant Everett Baxter advises that the suspect has been taken into custody and is currently located at the homicide office. Sergeant Everett Baxter requests that Officer Chris Click respond to the homicide office and photograph the suspect and take custody of her clothing. As soon as he hangs up the phone, he responds to Sergeant Everett Baxter's request and arrives at the homicide office at 1:20 p.m.

At the homicide office, Officer Chris Click goes with Inspector Whitebird to the Interview room where Clara is being held.

Officer Chris Click begins by asking Clara if she has any injuries that he needs to know about. Clara says she has all kinds of injuries and says it's because she sleeps on the carpet. While this conversation is taking place, Inspector Whitefield walks over to the far corner and removes the chair from this corner of the room.

Officer Chris Click says he will be taking a few pictures of her and will need her in several poses for the shots. While he is in the middle of telling her this, Clara's phone rings. Officer Chris Click tells her that she needs to tell whoever is calling that she will call them back. Clara obeys.

Getting back to the matter, Officer Chris Click asks if she has any injuries he should know about and Clara points to a small scratch, which extends vertically along the center portion of her left leg, just below her knee. Clara says that the wound is old. Officer Chris Click takes photographs of this wound using scales. The wound measures approximately 20 mm in length.

Officer Chris Click continues with the pictures. He asks her to put her hands at her sides for him. At this point he notices that the camera batteries are low. Officer Click takes out his cell phone and calls for someone to bring him some new batteries for the camera.

While waiting he fiddles with the camera and tries taking some photographs. When the batteries are delivered, he then proceeds expeditiously with the pictures, doing a close up of her hands and legs. He puts a scale next to her knees to show the measurement of the scars that appear there. He records this as an elliptical-shaped abrasion on the left portion of her right knee cap. It measures approximately 5 mm wide and 10 mm in length. He then records a circular-shaped abrasion on the lower portion of the right knee cap, measuring approximately 10 mmm wide and 10 mm in length. Clara says that she doesn't understand why they want pictures of old scars on her knees.

Officer Click doesn't respond. He asks her to turn sideways and face the wall and she does and he snaps several pictures of her in this pose. He next tells her to face the back wall and snaps pictures of her from this angle. She keeps moving her arms from grasping them in back and then moving them to the front.

Officer Click uses a flash and gets even closer. He then has her turn to face the opposite side wall and snaps several pictures in this pose. Next he tells her to face him and tells her to put her hands in front of her in an open finger, backs up, pose. He again takes a scale to measure a scar he sees on the back of her hand. He records it as an abrasion on the right index and right fingers just above the knuckles. He continues to take shots up-close of the back of her hands.

Officer Click next tells Clara to turn her hands over and spread her fingers. He takes close ups of her hands in this position.

Officer Click has her lower her hands and begins taking pictures of the tattoos on her body. The photographs include the following:

BIC: TAT L Lisa Marie, To B
CHE: TAT L Tear Drop
CHE: TAT R Freedom Wings
FGR: TAT L Top Index= H, Middle= R, Ring= M
FOR: TAT L FRT Pooh & Tigger Kissing
HAN: TAT L TOP Hardword
LEG: TAT R FRT LOWER= Gay Dancing Word Fag
LEG: TAT R FRT UPPER= Puppy W/ Wings
SHL: TAT L Freedom Wings, Tribal Art
SHL: TAT R Pooh Bear

SHL: TAT R BACK 2 Girls Kissing

WRIST: TAT L TOP 2 Female Sex Symbols

After he is done photographing her various tattoos, Officer Click asks, "Do you have any other injuries?"

Clara says, "No."

To make sure this is correct, Officer Chris Click says he has to be sure she isn't hurt."

Clara then says, "I'm hungry. Can someone get me something to eat. I have money."

Inspector Whitebird says, "Try to just hang in there".

Officer Click has completed his photographs and gathers his equipment. Inspector Whitebird opens the door and they both leave the interview room.

Clara is alone in the room. She makes another call. She rocks back and forth, waiting for someone to pick up the phone. After a while she disconnects the call and then dials another number. She continues to rock back and forth and checks the phone to see if she has the right number. No one answers so she disconnects.

Clara continues to rock back and forth. She dials another number and lays the phone in her lap. After several rings, she disconnects the call and puts the phone on the table, hugging herself and leaning forward. She crosses her legs high and leans her forehead onto the knee of the crossed leg.

CHAPTER 7: CLARA A. BLOCKER IS MIRANDIZED

(SEPTEMBER 16, 2010)

Law enforcement agents are required to read you your rights if both: you're under arrest, and they want to ask you questions. If the officers haven't arrested you yet, they can ask you questions without reading you your rights, and your statements will still be used against you in court. The core of the Miranda decision is the requirement that law enforcement officers advise suspects of certain constitutional rights before conducting a custodial interrogation. Once a suspect in custody has been read the Miranda warnings, he is free to talk with law enforcement officials or not. The suspect can change his mind once he's started to talk. At every stage, he retains the right to call a halt to the interrogation and request an attorney.

The exact wording of the "Miranda Rights" statement is not specified in the Supreme Court's historic decision. Instead, law enforcement agencies have created a basic set of simple statements that can be read to accused persons prior to any questioning.

###

Clara hears the door being unlocked and in a few minutes she is joined by Inspector Whitebird.

Inspector Whitebird takes the seat across from her again and says, "Where are we at?"

Clara responds. "I told you everything I know".

Inspector Whitebird then looks directly at Clara. At this point she is going to be put into custody so Inspector Whitebird begins reading Clara her rights.

"You have the right to remain silent. Anything you say can and will be used against you in a court of law. You have the right to talk to a lawyer and have a lawyer present with you during questioning. If you cannot afford a lawyer, one will be appointed for you."

"Do you understand each of these rights as I have explained them to you?" Clara says, nothing.

"Do you still wish to talk to me now?" Still no response from Clara.

Inspector Whitebird asks, "Who were you talking to on the phone?"

Clara leans her head down with her hand on her head and does not answer. Inspector Whitebird tells her she has injuries such as those that might result from an altercation and that she just got off the phone with a person named Laurie.

Clara breaks her silence and says, "I told you everything. I don't know what happened."

Clara says she has no reason to lie to him. Inspector Whitebird says she has been lying to him.

There is a pause as Clara obviously is trying to figure out what she wants to say. Then it begins.

Clara says, "I did get into an altercation with Erik."

Inspector Whitebird asks, "Did it have something to do with what happened to him?"

Clara replies, ""Erik got into an altercation with me. That was when he got a black eye, but that has nothing to do with him being dead".

Again there is silence and Clara says, "I'm scared!"

Inspector Whitebird says, "I'm scared for you!"

Inspector Whitebird adds, "You need to explain what happened."

Clara's phone rings and she looks at Inspector Whitebird and says, "It's my girlfriend calling from the county jail."

Inspector Whitebird not wanting to have interference when Clara is finally beginning to tell the truth. He says, "Disconnect the call Clara."

Clara complies.

Inspector Whitebird asks, "Clara, did you hit Erik with something or with your fist?"

"I don't remember. I hit him a couple of times." Then after thinking about it Clara says, "I didn't hit him with my fist".

Inspector Whitebird asks, "So what did you hit him with?"

Clara replies, "Probably the DVD player and a crystal ball thing, but that was it. Erik was still talking before she went to bed".

Inspector Whitebird says, "Start when you started drinking yesterday. It was you and him only?:

Clara says, "Yes".

"Where did you get the booze?"

"From Chase".

How long did Chase stay?"

Clara replies, "He didn't stay and he didn't' drink with us".

"When did Chase come to the apartment?"

"It was around noon, yesterday, and after he left we started drinking out of the 5th of Tvarscki Vodka".

Inspector Whitebird then asks, "What started the argument, Clara?"

Clara said it was Erik leaving the apartment door open.

Inspector Whitebird repeats saying, "You were confronting him about leaving the door open?"

Clara replies, "Erik said he didn't leave it open, it was locked".

Clara then says, "I didn't hit him with my hands."

"Where did you hit him," Inspector Whitebird asks.

"Erik was in the bedroom and I hit him with the crystal ball at the back of the head in the bedroom."

"Then what happened."

"The DVD was in the front room and I was folding my clothes and I hit him with the DVD in the eye."

"Was that a different time," Inspector Whitebird asks?

"It all happened at the same time after David came to get me."

He needs more clarification so Inspector Whitebird asks "Did you speak to any neighbors."

Clara replies, "I didn't talk to any neighbors".

Inspector Whitebird adds. Well, two girls described you to a tee and said you talked to them."

Clara says, "I don't remember. I was pretty drunk".

Inspector Whitebird asks, "Afterward you hit him, where did Erik lay down? Did he lay down right where you had hit him?"

Clara says, "I am trying to remember." She pauses. "He fell down and got back up. He didn't lie down. We went to 7-11 and got something to drink and then when we came back he laid down by the couch and I laid down by the door".

Next Inspector Whitebird asks, "Have you ever argued like this before?"

Clara says, "No. This is the first time this has happened."

After a bid, she adds. "How I hit him with the crystal ball and with the DVD player does not explain why he is dead. He was not dead this morning or dead last night."

Trying to keep her calm and talking, Inspector Whitebird asks now, "Were you wearing the same clothes you are wearing now?"

Clara responds saying, "No, I don't think so".

Inspector Whitebird confronts her. "You can't remember what you were wearing?"

Clara says, "I can't remember".

Inspector Whitebird asks her now, "Do you think David would remember?"

Clara says, "She doesn't know."

"Are those the same shoes you were wearing?"

This seems to spark her memory and Clara says, "I think I was wearing a pink tank top and the same flip-flops. I don't know what shorts. I was in a hurry as David was my only way to get to the Cricket store and get the minutes on my phone. The store was about to close."

Inspector Whitebird asks, "Are you saying that Erik was still alive when you came back at 7:30 p.m. on the evening of Wednesday, September 15. And Erik was still conscious when you returned from the 7-11?'

Clara responds to both questions. "yes, he was".

At this point Inspector Whitebird says let him get back to her. He leaves the room and locks the door again.

Clara again sits with her arms crossed this time across her chest and her head leaning against the wall. It is not long before Inspector Whitebird returns.

Inspector Whitebird begins again. "Clara what was the Crystal ball like".

Clara replies, "It wasn't solid and had water in it and Erik called it a dragon light. It broke when I hit him." She stops talking and then adds, "I really didn't mean to hurt him".

Inspector Whitebird asks for clarification. "Was anybody else in the apartment?"

Clara replies, "No one else was there."

"What did you do with the pink tank top? Did you put it in the hamper or in your back pack?"

Clara replies, "I don't know where I put it."

Inspector Whitebird seems satisfied he has all the questions answered and tells Clara he will need to take her clothes for evidence. He explains he will get her something to wear. He then leaves the interview room, locking the door again.

Clara unzips her wallet and reaches into her pockets, removing her money. Carefully she folds and organizes the bills and places them inside her wallet. She then removes something that looks like a key and places them in her wallet.

She stands with her head down and her hands in her pocket. and then slowly she raises her head thinking they are coming. She starts swaying back and forth and then pulls out other items she has in her pockets, including some more loose changes which she then places in her wallet.

She removes the paper money and piles it up, then puts it back in the wallet. Satisfied she puts the wallet down. After a bit she takes out the key and places it in another compartment of her wallet then as though trying to hide the money she places it in different areas of her wallet.

Finally she lays the wallet, along with her cell phone down on the table. It remains there for a little bit before she again picks up the wallet and moves her money around in its confines. That done Clara stands with her head down.

The door is unlocked and a woman enters the room. She introduces herself as Detective Moran. She tells Clara to change and put all her items in the bag which she has brought with her and now hands over to Clara. Clara's phone rings and Detective Moran tells her to turn it off. Clara obeys. Detective Moran tells her that she needs to remove everything out of her pockets first. Clara says, "I've already done that."

Clara is told she can keep on her underwear. Detective Moran stays in the room. Clara leans over and takes off her pants. She places them in the bag that she has been given by Detective Moran.

She next takes off the bandana she has been wearing to display that her head is shaved clean of any hair. The bandana is put in the bag.

Clara reaches over and picks up the orange pants that have been provided for her. She puts them on.

With the pants on, she next takes off her top. She is not wearing a bra. She puts her top into the bag. She reaches over and picks up the orange top and puts it on over her head. Like the pants, the top is large and ill-fitting.

Clara slips her feet out of her flip flops and puts on the rubber sandals given to her.

All evidence that is to be sent to the crime lab must be packaged to ensure that such items arrive at their destination intact, and without becoming contaminated, damaged or spoiled. Every piece of evidence needs to be properly collected and labeled so that it may one day, if necessary, be admissible in court.

Detective Moran knows this and is very careful to make sure the evidence is properly handled.

Clara puts her flip flops in the bag. Lastly she puts her wallet and cell phone in the bag. Detective Moran has watched carefully making sure that each item has been placed in the bag and that nothing remains.

With everything in the bag, Clara hands the bag to Detective Moran who then takes it with her as she crosses the room and knocks on the door for someone to open it for her. She waits and then knocks several more times before someone comes to unlock the door.

As soon as the door is opened, Detective Moran leaves the interview room. She will now go to record each individual item she has collected into evidence. Her list will show one black American Honey sleeveless shirt no size tag visible. One Old Navy brown tank top, size large. One pair of OP brown flip flops,

no size. One pair Faded Glory black denim jean shorts, no size.
One black leather belt, one pair of Fruit of The Loom boxers, plaid
purple and green, size L and finally one blue and white bandanna.

Detective Moran gives Detective Kim Vorel the bag that holds
Clara Blocker's clothing. Detective Vorel documents the contents.

When this is done, Detective Vorel takes the single brown
paper sack that now contains the evidence collected and signs it
over to Officer Chris Click.

Inside the interview room, Clara moves about and finally sits
sideways on the chair. She rests her shoulders and head against the
wall. It has now been almost three hours since Clara was placed in
the interview room. There is no doubt that Clara now is feeling the
strain of being in this room and at the Police Department.

###

One can only imagine what is going through her mind now
that she has admitted to the crime. Except she still seems unable to
grasp the truth that her actions lead to Erik's death.

The door to the interview room is unlocked and the person
who enters this time introduces himself as Detective Benavides.
Detective Benavides says, "Hi Clara. Detective Fiber asked me to
talk to you a little bit. What we do in cases like this is we would
like to get a sample of your DNA and what we use this for is to
compare to any samples found in the apartment. Do you think that
is something you are willing to do?"

"I don't even know what's going on. Do I need an attorney?
Am I under arrest?", Clara asks.

"I can't answer that."

After a little back and forth, Clara finally says, "You can take
a sample. I will do whatever you want."

Detective Benavides excuses himself and tells her he needs to
go get the kit.

When he leaves the room Clara rocks back and forth and then
lays her head in her lap, her arms inside the sleeves of her shirt.

In a few minutes she hears the door being unlocked and in
comes Detective Benavides again. He has the kit with him.

Detective Benavides begins by showing her the Q-tips and
then says he has to put gloves on so that they can't say it was

contaminated. He shows her the waiver of search of a body and asks her to move closer to the table so that she can see the form. He reads it, explaining and pointing out where she will need to sign and where he will sign the form. The waiver covers everything for collection and he clarifies that all he wants is just the buccal swabs.

Now Clara is feeling real pressure. It is obvious that by her next statement, she is no longer sure she can convince the police she is innocent. She is no longer processing what they say or ask of her anymore.

"What do you need it for?" She asks.

Detective Benavides again explains that they will match this sample of her DNA against what they find in the apartment. He adds that of course they know she has been living there.

Clara says, "I don't understand it. I don't understand what I am signing for."

Again Detective Benavides calmly explains that she is signing the form so that they can get the buccal swabs and that is all.

"Am I under arrest?"

He tells her that he can't answer that. That there is a good possibly that she will be arrested. The best thing she could have done was tell the truth. He knows it doesn't seem like it now but the best thing she could have done was come down to the station and be honest. Ultimately, he says, she did tell the truth.

Clara says, "I didn't kill him."

Detective Benavides just says, "I'm not saying that you did."

Clara says point blank, "I want an attorney."

Detective Benavides at this point tells her that he won't do this then. He adds that it is just something that they ask. He explains that she needs to help herself and that they cannot help her. Just because she's going to jail does not mean that she is guilty

Clara replies, that she would have told the truth but she didn't want to say anything about hitting her friend because it wouldn't have caused him to be dead. She adds that she has been in trouble before.

Even though Detective Benavides says he doesn't care about that, it doesn't stop Clara who says, "I was involved in a case where a man was stabbed and I had this attorney who said you are a stupid bitch. Don't you ever tell the police anything. So ever since then, whether I did something or not I don't want to say anything. I don't know how to take things. I know how to tell the truth. I was the last to see the victim, Victor alive and I told him to lay still and not move and today he is alive."

They have a little back and forth about telling the truth and what Clara has said the attorney told her. When she tries to explain about the current issue, Detective Benavides stops her explaining that since she has asked for an attorney they can't talk about this with her. He says, "Let's hold off on the DNA sample. I will go and talk to Detective Whitebird".

Clara says, "The lady came and took my clothes, my wallet; everything!"

Detective Benavides says to her that she is most likely going to jail.

Clara asks, "Do I have to sit in jail until I figure it out?"

Detective Benavides replies, "I know it's hard."

"I called to get him help. I did not hit him to kill him."

Detective Benavides says he will go talk to Inspector Whitebird. He explains that this is how things work. They have to find out why Erik died and that is done by the Medical Examiner's office and since she requested an attorney they will not be able to take the DNA samples and can't discuss anything about the case with her. Detective Benavides leaves.

Clara is again alone. She takes off her glasses and places them on the table and stares at her hands. She begins what seems to be cleaning out her fingernails as she sits there, again waiting for what will happen next. After a bit she gets up and moves to the corner of the room and stares into it and then taking her arms back out of the sleeves of the shirt, stands and leans against the back wall. She takes off the sandals they provided her and stands bare foot against the wall. She burps, and begins shifting from foot to foot. She glances about the small cubicle, fidgeting constantly.

After about ten minutes Clara eventually puts her feet back into the shoes and removes her hands from under the shirt. She looks at her hands and then puts her arms back into the shirt and removes the shoes once again. She looks at the shoes and then again slides her feet into them.

She is extremely restless moving from the back wall to the side wall and back again to lean against the back wall. She bounces back and forth. It is now almost four hours since she has been placed in the investigation room. She's tired, cold and hungry and though she has told the Detectives she is well aware of police procedures, she is not comfortable with any of this. Clara leans against the side wall and again slips her feet out of the shoes.

The only possession that remains in the room is her glasses and these she has left on the table. When she hears the door being unlocked, Clara puts the sandals back on her feet and places her arms back in the sleeves of the orange shirt.

###

From evidence and interviews, it became apparent that Clara Blocker had murdered Erik Saxton on September 16th at 12 noon. Officer Poindexter receives a call from Inspector Whitebird to come to the Oklahoma County Police Department, homicide office to transport Clara Blocker to the Oklahoma County Jail and book her on the charge of murder in the first degree.

Finally Detective Whitebird enters the interview room with Officer Poindexter. Detective Whitebird says, "Okay, Clara, this officer will take care of you." While he stands back Officer Poindexter tells Clara to put her glasses on so they don't lose them. He asks her to turn around and put her hands behind her back. He puts her in a pair of handcuffs. Then he walks her out of the interview room.

CHAPTER 8: CLEANING UP LOOSE ENDS

(SEPTEMBER 16 & 17, 2010)

One of the most important messages communicated has always been the notification of the death of a family member. The news spreads outward—like ripples in a pond—from family members to friends, to employers, and other individuals who knew the deceased. Various bureaucracies, too, must be informed, such as Social Security agencies, and voters' registration. A death notice announces a void in the social fabric and the survivors' entry into the bereavement role. Who delivers the death notification, and to whom it is delivered, reveals much about the nature of individuals' ties to the broader society. The order and nature by which notifications are made reveal a prioritizing of the importance of the social bonds between the deceased and his or her kinship groups, friends, work and civic associates, and the wider public. If the wrong approach is employed when informing someone of a death, as a distant cousin is informed before a sibling, people may feel slighted and ill feelings can result. Therefore, a "ranking" process usually exists with regard to whom the contact person(s) should be and the order in which survivors should be notified of a death.

Just as critical, the documentation is a very important part of the criminal investigator's job. Clear, concise, and correct documenting of the facts and circumstances surrounding the crime scene is essential. The documentation in this case is composed of field notes, photography, and crime scene sketching. The notes will become permanent written records of the facts of the case to be used in conducting further investigation, in writing reports, and in prosecuting the case.

###

While at the scene, Lieutenant Shubert has spoken with the management of the apartment complex where this incident occurred. He obtains Erik Saxton's emergency contact information and passed this information on to Detective Lyndell

Easley. Sergeant Jay Coffey includes this information in his crime incident report.

One of the names is for Juanita Tischendorf, Erik Saxton's mother in Rochester, NY. Detective Lyndell Easley calls the number and it is answered by an employee of a business who state she has never heard of Juanita Tischendorf. (It was later learned the phone number on file had the wrong prefix)

Marilyn Goodban was listed as a family friend, and Detective Lyndell Easley calls the number listed for her on September 17, 2010 at 9:45 a.m. He speaks with a person who identifies herself as Sharilyn Edlund, and advises she is Marilyn Goodban's roommate. Detective Lyndell Easley explained he is seeking next of kin information for Erik Saxton, and Ms. Edlund advises him that Marilyn Goodban was Saxton's former mother-in-law. Marilyn Goodban is unavailable at the time of the call, but Sharilyn Edlund provides the name and telephone number for Heather Goodban who is Erik Saxton's ex-wife.

Detective Lyndell Easley speaks with Heather Goodban on September 17, 2010 at 9:50 a.m. She provides a street address for Juanita Tischendorf in New York but is too distraught to give him additional information.

Taking the initiative Detective Lyndell Easley contacts the Rochester Police Department and speaks with Lieutenant Mike Van Roo. Detective Lyndell Easley identifies himself and tells Lieutenant Mike Van Roo that he is calling from the Oklahoma City Police Department. In the conversation Detective Lyndell Easley informs Lieutenant Mike Van Roo that he has an address for the individual, Juanita Tischendorf, who he needs to get in contact with.

Upon hearing the address, Lieutenant Mike Van Roo informs Detective Lyndell Easley that the address he has been given is in a suburb of Rochester called Irondequoit. After advising him, Lieutenant Mike Van Roo transfers the call to the Irondequoit Police Department. Inspector Scott takes the call.

In the pursuing conversation, Detective Lyndell Easley explains that he is calling from the Oklahoma City Police Department. He informs Inspector Scott that the reason for the call is that they need to notify Juanita Tischendorf of the murder of her son in Oklahoma City. Inspector Scott volunteers to handle the matter and Detective Lyndell Easley gives him the street address.

Inspector Scott lets the Detective know that he will call him back as soon as he makes contact with the mother. They then discuss the information concerning the case that can be shared with her.

Heather Goodban called Detective Lyndell Easley back after she had regained her composure and he explained that Saxton had suffered trauma to the left side of his head. Goodban stated Saxton was paralyzed on his left side and was incapable of defending himself. Detective Lyndell Easley asked for additional information and Goodban stated he could not use his left arm and hand at all and his left leg was disabled to the point he was only able to walk by pivoting this leg form the hip. Detective Lyndell Easley asked if this disability was readily apparent to a casual observer and Goodban assured me it was.

###

At a little before 6:00 p.m. on Thursday, September 16 a phone message was left at the Homicide Office for Detective Gary Damron. The call is from Thu Tran of Apartment C in the Hunt Apartments. She explains that she is calling regarding a call back card left in her door while she was out.

Detective Gary Damron returns the call on Friday, September 17 and speaks to Thu Tran. Thu immediately asks, "What is this about?"

"There was a death in Apartment E. Do you know the person who lived there?"

"I don't know anyone in Apartment E. I heard a noise between 11:00 p.m. and 12 midnight and looked out the window but I could not see anything and didn't hear anything either. I have a roommate. Maybe he heard something."

"Can I speak to your roommate."

"He's not here now, but I will have him call you.?"

"Thank you Ms. Tran."

Detective Gary Damron makes a note of the conversation.

###

At shortly before 2:00 p.m. on September 17, Detective Gary Damron receives a call back from Amanda McDonald who lives in Apartment F.

Detective Gary Damron informs her that the Oklahoma Police Department was conducting a canvass of the Hunt Apartments after finding the person in Apartment E was dead. Amanda informs him that her sister, Amber had spoken with a Detective at the scene.

Detective Gary Damron says, "What can you tell us?"

"Well, I did not know the person living in Apartment E but did see a female around the apartment on the night of Wednesday, September 16. It was around 6:30 p.m. that myself and my sister Amber returned to the apartment. As we were walking to the apartment we saw a white female in front of Apartment E. As we walked by her, she hit on my sister. She was talking, saying "hey homie", just trying to get my sister's attention. The female appeared to be high on some kind of drugs and wanting to get higher from the way she was acting."

"I let my mother know about her since she was coming to the apartment at 9:45 p.m. that evening. When my mother arrived, I went out to bring her to the apartment because of the female being in front of my apartment. While we were walking in the white female begins saying "hey baby girl." I ignored her and went to my apartment. As we were walking by Apartment E I saw a black male through the window. I hadn't seen him outside the apartment at any time."

"Later that evening my sister Amber was helping me fix the light in front of my apartment. When we went outside the female was walking around in front of the apartment talking on the phone. She was telling the person on the phone that she had one hundred dollars and asked if they were cooking. After the female got off the phone I heard her talking to the person inside the apartment telling him to let her into the apartment, but I did not hear the person inside the apartment say anything."

"At around 10:00 p.m. my mother and sister left my apartment to go home. I heard doors slamming during the evening but not very loud. I went to bed and around 11:00 p.m. I heard doors slamming very loudly. I also heard a female talking very loud but could not understand what was being said." At this point she stopped.

"Anything else you can think of?" Detective Gary Damron asks.

"No, I can't think of anything else."

"Well, thank you. You've been a big help."

###

At around 2:00 pm. On September 17, Thu Tran's roommate, Lan Phommachanh, calls into the precinct and asks for Detective Gary Damron. Lan says that he did not know the person staying in Apartment E and was not aware of there being a problem until they were notified.

###

At around 2:00 p.m. on September 17, Detective Lyndell Easley receives a call back from Heather Goodban, the victim's ex-wife. She is more composed and wants to know what happened. Detective Lyndell Easley explains that Erik Saxton has suffered trauma to the left side of his head. Ms. Goodban tells him that Erik Saxton was paralyzed on his left side and was incapable of defending himself.

Detective Lyndell Easley asks if there was any additional information that she could share and Ms. Goodban tells him that he could not use his left arm and hand at all and his left leg was disabled to the point he was only able to walk by pivoting this leg from the hip. Detective Lyndell Easley asks if this disability was readily apparent to a casual observer. Ms. Goodban assured him it was.

###

On September 17, 2010, at 3:10 pm. Inspector Whitebird enters the interview room and arranges one of the chairs to the left side wall. This room is set up opposite to the one that held Clara, but has the same walls and lack of furnishings beyond the small table with metal legs, and three armless, molded plastic black chairs.

Inspector Whitebird leaves and shortly returns with David P Elkins who is wearing a navy blue and white striped polo shirt, a blue baseball cap, blue jeans and sneakers. David is guided to the chair behind the desk near the back wall.

As he talks there are several points that are not correct. He says that Erik has only part of an arm on one side and that Erik is an epileptic. He also says that Erik had met Clara in a drug rehab program. Nothing on record shows this to be true.

###

Once seated, Inspector Whitebird goes through his notes. While waiting, David says, "I've known Erik for a long time. I use to give him a ride when he lived in the Brookwood apartments before moving to the gated community. Since Erik moved to the Hunt apartments I would see him walking to the CVS out there . I live out there myself."

Inspector Whitebird asks for his address and phone number and David willingly supplies that information. He next asks him his birth date. David is 64 years old.

Detective Whitefield asks, "Where do you work?"

David says, "I am a trim carpenter, but I am actually retired. I just do some jobs on the side".

At this point Inspector Whitebird tells David that he is being interviewed concerning an incident that occurred on Thursday, September 16 around noon and what he plans on asking him is about the day before which was Wednesday the 15th of September.

David shows Inspector Whitebird his cell that has three calls from Clara. "Clara called me at 6:36 p.m."

"Where were you when she called?"

"I was home."

After looking closer, David says, "Wait a minute, Clara called next on the 16th not the 15th and she called from here, the police department."

Inspector Whitebird asks, "How do you know Clara?"

"I met her through someone else who knew Clara and she at the time was in the Oklahoma County Jail. Clara called me and said that until she gets into a drug rehab program she needs help and asks if I would help her out as I had done for this other person. So I did and Clara stayed with me and goes to the program and does well."

David explains that he has lots of room and lives alone since his wife passed. He use to take in foster children and that is how he has had contact with the system.

He continues, "So she stays with me for a while and then leaves and it is quite a while before I hear from her again. She calls and says that she has been in a drug rehab program in the town of Washington, Oklahoma".

Inspector Whitebird is aware that the town of Washington is in McClain County, Oklahoma, about 40 minutes due south of Oklahoma City. This is a small town with a population of a little over 500 residents.

David continues, " Clara says she will be in Oklahoma City until September 17. She says that she knows she owes me some money and she will be getting her food stamps soon and will pay me back by buying groceries if that is all right with me. I tell her that is fine."

To explain, David says, "When Clara stayed with me before she had gotten into a fight and had broken her glasses. She couldn't see without her glasses so I felt sorry for her and took her to Optical Illusions where I get my glasses and bought her a pair. It costs me $200.00."

"Anyway", David says, "I hadn't heard from her for a day or two and then she calls me and says she needs to put some money on her cell phone because she needs to call her probation officer. Her PO came to visit with me one time. I forgot his name, but it was when Clara lived with me"

"So, in any case I told her I had $17 dollars in my pocket and I would go put that on her cell phone."

Clara has been staying with me for about a month when I tell her she needs to find some place to stay as I am getting ready to go out of town and will be gone for some time. Clara says she knows someone she can stay with and she mentions Erik."

"This is the first time I knew that Clara knew Erik. I assume that Clara met Erik in drug rehab. Although I didn't know, that Erik had a drug problem. I know Erik takes medication for epileptic though because Erik told me that.

When Erik is asked if it will be okay for Clara to stay with him for a while, he says, yes."

" Anyway, Clara goes to stay with Erik".

###

This is different from what was said before. It was stated by Clara that he, David had said to Clara he knew someone she could stay with and had called Erik to ask if Clara could stay with him for a while since he had to go out of town.

###

"Then I didn't hear from her for another couple of days and she called on the 15th of September to say she need to put some money on her cell phone. That her PO would call and she wouldn't be able to answer. So I asked if she had the money this time and she said, yes."

"I told her that I would come and get her. So this time I drive over to the Hunt Apartments to pick up Clara and take her to get minutes on her phone."

Inspector Whitebird asks, "When did you get the call from Clara?"

"It was 6:36 p.m. on the 15th of September."

"Is that a gated community?"

David says, "It is, but Erik's apartment is in front and you can pull up to the back door. But I parked out front."

'What type of vehicle were you driving?"

"I was driving my green van to the apartment."

"Did you see Erik at that time?"

"I didn't go in, instead I waited in the van and called Clara again and she came out to meet me "

"So you didn't see Erik?"

"No, but when I called her I could hear her talking to someone in the background and I assume it was Erik."

"When Clara got in the van she said that she doesn't know if Erik will let her back in or not, and I said, sure he will. I really didn't think much of it at the time."

"So she gets in the van and I take her to the Cricket store but I don't go in, instead I wait in the van. When we get to the Cricket store it is almost closing time. Clara comes out of the Cricket store laughing and climbs into my van and says, that the man behind the counter didn't want to take her money because she has been drinking. I asks if he did give her the minutes and she says yes."

"You said you have known her off and on for how long?" Inspector Whitebird asks.

"For about a year."

"Have you ever seen her drunk before?"

"No, never. I didn't allow her to drink at my house."

"Did she show any different characteristics. Was she louder, bossier?"

"She was a little mouthier".

Inspector Whitebird asks, "Did she say why initially she thought Erik wouldn't let her in?"

"No"

"Did she say they had been arguing?"

"No."

David says that he drove her back to the apartment and she went around the corner toward Erik's apartment. He left then as he was going to visit his grandkids out in Norman that evening. He was there for a while and when he got back in his van he saw that Clara had called around 9 p.m. But he didn't' speak to her. That was it. He never talked to her again. The next call about Clara came when Inspector Whitebird called him.

Inspector Whitebird asked David if he had talked to Clara while she was in the investigation room at the police department. David says that he did and that it was after he had spoken to Inspector Whitebird. Clara said, "David, Erik has died." and he told her he knew that because Inspector Whitebird had called him. Clara then said, "I don't know what happened." David said he told her no matter what happened you better tell the truth.

At this point Inspector Whitebird informed David that Erik apparently had some head trauma, but he can't speak to that until the medical examiner has a chance to examine him. Clara did admit to getting into a fight with Erik and there was enough evidence to take her into custody.

David tells Inspector Whitebird that Erik is pretty defenseless and tells him that they had a friend Steve who was rough and who came to Erik's place and a girl named Teresa Rene Stanfield who the police are holding now. Both of these people know Erik and know Clara.

It is as though David is trying to give some alternatives for who murdered Erik. David adds that Clara never mentioned to him that she and Erik had got into an altercation or anything.

Inspector Whitebird asks about Clara's demeanor and David says that she was drunk and acting odd. David says that she is not to drink as she is bipolar. He adds he knows about bipolar people as the church he goes to administers to bipolar people. As for her medication, David says they must have seen all the pills she has. Those are meds for bipolar and David shares that she gets her meds from the state as she can't afford them. He adds that Clara knows she shouldn't drink.

Inspector Whitebird says that being drunk is not an excuse for killing someone and David agrees. They have been in the interview room nine minutes, eleven seconds when Inspector Whitebird stands and says that's all they need for now. They walk out together.

###

During the initial investigation of this murder scene on September 16, 2010, Inspector Benavides left a contact card on the door of 3041 SW 89th Street, Apartment G. The resident of this apartment, Robert Blanchard, called the Homicide Office after hours on September 17, 2010 and left a message requesting contact.

Detective Lyndell Easley called Blanchard on 9/18/10 at 11:20 a.m. and asked him if he had been home on September 15, 2010 when the altercation between Erik Scott Saxton and Clara Ann Blocker was supposed to have occurred. Blanchard stated he was out of town on business during this time. He further stated he had only seen Saxton one or two times and had never spoken with him. Detective Lyndell Easley described Blocker to Blanchard and he stated he had never seen her around the apartment complex.

###

Heather Goodban, the ex-wife of the victim, Erik Saxton, contacted Detective Lyndell Easley on Monday, September 20 and advised she had located some property while cleaning out Saxton's apartment that she thought possibly would be evidence. He met with her at her residence on this date at 2:00 p.m.. Goodban turned over a handwritten letter to the victim, and apparently written based on the content of the letter by the suspect, Clara Blocker.

Goodban also had a gallon-sized zip-lock baggie containing numerous prescription and over-the-counter medications. The medication consisted of 13 round, white tablets marked with the letter R, 3 round red tablets marked I-2, 6 oval white tablets marked Bayer back and body, 8 oval white tablets marked IP272, 3 oval orange tablets marked B 293, 15 orange tablets marked B293 and packaged in a prescription bottle to Clara Blocker and marked Oxcarbazepine 300 mg; 10 oval shaped orange tablets marked 4 0 on one side and 1011 on the reverse side, packaged in a prescription bottle to Clara blocker and marked Citalopram.

Goodban also provided Detective Lyndell Easley with a photograph of the victim to be copied and placed in the case file.

Before he left the residence, he asked Goodban about the claim Saxton had been consuming alcohol the day prior to his death. Goodban state she was married to Saxton for eight years during which time she observed him to consume alcohol no more than six times per year and she had never observed him to have consumed alcohol to the point of intoxication. Goodban explained Saxton took the prescription medication Topamax to control seizures which prevented him from consuming alcohol.

Detective Lyndell Easley subsequently booked the above listed property into the OCPD property room under the case number.

Chapter 9: From Normalcy To Shock

(September 17, 2010)

When someone is murdered, the death is sudden, violent, final and incomprehensible. The loved one is no longer there — the shared plans and dreams are no longer possible. The loss of the relationship will be grieved in different ways by all those who felt close to the victim because their relationships with the victim are all different. Losing a loved one through a homicide is one of the most traumatic experiences that an individual can face; it is an event for which no one can adequately prepare, but which leaves in its wake tremendous emotional pain and upheaval.

###

It is Friday, September 17, 2010, and it starts out like any other Friday for me. I am up and about by 4:30 a.m. and meet up with my neighbor to begin our hour walk. It is a little chilly this morning as the temp is around 45 degrees, but after the winter we had, it feels good. It is a great way to start the day.

I put on my coat, hat and gloves, and I am ready by the time Gale knocks on the door. From the minute the door is open, we begin talking as we start out on our route that will take us around the neighborhood.

The hour goes by quickly and soon we are back on our street. We part ways and I hurry upstairs to take a quick shower and put on fresh workout clothes, then hurry back downstairs so that I have time to drink a cup of coffee with my husband, Mark, before he leaves for work. I know he will be leaving early as he plans to ride his bike to work this day, like any other day when it is not showing or raining.

As soon as Mark leaves, I climb in my car and drive the three minute distance down the street to CURVES. I do my half-hour workout then spend the same amount of time chatting with my friends.

By eight o'clock I am back home having a final cup of coffee and trying to decide whether to take another shower right away or wait until I finish cleaning the house. Friday is housecleaning and laundry day.

I decide to wait on that shower and just get to the cleaning. I begin upstairs, turning on the radio first, find a station with an upbeat sound and then turn up the volume to fill the house with music. Methodically I move from room to room lost in the music while I put my home in order, tossing the dirty linens and clothes down the laundry chute as I go. When the upstairs is back in order and smelling wonderfully fresh, I turn off the music and go downstairs where it all begins again.

I think about our upcoming trip. We are off to Dallas where we are invited to The Cooper Clinic for a book signing on-site. My book *The Madman, The Marathoner* in which Dr. Cooper so kindly prepared a foreword was about his patient, my friend, Don McNelly. For me it is an honor indeed to just have Dr. Cooper prepare the foreword for the book. When I am informed they want to hold a book signing at the Clinic, I am ecstatic and of course I accept. Kenneth H. Cooper, MD, MPH, is not only the founder of the Clinics but also the man who coined the phrase 'aerobics' and inspired millions to exercise for good health with the release of his first best-seller Aerobics.

It is all going as planned with no interruptions as I finish my cleaning and turn off the music. Before I do anything else, I need to eat something and rest a bit then take my shower. I am just about ready to sit when there is a knock at the door.

I can't help thinking, Murphy's law. 'If everything seems to be going well, you have obviously overlooked something'.

At first I think I will pretend I'm not home since we have a lot of politicians calling and knocking at the door. But that would be rude so I tiptoe over my freshly mopped kitchen floor and open the door. No one is there.

The doorbell rings again and I realize it is the front door. No one, but a stranger will go to the front door. It is definitely a politician.

In a loud voice I say, "Hello. Come to the side door, please."

I can hear footfalls and know that the person is now going down the walkway, heading toward the driveway. In a minute I see a well-dressed man coming into my line of vision and I politely say, "Hello". He responds in turn, then asks, "Are you Juanita Tischendorf?"

That throws me off guard. I reply, "Yes," hesitantly wondering who this man is since this is not the usual greeting from a politician coming to the door. I begin to think that this is maybe a customer instead. I run a computer business and an upholstery business and usually my clients call first, but some have come to the door. That must be it.

"What can I do for you," I ask. The visitor pauses a moment and then asks if I have a son.

Suddenly I feel strange and unsure what to say. Yes I have a son, but not in Rochester, New York. Erik lives in Oklahoma and his last name is still Saxton so whatever this man has to say, this must be a mistake. This person evidently is looking for someone else; totally forgetting that he knew my name. Whatever he came to say has to be a mistake. So, I say, "No" in response to his question.

"Mrs. Tischendorf," he says, "My name is Investigator James Scott of the Criminal Investigation Unit here in Irondequoit." He offers me his card and I take it, staring at it as if it holds the answer to what this is all about. Erik is 41 years old and has never been in trouble with the law, nor would I believe he is now. This has got to be a mistake and I need to call my son in Oklahoma to get to the bottom of this.

Investigator Scott waits patiently and then asks, "Is there anyone home with you?"

This is some kind of scam, I tell myself and I need to be more careful about opening the door to strangers. I feel my heart leap, but the feeling passes as I tell myself there is nothing to worry about. It's broad daylight and I can see my neighbor is outside so I tell him that my husband is at work and, I am alone at the moment. I figure he will ask if he can come back later.

"Can I come in?"

That I did not expect and I rub the card feeling the raised emblem and words on it, but anyone could make a card like this. I need a moment to think. I look down at the floor and ask if he can wait a second while I put the rug at the door, explaining that I have just finished cleaning.

"No problem," he says. He waits patiently and I have only a few moments to decide what to do. If he wanted to, he could have just opened the door and walked in while I fiddled with the rug, so maybe he is legit.

"Can I see some ID," I ask.

Patiently he reaches inside his pocket and pulls out his wallet. I watch as he flips it open, but his next words let me know he hasn't made a mistake and I am who he is looking for.

"Do you have a son by the name of Erik Saxton in Oklahoma City?"

There is no way he would know this! I move aside and allow Investigator Scott in. As soon as he is in the kitchen he says, "Mrs. Tischendorf, I have some bad news. Would you like to sit down?"

Left to themselves, things tend to go from bad to worse is Murphy's law playing itself out now. Somehow I know that whatever he is about to tell me is beyond my comprehension of 'bad to worse'. So I panic and at that second my heart is in my throat blocking my air flow and I feel the first real sense of something being dreadfully wrong. My mind rewinds back.

My son Erik is a dwarf. As a child he was diagnosed with fluid on the brain and at the age of ten he had brain surgery to remove a cyst. Since the surgery he has been prone to having seizures. I know he has had a couple since moving to Oklahoma, but his medication has kept him from having them often. Maybe he had a seizure?

Good treatment with medication is a tricky balancing act. You need enough of a medicine to stop the seizures. But if you have too much of it, you can have a lot of side effects. The key is to find a happy medium and that is not always easy when you are a little person. Erik has dealt with this for a long time and has been lucky to find that Topamax works for him. So maybe Erik asked that I be contacted and told he is in the hospital?

When Erik was married I was able to relax some and not worry so much about health issues. Then when he divorced it all came back again. The thought of him being alone and having something go wrong and with me so far away from him was a constant burden on my soul. I know he's forty-one, but he is still my baby.

I have all but forgotten the man standing in my kitchen as I try to figure this out on my own so that I am able to control myself. So, did he have a seizure and was he in the hospital? Was this what the Investigator has to tell me? Erik had a seizure and is in the hospital.

I begin to tear up, waiting for the Investigator to tell me more. I want to know if Erik is all right, but I am scared to hear what he might say next.

"Maybe we should call your husband."

Shakily I say, "He's at work. He rode his bike to work this morning. Please tell me what this is about."

Investigator Scott guides me into the great room and has me seated before he shares more.

"It never gets easier to bring bad news to a family", he begins. "There never seems to be a right way to say it."

He pauses and then he says the words. "Mrs. Tischendorf, your son, Erik Saxton was murdered!"

This is the moment that marks a time in my life when there is no time before and no time after. Every moment is in this now!

"Murdered!" What is he saying. Why is he saying this. Who would murder my son. I try to focus, but can't. I try to speak, but couldn't. This couldn't be happening. This has to be a mistake, but as I sit there unable to push the lump in my throat down so that I can swallow, or speak, I know this is happening. This is really happening.

But then, I think, maybe this is all a mistake. Maybe it isn't Erik after all. I mean there are a lot of distinguishing features, but none have been mentioned. Yes, I think, it is a mistake. The tears will not stop and I need to ask questions.

"How do you know its Erik," I manage to say.

"He had ID on him."

Okay, I think, but then someone could have stolen his ID and, and…

"Are you all right? Can I get you some water? Can I call someone for you? Can I call your husband?"

Investigator Scott is full of questions and I can't even remember my own name at the moment. Obviously I have replied to him because he brings me a glass of water and I drink it while he stands by the table dialing his phone. I hear him say, "Is this Mr. Tischendorf?"

He walls into the kitchen and talks low into the phone. I can't even remember giving him the number. I can't remember much since hearing the word, MURDERED. I look up and Investigator Scott stands beside me. He says, "You're husband is on his way."

That's funny. I find that so funny. Mark rode his bike to work and he is on his way. I want to laugh out loud at the picture of him hoping on his bike, strapping on his helmet and pedaling home. Only I can't get the laugh out. All I can do is cry so I settle for a few more gulps of water.

Drinking the water stops that choking feeling. I begin to calm myself. I have to get myself together. I need answers and I need to ask the questions to get the answers I need. Only Investigator Scott has a question.

"Do you know a Clara Ann Blocker?"

I allow the name to sink into my brain. Clara. I don't know any Clara. Blocker is a strange last name, so I am pretty certain I would remember it if I had heard it. Besides where does he think I would have heard this name.

"No, I don't know any Clara Blocker. Who is she."

His next words I know will remain with me for the rest of my life.

"She is the woman who murdered your son!"

That opens a whole now mass of feelings. My heart is pounding in my chest and my head is spinning not allowing me to think or know what I should do. There is no more room for words to enter my brain. It is becoming too real to handle and so I let myself be silent and cry.

I have a right to cry. I am filled with intense grief, and a lot of stress that needs to push its way out. That is when the Investigator helps me up from the chair and just holds me until I am able to breathe again.

Time has no meaning but there is something that does. I think, Erik needs me and with that I can feel control return.

"Thank you. I feel better now."

I sit back down. "Why, " I ask. "Why did she do this?" Even as I ask I know there's not an answer anyone will be able to give. How could there be a reason to murder my son. If you want something from him all you have to do is ask and he would give it freely. This has to be a maniac, a sub human who just wanted to hurt someone!

Investigator Scott has been listening to his radio, cell phone; not quite sure what it is. I wonder if he has heard my question. He seems to be fidgeting with this thing as though his life depends on it. I am about to pose the question again when he finally looks up.

"I'm trying to reach Detective Lyndell Easley in Oklahoma City. He is the one who called our offices and he will be able to tell us more." He pauses a movement and then he adds, "Detective Easley apparently found something in the apartment or on Erik that listed you as his mother. He also has information on other close family members that need to be contacted before your son's name is released. As soon as I get him on the phone I will let you speak with him."

Am I ready to hear more. The thought of knowing what happen will make it real and I don't know if I am ready for that just yet. But I have to know, I have to see where it happened. It was at that instance I knew we were going to Oklahoma.

I am forced out of my reverie when Investigator Scott asks if I have any contact information to help them reach Erik's father. At first I tell him I do not, then think about it a moment. "Yes I have his sister Dorothea Saxton's phone and home address. She should be able to reach her brother or give you the information." I excuse myself and go to my office. It feels good to be away from the Detective. As I enter the office I take a moment to catch my breath, then go about trying to find the address.

It feels good to be doing something and not having to sit and hear the news that is ripping my heart apart. My baby is dead and I am so far from him. I take a moment for myself, then take the mouse, click away until I have my address file open. I scroll down and find Dorothea's address and write it down on a piece of paper. I write down the phone number as well.

I look at what I have written and wonder if I should make the call myself. I still care for Dorothea but it will probably be best if I let the detective handle the call because if she starts crying I will not be able to console her. Finally I get up and go back into the great room to give the detective the piece of paper with the information.

"Would you like us to call anyone else," he asked.

"No, I should call my family here. They should hear it from me."

I then mention that Erik's ex-wife lives in Oklahoma and did they want to contact her.

"No, that's not necessary," he says. Then he pauses and adds, "Well, if you have her contact information, I will give her a call. What's her name?"

I knew that was coming and I sit there for a moment trying to remember. I had removed the address and phone from my address book since on several occasions Heather had emailed me frustrated. She wanted me to stop people from sending Erik cards and things to 'her' address. She no longer wanted people asking her how to reach Erik.

Remembering this I think to myself, maybe she shouldn't be contacted. Besides I can't even remember her address anymore.

I am shaken back to reality when I hear the detective asking, "Do you know her maiden name?"

Like right, I think, like I am going to come up with that. Then I remember I still have her mother's address and phone in my address book. I didn't want to remove them from my life as Mark and I both liked them a lot. And thinking about her and knowing her mother's name, it pops into my head. "It's Goodban"

At that moment Mark walks into the kitchen with his bike helmet in his hand. His face and neck are red from the obvious fast bike trip home and I can see he is trying to catch his breath as he moves toward me.

Until that moment I hadn't thought of how dangerous it could be for him to try and get home quickly on his bike. He could have been hurt. The thought of putting him in danger releases a fresh flow of tears as he comes to me. In a flash, Mark is at my side consoling me.

Mark introduces himself to Investigator Scott. After easing me into a chair, Mark stands beside me and listens as Investigator Scott reviews what he has already told me. Mark listens intently while keeping a comforting hand on my shoulder. I am only half listening now, glad to have someone else be the 'sounding board' as Mark asks questions of Investigator Scott.

Then Investigator Scott's phone rings. "I need to take this," he says. "It's Detective Easley in Oklahoma".

Investigator Scott steps out of the room and speaks too softly for us to hear. Then, he returns and hands me the phone. "Detective Easley would like to speak to you," he says.

At first I just look at the phone in his hand. Then Mark says, "Do you want me to speak with him?" I want to say 'yes' but I have to do this so I smile at Mark and finally take the phone

"Hello, Detective Easley," I say.

"Is this Mrs. Tischendorf?"

"Yes."

"I'm sorry for your loss."

"Thank you."

"As I am sure Investigator Scott has shared with you. Your son, Erik Saxton was murdered by a woman named, Clara Ann Blocker. This woman called 911 and asked the police to make a welfare check at 3042 SW 89th Street, your son's address. When the officers entered the apartment they found Erik and transported him to the hospital."

I am silent listening intently.

"Are you okay? Do you want me to go on?"

"Please."

"Clara Blocker remained at the scene and the officers spoke with her and finally transported her to police headquarters where she finally admitted to the crime. She was taken into custody"

I am about to ask the question that I dread asking, when it is answered for me.

"Erik died at the hospital and Clara Blocker was charged with 1st degree murder and is now being held without bond."

When Detective Easley tells me to call him, I ask Mark for a piece of paper and then tell the detective, "Go ahead." I write down the information and then give the phone to Mark who bobs his head as he listens to the instructions. Then Mark hands the phone back to the investigator.

"She just left him there alone to die," I say to Mark feeling the tears of helplessness coming upon me again. How could anyone be so cruel.

When I am able to get control of myself, I tell Mark that he did not die alone because he was alive when the ambulance took him to the hospital. I try to find comfort in this.

###

Mark entered my life when Erik was 24 years old and living in California. They would meet when Erik came home to be at our wedding in 1995 and they got along just fine. As the years progressed Mark was always willing to help Erik in any way he could and Erik grew quite fond of him. Mark would go with me in Oklahoma and we helped them fix what needed to be fix in their home. We made many trips to Oklahoma for visits and Heather and Erik took us around to see the area.

On one of our trips we went to the Alfred P. Murrah Federal Building which was a US federal government complex located in Downtown Oklahoma City, Oklahoma. The building was the target of the Oklahoma City bombing on April 19, 1995, which killed 168 people, 19 of which were children under the age of six. The Oklahoma City National Memorial was built on the site. The first thing that catches the eye as you arrive at the site is the Jesus Wept statue across from the OKC National Memorial in Oklahoma City, Oklahoma. Once parked, you enter the Gates of Time which are the twin gates that frame the moment of destruction – 9:02 a.m. –

and mark the formal entrances to the Memorial. The East Gate represents 9:01 a.m. on April 19, and the innocence of the city before the attack. The West Gate represents 9:03 a.m., the moment we were changed forever. Inside the Gates is the Reflecting Pool, a shallow depth of flowing water . Then comes the Field of 168 empty chairs that represent the lives taken on April 19, 1995. They stand in nine rows to represent each floor of the building, and each chair bears the name of someone killed on that floor. Nineteen smaller chairs stand for the children. On the east end of the Memorial stand the only remaining walls from the Murrah Building to remind us of those who survived the terrorist attack. The Memorial Museum is an interactive learning experience that takes you on a chronological self-guided tour through the story of April 19, 1995, and the days, weeks and years that followed the bombing of Oklahoma City's Alfred P. Murrah Federal Building.

On other visits we would go to the historic Bricktown Canal in the heart of the Bricktown Entertainment District. Here there were lots of shops and good food. We also enjoyed going to the walking parks and to Wynnewood, Oklahoma, a very small town about 66 miles from Oklahoma City. It is quaint, quiet and where Heather's parents live. Other times her parents would come to Oklahoma City to visit with us.

When Erik was faced with going through a divorce after seven years of marriage, Mark was the supportive one. This came as a shock to me. Heather and Erik were both dwarfs and both ambitiously trying to find jobs and live a normal life. I thought of them as the perfect match. Obviously I was wrong, but the experience of marrying and owning a home were two of Erik's hopes for the future and he had accomplished them.

###

Now here again Mark is being my rock. I listen as the investigator tells Mark he can bring up a website for him to read, but Erik's name has been left out until next of kin are notified. He gives us the web address and Mark writes it down.

"Is that all you can tell us, Investigator Scott", I ask.

The investigator is intent on his phone again and says, "I am waiting on a call from the medical examiner's office now," he informs us. "Let me try and dial his number again."

Investigator Scott moves about as he continues to try and make contact. Every now and then Mark and I can hear voices coming from, maybe the radio on his belt. Then finally Detective Scott is talking on his phone and we know he has made his connection. He talks for a while and then hands me the phone. I take it without hesitation.

"This is Eddie Johnson, the medical examiner in Oklahoma," the detective states. "He hasn't completed his autopsy, but maybe he can tell you something."

I manage a mumbled, 'thank you' and then take the phone and put it up to my ear.

"Hello Mr. Johnson," I say.

"Is this Erik Saxton's mother," he ask

"Yes. Have you seen Erik?"

It's natural to want to shun suffering… to avoid it at all costs. No one in their right mind would choose to suffer. So it is natural for me to grasp at even a peek at hope.

"Yes, I saw your son when they brought him in," Mr. Johnson replies.

"How do you know it's my son, Erik," I ask.

"It's your son". He says positively. "He was found in his apartment and his identification identifies him as Erik Saxton."

He has not said the obvious and the first peek at hope seeps into my soul. I want this to be a point of mistaken identity. I want this to turn out for the best. I turn to the Investigator and say, "This might not be my son. He didn't say he was a dwarf and he could tell that my looking at him. It might not be Erik."

The Investigator takes the phone from me and puts it to his ear. He talks to Mr. Johnson, then turns to me and says, "It is your son."

I share with Mr. Johnson that we will be coming to Oklahoma and hand the phone to Mark who gives the details on our visit and then writes down information from Mr. Johnson who tells him he will be available to talk with us when we arrive in Oklahoma. He explains that he needs to release the body after the autopsy and wants to know if we have a place in mind. Mark informs him that we have no idea what is available in Oklahoma but that we want the body cremated. Mr. Johnson then tells Mark of his suggestion and then shares the information with me. I agree.

When Mark asks how long this can take, Mr. Johnson explains that the whole process takes careful work. An average autopsy case takes about four hours. That's including all the paperwork. There is about a half an hour before and after the autopsy for doing the external examination, the dictation, the paperwork.

###

After hearing Mr. Johnson, I know deep down that it is true. This is my son and he is dead! It's normal to act as I am acting because when we get bad news, the first thing we want to do is verify it but once it is proven to be a fact it is time to deal with it. There isn't any other choice you can make. I feel like everything has come crashing down around me and I am alone, but I am not. I strive to stay focused on getting through this. I must be strong but I can't hold back my emotions. There is nothing I can do about what has happened and I know I must try and get on with life. This I keep telling myself.

I watch as Mark concludes his conversation with Mr. Johnson and hangs up. He hands the phone back to Investigator Scott.

The detective pulls out the article in the Oklahoma paper and hands it to Mark. I stand up beside him so I can read it too.

Oklahoma City Woman Arrested On Homicide Complaint

Police have arrested a woman on a homicide complaint. The woman had called police to report a man's death in a Southside apartment.

###

FROM STAFF REPORTS

Published September 17, 2010

Oklahoma City police have arrested a woman who called them Thursday asking for a welfare check to be conducted on a male acquaintance. The man found in the apartment was pronounced dead at the hospital, Sergeant Jennifer Wardlow said.

Clara Ann Blocker, 38, of Oklahoma City, is in the Oklahoma County jail on a homicide complaint. The name of the male victim was not released pending notification of relatives.

About 10 a.m. Thursday, Blocker called 911 and asked police to make a welfare check at 3042 SW 89th Street. After the man was found, Blocker was taken into custody, questioned at police headquarters and arrested, Wardlow said.

Police did not say how the victim died. Wardlow said cause of death will be determined by the medical examiner's office.

Blocker was convicted in 2009 on a trafficking cocaine charge in Oklahoma County and is serving a 12-year suspended sentence.

In 2006 she was convicted of larceny of merchandise from a retailer, court records show.

###

Investigator Scott points out the address and it matches the one in my address book. I know he is trying to help me accept what I now know in my heart to be true. He then asks if we are going to be okay and we tell him we are fine, though we are far from fine!

Investigator Scott says that we need to call relatives as the name will be added to the news report and in their incident report as well. Before he leaves, Investigator Scott gives us a copy of his incident.

###

Incident #: 10-77977

Victim: B/M – no next of kin notified

Arrested: Blocker, Clara (W/F 1-17-72)

Yesterday morning (September 16th), at approximately 10am, Oklahoma City Police responded to a check-the-welfare call at 3042 SW 89th #E. This call was in reference to a man down inside this residence. This man was transported to an area hospital, where he was pronounced deceased.

Clara Blocker was the individual that contacted 911. Officers took her into custody at the scene. She was brought to Police Headquarters, where she was interviewed by Homicide investigators. At the conclusion of the interview, she was booked into the Oklahoma County Jail on one count of 1st Degree Murder.

The victim and Ms. Blocker were acquaintances. Victim's cause of death will be determined by the Medical Examiner's office.

Sergeant Jennifer Wardlow

Update # 1:

Victim: Saxton, Erik Scott (B/M 4-10-69) Next-of-kin has been notified.

For additional information, see original news release below.

Sergeant Jennifer Wardlow

Like me, other survivors tell of remembering, in detail, events of the notification. They recall every word delivered, the tone and voice inflection, even years later. I don't understand why, but I can theorize that it is because each one of us looks for a loophole in the information being delivered. It is that hope that this has all been a mistake that chisel's the moment in our memory.

Mark and I are alone, wondering what to do next.

"What do you want to do," Mark says.

"I want to go to Erik.

Mark is quiet, thinking and then says, "The Investigator said that we would probably get nowhere until after the weekend. Why don't we continue with our plans for the book signing in Texas and drive from there to Oklahoma."

I think about what he is saying and know he is right. We will go to Texas as plan and check into our room at the Cooper Institute and then drive to Oklahoma. There really isn't any other course to take.

That settled it is time to make the calls. With the address book in hand, we begin contacting family members. We call friends of Erik's who are local. We continue with calls and waiting for callbacks as long as we can before we must be on our way to Buffalo to catch our plane. Most of the family and friends have our cell phone if they need to reach us, but there is not much more we can share at this point.

My heart and my mind is full. If it wasn't happening to me I would wonder just how it is possible to go on with life at a time like this, but we must for many reasons.

###

On Friday, August 13, Mark and I traveled to Buffalo to take my mother-in-law Rita, to meet with her new doctor, an oncologist. It is at the end of that visit we are informed that there is a chance, Rita has colon cancer. Several days later, it is confirmed and treatment begins.

It doesn't seem real as we receive reports from my sister-in-law, Holle, how mom is doing. At first it seems hopeful. Rita is fighting the cancer with chemo tablets and radiation, since surgery is not recommended at this time.

It is over labor day weekend that we are next in Buffalo for a visit. We plan to take Rita with us to the labor day weekend family get together. When we arrive, Rita seems exhausted and says she hadn't been eating much. So unlike her, Rita says she needs to lay down for a while. A little over an hour later she is up and going about taking care of a few things she needs to handle and then sits down to play a game of pinochle with me. She explains that she doesn't feel like going to the labor day picnic but that we should go. Then, as I sit across the table from her I notice her arms shaking. It frightened me.

We know Rita is tired from the chemo or radiation and needs to rest, but we didn't think this shaking is a symptom of that. We call an ambulance.

That marked the beginning of her next hospital stay, beginning on the sixth of September and still continuing. So along with the recent news, we must be with Rita, too.

###

On Friday, September 17, 2010, Mark and I drive to Buffalo. We spend hours at the hospital hoping to see some improvement or talk with her doctor to see what he thinks. With Mark's sister there, we are getting daily reports but we want to be there as much as we can.

Having gone through this before when my mother was diagnosed with colon cancer, we know that acceptance is absolutely necessary not only for our wellbeing, but for our parent as well. This time is different because the recovery will drag on. With my mother, Blanche, who was also diagnosed with Colon cancer they were able to surgically remove part of her colon and she never required radiation or chemotherapy. Each checkup after the surgery found her free of cancer.

Because of her age, Rita has chosen oral-chemotherapy, along with radiation therapy that targets energy to destroy cancer cells.

We stay in Buffalo overnight and then return to Rochester on Saturday September 18 so that we can pack and be ready to catch a six o'clock morning flight on Sunday to Dallas, Texas.

###

Back home, we spend most of Saturday on the phone. We talk to the medical examiner and to the detective in Oklahoma City with each giving us the same information. There would be nothing done or anything to report until Monday.

Mark and I begin preparing for our trip. Since June of this year we have been working on a book signing at the Cooper Clinic in Dallas, Texas. Dr. Kenneth Cooper who owns the Cooper Clinics wrote a foreword for my newly released book, "The Madman, The Marathoner" and he has asked if we would have a book signing at the Clinic. We agreed. The book signing is scheduled for Tuesday, September 21st at noon.

We have done all we can for our mother and all we can do for the time being for Erik. There is no need to disappoint The Clinic after they have been so supportive. The plan is to go to the Cooper Clinic in Dallas first since we won't be able to meet with anyone in Oklahoma until the weekday. Once we arrive in Texas, we will rent a car and use it to drive to Oklahoma City on Monday, September 20. There we have arranged to meet with Detective Lyndell Easley who has handled the investigation in Oklahoma and he will more or less give us directions on what we can do at this point.

###

My nephew Dennis arrives at our home at 4:30 a.m. on Sunday, September 19 to take us to the airport. I climb into the back seat of his SUV and buckle my seatbelt while Dennis and Mark put the luggage in the back, before climbing into the front seat and buckling their seatbelts. I can hear them talking in the front seat, but my mind is too far away to make sense of the conversation.

I look out into the darkness of the night, staring and trying to focus and make out shapes along the way. Every now and then I hear my voice saying something in response to a question, mechanically, but appropriate since neither Mark or Dennis turns and stares in surprise. Then we are pulling up at the Delta entrance. I climb out of the car and join Mark and Dennis at the back where we take out our luggage and say our goodbyes. I can sense Dennis wanting to say something more than just goodbye, but I am not ready and make the goodbye quick.

It's a blessing to start out here as The Greater Rochester International Airport is small. The airport's main terminal building has only two levels with the upper level for ticketing and boarding gates and the lower level for baggage claim and rental cars. To improve the flow of passengers in the terminal, the airport has constructed a centralized security checkpoint to replace the checkpoints at each concourse entrance.

The airport is practically empty as we enter the terminal. We have handled all the pre-boarding requirements online so all that remains is for us to go through security. We enter the six lane security check point and I fumble around in my purse to pull out my wallet and take out my license. I then get out my one quart plastic bag and keep that in my hand. Mark is the official holder of the boarding passes and he hands me mine.

Due to the heightened security measures after 9/11 the Transportation Safety Administration, or TSA, has revised its guidelines numerous times, but most regulations remain firm such as no firearms, explosives, dangerous chemicals, etc. Then there is the weight limit on luggage that has people stepping in and out of line at the airport, followed by the oversized carry-ons that have to be dealt with—all making the process painful and stressful. The rules of 3.4 ounce (100ml) bottle or less (by volume) ; 1 quart-sized, clear, plastic, zip-top bag; 1 bag per passenger is indeed limiting and quite frankly impossible for those going on long trips. But it just means that if you plan on staying for a while you have to consider purchasing items you need once you get where you are going.

I had to renew my license just last year and had thought possibly my full name would appear on the new license. Wrong! Because we had flown in July to Jamaica, I still have my passport in my purse which proves to be a blessing because once showing my driver's license, I am asked if I have anything with my full name on it. As unbelievable as it is, because my name is so long and I have added the initial of my maiden name as my middle name, my license is issued as J. B. Tischendorf. My passport carries my full name and once produced, we are able to go on our way.

As we pass through checkout, we are early and take our time walking through the airport. We pass the 'show stopper' Brass Tree by local artist, J. Pat Bucey, a nine-foot tall tree made of brass and adorned with over five thousand shimmering brass leaves but it holds no appeal for me today.

Then we see the larger attraction, the unique 'Clock of the Nations' which was once the focal point of Midtown Plaza mall in Downtown Rochester and it stops me in my tracks. Standing there before it, my eyes tear as I can't help remembering the times during the holidays we would take Erik to ride the monorail in Midtown Plaza and stand and watch the clock. Visitors gather each hour and half-hour to watch the doors on the 12 clock pods open to display the animated dolls as they dance to the music of the represented twelve nations. It was a sad time when Midtown Plaza lost tenant after tenant until finally it was a ghost town. Nothing could be done as the plaza, empty, soon fell into disarray. After the sale of Midtown Plaza and the decision came down to demolish the building, the Clock was moved to the airport. I feel a tug on my arm and soon Mark gets me walking again.

Inside the terminal there are plenty of seats and plenty of time as we make our way to our gate. We check the monitors and note that our Flight 4985 is 'on time'. Mark finds us a couple of seats and I pull out the book I have been reading, while he goes through magazines he hasn't had a chance to read at home. Every now and then I glance up and watch. I see them as I sit there at the gate, these stewards whose primary role is to ensure passenger safety. As I watch the crew go through the doorway that leads to the plane

I can view through the window, I glance at my watch. It is almost time and I know soon the boarding will begin.

When we hear our zone called, I roll my regulation size suitcase and with my purse over my shoulder join the line of passengers at the door entering the jet bridge to the plane. Mark has a carryon over his shoulder that has the extra things I need but couldn't fit in my purse. That along with his cloth duffel bag that seems more than half empty makes it easy for him as he moves swiftly down the jet bridge. As I arrive at the platform before entering the plane I am stopped by an attendant who says the overhead bins are full and I need to check my bag here.

I panic. I know that my luggage meets airline requirements. The attendant must have read my thoughts as she quickly explains that the bag will be put in the cargo area of the plane and once we arrive in Atlanta the luggage will be delivered to the jet bridge there. I will not have to pick it up in baggage.

I breathe a sigh of relief. I am happy with that and take the stub she gives me to use in collecting my luggage once we reach Atlanta.

We board Delta Flight 4985, a CRJ 700 plane. As I carefully move down the nineteen inch aisles of first class, I pay attention to the motion of my large, heavy purse that I have over my shoulder, worried that if it swings and hits someone it could hurt. We are seated in row16 which is in the back of this 18 or 19 row aircraft that holds a total capacity of maybe 60 passengers.

The progress is slow as the people ahead of us are still trying to get their luggage to fit in the bins and take their seats. Once through first class, the aisles are even narrower and I feel as though I am folded in half lengthwise, trying to keep everything either in front or in back of me at all times.

I watch ahead of me as some passengers struggle with their luggage and I think, there is no way that bag of theirs is going to fit, and mine is under the plane because of them. This lows the progress.

Along with this delay, some passengers who are seated have to enter the aisle so that the passenger that has the inside seat can be seated.   With each moment I feel anxious and I just want to sit down.

I try to be patient for a bit longer as I watch Mark take his soft sided duffel bag, plus the over shoulder cloth bag and easily fit both under the seat in front of him. My seat is directly across the aisle from him. I squeeze my purse under the seat in front of me, then pull it out again to make sure my book is in there even though I doubt I will stay awake long enough to read.

It turns out that this is a full flight, but the window seat next to me is empty. I opt to keep my seat belt off in case someone is still coming to sit here. While I wait, I watch the passengers as they crawl down the narrow surface of the aisle and then I tune into a conversation taking place in front of me.

In the seats in front I can see the head of an older woman whose silvery gray hair is illuminated by the overhead light. She is by the window and a younger man sits next to her, his hair a dark brown and almost the exact shade as that of the little boy seated on his lap. The conversation is not between the two of them though, it is between the younger man and a woman who sits across the aisle and one row up. I hear snatches of what they are saying and soon know that they are a husband and wife travelling with their two young children. The man in front of me is sitting with the grandmother of his son.   The woman, his wife who he is conversing with is sitting alone with their daughter, but his wife for some reason wants the little boy.   I listen to the private conversation that is loud enough for all of us to hear.

"...but she won't settle down until she sees her brother. I don't want her screaming all the way to Dallas."

"...no...he's fine here."

"Give me him, I can manage both of the kids," the woman says.

"No, he's fine with us," her husband replies."

The woman's head disappears for a moment and then she's back, lifting herself out of her seat and making her way toward her husband, whereupon she leans into his space. I'm not sure since I can't hear her, but I think she is whispering her next command in his ear.

Whatever she has said, he is relenting to her. He lifts the little boy up from his lap. His wife straightens up quickly, smacking the back of her head on the overhead bins and a laugh spills from my mouth before I can stop it. I tuck my lips into my mouth to keep it from happening again. "Are you all right?" her husband says. His wife shakes her head and reaches over to pull her son into her arms.

There are now other passengers in the aisle and the woman squeezes by them to make her way to her seat where she turns around so she can slide into her seat, but before she manages this, she smacks the little boy's forehead on the front of the bins. It's not funny, but I laugh again. It's like a cartoon skit and I can't help myself.

I am so involved in the drama unfolding in front of me that I don't feel Mark tapping my arm right away. "Nita, this woman needs to get in."

"Oh, sorry, I say as I slide out of the row and wait for her to get into her seat. I hook , my seat belt and then turn to say hello. The woman who now sits in the window seat waste no time in opening her cell phone and begins texting. I can see she is lost in her electronic world and not interested in any introductions so I lean back in my seat and look across the aisle at Mark. He is engrossed with reading the airline magazine so I look about the cabin again.

This aircraft doesn't have audio, video, or laptop power. Usually I opt for a window seat which are always the first taken, but on this aircraft the windows are misaligned so that passengers will need to lean backwards to look out the window. I toy with the idea of trying to read, but it is dark outside and the light inside the cabin is not the best for any serious reading.

In the front, standing in the aisle is a stewardess, announcing that we will be taking off soon. She asks for our attention as she begins the pre-flight safety demonstration. On a small aircraft such as ours, the demonstration takes place in the form of a live briefing performed by one flight attendant standing up in the aisle, while another flight attendant narrates over the public address system. I am not really sure if this is a live voice or a recorded one.

They begin reminding us to review the aircraft safety card, and then with a sample in her hand, demonstrates how to hook and unhook the seat belt. They suggest that we keep our seatbelt fastened at all times in case of unexpected turbulence.

Then we are provided a seated tour of the cabin. The steward begins pointing out the location and use of the emergency exits, evacuation slides and emergency floor lighting. With a sample in hand, she shows us how the oxygen mask will fall from the overhead compartment on its own when necessary, then demonstrates how to use the mask.

Next it is on to explaining the location and use of the life vests, life rafts and the use of our passenger seat cushions as flotation devices. With all the safety features covered, it is on to a reminder not to smoke on board, including in the lavatory. It is stressed not to tamper with or disable lavatory smoke detectors.

As she winds down the demonstration she reminds us to stow luggage under our seat or in an overhead compartment and finally she announces, "We are ready for departure. Please return folding trays and seat backs to the upright position, and turn off electronic devices such as laptops and cell phone until we are airborne."

Now there are two attendants moving down the aisles checking that the overhead bins are shut snugly and that all seatbelts are fastened. When she reaches the seat where the lady sits with her two children she says, "Miss, you can't have two children in the seat with you without another adult."

The woman asks, "Why?" I hear something about oxygen masks.

The husband in front of me says, "Evelyn, give me Jacob, I can hold him back here." The steward looks from one to the other waiting. Finally the woman whom I know now is Evelyn hands little Jacob over to the steward, who carries him to the husband and lowers him onto his father's lap. Satisfied, the stewardess gathers up her demo equipment and then disappears from my view.

Our plane leaves Rochester at 6:00 a.m. on Sunday, the 19th of September. As we transition from the gate to taxiing, I lean back and close my eyes. I can feel the sensation of the aircraft making a turn onto the runway for our departure. There is a stationary period, then the aircraft picks up momentum as it travels down the runway until we are airborne.

Once in the air, the pilot introduces himself over the loudspeaker and discusses the weather conditions.

"We are expecting a calm start in our flight pattern but the radar shows we will run into some turbulence ahead. It won't be much, but for safety I will ask that everyone return to their seats and fasten seat belts. We are slightly ahead of schedule and will arrive in Atlanta a few minutes ahead of our arrival time of 8:16 a.m. Our air time will be two hours, sixteen minutes. Sit back and relax and Welcome aboard."

The flight attendants are up and moving about the first class cabin. Eventually they will serve drinks and a snack.

The rest of the flight is non-eventful with our Delta Airlines flight leaving precisely at 6:00 a.m. on that Sunday morning of September 19, 2010. Once on board, unable to spend the time reading I have been writing to keep my mind occupied.

Now that the cabin is quiet, I close my eyes hoping I can drift off to sleep, but my mind is working overtime. I wonder if I should have cancelled the book signing and we should have gone to Oklahoma right away. Maybe there is something we can do beforehand.

Then I think about how much cheaper it is to fly from Rochester to Texas than from Rochester to Oklahoma City. Besides that, where would we stay once we arrived as we hadn't made reservations anywhere in Oklahoma. It is indeed too late to worry about that now. What I try to do most is keep from thinking about what we will find once we do get to Oklahoma. Will I be able to deal with it!

###

As we touched down in Atlanta, Georgia, the heat of the day is well on its way to the 90s. It would be several minutes before we will find standing room in the aisle, so we remain seated.

I watch the passengers as they struggle out of their seats and try to get their luggage out of the overhead bins without losing their place in line. Some smile, others look as though they are mad at the world; no one looks just sad. No one looks sympathetic. No one looks as though they had their life sucked out of them. That, I envision, is reserved all for me.

Finally we are able to weave our way to the front and depart into the jet bridge where the first blast of cold air hits us as the air conditioning filters into the jet bridge from the terminal. We stand in line with the other passengers who need to retrieve luggage and when we have my bag in tow we hurry up the jet bridge.

The terminal is a bustle with people moving in every direction, making their way to their gate or in search of food. This is what an airport looks like, I think. Our airport is no way as bustling as this one and that wasn't really a bad thing.

Mark and I move into the flow. "Are you hungry," he asks. "No, but I will have coffee while you get something," I say. "You need to eat." "I'm just not hungry right now." Mark let's it go.

With all these people, I am surprised when we not only find a place where Mark can get something to eat, but we find a couple open seats that I claim while Mark heads to the counter to place his order.

I sit with our luggage watching the travelers as they move about the airport. I had read somewhere that the world's busiest airport by passenger traffic is Atlanta International Airport and it has remained so every year since 2000. Now I am seeing it in action.

Then I think, who, I wonder, can be in Atlanta and not reminisce about the book or movie of "Gone With The Wind" by Margaret Mitchell. Now as I sit here I am curious, wanting to see the historical city that is just beyond the airport. Just to even tour the apartment where Margaret Mitchell penned her world-famous novel would be a memory to cherish.

I am pulled back to the present when Mark returns to the table. "Are you all right?" he asks.

"Yes, I'm fine. This is really a busy airport."

"That it is. Too crowded for me."

"Me too."

Mark eats his bagel but he cannot hide his concern over my lack of appetite but he doesn't push. I pull out my cell phone and check the time. We arrived in Atlanta at 8:16 a.m. and our flight from Atlanta leaves at 9:45 a.m. I am shocked! It is already after nine o'clock!

Mark finishes his bagel and we are on our way through this metropolis of an airport, squeezing through passengers, taking the automated people movers (apm) at a fast clip until we are at the plane train embarking area. This will take us to the Concourse Terminal for our departing flight.

We line up in front of one of the many door location areas and in seconds the train arrives and the door opens. We wait as the passengers debark and then enter. There is only one seat open and I take it. Mark holds on to the bar above his head for support.

Inside the trains, LED displays deliver station information in several languages. It begins its announcement the minute we board. ""Welcome aboard the Plane Train. The next stop is for ..." We are on Concourse B and our departure flight is on Concourse T. When we arrive at our concourse, we disembark and follow the arrows to our departure gate.

On the way to the gate we stop to check the flight information display board and find that our Flight 2511 is shown as 'on time'. We continue on our way. It feels as though we have traveled over a mile just within this airport, but finally we arrive at our departure gate.

We stop at the restroom and take turns. Mark stands with the luggage while I go into the ladies room and luckily find there is no waiting. Then we exchange places. It's me with the luggage while Mark goes into the men's room.

While I wait, I watch all the people going their merry way and I wonder if anyone else is about to face the most devastating event of their life. I know the odds of me being the only one is slim; especially amongst so many people. So I scan faces to see if I can identify anyone who appears depressed. I have been dealing with overwhelming depression and anxiety. My husband is my very best friend and the person I turn to when I am most scared or upset yet it is still the scariest and most helpless feeling that I have ever felt.

It's like the sadness takes over my existence, affecting my sleep and leaving me feeling fatigue nearly every day since getting the news. I am riddled with guilt though I know this feeling is inappropriate to the situation. This was not something I could have prevented or controlled. Yet I do feel guilty. And I can't relax because I feel anxious. Now as I look at those faces milling about I am sure that my face shows what I am feeling and that there's will too.

I hope that once I have completed the visit to Oklahoma City these symptoms will lessen because I am sure they will not disappear. By the time Mark is back at my side, I have controlled the urge to cry by focusing on those passing faces.

The departure area is packed with people and we scan the area to find an opening space to just stand before we then make our way with our carry-on luggage, trying not to nudge any passengers along the way. There are people in the seats, others sitting on the floor and still others standing in any space they can find near the exit doors for the flight. Mark checks our seat boarding zone and shares his findings with me.

The scene is always the same.   Eager passengers line up outside the gate before those on the incoming aircraft have even deplaned. They rush down the jet way, roll aboard suitcases trailing behind them. They squeeze their luggage into the overhead bin before a flight attendant can say "gate check." So many passengers are carrying on more bags, making the overhead bin a hot commodity.

Finally the boarding starts and the gate agent calls out the first boarding zone. First class passengers and those in the first row of coach are in Zone 1. Zone 2 is for Delta's elite frequent flyer members. Zone 3 is for elite members of Delta's partner airlines. After first class and elite passengers, Zone 4+ are designated based on seating assignment, from the back of the plane to the front. We are in Zone 5.

People pass by saying, "Excuse me, Pardon Me," as they make their way into the line that has formed in front of the doors to the plane. We listen while trying to stay out of the way of those who need to board before us until finally our zone is called.

I look around us at the other passengers that will be sharing the plane with us and wonder what is their final destination, where they have come from, and their reason for traveling. We are in Row 23 which is not a bad location on this larger plane, and it gives me time to lose myself in thought.

Mark hands me my ticket when our zone is called and we move into the line that goes slowly toward the doors that will take us to the plane. At the threshold of the doorway I hand the gate agent my boarding pass and watch as it is passed through the boarding pass machine and is then handed back to me. This time I am not stopped, but proceed with both my carry-ons to board the plane.

I move done the aisle trying not to hit someone in the head with my purse that swings gently on my shoulder, or roll over a foot in the aisle with the bag I pull behind me or finally to not bump into the person in front of me as they stop to deposit luggage in the overhead compartment. This need to concentrate is good medicine, making it easy for me to return the smile or nods as one or another passenger happens to look in my direction at the same time as I look at them.

At our seats Mark puts his bag in the overhead bin then reaches for mine and places it next to his. I slide into the aisle of our seats so that he can get out of the way of boarding passengers. We place our other bags under the seat in front of us.

We are not at a window seat so we need to wait to get settled for the other passenger and when she comes, we step back into the aisle so that she can get to her seat. This time when we are seated, we hook our seat belts for departure.

When everyone is seated and the preflight check is done, we finally are taxiing down the runway. Once airborne I listen as the stewardess appearing on the monitors provides us with the standard safety presentation.

I'm like a student, listening as though it is something I have to learn and memorize. In my hands I have the card provided in the back of the seat ahead of me and I look at it at the proper moment on the proper side during the presentation. I am mesmerized by this routine that I have heard or almost heard over and over again, only this time it seems important to be attentive. It seems necessary that I pay close attention to what is being said. When the monitor goes blank I look at Mark and he smiles at me. I smile back.

Inside the plane the air is stifling so I reach up to turn the control on the overhead panel. Nothing happens. I wait a few minutes and try again, thinking I have turned it off. Nothing happens. I can feel my eyes filling up again as though this is a personal offense, but before I start bawling, the air starts to come out. I lean back and calm myself.

Feeling more in control again, I reach under my seat and rummage through the bag until I find my book. I am reading "Look Again", by Lisa Scottoline and finding it a real page turner. That first paragraph begins, 'Ellen Gleeson was unlocking her front door when something in the mail caught her attention. It was a white card with photos of missing children, and one of the little boys looked oddly like her son. She eyed the photo as she twisted her key in the lock,...' From that beginning I have only been able to stop reading when it is imperative that I stop and now it takes only a moment for me to immerse myself in the pages of this book.

I am swept up into a whole new universe of feelings, memories, pain and confusion that allows me to forget everything going on around me. Yet, a part of my mind remains in the presence as I am aware of the activities going on in the plane. It may be that I have been exposed to what takes place often enough that now I can sense the flight attendants are on the move pushing that big rectangle compartment down the small aisles. I know without really listening that they are asking each passenger what they want to drink and giving out a snack.

"Miss, what can I get you to drink?"

"Nita!" I hear my husband say. and I realize it is my turn. I smile at Mark and reply to the stewardess. "Just coffee, black." Then I busy myself with getting my tray down while she pours the coffee and then reaches inside the compartment, pulling out a napkin that she wraps around the cup before offering it to me.

I take the cup and place it on the tray and start to shake my head, 'no' when she asks me which snack item I would like, but

Mark leans over and says, "Get the peanuts." So I do and turn them over to him.

Mark is tall and thin, but he eats well and often. After fifteen years of marriage I have noticed and sometimes been upset that he can eat and not gain weight while I have to watch each mouthful.

My mind is open and before I can stop it, I begin thinking of Erik when he was little and just learning how powerful his smile could be. He would flash that smile at a drop of a hat and know that whatever it was he wanted or needed would soon be his. He was...

I have to stop myself or I will start crying so I quickly pick up the kindle and start reading again. In a matter of minutes the story engages my whole attention as I live the crisis of the reporter Ellen Gleeson as she not only realizes that the boy on the flyer looks just like her adopted son, but that she must investigate, following a trail of clues no one was meant to uncover.

My eyes begin to tire and I force myself to take them away from the screen of my kindle. In the small space of my airline seat, I try to stretch, then move my neck from side to side to ease the tension after spending so much time looking down at the screen on my tray. I like reading on the kindle when I travel because it takes up less space, but when at home, it is the book itself that I like to read and turn the pages, allowing me to forget everything that's going on around me.

It is a little over an hour flight from Atlanta to Dallas. Now as I stretch I hear the pilot make the announcement that we are about to land. I watch as the flight attendants make the final round to collect any leftover cups and napkins from the passengers and I look over at Mark and see that he is sleeping.

I take my cup and place it on my husband's tray, picking up his napkin and placing it inside his empty cup. I then put his cup inside mine, just before the stewardess arrives and Mark wakens in time to put our stuff into her waiting garbage bag.

I hear the announcement to fasten seatbelts, secure the trays and put the seats in the upward position. At that point I turn off my kindle and lean down to pull out my bag that is stored under the seat in front of me. I put the kindle inside and using my foot, push it back in place under the seat. With that done, I lift up the tray and press it into the back of the seat, then place the latch in place. I am ready.

I look over at Mark and see that he is waiting for a passenger to make it pass his seat. When the aisle is free, he slides out and opens the overhead bin to get into his carry on where he places the papers he removed prior to takeoff. With the papers stowed away, he sits down and fastens his seat belt again.

"How are you doing," he asks.

"Fine."

Soon we are landing and once on the runway, the passengers are in action. People are pulling out their phones to contact the person who is meeting them or maybe to check on their next flight. Others have moved to the edge of their seat and with hands resting on the arms of their chair, they seem ready to propel out into the aisle the minute we are at the gate.

I am glad for this activity since it keeps my mind off my problems for the time being. When we arrive at the gate, Mark enters the aisle and gets our luggage from the overhead bins, placing them on his seat, while he continues to stand. I reach under the seats and get our other luggage, placing them beside the ones from the overhead bin. Now we wait.

At first there is little movement ahead as everyone is busy with gathering their belongings. Then I can see the line moving. Mark takes his bags and I get mine out of his seat., then squeeze into the aisle in front of him.

This time there is little worry of hitting someone on my way down the aisle as most of those in front of us have already disembarked. A few linger in the rows for what reason I do not know. In any case I have no problem making it to the jet bridge and then into the Texas airport where I stop and wait for Mark to catch up with me.

The air inside the airport is quite cool as we move toward the aisle and try to fit into the rapidly moving crowd in front of us. It is a little after 11 o'clock in the morning and the airport is bustling.

Once in the airport with our baggage in hand, we follow the Rental Car signs that take us to the lower level of the Airport terminal. I trail behind Mark as he goes to the rental car counter to pick up the rental agreement and vehicle keys. With that complete, we are on our way.

We find ourselves in a massive garage where we search for our rental agency area and then try to locate the rental car. Luckily the expanse is well marked and it turns out to be quite easy to find the car. Soon we are putting our luggage into the trunk, then I climb into the passenger seat and watch as Mark gives himself time for a quick lesson on the operation of this vehicle before turning it on.

"Can you set the GPS for the Cooper Clinic?"

"Sure, no problem". I take out our GPS which I brought with us, just in case one was not available in the rental. Having already programmed the address in the GPS, I now quickly locate it and press the button. By the time we are exiting the car rental garage, it is ready to give us directions.

Once there we will first need to check into the Cooper Guest Lodge on Preston Road, which is located on the property.

Right now, this is what I need. We are someplace we haven't been before and on our way to stay where we have never stayed before. It is all new, making it easy to put the past aside as we drive to our destination. It is hard to not get excited at the prospect of seeing this place that my customer, friend and subject of my book, Don McNelly, has told us about.

The Cooper Clinic isn't Dr. Cooper's first breakthrough in the world of health and wellness. Two years before its founding, he introduced the world to a new word and a new concept—aerobics—launching a global fitness revolution.

We exit the airport and wait our turn to pull out heading north on International Pkwy. After about three miles the GPS tells us to get into the middle lane and we do. To get to our destination we will need to go 20 miles and I am thinking that the traffic will be heavy, but surprisingly, it is not that bad. Soon we are turning on the I-635 exit off this road and in a mile and a half we continue onto I-635-E, which marks the longest leg of our trip. The sky is quite clear with just a few wispy clouds as we make our way along this fourteen mile stretch where this is nothing much to see out the car window.

The GPS tells us to take Exit 21 toward TX-289 which will be Preston Road where the Clinic is located. The first entrance into the property we take is the Cooper Institute entrance only to find we can't go through to the other area as the roadway ends so we go back out to Preston road , go down the road a bit. I look out the window and see the low red brick columns connected by the white wrought iron fencing. On either side of the entrance there is another set of columns connected by a red brick low wall that reads 'The Cooper Aerobics Center'. The fence surrounds an area of lots of trees and greenery.

Straight ahead is the Cooper Clinic, but a sign directs us to the left to find the Cooper Hotel I which is where we are staying. Mark takes the left. We pull up and park in front of the Hotel, trying to get under a tree so that the car interior won't be hot when we need to use it. We get our luggage out of the trunk of the rental and go into the building in front of us.

The interior of the lobby is cool and it looks like a grand hotel with sweeping staircases to the upper level and an elegant lobby. We walk over to the front desk and check in, receive the key to our room which is located on the second floor and a packet of information on the complex.

We take the stairs up to our room, walking along the wide hallways that are tastefully decorated. When we open the door of our room it too fits the age and style of the building, and has an inviting air about it. Once settled in, we call down to the front desk to see if Don has checked in. We are informed he has not.

This seems strange since he's purpose in coming here is to first have his annual physical and of course later to attend the book signing. I put it out of my mind for now and instead turn my attention to the packet of information we were given.

Inside the packet I pull out an information sheet and am surprised to learn that the property is a 30 acre complex dedicated to health research and education. Within the Cooper Aerobics Center, are several buildings that include the Hotels, the Gastroenterology building, the Fitness Center and Spa and the

Cooper Clinic. The main entrance area has a one mile, half mile and quarter mile track layouts that we decide to follow around the property so that we can see where everything is located.

It is hot, steamy hot as we follow the walking and running paths meandering everywhere that we follow stopping first at the pool between the two hotel buildings. We then check out the location of the executive offices where we will meet up with the person who is coordinating the book signing.

As we traverse the path we walk by the tennis courts and pull out our property map to get a handle on where we are and which way we need to head to get to the conference room area where the book signing will take place. We are pretty proud of how easily we find the locations, then just spend time enjoying the area. It is so peaceful and not a bit like a place one is staying for a medical checkup. As we meander through the buildings we find another swimming pool, a gym, snack bars, and just about everything one can imagine or expect to find at a resort.

It is beautiful. There are so many trees and flowers to enjoy and even a bridge over probably what might be a manmade lake across the south side of the property with lots of vegetation. and even ducks.

When we return to our room, Mark calls the front desk to find out what room Don is in. When they inform Mark they did not have his name on a reservation, I finally remember that he has arranged to stay with a friend, but which one he would be staying with, he is unsure when he shares this information with me. It is one of two friends that always come at the same time to the Cooper clinic for physicals. Even if he had given me a name, it was loss to me now, but luckily the front desk finally traced Don's room number. Soon Mark is talking to Don and making arrangements that evening to meet him for dinner.

We have time to kill and decide to find our way back to the snack bar and try one of the health shakes. We get it to go and walk over to the gift shop. Inside there is all kinds of Clinic clothing items and duffle bags. In another section are copies of Dr. Kenneth Cooper's many books and in yet another area are the vitamins he has formulated and now sells.

A check of our phone lets us know we need to get back to the hotel and change for dinner. So we make our purchases and head back. Once inside our room we take turns showering and once we are dressed we head out again, going straight to the restaurant. We enter the dining room and see Don waving us over.

It is pleasant in here and I lean back, enjoying the conversation at the table as Don introduces us to his friend and us to him. He then tells us about the physical he has gone through. I only partially listen as I have heard this before and have seen the oversized booklet from his last physical.

I enjoy looking at the people around us and then when I hear my name being called, I focus on our table, giving my order to the waitress and adding a little to the conversation.

When the food arrives, the table grows quiet. It has been a long day for all of us and the appetites are heighten. The food is not only healthy, but taste great and we comment on this before we finally leave. This time Don leaves with us while his friend heads out to join Don later. This gives us time to tell Don about our plans.

"Don," I say, we are going to drive to Oklahoma ;first thing in the morning. Is there anything we should take care of before we go?"

"No, everything is being handled by the office and I checked in with them to see if they needed anything and they said that the books had arrived and they also had the promotional packages you sent."

Even though it is still quite early, we are tired and decide to go directly to our room and rest a bit before trying to get a good night's sleep.

"Good night Don."

"Good night."

"We'll call you as soon as we return."

We take our leave, heading directly back to the hotel, stopping only once to watch the guests swimming in the pool between the two hotels. Once inside the lobby we take the stairs up and go down the hallway to our room. In the room we change out of our clothes and get ready for bed, then just sit and relax.

An Unfair Advantage   By: Juanita Tischendorf

Mark turns on the television and I sit beside him on the couch, not really watching the program on the screen, but just enjoying being able to not think about anything for a moment. I know that tomorrow will bring the reality of the past and put it in a new perspective that will force me to accept and then to do what must be done. I just hope that I am strong enough because I am the only one that can make sure that all is made right for Erik. But now I need to rest my body and my mind.

It isn't long before we both turn in and I must have instantly fallen asleep because I can remember nothing more.

###

On Monday, September 20, 2010 we wake early as is the usual case with us. I wake at 4:30 a.m. almost every morning, no matter how early or late I retire. It has been a habit for as long as I can remember. Mark accustomed to my early rising usually is up right behind me. He also is attune to my feelings and knows that this morning I am anxious and wanting to keep me from stressing out, he is ready to get in the shower when I come out of the bathroom. As I move around the room getting out my clothes, I start to cry, and I try not to let it get too out of control.

I try raising my eyebrows as high as I can making it easier to hold back the tears. Then I hold myself perfectly still and without moving my head, look up with my eyes. It is almost impossible to cry when you do this.

I stand still for a second and look up at the ceiling. I think about how I am going to get through the situation ahead. I am well aware that I can't run away from the matter and if I could it would only make getting over it harder to do later.

I feel more in control now. I know that crying is not running away, but what I need to focus on now is a means for dealing with the issue at hand so I distract myself by thinking of plans and ideas I need to make so that I don't leave anything unfinished. After a few seconds of stillness I am able to continue getting ready .

I move about in this unfamiliar hotel room and try to remember where I have stowed my belongings. I'm fragile and I know it to be true; especially when I find myself tearing up

112

because I can't find my underwear. Before I burst into fresh tears, I pinch myself, hard. "Ow!"

"What happened," Mark asks as he hurries into the room.

"Noth... oh, I closed my hand in the drawer. It's okay, though."

Though he doesn't know it, he has just cured my tears and I am able to finish getting dress without another episode.

While Mark finishes dressing, I cross the room, turn on the television and search for a news channel. I then open the balcony door of our room, letting in the intense heat that is apparent even this early in the morning.

I can see the well-manicured lawn move slightly in the warm breeze under the sky that is a bright blue layer in the humid air. It is beautiful if not comfortable outside. The lush green of the lawns, trees and hedges outside our window emphasize the beauty of the flowers. I can identify blue daze with their pubescent gray-green leaves and one inch wide blue flowers and the Copper Canyon Daisies that are heavily covered with yellow daisy-like blooms .

The city of Dallas has a humid, hot climate and is often prone to storms. On the television they are broadcasting the weather so I turn my attention to what is being reported. The weatherman is saying that the temperature is already close to 90 degrees and the morning is just beginning. I step back into the room, locate my purse and check to make sure I have a pair of sunglasses in it. I do.

"Babe, make sure you have your sunglasses." I say.

"Got them", he replies.

I dig into my purse and get out my GPS, a Christmas present from Mark that I sorely needed as I have no sense of direction. When I needed to replace my car back in 2000, one of my requirements was to have a compass in my car so that when I downloaded a map from Expedia or Google, I could check to make sure that I turned the right way and was heading in the right direction. Early on these maps gave compass point directions and not 'left turn, right turn' which did me no good.

I go to my carryon and pull out the folder I have arranged for this trip. It has all the addresses, phone numbers and contact people listed. I thumb through the pages while I wait for the opening screen on the GPS to appear, then stop and responded to the warning screen and the GPS soon shows the opening menu. I searched for the first address of our destination in my address list and then I press the Where To? Button.

This is working. It is the perfect distraction as I have to concentrate on what I am doing and there is no room in my mind to think of anything else. I select the Change/State/Country and then select the Spell state or Province. I began typing in 'Ok' and the GPS showed my choices. I select Oklahoma. Next I select Spell City and began typing 'Ok' and the choice comes up Oklahoma City, OK. I select this and then the choice to type the address. I enter the 1500 when asked for the house number and then press, Done . I enter NW 40th and the choice appears with the right zip code. I stop there so that later in the car all I need to do is press 'Go'.

"Damn,"

"Are you okay," Mark says, the concern in his voice.

"Yes, I am. I just put Heather's address in the GPS and…"

"I know," Mark says as he comes over to give me a hug.

This was the home address of my son when he was married to Heather. After the divorce she remained in the house and Erik found an apartment in the same vicinity, but then after a bad situation with a roommate, had moved to a 'safer' place or so he thought….

It's easy to quickly find a way to blame someone for what has happened and at this point I find myself blaming Heather. No, I reprimand myself, this is not right! Erik and Heather divorced and just like when I divorced Erik's father, I couldn't continue to live with him. This is not Heather's fault no more than it is Erik's fault. Besides when Erik told me he was moving out of the house, he had said he didn't want to stay there.

I have to admit that it was upsetting as Erik and Heather were obviously in love in the beginning. They had a lot of differences, but I know they loved each other. When I heard from my son that he and Heather were going to get a divorce, I did not understand because to me they had seemed a perfect match. Now as I think about it I know that was not true. The perfect match came from the fact that they were both little people and for Erik in those times it was uncommon to actually find another little person. You could travel about from state to state or job to job and never once run into another little person. But to make that the ideal perfect partner now seems ridiculous.

Having gone through a divorce myself, it was the last thing I wished for my son to experience. Divorce can be the largest single mentally straining and financially draining transaction of most people's lives, raising important questions that demand immediate answers. I know Erik was not happy getting a divorce but he did not make it hard on her. Though Mark and I had given them the money to help purchase a house in my mind now I see it as having given the money to Erik and he was no longer benefiting from the purchase. I know it's wrong to think like this and I know that when we gave the money it was not just for Erik. It is what Erik decided that matters now and not what I am feeling at the moment.

They did not have any children thought they had both wanted them. This in one way is a blessing, but in another it means I will never have any grandchildren.

I have been my son's protector for most of his life and I know that Erik has run into many situations where he is taken advantage of because he is a little person and because he is the type of person to give you the shirt off his back. I witnessed many times how Heather was able to 'boss' him around. That was my view and not Erik's. When Heather said that Erik had given her the house in the divorce, I am sure he did. He would not fight it even though he knew that she should have 'bought' him out by settling his investment in the property.

I am also sure that his roommate saw this 'flaw' if you will, in his personality and took advantage by not paying the rent and when it lead to them both being evicted, took everything he could of Erik's. He knew Erik would not call the police or make a big deal of it and he was right.

I raised Erik to be considerate and understanding so in a way it was my fault. Maybe with him being a little person I should have managed to embed these feelings differently. Maybe for him I should have said to look out for No. 1 first and then react to others. I don't know. As I said earlier, I had to learn as I go on 'same' and 'different' methods of raising my child.

This train of remembering brings fresh tears to my eyes. I know Erik believed the roommate would pay him though several months passed and the promise was still words in the wind and not a cent had changed hands. He should have thrown him out after the first month of no payment, but that is not Erik. So by the time he realized it would never come to be, he himself was in jeopardy.

So from the end of his marriage and having to start all over again, when he felt he was getting back on his feet, Erik had hoped for the best and ended up again in the position to have to start anew.

I played the wrong hand with my son but it is hard to stop giving advice to someone who you have always given advice too. It would take only one call and I would send him whatever he needed, but along with that I was unable to keep from giving my advice on what he should do.

It had gotten to the point where I was practically insisting that he come home and live with us and get a fresh start. Erik, I am sure was aware of what he had done wrong. He also knew that if he was to stand on his own feet, it would be harder if he lived under my roof.

Now I wish I had just given him what he asked for and kept my thoughts to myself. There was a period of at least two months where Erik was 'in the wind' with no address or phone contact information available. I wish I could put that on someone but it was my own fault. I had forced Erik to stop contacting me so that he could find his way on his own and when he had settled into the Hunt Apartments and feeling as though he had his life under his control, he finally gave me a call.

"Are you ready," Mark asks, breaking my train of thought once again when I needed to be pulled from the reverie.

"Yes, I'm ready."

Now after we double-check each other, we make our way out of our room. Mark juggles his bag so that he frees his hand and locks the door and then we head down the stairs.

It is very hot and humid outside. "We have time, let's go to the snack bar and get something to eat," Mark says.

We turn right and follow the path pass the pool and near the Cooper Hotel II situated behind us. There are several individuals out on the running path and I think it smart to get up and out early before the sun makes it impossible to enjoy a walk or a jog.

We reach the snack bar and welcome the coolness inside as we enter to stand in the short line that has formed in front of the counter. This gives us time to decide what we want before it is our turn. As we stand there we look around the interior deciding where we want to sit. There are several seating areas to choose from and by the time we are at the counter we have already chosen seats and we place our order for muffins and coffee.

Mark pays for our purchase and I follow him over to one of the tables near the television set so that we can hear the news while we eat our muffins and drink our coffee. It is now 6:30 a.m.

We finish and carry our trays over to the trash bin to toss away the papers and then place the trays on the self on top of the trash before heading out the door. The heat is apparent from our first step out on the path that we follow all the back to our rental car.

We waste no time as we climb inside to feel the car interior which is insufferably hot. Even though Mark had tried to find a shaded spot for the vehicle the sun still managed to heat up the interior so we have to sit with the doors open until the air-conditioning kicks in. Finally we can close the doors.

The clock on the dashboard registers 7:00 a.m. as we drive through the parking area at the front of the guest house for the Cooper Clinic. We pull out onto Preston Road and turn left unto I635, also known as the Lyndon B. Johnson Freeway which we will stay on for the first five miles of our trip before taking the exit onto I-35E.

With the address already entered, I start to put the GPS in its holder on the windshield for Mark to easily view, then remember this is a rental and the holder is in my car at home. I then lay it on the console where I can see it. The voice is quite loud so there will be no problem hearing the instructions from the woman's voice as she guides us on our way.

"How many miles does it say," Mark asks.

"203," I reply.

"Well, that will take us about 3 hours to get there."

"I didn't think it was that far," I say but I really had no idea of the distance whatsoever.

The Dallas metropolitan area is encircled by Interstate 635 and the President George Bush Turnpike. Interstate 635, also known as the Lyndon B. Johnson Freeway wraps around the northern and eastern fringes of the city. The stretch of roadway between the Central Expressway and Interstate 35E is six lanes wide, something not seen back home in Rochester and I can't imagine the delay time of some drivers who wait until the last minute to cross over to an exit.

As we drive, we see some drivers manage to just slow the traffic from lane to lane, while others do not make it all the way. When that happens the traffic is backed up even more, barely moving as the emergency vehicles arrive at the scene and close off sometimes one, sometimes two lanes. At that moment I think, this is going to be a long ride.

Mark plays it smart and keeps to the right as the exit we want is not far and he did not want to attempt to squeeze into the already congested lanes. It is slow going with Mark having to drive extra cautiously and we manage to exit at 27B onto I-35E without mishap.

I listen to the voice of the GPS giving the instructions and doing it in a way that an idiot could feel confident getting from point A to point B. For me even with all my faculties this would be the only way I would manage to get through Texas.

We drive down Interstate 35E and Mark says, "This is going to split up ahead so I think I'll stay in this lane."

We have been driving for almost a half hour now in a boat load of traffic when we finally come to the split in the highway and soon it rejoins itself to become just I35.

"Well, we will be taking this all the way to Oklahoma," Mark says and I can see his shoulders relax now that we have gotten through the city and ahead the highway seems to be less congested. The view on either side of the highway is of the tops of high rise buildings as we are going over bridges on our way out of the city.

"Can you believe this traffic, Babe?"

"Yes I can believe it. Dallas is the ninth largest city in the United States and with over a million in population. I imagine driving is like this every day."

Looking out the windshield the high rise buildings sprawl across the horizon for what must be miles and the small structures that are sprinkled here and there lose their appeal. Just as awe inspiring are the tangled mass of highways. There are so many bridges going over other bridges that we never seem to be at ground level as we travel the expanse of cemented roadways.

We can see flashing lights ahead and Mark tries to move over to the center lane which seems to be the only open lane besides the specialty marked HOV lane which we hadn't a clue what HOV stood for. We will pass by two more accidents before we finally are moving at the speed limit.

"Babe, look at the sign over there."

"I can't, I'm driving. What did it say."

"It says the speed limit during the day is 70 mph and 65 mph at night!"

"That's different," Mark acknowledges. "I can't say I've seen two speeds on a highway before, but this is Texas."

While Mark concentrates on driving, I start wondering even though we called ahead what if anything we are going to actually accomplish once we are in Oklahoma City. Mark breaks the silence and asked if I should try Heather's number again. We have been having trouble with the phones even though we switched from T-Mobile to Verizon for the specific purpose of having no signal in the places that we frequent. Now, we are experiencing the same problem and again we can't get through.

Mark continues to drive and looks at the clock on the dashboard to see that it might be possible to reach someone now. "Can you try to call the ME's office?"

"Sure," I say. I pull out my cell. I have stored all the necessary phone numbers in my contact list which I go to now, find the ME's listing, click on it and wait while it dials. Not really thinking it will connect, I am surprised when it does. I speak to someone in the ME's who informs me what time works best for him. I jot it down, disconnect the call and return to the contact list. I again locate Heather's number and press to connect but I am still unable to reach Heather. She is the one we need to contact first. I know my ex daughter in law does not appreciate someone just dropping by unannounced and I bet that even under these circumstances we will not receive a gracious welcome if we don't call first.

I hear my husband's voice and turn my attention to him.

Mark says, "We have crossed the Oklahoma line and if this thing is right, we are 40 miles away from Heather's. You might want to try her again".

Mark is well aware of the need to reach her before reaching the house. I try the number again, but get the same message that the call cannot be connected.

"No, still can't get her", I say. This makes no sense. We should be able to reach her now but it is not connecting. This frustrates me and I make a note to call Verizon when we get back to New York and ask for an explanation Here we are in Oklahoma and we can't call someone who lives here.

I give up and now as I look out the window I begin to recognize the scenery. This is the road we had taken to go get takeout once with Heather and Erik. We turn the corner and I recognize the street we had gone down many times to go to their home or to take them to the store or out to eat. We are definitely in the area, so close to where my son had lived when he was married to Heather. So close to where he had achieved his dream of being married, but not his dream of having children This was the last place that I had actually visited him at home because after the address changes, it wasn't until he was situated in the suburbs, did he call and we had made arrangements to visit later that year. If only....no, I won't go there..

I look out the window and see the sign for Classen Blvd and soon Mark turns left onto NW 40th Street and we are on the first block before the house. Even though the car is air-conditioned, I can feel sweat dripping down my back as we drive closer and closer and then we pull into the driveway at 10:25 a.m. just as Heather is coming through her front door with a pizza box. She looks up and sees us and before she has a chance, we notice the expression on her face that reads, "you should have called first!"

She's right and as soon as the car has stopped, I get out and walk over toward her, apologizing. "Hi Heather. We are so sorry to arrive unannounced but we couldn't get our phones to work. We tried and tried to call you but even though we have bars, it wouldn't connect the call. So sorry".

As I explain the situation I can visibly see Heather's face softening. I continue to walk towards her as she says, "I wanted to clean the place before you came," and I tell her I understand. We are now standing in front of each other. Heather has deposited the pizza box in the trash can and she has her arms hanging at her side. I can see she is tearing up and I approach her. We hug each other as Heather says, "I'm so sorry, so sorry," over and over again.

I know she means it. I know that even though they are divorced they were married long enough for her to feel a loss too. This is not always true, I'm sure, but when the divorce is not nasty there remains a connection just because of years spent intimately together.

"I know, I know," I pat her back sure she can feel the sincerity in my words and touch. I don't blame her for what has happened. It is not her fault. Even as I think this, I again wonder if she had allowed him to stay here until he found a place..." I wipe that thought out of my head. That's water over the bridge now and no need to revisit the situation.

Mark comes over to join us and we stand in the hot sun, its rays so bright it hurts our eyes to raise our eye lids. I look at what was the lawn and I feel resentment because Heather is not keeping up with the outside of the house. There are weeds growing in what was a flower bed. A tree seems to be surviving on its own but looking in need of attention. The grass is brown and patchy with weeds more prominent than the grass. I know it is hard in this climate, but Heather's training is as a horticulturist so I expect more from her.

Heather has seen me appraising the area and says, "I try to keep up but my grandmother has been sick and I haven't been home much."

Her grandmother is one of the sweetest people I know. I met her on several occasions and found her to be charming. Actually, I have found Heather's parents and her grandmother to be wonderful people and every chance we got when we were in Oklahoma, we looked forward to going out to visit them or to meet them at Heather's. From first meeting her parents, we felt as though we knew each other. Later we realized it was because we began with a common understanding of what it is like to raise a little person and the special considerations that we needed to deal with along the way. It gave us something substantial to build a relationship on.

But that was all before the divorce.

###

When I first met Heather I felt as though I was meeting the one person in life who understood my son. I can still remember that day when I picked Heather up at the airport in Rochester. She entered the airport with a look of all I can describe as 'power'. It was as if she was defending her size against all the people pushing by her and yes, some stopping to stare at her. She wasn't about to show that this made her uncomfortable. She was not about to have them think she was not able to take care of herself. She walked with purpose, her head up as though she were trying to appear taller and the other passengers parted a path as she made her way across the airport to where I stood waiting for her. As she looked ahead, I could see the slightest move of her head as she tried to find me who she had yet met, or Erik, who I had told to wait in the car. I smiled at her and that was just what she needed to know she had finally found me.

We chatted about I don't know what, but I remember when Heather opened the car door and saw Erik, his face lit up and when she climbed in, he reached over to touch her. They both smiled a special smile at each other all the way back to our house, and even though the engagement took place later, I felt as though they were already married.

That was my first impression of the two of them together and later that would remain the same each time I saw them for maybe the first three years. After that point I began to notice that Heather had realized how easy going Erik was and how he was not one to ruffle feathers. He seemed to be the busy one whenever we visited. He would cook the dinner, help set the table, do the wash, straighten up, and do the dishes. It never changed. Heather would sit with us and chat while Erik joined us until it was time for a meal or something else had to be done.

I didn't blame Heather because Erik could have refused or asked her to help out more, but he didn't. It did not seem right to me and once when I approached Erik with the subject, he said that Heather had weak ankles that made it hard for her to stand for long periods of time so he tried to take care of things for her. Knowing my son, I knew he didn't mind doing it and therefore I should let the topic be.

###

"I'm sorry," she says and I believe she is as I try not to think about the fact she threw him out and has recently told me to tell the family and friends that Erik does not live in the house anymore and that she is tired of getting mail and other things for him. She punctuates it with if she does receive things for Erik she just throws them away.

I get control of myself and say to Heather that we need to make a call to Detective Lyndell Easley, of the Oklahoma City homicide Unit. "He is assigned to Erik's case, but our phones aren't working.

"That's okay, you can use mine," she says.

It's still hot and even here not a breeze blows and the heat is stifling. I follow Heather up the stairs, glad to get out of the heat that seems to be beating down on the top of my head. Mark follows and I can see he is feeling the heat too, though he does have more tolerance than I do. Before opening the door, she turns to say, "Don't mind the mess. I've been away and haven't had a chance to clean up."

I gratefully walk into the coolness of the front room and stop immediately. The smell is overpowering. .

Mark and I had not been to the house since the two of them had divorced. Something I have known all along was that keeping the house clean was not Heather's forte, nor was doing the wash.

Now as I stand there I start thinking of Erik sliding across the floor on his butt as he polished the legs of tables, and chairs for me, working as a team to get the house clean when we lived in Henrietta, New York. I remember how neat he kept his room; neat even though his friends were coming and going daily from that room and the smell of teenage boys made it hard to appreciate the neatness. Thinking of Erik again has tears already forming in my eyes which I have tried to eliminate, knowing that I must be strong if I am going to help Mark get us through what we need to take care of in Oklahoma.

Even aware of who was the housekeeper in this relationship, I am still shocked when I enter the house. As my eyes focus, I can see the room is a mess of clothes and matter I don't care to mention.

Mark, whose sense of smell is gratefully less than mine, is also overcome by the smell and immediately says, "I'll wait outside."

I start to say something about the state of the house, but catch myself as I am a guest here now. I take the cell phone that Heather offers and place the call to the Detective. He answers on the second ring.

"Where are you?" he asks. "I am at Erik's ex-wife's house right now," I reply, "Do you need the address?". "

I have the address. Stay there and I'll be right over," he says.

I turn to Heather and say, "Thanks, Heather, the detective is on his way over."

Slowly I edge toward the door anxious to get outside, hoping she does not see a critical eye or movement from me.

Heather follows after me and once outside, we stand on the front lawn waiting for Detective Lyndell Easley.

Heather says, "This whole thing doesn't make any sense. If she had wanted something, all she had to do was ask. Erik would have given her whatever she wanted. She didn't have to fight him." I nod in agreement. "People were always taking advantage of him," Heather added.

"You're right. He would give the shirt off his back if someone asked for it. It was unnecessary."

Tears stream out my eyes and I can't stop myself as I continue. "All she had to do was walk away. He wouldn't have been able to catch her or even defend himself against her. My God, he wasn't able to lift the left arm up above his head or run for that matter. She could have just taken what she wanted and left.

Now we stand silently, each caught up in our own thoughts and not feeling the sweltering heat. It's not easy for me to be here, and hard to keep silent. I find myself saying, "Heather, can I ask you something?"

"Sure,"

"Why didn't you let Erik stay here when he was between apartments? I mean, after all the house is half his."

"No, the house isn't half his. He signed the house over to me as part of the divorce settlement. I can show you the papers if you don't believe me."

I have an inkling that she wouldn't even be able to lay her hands on the papers. "No, that won't be necessary. I'm sure he did".

I don't know which heat was the most intense at this moment because the heat of the sun was barely a match for the seething heat inside. Yes, people took advantage of him. In the same breath that she accused those others of doing just that she had done the same.

"Water under the bridge, water under the bridge," I say silently to myself fighting to hold back tears of regret. Children are a reflection of their parents and if he allowed people to run all over him it was because of something I did wrong in his upbringing. I should have made him stronger. I should have told him it was all right to look out for himself first. I should have, I should have... Just then a car going slowly by the house catches my eye.

"Mark, do you think that's the Detective?"

"It could be. It wasn't a police car though."

I cross over next to Mark who is looking up the street at the car that is now turning around and coming back towards the house. The car moves slowly and when it is in front of Heather's house, it moves over to the curb and parks.

We watched as the man gets out of the car and starts across the lawn toward where we are standing. When he is directly in front of us he says, "Mr. and Mrs. Tischendorf?"

"Yes, I reply."

In front of us stands the man who has been at Erik's apartment. Was he the man who had identified the person in that apartment as Erik Saxton? Could he have assumed because the person was in Erik's apartment it was him?

No one has mentioned that the man was a dwarf or that he was paralyzed on his left side. Wouldn't they have noticed this; I keep this to myself as I look at this person who may have seen my son at his last moment.

Was he alive when Detective Lyndell Easley arrived? Did Erik say anything-- was he in pain. Oh my god, what am I doing here. I have to stop this or I'll not be able to help my son.

I finally tune out my brain and begin listening to the conversation. Detective Lyndell Easley is apologizing to Heather who has said that she was hurt when they had said she didn't count just because she was the ex-wife.

Detective Lyndell Easley explains that it wasn't meant the way she took it. Indeed what they meant was that they usually didn't contact the ex unless they had reason to assume they may be involved or know what had happened. In this instance it wasn't the case.

"Well, I think I can help," Heather says. "I was married to him for almost 8 years so I know him better than his mom would; I mean as a man. I think that you might want to know what he was like."

I want to slap her. I don't know why, but that is what I want to do at that moment. Whether or not she wants to seem more important or not, it is not the time for this. She has turned her back on him when he needed her and...

I have to stop this way of thinking. I really have to stop it.

Detective Lyndell Easley handles the situation, breaking the silence by acknowledging what Heather says. He asks when were they divorced and Heather replies in 2009. He goes on to say that what they need to find out about Erik is during the year after the divorce. That is the period of his life they are now interested in and yes, he acknowledges, that there may be information she can supply.

I stand and listen as Heather talks to the detective saying that she has helped Erik move into the Hunt Apartments and even the apartment before he moved there. She has taken him to file a change of address and that is the extent of her contact with him after the divorce. She tells the detective they were friends after the divorce.

I listen and wonder if what she says is true, but then think, why she should lie.

Detective Easley asks Heather about the possibility of Erik taking drugs and she replies that Erik didn't take drugs. He asks if Erik drank and Heather replies that he didn't have more than a beer and that would be if someone came over and he would have a beer with them, but no more than one because of his medications.

Finally the detective finishes asking her questions and tells her he will call if they need anything else. He then turns to me and asks how he can help us. To this Mark says that we have the GPS, the addresses and contact information we need and should be able to get where we want to go.

Detective Easley mentions the people we need to see and we assure him that they are on our list. We tell him that we plan on stopping at his office too. He makes sure we have his contact information before he climbs back in his car and drives down the road. We will meet up with him later.

It is now time to go to Erik's apartment. Heather asks if she can go with us and seeing no reason why not, we concede. Besides, Heather has been to the apartment and can help direct us there. At this point we do not know that she has been there even more recently.

Heather goes inside to get her things and lock the door. When she returns, all three of us climb into the car and we are on our way.

I don't know what to say as we drive to Erik's apartment and the awkward silence feels uncomfortable as we all sense the reality of the moment. This is it, the significant point of no return. This is not just a visit to Oklahoma. This will mark the last visit to Oklahoma to see Erik.

Oklahoma has taken my son away from me. I know as I think it that this is not true, but it feels as though the city is at fault. It is here that this person, who's name I can't bring myself to say, has ended his life. I so want to hold on to it all being a mistake but if I am to survive the day, I need to prepare myself and that means not being in denial.

I will return here, I know that because I need to make sure that this monster pays dearly for taking the life of my son.

###

It is hot, so very hot in the car. I look over at the controls and see that the air conditioner is set at the highest point. I reach out and check the vents and they are open. It is the heat from the sun coming through the windows that is overpowering the air conditioner.

I try to sit back and relax but I can't. I wish I hadn't said, yes to Heather's request to go with us to Erik's apartment. We did have the GPS to help us find the apartment so we didn't really need her. Why did I agree she could come with us when in my heart I can't let go of the fact that she could have prevented this all from happening. It's wrong to feel this way but she is the only other person besides myself that I can blame for this tragedy.

I look out the window trying to prepare myself, but also trying to ignore the fact that Heather is sitting in the back seat of our rental car. I know it's not Heather's fault and I know after my divorce I cared what happened to Erik's dad so I should understand that Heather cares too. I remind myself that they were divorced before this happened and if Erik's dad had wanted to stay with me after our divorce I don't know that I would allow him to.

As we drive away from 1500 NW 40th Street for the last time I recall the first time Mark and I pulled up in front of my son's first home. It was built in 1945 and was a traditional style dwelling We thought it could be charming, but it was in need of repair. On either sides the houses were close but this house was elevated above them.

The exterior was impressive with large windows on the left and right of the doorway that set under a covered porch. The white vinyl siding and the grey shingled roof required attention, but the general appearance was cozy and inviting with a fenced in area on the left side and a one car garage on the right. The single-family 1,368 square feet one story house sat on an 8500 square feet lot that was definitely in need of some tender loving care. The lawn was more weeds than grass and the front porch needed the posts replaced. Even the driveway needed attention. Yet, it deserved a look see since the price was right.

So we all entered the premises and was surprised to see the interior had all hard wood floors that were in good condition so with this encouragement we stepped inside. The front room was quite spacious and seemed appropriate as the living room. Behind this room was a wide doorway that lead to a large dining room area. Off to the right of the dining room was the kitchen. It was not large, but it was big enough with plenty of storage. Behind the kitchen was the laundry room and it was through this room you could access the back yard. Here was an interesting view of wild flowers and overgrown grass, yet it held charm; especially because of its depth and a surprising low red brick wall that seemed to separate the immediate lawn area from a field that also was part of the property.

Back in side, behind the dining room was a spacious room that could be a family room or even another bedroom. Retracing our steps through the dining room and into the living room area there was a side doorway entrance to a hallway that lead to a good size bedroom, a full bathroom, an office or possibly another bedroom that had a built in storage unit, and off this room a half bath.

We returned many times to help get the place in order, with Mark doing a lot of the work himself, except when it came to the bathrooms, which we paid someone else to handle. It took time, but when it was done, it was quite lovely; especially when all the furnishings were in place.

After a glimpse of it inside now, I know that it will take a lot of time and a lot of money to ready it for sale, if indeed that is what Heather plans to do.

###

Later I learned I was right as it didn't sell until 2012 and from pictures online, extensive remodeling and repair work had been done. Even then, the house sold for $45,000 which was low compared to the estimate value of $123,000.

###

My attention returns to the present as we turn onto Route 44 and I hear Heather say that she hadn't realized how far it was to Erik's apartment. I start to comment, but stop. Earlier she mentioned she had made several trips here and recently picked him up and brought him to her house to go to a family event that he had been invited to. She may be trying to make conversation now or maybe with someone else driving it seems longer.

I resume staring out the window and see we are moving along quite briskly as the traffic is minimal. The view is more open now as we leave behind the congested city area neighborhoods. Soon we take the exit ramp and I hear the GPS say we are to continue on I44. We all seem preoccupied as the silence continues. I wonder what to expect when we get there.

From avidly watching the police procedural, or police crime drama, programs like Criminal Minds, and the Law and Order genres I now think this is not going to be easy, especially if the premises has not been cleaned. What if it hasn't been cleaned!

I want to prepare myself because there is a lot to be handled in such a short period of time and if I want to take care of my son's final needs, I must be strong. No matter what shape the apartment is in, I can handle it.

We turn onto S.W. 89th Street and I hear Heather say we are very close now. I take a deep breath and feel Mark's hand cover mine. I smile at him as we approach the big brick sign at the entranceway announcing the Hunt Apartments and feel the motion of the car as we take a left.

We enter the drive to the parking area of the Hunt Apartments, at 3042 S.W. 89th Street and I think, to myself that anyone coming here would think it is a very nice Oklahoma City neighborhood, with its limited access gate entry and green lawns. Yes, that was the impression one had but I saw the place as evil, knowing what had taken place here.

Mark parked the car and I opened the door on my side of the rental and immediately feel the heat of the day smack me in the face causing me to reel backwards. It is so hot that it feels like my skin is burning and all I want to do is get inside where it must be cooler. I don't even want to wait for the others.

Mark has the same reaction to the heat, but Heather is more accustomed to it and does not seem to notice this drastic temperature change from the air conditioned car to the outside world. I stand patiently waiting for everyone to join me on the sidewalk and we walk unitedly together through the doorway of the office building. I take one more deep breath before we enter the office area and I think, this is where it begins.

The woman behind the desk seems friendly, I reach out my hand and say, "Hello, my name is Juanita Tischendorf. I believe Joann is expecting us." From somewhere off to the left, I hear a voice and before being summoned, Joann enters the front office. She immediately introduces herself and expresses her sympathy for our loss.

"I really liked your son and so did the tenants here. He was very personable and everyone here willingly helped him. We put Erik in an apartment near the office which made it easier for him to come and go and if he needed something to come to the office."

I respond with a 'thank you', but at the moment I am focus on going to Erik's apartment. I don't understand this feeling because he's not there. I will never understand why I am anxious to step across the threshold of the place where it happened.

It is as if Joann can sense the urgency I am feeling. She reaches in her desk and I hear the sound of keys jingling before she says, "Let me take you to the apartment. They have been working on it and the lock has been changed, but it should be open. But in case it's not, let me go over with you."

We follow Joann out the office door, across the driveway and to the sidewalk on the other side. Two doors down and we are standing in front of Erik's last resident, Apartment E.

I don't know if it is the heat or the fact that I am standing outside the door where someone has taken the life of my son but at that moment I experience a chill go through my body. I sway on my feet and feel as though I am going to pass out so I lean against the wall of the little porch in front of the door.

Joann first turns the door handle and finds it to be locked, then she tries her key, only to find that it doesn't work. She tries it again, but no deal.

I hear Heather say, "Erik doesn't want to let us in!" and I think, she's right.

Joann excuses herself and says she will be right back. She goes to find the maintenance man who had changed the lock. Soon she rejoins us and introduces us to the maintenance man who's name I quickly forget. Not because he isn't important enough to remember, but I know this is the only time I will meet him and as it is I have so many other new names to remember.

He tries his key. No dice, it doesn't work.

I try not to panic as I stand there waiting and wondering what happens next as we watch the maintenance man take off , leaving us still standing there, waiting to get in. I want to scream out at him to let us in, even though I know he has tried.

"This is ridiculous," I say more to myself. Mark steps over beside me and gives me a hug.

I wait like everyone else, and the maintenance man does return and when he does he has a reciprocating saw in his hands. He says, "Step back", and we all step back in unison to give him room.

He begins cutting through the lock on the door. It's so hot and I am becoming even more irritable so I concentrate on preparing myself for what I will see when we finally gain entry. I know now that work has been done inside so it may be cleaned already and I won't be faced with more than I can handle. I think about the forensic shows I constantly watch and wonder if there will be crime scene tape and blood because they have been instructed not to touch the area.

Finally the lock gives and the maintenance man pushes the door open and steps aside to allow us entry. Joann says, "I'll leave you now. Stop by the office when you are done." I nod and she heads back in the direction of the office while Mark, Heather and I step into Erik's apartment.

The apartment is much cooler than the outside and I take a moment for my eyes to adjust to the interior and to prepare myself before moving forward. At this point I am only aware of me. I see nor hear Mark or Heather once inside the apartment.

I can see all the way back to the kitchen area separated by an island from the living room where I stand. There is light carpet on the floor in this room and I force myself to lower my eyes and look, trying to take in bits and pieces at a time and not the whole area. As my eyes move across the room I see a stain that is faint but obviously blood.

I draw in my breath and tell myself, I can do this. It is not as bad as I thought it would be. I can do this. After a few moments I am able to move a step forward. In the same room I notice the sofa has been moved up so that instead of sitting on all four legs it sits on two with the back of it leaning against the kitchen island. I'm not sure whether this is done by the cleaning people or the investigators at first until I notice that around the area where the stain remains, there is debris, medical debris.

This is evidence that paramedics have been here and worked on Erik because there is an empty saline drip bag and litter from packaging laying on the rug and for me at that moment this means only one thing. Erik was alive when he was found. He was alive and didn't die alone and that gives me a little relief. Someone was there with him while he struggled to live. I am glad to know he wasn't alone and left to die here on the carpet. This gives me the strength to go on.

Now I see a chair near the door and on it is a back pack and on the far right the closet is open exposing Erik's things. I don't know why, but I immediately walk over to the back pack and take a look. It belongs to her. Inside are prescription bottles, lots of them, with her name on them. There is a change of underwear in the bag as well that speaks to the fact that she didn't live here. Who lives at a place and keeps a change of underwear in her backpack, I think to myself.

This looks like the way my son would keep his place, less the mess made by the police. What I can see so far it is neat and clean, very well taken care of. It is obvious that they have gone through his papers and closets and I wonder what they have taken from this place. Did they find enough evidence here to make their case?

I try to keep my eyes forward and I begin to tear up as I reach the area where my son fought for his life. I pause ever so slightly and then with determination I enter the bedroom, which is the room off to my left.

Here there are signs again that someone has gone through his stuff. Mark is in the bedroom and checking through the papers on one side of the room. Heather goes through papers across the bed from him. I check out the closet and again there are only Erik's things in the closet. I reenter the front room and rummage in that closet. Still only Erik's things are in the closet and I can find nothing that belongs to her.

I come across a shoe box and I open it. Inside the box I find bill receipts, a list he has made of the bills he needs to pay that month and tucked in the bottom is a folded piece of paper. I opened it and leaning against the wall I read its contents.

Emails To Obama! Creating Change For People With Disabilities!

Posted on *13 November 2008*. Filed under: Advocacy, Email Obama! | Tags: deaf rights, disability rights, human rights, Convention on the rights of persons with disabilities, CRPD, Obama, Barack Obama, Bangladesh, Uganda, Email Obama!, Advocacy, campaign promises, Kosovo |

My name is Erik Saxton. I am disabled and on Social Security. I am finding it difficut to live on my income, not to mention Heath Care costs being added.

Sothing needs to be done.

Also I need help in finding a job. I have been going to school but only because no companinees will hire me full time.

I have penty of skills

Sincerely,

Erik Saxton

Erik Saxton
24 May 2009

This is so like my son, not giving up and just sitting back and taking it. Erik is expressing his need to be seen and treated as equal by all those around him. I cry for him, for what he deserves but has trouble obtaining because he is handicapped and he is a little person. It doesn't even come to the fact he is also Black.

It takes me a while to get the strength to continue as I peer into my son's life. I put the shoe box on the floor so that we can take it with us and then I walk back through the living room and into the kitchen.

Here I can see his step stool, a necessity for any little person living in our world. At least at the house we were able to rebuild the kitchen and bathrooms to accommodate their height, but this would be impossible to find in a rental.

I check out the kitchen drawers. Silverware, knifes and nothing more. I begin opening cabinets to see dishes, glasses and in the lower cabinets his pots and pans. Nothing extraordinary tucked anywhere so I turn and open the refrigerator door. I don't know what I am looking for as I stare at the contents within and see only a couple bottles of pop, some wrapped leftovers and a bottle of water.

I close the refrigerator door and turn to lean on the island, looking out into the living room and I see the computer near the window and go over to it. I try to turn it on but find that the one thing they have done is turn off the electricity. I consider contacting Joann and asking her to turn it on, thinking there could be something of interest stored in it, but I taught my son to use passwords that had no personal connection to anything or anyone: in other words 'unguessable'. This would keep his equipment safe. but unfortunately I wouldn't be able to access anything even if I could turn it on.

Next to the computer is his portable television. It sits on a stand with a shelf underneath where I would assume he had a DVD player, but the shelf is now empty. Not only is the shelf empty, I look around and notice that the walls are empty too.

This is the first time I notice this. There are no pictures anywhere that give a personal quality to the room. It could be because it would be hard for Erik to hang pictures or it could be that he wasn't totally settled in.

I return to the bedroom and Mark says, "I've found some pictures you might want."

I go over to take a look at them. "Thanks, babe, I do want these." I leave to search for something to put his possessions in that I plan to take with me.

Heather has a request for some things as well so we pile everything in the corner while we continue to go through Erik's belongings.

###

The apartment is scarcely furnished and I begin to wonder what happened to all the things I purchased for him to replace those that he had to leave behind at the house. I ask Heather if she knows. And she tells me that at Erik's last rental, his roommate had ripped him off. I remember Erik telling me about this, but he didn't specifically say it was his furniture and other personal effects.

In a sense he did say that he had taken his things, but I had always told him that these were just things and the items that where personal like his pictures or other prized possessions no one would take since they only held value for him.

My mind takes me back again as I think about the roommate not paying his share of the rent and still having the gall to take what wasn't his. In our conversation Erik told me he needed my help as the landlord was going to throw him out of the apartment because he didn't have his rent money either since his roommate had taken it, too. I remember sending him the money, but for some reason he was still evicted.

What's done is done, I had told myself, so there was no need to question him on why he was thrown out. What was important now was to find a place for him to live. That was when I mentioned to him that he still had a house. He could move in with Heather until he found something. After all the house still half belonged to him too. Little did I know.

After seeing the condition of the house, I now realize that when he said he couldn't live there it probably had something to do with the state the house was in when Mark and I saw it. It was even beyond my capabilities to clean, let alone Erik's. I think that is why he searched and found this place and it was a better alternative, then.

###

I can't feel him here. I really expected to feel him here, but I can't. Is it because I never saw my son in this environment?

Instead I just feel sad because he was here and he was hurt and I wasn't able to help him. My son was 41 years old so there is no reason for me to feel that I should have protected him, only tell my heart that.

I manage to do what we came here to do. I have seen all there is to see and now I help gathering possessions that we wish to take with us. I am glad when we are ready to finally leave.

While Mark puts the items in the car, I go into the office to sign a form that gives my permission for them to take possession of Erik's belongings that we are leaving behind. There is nothing more that we can take since we are going to ship it home. Besides it will be of use to someone else so we donate the kitchen contents, furniture and other items.

When I return to the car Mark and Heather have already put the items we are taking in the trunk of the car. They sit patiently waiting for my return. I climb into the passenger's seat and appreciate the coolness within. They must have been settled for a while waiting for my return. As soon as I am seated and belted in, Mark says, "Heather knows the location of a UPS store so we can send these items home."

"I nod my head."

We then head toward the UPS store to send the items we want back to Rochester. I look at the clock in the car and note that there is plenty of time before our next appointment. As we drive away a saying comes to mind. "Leave the yesteryears alone, it is the todays that count since you can't change what happened in the past". I can't recall where I heard this before, and I ponder, if only it was that easy to move on.

Erik is gone. I don't want it to be true but I am beginning to believe it is so. This is not right. I was to go first. Not the other way around. Now I am here and he is gone. They took him and there is nothing I can do about it. I am here and he is gone. All I can do is make sure he is never forgotten.

###

I make a decision. We will go to the UPS office and then drop Heather off before we go to the Funeral Home. There really isn't any reason for her to go with us and she should understand that.

Heather is quiet as we drive to the UPS office near her home and where she usually goes to drop off packages. When we arrive, I watch as she talks with the attendants that she seems to know quite well and who seem to like her. Mark and I get boxes and begin packaging the belongings we intend to ship to Rochester. It takes a bit to try and organize the contents to get it all to fit in the one box, but finally we have the box secured and make our way to the counter. There we fill out the forms and provide the necessary details.

When we are done, I check to see that Heather is still conversing with one of the UPS people so I say to Mark, "Let's take Heather home now. I cannot think of a reason for her to go with us to any of the other appointments."

"That's fine with me."

I call out to Heather, "We're ready to leave now."

Heather says goodbye to her friends and all three of us leave together. Outside we climb into the car and settle in, then we drive in total silence the short distance to Heather's house.

We sit in the car in her driveway. Heather releases her seat belt and asks, "Are you planning on having a memorial service in Rochester?"

"Yes, we do."

"You know Erik wanted to be cremated because the thought of being buried did not appeal to him."

"Yes, you told us."

"So, you will be spreading his ashes at the Henrietta townhouse you lived in?"

"Yes."

"Good." Heather climbs out of the car then adds, "I will have a memorial service for Erik here in Oklahoma."

"That's fine. Thank you."

Whether or not she really has a memorial service here, is no matter. I know that this will be the last time she has any dealing with Erik or with me.

###

I set the GPS for 1145 W. Britton Road in Oklahoma City, the address for the Demuth funeral Home. The GPS says it will take us 15 minutes to get there. We head north on S Agnew Ave and turn left to merge onto I-40 W. We drive a little ways and then we are taking exit 147B to merge onto I-44 E and heading toward Tulsa.

Tulsa is the second-largest city in the state of Oklahoma and 46th-largest city in the United States. Tulsa is only 47 miles from Bartlesville, Oklahoma where Erik's father's family live. On visits to Bartlesville, we often would make a trip to Tulsa that has many art deco masterpieces in downtown buildings and churches and a must see beautiful river parks. We once went to see a musical at the Performing Arts Center.

AN UNFAIR ADVANTAGE   BY: JUANITA TISCHENDORF

Several other highway numbers later and we are exiting on to W Britton Rd and I see the Demuth Funeral Home on the left. This is where Detective Lyndell Easley had informed us that we could see Erik.

We stop next to a sprawling brown brick building that could easily pass for a large home except for the identifying sign at the left front corner . We drive to the side parking area. Here we stop. I sit there taking deep breaths and try to convince myself that I can do this. Then we both get out of the car and take the walk along the side of the building to reach the front awning entrance.

Erik was sent here, once we learned from Heather that Erik wanted to be cremated. It bothered me a little that I had to rely on Heather for Erik's wishes, but discussing funeral arrangements with my son had not been a topic at any time. I know that I have told my husband my wishes so it stood to reason that Heather and Erik had discussed this at one time, too. I have to believe that Heather did know and trust what she says to be true. She has no reason to lie about something so important.

Demuth is a crematorium and unlike the wide inviting entrance hallways of a funeral home, here the front lobby leads to rooms that are down a smaller hallway. This is where Erik was transported after leaving the medical examiner's office.

When we reach the front door, I touch Mark's arm and we pause. I take a deep breath and then I am ready. We walk through the front door and are engulfed by the silence of the air conditioned room. The furnishings in the area is not as fancy as those found in a funeral home, but is still tastefully decorated. Since entering, we seem to be the only ones in the building.

There is not a sound to be heard in this well-furnished entrance way. We walk cautiously ahead toward the hallway and soon we are noticed by an individual who guides us to the office. She asks, "Can I get you something to drink?"

"I'm fine", I say.

"I'm fine, too", Mark says.

"Well, have a seat and I will let Mr. Demuth know you have arrived".

The office is what I would expect. It has two quite comfortable chairs situated in front of a large dark wood desk with only a few items on the surface. There is a high back chair positioned behind the desk. On the fall wall there are several samples of urns and some kind of certificates on the other walls.

In a few minutes we are joined by Mr. Demuth who enters with a folder in his hand.

"Hello, I am Mr. Demuth. I am so sorry for your loss."

"Thank you," is all I can say.

I watch as Mr. Demuth goes to sit in his chair and once he is seated, I ask, "Can I see Erik?"

I see the hesitation in his face before he has a chance to recover. He takes a minute to adjust the folder on his desk.

I had done my research and know that Erik may have been placed in a cardboard coffin since he is to be cremated. They have not been notified of any memorial service to be held in Oklahoma or that the body will be shipped to Rochester, prior to being cremated.

I have also read that arrangements can be made at the crematoria to visit Erik so I am in my right. I am about to mention that I have a right to see my son, but it is unnecessary.

I watch as Mr. Demuth makes a call and talks quietly into the receiver. When he hangs up he says that they will get Erik ready.

Mr. Demuth informs us that they were notified immediately at the time of death of Erik, and his body was transported to the crematory facility where he has been held until the death certificate and cremation permit were issued by the State Medical Examiner's Office. They now have the documentation so Erik's body has been readied for cremation. I'm not quite sure what this means.

"What does this all mean?"

"We have onsite refrigeration facilities where the body has been kept."

"Can we take care of the paperwork and then I will answer any questions you have and take you to see Erik."

"Yes."

Mr. Demuth explains that when someone passes, the death must be registered with the local or state vital records office within a matter of days so that the vital records office can then issue copies of the death certificate. This is why I was asked over the phone to supply the personal details that they did not have.

He continues saying that as the person in charge of the deceased remains they are supplied with a copy of the death certificate, which they have, but would like us to look it over before they file the record with the State Registrar.

I watch as Mr. Demuth takes out a sheet of paper and hands it across the desk. I reach out and accept it.

I look at the paper in my hand. Across the top it says, 'Board of Medicolegal Investigations, Office Of The Chief Medical Examiner'. I scan down to the bottom and see the name, Chai S. Choi, M.D. I close my eyes and return to the top of the document. There, under Decedent is his name, Erik Scott Saxton. I stare at it. Mr. Demuth hands me a Kleenex and I catch the tears before they spill on the document.

"Sorry."

"That's okay, Mrs. Tischendorf. Take your time."

I focus and slowly check each piece of information to make sure it is right, I notice something that needs to be addressed, but continue on until I have looked over each text box. A Dr. Boren at the Southwest Medical Center saw my son on 9/16/2010 at 10:50 a.m. but that was later as it shows that Erik passed at 10:42 am. It's a maze of information and some is still missing.

I return to the bottom and just before the box showing the medical examiner's name and location is the Probable Cause of death.

Probable Cause of death? Are they not sure what caused his death, even after the autopsy. I read, Subdural Hematoma due to blunt force head trauma. I have an idea what that means, but now, just under this I find what takes away any doubt that this is my son.

'Other significant medical conditions. Neck injury, dwarfism with left upper extremity hemiparesis, status post craniotomy with cranioperitoneal shunt.'

I am well aware of these medical terms from past experiences. They mean he has a weakness of the upper left side of his body and has had brain surgery after which a shunt was surgically installed.

Tears flow, uncontrollably from my eyes. It is Erik. I can't doubt it any more. This is my son.

I force myself to get back in control so that I can complete this first task given to me in taking care of my child.

"It seems in order, " I say. "but there is some missing information."

"Yes, I know," Mr. Demuth says. "That will be filled in before the copies are issued and the official stamp is applied. Did you find anything incorrect?"

"Yes, okay. I think the place of death is incorrect."

"What is the correct location", he asks.

"It should be 3042 SW. 89th Street, Oklahoma City, Oklahoma 73149. The address you have is the one for the house he shared with his ex-wife. I'm not sure how that got put on the certificate."

Mr. Demuth writes down the correct address and when I hand him back the copy, he writes the change on the copy. I watch as he writes the information in the two places on the certificate, then hands it back so that I can check the accuracy of the change.

"That's correct."

"As soon as the official copy is ready you will be sent copies." He continues explaining that we can get either informational or "certified" copies of the death certificate. The Informational copies are for personal records and the Certified copies bear an official stamp, and are necessary to obtain a permit for burial or cremation and for transfer of the deceased person's property. Since it is our responsibility to provide a copy to the Social Security Office, you won't need one for them. "Do you know how many copies you'll need?"

Mark says, "We'll order three. Can we get more if we need them later?"

"Yes, you can order more copies of the Death Certificate by mail. You will need to download an application form to fill out to request additional copies. Just complete the application in full, enclose a photocopy of your photo ID for identification purposes, enclose the correct fees and mail it to this address." He hands Mark a card with the address on it.

"Thanks."

"No problem. You will have to pay for each copy of the death certificate and that should be fifteen dollars for each copy you request." Mr. Demuth pauses and then adds, "Any more questions on this?"

We tell him no.

Mr. Demuth opens up his folder and pulls out a form. He then begins filling in information on the form while we wait. When he is done he turns to us and says, "The charge that you will need to pay today is $1,370 for the cremation and the death certificates you wish to order now. This allows for all aspects of the cremation to be handled by us."

"That's fine," Mark replies.

"The 'ashes', can be sent to you in a temporary container at no cost or you can purchase an urn."

I think about this for a moment. Mr. Demuth has handed Mark a pamphlet which he opens and leans over so that I can see the information. This gives a list of prices that break down the initial cost quoted to us as well as a price list for urns.

While Mark continues to look through the pamphlet, I again make my decision according to what Heather has told me; especially since I feel this is my son's wishes. Heather has said that Erik told her once that he wanted his ashes to be spread in the woods at the townhouse where we use to live.

Erik was the happiest little boy when we lived there. He was young enough that his size did not matter. He had not experienced the paralysis until much later, and he had so many children his age to play with. Yes, I am sure this is where my son will want to be. Not only was this place a fond memory for him, it was also a fond memory for us as a family.

"I won't need an urn," I say.

I watch as Mark hands Mr. Demuth his credit card.

Mr. Demuth stands up, taking the folder and the completed forms with him as he says, "I'll be right back."

I watch as he goes ;through the door, closing it behind him. When he is out of the room, I turn to Mark and say, "I have to see him."

Mark responds, "I know."

He is gone for some time, or so it seems. It may have been only a few minutes, but I am now anxious, wanting to see my son.

When the Mr. Demuth returns, Mark tells him that we want to see Erik.

Mr. Demuth hesitates for a moment than explains, "I want you to realize that he will not be in a casket and his body is downstairs." He pauses and says, "Are you sure?"

"Yes, I'm sure. I have to see him."

"I want to make you aware that his body has been frozen for the last few days."

Erik is frozen! The words come back to me now, "We have onsite refrigeration facilities where the body has been kept."

I heard those words, but it didn't sink in until now. I try not to let my feelings show as I say pleadingly to Mark, "I want to see him."

"Yes, we still want to see him," Mark says again.

Again Mr. Demuth excuses himself. "I'll be right back." He says as he gets up from his chair. He opens the folder he has on his desk and places all the papers inside. He excuses himself and with the folder in hand, goes out the door, closing it behind him.

I sit there wondering what all is in that folder that he keeps with him. I wonder if I should ask to see what information he has in there, but then decide against it. What does it matter anyway.

We are alone. I look at Mark and he smiles at me. I want to ask him if he knows what we are in for. Will Erik be lying on one of those metal tables, covered with a sheet, behind a plate glass window, where we are standing on the other side? Or will we be lead into a room that has oversized drawers on a wall and we will stand next to one and they will open it and under a white sheet pulled up over his head, there will be Erik?

I find I don't care which it is. Just as long as I can see my baby just one more time.

Mr. Demuth opens the door to the room we occupy and stands at the entrance. "Mr. & Mrs. Tischendorf, please follow me."

This is it. I stand up and wait for Mark to do the same. I inhale quietly as Mr. Demuth steps aside to let us pass. He then walks beside us, but not toward another room. Instead he leads us to the front door, where he again stands back to let us pass.

We step outside into the stifling heat of the day, but I barely feel it because I am inside myself thinking I will see Erik and this will be the very last time I will see him. I walk behind Mr. Demuth and beside Mark as the sidewalk slants down along the right hand side of the building until we are all the way in back of the building.

Mr. Demuth stops and we are forced to stop behind him. We are now at the back side of the building. Everything around me looks so out of place. There are pallets piled up back here and there is machinery that belongs in a factory building. From inside a gaping hole in the side of the building, I see a man walking out in coveralls.

Coveralls?   I   think!   Here   is   Mr.   Demuth   dressed professionally like I would assume all funeral home employees where to dress, but not this man.

While Mr. Demuth confers quietly with the gentleman in the overalls, I lean forward and try to see inside the back of the building, but it is very dark in there and I can't make out anything from this angle.

"Mr. & Mrs. Tischendorf, this gentleman will take you to Erik."

"Please follow me," the man in the overalls says.

It is only a few steps before we are led by this stranger through the wide opening in front of us. We step over the threshold and once inside it is still dark and I am unable to make out anything. We stand just inside the building and I look down and notice that we are standing on a dirt floor in this dank area. I wait for my eyes to adjust and the first think I notice is that off to my right is a huge furnace.

This is not a furnace to keep the building warm! This is where the cremation process takes place. I could have gone all my life without seeing this and knowing that Erik will be put in there. This is frightening and I want to change my mind. This is just too frightening. I am about to say this when I remember. This is not for me to choose. Erik has made this choice and I must abide by his wishes.

Cautiously I walk deeper into the darkness that reveals much of what I saw outside the area. There are piles of pallets on my left like the ones used to stack fire wood on and I figure that is their purpose here too.

I walk cautiously further into the area being careful not to trip and wondering where the door to our final destination is. I have to wonder no more as the man stops leading us and I stop, knowing somehow before he says anything that Erik is here.

I look at the pile of pallets on my left, letting my eyes slowing work their way to the dirt floor and I feel my strength drain. Mark is right there beside me holding me upright as I stand frozen in this spot.

There, at the base of the pallets, I see him. I see my son, lying on a pallet on the floor of this dark, foreboding place. His body is covered with a sheet just below his shoulders. I try to scream but nothing comes out!

This is not what I expected. I expected Erik to be treated with respect, at least just for me to see him. I don't want to see him this way. They could have put him on a table or done something to show respect for him. It disturbs me deeply to see him like this, laid out like a piece of meat, on a pallet next to the furnace that will engulf him in flames. No, this is not how I want to remember him.

I am sobbing and I want desperately to stop so that I can see him clearly, but the tears will not stop as I lean over him. This is my son and I need to see him under whatever circumstances and surroundings.

Erik's eyes are open as if he is looking at me. I stare down at him, first noticing that his left eye is swollen and has a purplish bruise. I glance up at his head, noticing that his hair has begun to turn gray. The last time I saw him his hair was still black with no gray.

It is there that I notice the right side of his head is caved in. Caved in! How hard must someone hit you to cave in your skull!

I just let the tears come now as I lower myself so that I am able to see him up close. I reach out and touch his dear face, ignoring the coldness of his skin on my hand. "I love you, Erik. Mommy loves you!"

I am bawling uncontrollably as I touch him once more and talk to him, telling him that I am here and so sorry I wasn't here earlier. I say that I know he wasn't alone when he died, and I hoped that he didn't suffer, but I believe that he had. That I could tell by looking at him. His left eye so bruised, black and blue and swollen shut. The deep indentation mid-way on his forehead above the eye while the right side of his head had sunken in.

I lean over and kiss his cheek and can see evidence of blood having been present in his ears, his mouth and his nose.

I tell him that I am so sorry, so sorry that this happened to him and that I would make sure that the person responsible for taking his life will have her life taken from her. I will not rest until that is done.

I whisper to him, trying desperately to choke back the tears as I tell him that I will remember every moment of his life and keep his memory alive. I will find out about the moment when his life was taken. I will write his story as I did once before so that people will know how proud I am of him and that this person took the life of a loved and wonderful person.

As I stare down at my child I wonder if anyone cared about him during those last moments and did they show it. Or did he seem to them to be just a body. It would be important for me to think that as they worked to try and save him that they saw him as they felt his last breath leaving his body.

"I love you Erik and I won't forget you. I won't let anyone forget you."

I feel Mark as he helps me up and starts walking me away. I don't turn back. I can't, but even under the circumstances I am glad I had a chance to see him once more and to know, without a doubt that this is my son.

Mark helps me in the car and asks if I am all right. I let him know that I am. I stare straight ahead trying to gain control of my feelings so that I can do what I must do next. It is not my time to need consoling, not yet. By the time Mark climbs into the driver's seat I am able to say, "We need to get to the Medical Examiner's office

###

We leave the Funeral Home and turn right onto the Broadway Ext Service Road that will take us to US77.   Mark drives, following the directions of the GPS as he is told to take exit 1F and turn right onto NE 6th Street and I gaze out the window but am not really seeing anything. I feel the motion of the car as Mark makes a left hand turn onto North Oklahoma Avenue and in less than fifteen minutes we are at our next stop on 901 N. Stonewall Avenue, just over 3 miles from the Demuth Funeral Home.

###

We drive in front of the building of white brick with the words, "The Office Of The Chief Medical Examiner printed in big black lettering on the right hand side of the building. There are several tall trees that decorate the flat lawn and roofline of the building with a very big one at the edge of the sidewalk.

The wide staircase entry has two gray cinderblock railings framing it and the impressionless building seems to be as it should be, somber and sedate. Mark finds a parking space along the right side of the building and we park. He looks at me and asks, "Are you ready?"

I shake my head to let him know I am. After what I have gone through, nothing here could be as frightening. We get out of the car and walk around to the front entrance, no longer thinking about the heat as we continue to be going in and out of it constantly. I know that here at the medical examiner's office we will have our first look into what has taken place in Erik's apartment.

In moments upon entering the building we are lead to the medical examiner's office.   We are asked if we would like something to drink and we settle on water. Soon we are seated in front of Dr. Choi's desk. After introductions, we wait while he goes through the folders on his desk until he finds the one that has information on Erik.

Dr. Choi looks over the information in the folder and then begins. "It is the sole responsibility if this office to investigate sudden, violent, unexpected and suspicious deaths. It is the information gained from these investigations that is frequently required in the form of evidence and expert testimony in both criminal and civil proceedings."

"As a physician I am also specially trained and certified in the field of Forensic Pathology and I also perform autopsies to determine the cause of death and the manner of death."

"The determination of the cause of death can be straight-forward or may be more complicated, requiring the assistance of toxicology tests, laboratory reports, hospital records, histologic examination of tissues, and other studies."

"After reviewing the scene details and the autopsy findings, I have listed your son's death as a homicide of violent and unusual or unnatural causes. These findings will lead to a formal investigation into the case."

It was a violent attack which I already know since seeing Erik. I can't help wondering what kind of person was this woman! I know my feelings are written all over my face and if I want the examiner to continue I need to pull myself together. I take several deep breaths and manage to look at the medical examiner without exposing my thoughts.

"Can I have a copy of your report," I ask.

"As I mentioned, this will be used as evidence in this case and I cannot release that to you now."

"I understand." I really don't, but what else can I say.

Dr. Choi picks up from behind his desk one of those plastic hospital bags that they ask you to put your belongings in before getting into the hospital gown I'm sure Erik was not the one who put the items in the bag. Now I watch as Dr. Choi removes the contents. It consist of Erik's driver's license, shorts, gray Hanes underwear, a dollar and twenty-one cents in change, one 7/11 receipt, a piece of glass found in his pocket, and a pair of tennis shoes.

"Can I have these?"

"No, sorry, this goes into evidence. I was told that you would probably want to see these so I had them put in my office. What I can do is notify the proper office that you would like to claim these later."

While Dr. Choi puts the items back in the bag, I think about Erik and how surprised I was to see he has gray in his hair. It hadn't been that long, a year, maybe a year and a half since I last saw him. But he had the same face, the same dear face. He was older, but he was not old enough to die.

I draw my attention back to the medical examiner who is saying that on site and later in the ambulance they had performed several medical procedures in an effort to save his life and those procedures continued when he arrived at the hospital.

"Can I see the report?"

"It's not completed, yet. These are just my notes, Mrs. Tischendorf." If you want I can read what I have here to you.

"Please," I say.

"The medical application included an endotracheal tube through mouth, intravenous needle placement over the right subclavian region, needle placement over the left subclavian region, bilateral chest tube in place, needle puncture mark with tape over the dorsum of the right hand, identification band around the right wrist, intravenous needle placement over the right tibia, two electrode pads over the chest and abdomen and six monitor pads attached over the chest, arm and abdomen."

He shuffles his papers and finds what he is looking for. "The injuries were over the left eyelid, a purplish contusion with edema. Just above the eyebrow, there is an ill-defined purplish red contusion. At the lateral angle of the eyebrow, there are two vertical red abrasions. On the back of the neck region there are several superficial linear abrasions. Underneath the abrasions, the skin shows subcutaneous hemorrhages. There are purplish contusions over the back of the right forearm and the dorsum of the right hand. On the back of the right shoulder there is a fine petechial contusion that shows extensive subcutaneous hemorrhages. Over the left back, there is a somewhat V-shaped horizontal linear red abrasion. Over the dorsum of the left hand there are fine linear red horizontal abrasions "

"Finally, the summary will state, the decedent is a 41 year old black male who lives with his girlfriend. It was stated that the decedent had been drinking vodka all day long yesterday (September 15, 2010) and had a history of seizures due to his drinking. Around 1800 hours, the decedent was found to have allegedly beaten. Today at 0800 hours, it was stated that the girlfriend checked on him and he was okay. When she checked on him later, she found him unresponsive. 911 was called and he was transported to Southwest Medical Center where he was pronounced dead."

"Complete autopsy showed a blunt force injury of the head with a large subdural hematoma with multifocal subarachnoid hemorrhages. This is bleeding in the area between the brain and the thin tissues that cover the brain, along with cerebral edema. This is excess accumulation of fluid in the spaces of the brain. with focal cortical contusions which is a form of traumatic brain injury; a bruise of the brain tissue, if you will. In addition, I noted previous craniotomy with scar formation of the right temporal region and has a shunt placement. There are blunt force neck injuries with hemorrhages".

"I noted the decedent is a dwarf and has a history of left upper extremity hemiparesis, muscle weakness on only one side of the body, for a brain tumor operated on at the age of 10 years old. It is felt that cause of death is a large subdural hematoma due to blunt force head trauma. The neck injuries and the underlying natural disease of dwarfism with left upper extremity hemiparesis would be participating factors to this death. The manner of death is ruled a homicide. Postmortem toxicologoical studies were negative for ethanol and drugs."

"This changes the report that Erik had been drinking?"

"Yes it does. A negative value usually means that alcohol, prescription medications that have not been prescribed, and illegal drugs have not been detected."

"Who said that this was a girlfriend?"

"That either came from the police or from the suspect?"

This ends our time with Dr. Choi. As we ready ourselves to leave, Dr. Choi tells me that he knows how hard this must be and that I may find I have other questions that I didn't ask. If I do, he offers me his card so that I can call. He walks with us to the door and we say our goodbyes.

###

Was this a 'girlfriend'? I do not know, but this is something I need to check out further.

We were finding out Erik's side of the story. Since he is not here to tell it. Each stop on our trip to Oklahoma City will reveal a piece of the puzzle into what happened, why it happened, who did it and how. I need to face the reality that this will not be easy for me to see or hear the details such as this visit to the Medical Examiner. I must keep it in mind that all of this is how Erik will be able to tell his side of the story.

By the time we arrive in Oklahoma, this woman, Clara Blocker, had confessed to doing the crime and the evidence support that claim. But, I needed to know more than just she did it. I needed to know why. I needed to know how Clara and Erik knew each other. So I have to be willing to see, hear, read and keep an open mind.

###

Mark and I have one more stop to make and that one is to meet with Detective Lyndell Easley at the Oklahoma City Police Department, Investigations Bureau on Colcord Drive. At the car, I stand waiting for Mark to open the door and thinking how exhausting this trip has been and we're not done yet. As I slip into the passenger seat and hook my seat belt I wish that we had more time to cover all the bases instead of this rush, rush merry-go-round we're on. Yet, I have to admit we have been spending our time wisely and what more would be gained by having more time.

I program the GPS for our next stop, the Oklahoma City Police Department at . 701 Colcord Drive and the GPS informs me that it is ten minutes away. By the time we pull out of the parking space at 901 North Stonewall Avenue, the GPS is ready to give us directions. Mark drives south on N. Stonewall Avenue, heading toward northeast eighth street. When we reach the turn, we turn right and continue onto Harrison Avenue, until we are instructed to make a slight right onto northeast fourth street. We drive a short distance and then turn left onto N. Shartel Avenue and before we know it we are turning left onto Colcord Drive. The GPS informs us that our destination will be on our left.

The six story stone building sits back from the road on Colcord Drive taking up a good city block. There are large windows at the front entrance that is accessed along a paved walkway that leads to the white railed front porch entrance.

Several full grown trees dot the landscape along with several spaces of greenery breaking up the wide sidewalk and drive. On the right side of the building is a white structure, just above ground and in the opening you can see it is a parking garage. As we pull up in front of the building we are in luck and find a parking space on the driveway just before the entrance way.

On opening the car door. the heat smacks me in the face, as I sluggishly force my body out of the car. The moment I stand outside, my body starts a battle to keep cool. I feel my heart beat faster as it tries to increases the flow of blood to my skin and I am uncomfortable, feeling the sweat dripping down by back, increasing at each step as we make our way to the front door. We walk side by side down the sidewalk and up to the front entrance railed porch until finally Mark opens the door and we enter the building.

Inside the building is cool as we proceed to the front desk, ask for Detective Lyndell Easley and then take a seat. In short order, Detective Easley joins us and takes us back to his office. Here there are two chairs seated in front of his desk that is full of papers and folders that cover most of the desk top area.

"Would you like some coffee or water?" he asks.

Mark and I both say, "Water."

Detective Easley excuses himself and goes to get us some water. As we wait, I think the parents who 's child is murdered and they have no justice because the person who committed the crime has not been caught. I am lucky in that sense. They know who did this and have that person in custody. That has to be because the police acted quickly and followed the procedures leaving no stone unturned. This boosters my determination to keep on going, knowing that if the police had taken a break, this may have turned out differently and I might not ever know who killed my son. If they can keep going, so can I.

I can't help thinking about how I viewed my son's body. The only explanation has to be that the Demuth Funeral Home did not know anyone was claiming the body and probably did not expect anyone to come and see him. Yes, I think that must have been the case.

Detective Lyndell Easley returns with two bottles of water and hands one to each of us before he walks behind his desk and sits down. I watch as he shuffles the papers and folders on his desk until he finds the folder he is looking for. This he places in the empty area of the desk, right in front of him.

He clears his throat and opens the folder, apologizing for the 'mess' as it has been busy. When he is ready, he says, I don't know how much you wish to know, but I am willing to fill you in on what has taken place to date.

"Please tell me what you know." I reply.

Detective Easley pauses, obviously to refresh his memory and then begins.

"I had received a call on September 16, 2010 at around 10:00 p.m. from a female who said we needed to do a welfare check at 3042 S.W. 89th St. Apt. E. When I arrived, the first responders, Emergency Medical Services were administering first aid and I was informed that Erik had a pulse and they were going to transport him to Southwest Medical Center. I was also told that Erik appeared to have been beaten and that his left eye was so swollen shut that they couldn't even force it open. At that point I took a closer look, while keeping out of their way. I agreed with them, that Erik had been beaten."

"I was told that the woman who had made the call was standing outside and I immediately went to find her. Standing off to the side was a tall woman and I introduced myself and asked if she was the person who had made the phone call. She said she was and that her name was Clara, Clara Blocker. I asked if she could tell me what happened and she began stumbling over her words as they flowed quickly from her mouth."

"So how did he know this person," I ask.

"She said that she had known Erik for a year and had been living with him on and off for about a month."

"What does she say happened?" I ask.

"Well, on the 15th at noon one of her friends had brought a bottle of vodka and the two of them drank until she left with her friend around 6:30 p.m. and he took her to the Cricket store to put more minutes on her cell. They left Erik alone and returned around 7:30 p.m. and she went in to find that he had a swollen eye so assumed he had fallen after drinking so much. She said that later she and Erik walked to the 7-11 to get a coke and when they returned he passed out on the living room floor. She left him there, but when he was still there in the morning she called 911."

"So did she say she beat him up?"

"No, I recorded everything she told me and was finding that it didn't add up. Because I had seen Erik and agreed with the first responders that he had been beaten, I contacted Lieutenant Shubert who contacted the police department of assaults, who are responsible for handling these type of cases. When later the police department was notified that Erik had died, this became a murder investigation and the matter was turned over to the Homicide detectives, which includes me. I then had her taken into police headquarters for further questioning and after several hours of interviewing by my partner, she finally confessed."

"So Erik was alive when you got there?"

"Yes, your son was alive. He died in the emergency room of the Integris Southwest Medical Center. The cause of death was later learned to be blunt force injury to the head but along with this injury there was contusions and abrasions on the back of his neck. They did everything they could to save Erik on site and later in the ambulance before the hospital took over."

"How did you find me. I'm glad you did, but I can't imagine how hard it was to trace me, his mother, with a different name and living in a different state."

Detective Easley replies. "While the detectives conducted their investigation, Lieutenant Shubert had gone to the apartment manager of the complex where the crime had taken place. He obtained Erik's emergency contact information and passed this information on to me. This is where they obtained your name as Erik's mother living in Rochester New York, but they did not reach you on September 16 as the phone number had been entered incorrectly at the manager's office and when they called the number they reached an employee of some local Rochester business who stated she had never heard of Juanita Tischendorf or Juanita Saxton."

"So at that point I began making the calls, anxious to contact a relative or friend. I found Marilyn Goodban was listed as a family friend and called her number. I spoke with Sharilyn Edlund who stated she was Marilyn's roommate. I explained to her that I was looking for the next of kin information for Erik Saxton. Ms. Edlund said that Marilyn Goodban was Erik's former mother-in-law and that she was not presently available. Ms. Edlund provided the name and telephone number for Heather Saxton, saying that she was Erik's ex-wife, but might be able to help us."

"So that is how Heather came into the picture," I say more for myself.

"Yes. I called Heather's number. She at first was upset with me for calling about her ex and so I told her the reason behind the call was that Erik had been murdered and I needed to reach his mother. She was quiet and then I could hear her crying. When she finally spoke I could hear her rustling papers, then she gave me the street address to reach you at in Rochester, New York. She said that she did not have the phone number. I asked if she could talk with me further, but she was too distraught to give me any additional information so the conversation ended."

"So, having your addresses I contacted the Rochester Police Department and spoke with Lieutenant Mike Van Roo. Lieutenant Van Roo informed me that the address he was given was in the suburb of Rochester called Irondequoit and he put me in touch with Inspector Scott. The search ended at that point with Inspector Scott volunteering to make notification of Erik's death."

"On Friday, September 17 I received a call back from Inspector Scott. and he told me he had notified you and was presently at your home. It was then that I first spoke to you. I then had the information I needed to give to the Oklahoma State Office of the Chief Medical Examiner's for releasing the body. That was when we exchanged information for your trip to Oklahoma which I suggested that you sit tight until after the weekend so that you could make contact and meet with the concerned parties."

"We were at the apartment and there were things there that I touched and that could be maybe, evidence you need."

"We have already gathered physical and forensic evidence from inside and around the apartment. We have everything we need to make the case of murder."

"So what happens now," I ask.

"Well, we are processing the evidence, I believe we have interviewed all the neighbors and any other individuals that came in contact with Clara on the 15th or 16th of September, and we would like to add anything you have to share."

I tell Detective Easley that Erik lived alone, as far as I know, in this apartment. I add that Erik was partially paralyzed on the right side so that he would have been unable to defend himself in an attack. I tell him that Erik was not a drinker, nor did he take drugs. He did have to take medication for seizures, but that was the extent of his use of any substance. I also share with him that my son was an easy going individual and would have given anyone, anything that they asked for. He would not fight to save his possessions but would have given them willingly so there was no excuse for anyone beating him and definitely no reason for anyone to murder him. By the time I finish sharing this information, I am in tears.

No one says a word as they wait for me to give a signal I can go on. Detective Easley lifts up his tissue box and extends it towards me. I smile gratefully and taking a tissue, I wipe my eyes, blow my nose and am ready to continue.

"Is there anything else you want to know," Detective Easley asks.

"Yes, why did she do it? Was it money or what?"

"We don't have an answer for that yet. She has not told us why she did it, only that she did."

###

I now know a lot more than I knew before. They had the murderer in custody and the evidence to prove that she had done this. She and even confessed to doing the crime. She had even confessed to being the person who called in for a welfare check on Erik. But why would she do any of this and then hang around. It didn't make sense to me. None of this makes sense without knowing her reason for doing this.

We have done all we can here and I am more than ready to leave Oklahoma City. I wish that I would never have to set foot in this State ever again, but I know I will have to return. I trust the people I have met, but I must be involved and aware of everything that is being done and I must come back for any court proceedings. Then I can say I will never step foot in this State again.

I realize that this sounds harsh, but it is based on my personal experience. Erik's father was born in Bartlesville, Oklahoma and we visited that city along with Tulsa often, so my dislike stems from years of exposure to Oklahoma in the past. What turned me off back then was the open discrimination and the lack of confrontation. Is it still the same? I don't know but it doesn't matter as I will not be going back.

Yet, I have to say that since coming to Oklahoma City, which has been during the last seven years, I have gained respect for this city in Oklahoma. They have proven their lack of prejudice by working hard to solve my son's case in less than 48 hours—maybe even less than 24 hours.

I watch crime shows and know that this does not often happen that everything falls into place in such a short period of time. I know this is the result of good police work and I appreciate it. Detective Lyndell Easley has changed my opinion and I now have faith in at least Oklahoma City's police force. I will reserve my opinion of the courts until later. It is getting late and there is nothing more we can do here so we climb into the car and head back to Dallas, Texas.

###

We arrived in Dallas on Sunday, Sept 19, checked in at the Cooper Clinic, got our bearings and turned in for a good night's sleep so that we could rise early on Monday, September 20 to drive and spend the day in Oklahoma City. Now that I have been successful in taking care of what could be handled in Oklahoma, I need to focus on the book signing that is set to take place on Tuesday, Sept 21.

This is where my mind is as we drive back to Dallas. I know I am not much company to my husband but I also know he understands. Since the return trip is uneventful it allows me to get my head straight so that by the time we reach the Cleveland Clinic I am in control, able to set aside my personal situation and focus on this upcoming event.

As we drive up to our Hotel we park the rental again under the shade of a tree though we know now that it doesn't much matter. Then we hurry in and up to our room. We need to take showers and dress for dinner with Don later that evening, but now I can spend time going over my details for the book signing.

Book signings are not new to me. Over the past years I have had several book signings for books I've written. My very first one was at Barnes & Noble where I not only was there to sign books, but also to read passages from my book. Now that was kind of scary, but it prepared me well for those that followed. I've done book signings in the back yard, in Orlando, Florida, Erie, Pennsylvania, and other locations and always I walk away feeling good about the book and myself.

But I know that if I want to have a successful book signing I need to concentrate and do my upfront work. Sure the venue is set, but I can't waltz in, set up the table, and expect to sell. I need to prep the audience, the room, and myself. So I need to get my head into this now. Dr. Cooper and Don McNelly, who the book is about, are counting on me and I can't let them down.

I spend most of my time going over my one-page introduction that I hope will set the tone for the event and provide the information that I want the audience to have, which includes making them aware of the connection between the Clinic and the subject of my book, Don. This is important. I read and re-read until I am comfortable with the introduction.

That done, I next review the selections I have made in the book to read out loud and I practice until I have it almost memorized. I know that Don, with the amount of time invested in his physical will not have much occasion to spend on his talk so since this is about his life, I have listed points that he can talk about.

That is as much as I can do now. I still need to check out the actual room prior to the event and discuss how sales will be handled. I have the business cards, handouts, bookmarks and fliers that were sent ahead, but I need to check they have been received, I know the books arrived from an email sent to me earlier.

It is as if I have entered a new dimension where nothing bad can touch me. The now, I am in is what I am used to. Anything as sensational as murder and investigations is not a part of my repertoire and I didn't know what to do or how to act.

We meet up with Don and another friend of his who also came for a physical. All four of us go to dinner in the dining room of the Clinic and conversation flows freely. I find it easy to laugh and enjoy myself and Mark does too.

Most of the conversation has dealt with the extent of the physicals the men have been involved in for most of their visit, but it changes when Mark asked if they know what the initials 'HOV' on the highway stand for.

"Yes, Don said, "It stands for High Occupancy Vehicle lane. They are designed to help move more people through congested areas. "

"So who is it for? We saw cars with only two passengers in that lane, as well as bus loads."

Don replies, "Vehicles carrying at least two people may enter and exit the HOV lane".

Mark looks over at me and I look back at him and smile I know what he is thinking.

"Never knew two was high occupancy!" he says.

Don's friend has to leave and after he departs our conversation turns to the upcoming book signing. Don says that Dr. Cooper has invited guests and employees to the talk and says that he has prepared a few words, but figures I should do most of the talking while he responds to questions about his life. That is acceptable to me so we leave it at that.

When we leave the dining room Don walks with us around the campus taking us in and out of buildings and explaining what is done at each location. The place is massive. There are the two hotels, two pools, tennis courts, a clinic building, fitness and spa center and the clinic of gastroenterology, which Don explained as dealing with disease and health of the digestive system.

As we continue, Don tells us he has been coming to the Clinic for many years because another marathoner had told him that the Cooper Institute is dedicated to scientific research in the field of preventive medicine and public health. The Institute's founder, Dr. Kenneth H. Cooper, is known as the "Father of Aerobics," who became interested in exercise to preserve health. When he published his first best seller, Aerobics, in 1968, he introduced a new word and got millions to become active.

As we work our way around Don points out the many running and walking tracks labeled as quarter mile loop, half mile loop, and the one mile track. We had seen these tracks earlier, but now they are put to full use as we pass one runner after another.

We cross bridges over small streams, see all kinds of vegetation and trees along the way for runners and walkers to enjoy. It is all so beautiful and inviting.

We end our tour at the gym and I have my first face to face introduction to Dr. Cooper himself. Until this point it has all been emails and phone calls. Now as we shake hands and go over the next day's book signing, he tells me that he has read "The Madman, The Marathoner" and thoroughly enjoyed it. I am happy, filled with a feeling of accomplishment from his praise and the events of the days preceding recede even further I sleep well that night.

The next day is busy. Before coming to Dallas, Don and I have autographed several copies of the book and I sent them ahead to Amy George, the Cooper Clinic Promotion & Advertising manager who I have yet to meet. That is our first appointment today, so, after waking, we shower and dress and head out the door to go to the little deli on the property for a light breakfast.

I feel a little nervous now, knowing the time is close for our event. Mark and I leave the deli and head toward the back of the property where the promotion and advertising office is housed. We are early, so we sit outside Amy's office to wait.

Mark flips through a magazine he has brought with him while I take in the area. It is well decorated and very comfortable, from the choice of color on the walls, to the furnishing it is obvious that a lot of thought went into designing the area.

We have been waiting maybe five minutes when I see a stunning woman approaching. She has medium length bouncing brown hair and a trim figure, wearing high heels and a warm, sincere smile on her face. I can't help but smile as she moves confidently toward us and when she is in front of us she stops. Mark and I stand up at the same time.

She extends her hand, her smile reaching up; to her brown eyes and we take turns grasping her hand in a firm friendly shake.

"Hello, my name is Amy George, the Cooper Clinic Promotion & Advertising manager ."

"I am Juanita Tischendorf and this is my husband, Mark."

Amy seems to ooze energy and optimism and I find myself feeling confident in her capabilities. She guides us into her office and after we are seated she begins explaining how many people they expect to attend the book signing. She assures us that the books and the publicity items have been received and that she unpacked them and found them to be very well done. She then stands and following her lead, we rise from our chairs. Amy says, "Let's go over to the building so you can see the layout of the room."

We follow her through the property and listen as she tells us how much they have been looking forward to holding this event. She says that she as well as Dr. Cooper are proud to know Don and are glad they have a chance to meet me and to read the book. She says that only Dr. Cooper's books that he has written have been presented at the clinic so this is a first.

We are at the building now where the book signing will take place and Amy takes us to the room that is more like a lecture hall with desks and chairs situated stadium style. There is even a podium on a slightly raised area in front of the seating area. She adds that refreshments will be provided and that she will have the books brought to the room for us.

"Where would you like the books placed," she asks. "Maybe right here on the left of the podium we can set up a table and stack some, with others standing on top of the pile." She pulls out a sample of what she is describing.

"Yes, that will be perfect," I say.

"I have an easel that I will bring over and at that time I can place the promotional materials." Can I do that maybe an hour before?"

Amy checks her calendar and says that I can come over a half hour early to set up and she will come to help me. That's when the room will be available.

We shake hands with Amy then Mark and I leave Amy in front of her office and continue on through the complex. We have time before the book signing so we go back to our room to change and head to the gym for a workout.

###

The day goes quickly and soon I am getting ready for the book signing. When Mark and I are ready, I place a call to Don's room to let him know we are leaving and we meet him in the lobby. Don looks great, especially after knowing that he has spent the last five days having his health evaluation. I could not imagine an exam that takes five days, but Don speaks highly of the thoroughness of this exam and I agree. Don gave me a copy of the report from his previous year exam and it was book size. The report had information on every inch of his external and internal body.

Don, Mark join me and we walk to the conference room. I can't speak for Don, but I am feeling confident and glad that the moment has arrived. When we enter the building, I walk confidently to the room and I squeeze Don's hand, saying "This is going to be great."

Don nods in return. He has spoken in front of many crowds so I know he can do this, plus he knows the material better than anyone. It is his life, after all.

Inside the room has been set up. There is a table with books displayed beautifully and another table with water, and staged layout of flyers, business cards and bookmarks. Behind the table is my poster showing the book, a picture of myself and one of Don. We are ready.

Shortly after entering the conference room, the guest arrive and after an introduction by Dr. Cooper, it is time to begin.

I know my audience, not personally, but what will hold their interest, which makes it easier to present segments from the book that they will consider interesting. I begin by introducing how I came to write this book and how Don and I came to be friends. I then explain how I picked the title, 'The Madman the Marathoner' then briefly share what the book will reveal about Don and his history entering marathons.

When I start all eyes are on me and when I finish five minutes later I can sense the interest in the room. That is when I introduce Don who answers their questions.

###

No matter what is going on in my personal life, I have managed to put it aside and do what is expected of me. I know that I must go on and I know that if I had cancelled or let my hurt take control of my faculties, it would only serve to hurt those who were counting on me. There would be nothing to gain, but a lot to lose.

##

That night my sleep is restless as I toss and turn trying to decide exactly what I can do for my son and how can I help if I am all the way in Rochester, New York. Now that my mind no longer has to deal with the book signing, it is free to ponder what lies ahead. By morning, I am still fighting issues, wondering just what I can do. I pray to God to help me find the path I should take. Why should I know what to do when this is my first confrontation with a murder?

When morning comes, I am tired but believe in myself. I faced the challenge of raising my son, a dwarf, and preparing him for this world and, I did a good job. Back then I only had the help of God since there wasn't the internet to provide me with connections and information. ARPAnet -- the world's first multiple-site computer network -- was created in 1969, the year of

Erik's birth and the original ARPAnet eventually grew into the Internet.

So now I am dealing with something just as unexperienced by me, but not so foreign to the world and with the help of God, and the internet I can discover what I need to do.

We again rise early, climb into our rental car and head for the airport to catch our plane home.

CHAPTER 10: FINDING MY WAY

(SEPTEMBER 19, 2010)

The number one problem facing people today is grief and loneliness. People encounter major losses in their lives, and some may never get over them. Coping with the loss may be one of the hardest challenges that many of us face. When we lose a spouse, sibling or parent our grief can be particularly intense. To lose a child, well there is no words to explain the intensity of that pain. Loss is understood as a natural part of life, but we still are overcome by shock and confusion and it can lead to prolonged periods of sadness or depression.

But everyone reacts differently to death and employs personal coping mechanisms for grief. The first thing we must do if we want to deal with our grief effectively, is to allow our grief to exist by acknowledging it. The tasks of mourning begin with the acceptance of the reality of the loss. Being present at the death, seeing the body after death, and the rituals of a funeral can help.

###

The whole thing just seems like a terrible, terrible dream.

One minute I'm watching my son blow out the candles on his first birthday cake, and the next minute he's lying there, staring up at me with unseeing eyes. I'm in shock. Never did I think a day like this would come. Never did I think I'd someday have to say goodbye to my child. This pain, this excruciating pain—it's unlike anything I've felt before.

Losing a loved one through homicide is one of the most traumatic experiences that an individual can face; it is an event for which no one can adequately prepare, but which leaves in its wake tremendous emotional pain and upheaval. As the parent, it's the worst thing imaginable. Your own child, suddenly gone. I'd give anything to have him returned to me. I still can't believe it's real. I thought saying goodbye to my mother was hard, but nothing can prepare you for this. Mom was older and had lived a long, prosperous life. But my son, he died in such a violent way and at a young age.

In this case the police identified the murderer and have enough evidence to file criminal charges. In other cases a suspect may not be immediately identified. Police keep the case files for serious crimes open for a long time and this keeps the police busy. That is good, but I want to be sure that nothing is missed in Erik's case and that the case is ironclad. The police will not stay in constant contact with me, but I can contact them regularly.

Now that I am home and away from Oklahoma City physically, mentally I have a hard time putting reason to all of this. Erik suffered a violent death and there will be lengthy investigations and court trials ahead so I need to find 'my place' in all of this if I want to face his murderer and watch as her life is taken from her. I want those who are making his case to know that though I admire their work on this case, I will not rest or let them rest until she is tried in court and found guilty.

They are my link to keeping informed on what they know or have found out about this case because I am over 1300 miles, 20 hours 39 minutes away. I need to know and trust them to make sure it all goes the way it should. I want justice.

Back home in Rochester I try to figure out what I need to do but I do not know where to start so I do whatever comes to mind. I write emails and send letters to those people I have met over the years who have done publicity interviews or segments for me. I guess what I am thinking is that it is not enough to have the news coverage in Oklahoma, I need it to reach the east coast too.

I preparing details for a news release to the local television and newspaper stations.

An Oklahoma City woman has been charged in Cleveland County District Court with first-degree murder in the Sept. 15 death of a male acquaintance.

My name is Juanita (Saxton) Tischendorf and on September 16, 2010, my son, Erik Scott Saxton was murdered in Oklahoma On Friday, September 17, I was notified of his murder by Inspector Scott of the Irondequoit Police Department.

In 2006 I celebrated my son's life in my book, **"Who Says I'm Small"**. Erik, as an Achondroplasia dwarf who would later become partially paralyzed, managed to adjust to his life and be happy. I want to be sure no one forgets him. I have been trying to reach his friends in Rochester, but have not met with much success. A news report on your station may help us to reach those who his life has touched. Erik was a graduate of **Rush-Henrietta High School, Class of 1988**. He was born and raised in Rochester New York. Please feel free to release the following contact information: (Included my name, address, phone and email address)

Updated news reports on the murder appear on the internet, like the one that follows:

Clara Ann Blocker

By JANE GLENN CANNON NewsOK.com

Published: 9/24/2010 10:51 AM

Last Modified: 9/24/2010 10:51 AM

NORMAN — An Oklahoma City woman has been charged in Cleveland County District Court with first-degree murder in the death of a male acquaintance.

Clara Ann Blocker, 38, is accused of hitting Erik Scott Saxton, 41, in the head, causing fatal injuries. Blocker called 911 on Sept. 16 asking Oklahoma City police to check on Saxton in an apartment at 3042 SW 89.

According to a court affidavit, Blocker told police she got into an altercation with Saxton on Sept. 15. The woman gave inconsistent statements about the fight, but said she hit the man with objects in the apartment, according to the affidavit.

The woman told police she called 911 when she discovered Saxton was not breathing on Sept. 16, the affidavit states. Blocker was convicted in 2009 on a trafficking cocaine charge in Oklahoma County and is serving a 12-year suspended sentence.

In 2006 she was convicted of larceny of merchandise from a retailer, court records show.

I jot down names of people and locations to contact that I feel can help me in reaching his friends. There are so many people who knew Erik and they need to be informed of his murder. This is the only way I know to do this.

Within a few days I am approached to do interviews and then see the interviews run on television. Other local media pick up on the information and call for an interview or just details that they present to the public. I am confident that this will help me reach people I have lost contact with.

Doing this keeps the reality real for me because since I viewed my child for the last time it still feels like a dream. The reality is that he is not coming back and I will never hear him laugh again or see his smile. I will not hear his voice or have anyone call me 'Mom' anymore.

With all my efforts expended toward getting the news out, it is now time to do what I dread most.

###

I need to prepare his memorial service. I ponder the idea and decide I need to make a list of people to notify. That is where I run into my first problem. I've always made it a point of knowing who Erik's friends were and at least try to get to know them a little, invite them in for dinner, or sit and chat with them. But there comes a time when it is not possible to get to know all his friends. We had a party for Erik's sixteenth birthday. It was a swim party and BBQ. There must have been thirty kids in the back yard and at least half of them I didn't know. Yet, all the parties up until he was twelve, would have at least twenty children and I would know them and their parents well.

Things change. They change so much that for every girl Erik knew at a young age, they may now have a different last name. And, the unfortunate truth is that just like myself, not only the kids, but the parents may have moved too and I only have update information on a few.

Personally I figure it's my job to notify his friends as well as mine. I know it isn't going to be easy. Erik has friends from church, school, camp and the neighborhood. His father has been gone from New York State for quite a while so he won't be able to help. His aunt in California may be able to assist in notifying any friends he made there as well as his father's family members.

So this is where I start. I call my ex sister-in-law who has already been notified of Erik's death and tell her I need to have her prepare a list of friends and family on her side so that I can notify them of the memorial service.

She agrees to do this and is willing to take care of sending the service details to them once I have set a date. I thank her for her help. I know she wants to talk, but I am not ready to handle more than I am doing now and I know she understands.

I next begin making a list of the schools he attended, the Rotary Sunshine camp where he went every summer, his friends in our neighborhood in Henrietta, and all the places we lived during his childhood years. The list keeps growing as I try to remember everyone and every place I need to contact. When done I go on to my next step.

I have a little experience with arranging a memorial service. Along with my sisters, I did this for our mother. Now, as I search my hard drive for those files I stop and jot down a note to check the internet for information on what needs to be done so that I don't forget anything. I call our church and obtain a date for the service. I then sit down and write what I wish to say in announcing the memorial service.

On September 16, 2010, Erik Scott Saxton died in Oklahoma City. A memorial Service for Erik will be held on Saturday, October 30, at 1:00 p.m. at the Irondequoit United Church of Christ, 644 Titus Avenue, Rochester, NY 14617 (585) 544-3020. In Lieu of flowers the family asks donations be made in his name to any of the following charitable organizations: the National Headquarters, Little People of America, Inc., 250 El Camino Real, Suite 201, Tustin, CA 92780, (714) 368-3689, E-mail: lpaonline.org; Rochester Rotary Sunshine Camp, Administrative Office: 100 Meridian Centre, Suite 304, Rochester, New York 14618, 585-546-7435, www.sunshinecampus.org. Both organizations provided Erik happy moments in his life. Erik Scott Saxton was born on April 10, 1969 in Rochester, New York to Harold E. Saxton and Juanita (Saxton) Tischendorf. Erik attended

Rush-Henrietta High School. He continued his education at Rochester Institute of Technology, Silicon Valley College in California, and Oklahoma State in Oklahoma City, Oklahoma.

"Oh my God," I say aloud. "I need to put in his birthdate so that they are aware of the time he would have been at these locations. I write a brief email of the details of his death, and share Erik's age so that they know who would have been in his class, or at the camp when he attended. I use the internet to track down the websites for the schools, church and the camp and send this information to each location.

I am restless, unsure I am doing the right thing because this is all new to me. Before I even know why, I get in my car and visit the neighborhoods where we lived. I drive to Stoney Creek Development on Stowell Drive in Greece, NY and can find no one I knew in this townhouse development. I know that I will not find anyone left at North Glen Apartments as this is usually a temporary stop for people looking for a home. So I leave the Greece area and drive to Country Hills Estate in Henrietta, New York, the place where Erik wants his final resting place.

It has changed. As I drive through the townhouses I find where we use to live and pull into a parking space. I get out of the car. I am hoping that someone I know will appear, but that is not to be. I walk down the sidewalks and go into the woods and just stand still with my eyes closed and feeling the warmth of the sun as it shines through the trees. It is so peaceful and it seems as though I can see Erik running with his friends and his puppy without a care in the world. I cry noisily, making loud, convulsive gasps until I can cry no more.

The tears are still streaming down my face as I make my way back to the car. There is still one more place I need to go and that is Beaconsfield Road where we last lived together.

I drive with purpose feeling that there may be more hope in seeing someone still living in their home in the old neighborhood. This is a housing complex and people buy houses to stay in. I enter the road and continue down to our block and park just a ways down from our old home. I get out of the car.

I start walking through the neighborhood and I am shocked to see that the children playing are so young. It's like the neighborhood is starting over again with new families enjoying the homes instead of the original owners growing old and inviting their children back with their families.

Why, I wonder. This was my best chance at running into friends here and yet, even this area has changed. Nothing is as it should be, I think as I go back to my car and climb in. Nothing is as it should be.

As I drive back home I know that what I have already set in place is probably the only way I will be able to reach these friends. I can call the ones I have in my address book, but I have to rely on the media to reach the others.

At home I arrive in time to see the UPS truck driving up to our door. I don't want to get my hopes up but since I haven't ordered anything lately, I am thinking that the lost shipment of items we wanted from Erik's apartment has finally made its way to us. I watch as the driver comes up the walk carrying a large cardboard box. He asks my name to confirm he has the right house and then says if I can open the door, he will put it inside for me. I do this.

The UPS guy then says, "There is one more package." He turns and heads back to his truck.

I stand at the door and wait until he returns and places the last box on the floor inside.

"Thank you, " I say.

I stand there looking at the boxes for quite a while, then I get out the scissors to cut through the tape on the boxes. Slowly I pull back the flaps on the first box and then begin removing the items from the box. When done with this one, I immediately move to the next, this time moving quickly, anxious to take a closer look at each item. There are photo albums, his coin collection, his knife collection, his address book, and invention papers

I look through the photo albums first, reliving each day of his younger years. There are pictures of his birthday parties, our vacations and his dog. There are pictures of our picnics and swimming in our pool in the back yard. So many pictures with so much joy on his face.

I know I am crying, but I feel I have a right to cry so I ignore the tears and keep on going through the albums that include pictures from his stay in California with his Aunt with people I don't know, but feel as though I do. One picture holds my attention for a while. It is Erik at seven years old, sitting at the table in our townhouse in Country Hill Estates and he is in his pajamas. I remember the moment so well.

"Erik, turn around and say goodbye to mommy."

Erik turns and lifts up his hand and waves at me. I

I am laughing and crying at the same time as I remember that moment and look at this picture. I know then that I will use this picture as his way of saying goodbye to all of us.

I have to get control of myself so that I can look at the other treasures in the boxes. When I have wiped the tears from my eyes and have myself in control, I look at his coin collection, his small collection of knives, the sheet that shows his budget and the bills he needs to pay. I look at all of this before setting them aside and picking up the address book.

I slowly look at each address and any notes he has made. In this book are the names of people in Rochester that he has still been in contact with. I take out a piece of paper and write down these names and address and any other references to individuals that I feel may be his friends.

When I am done, I feel as though this day has not been a waste of time. It is like Erik is looking down and trying to help me. If you have ever lost someone you truly loved, you may feel their presence with you still. Many a time they will also be leaving you signs that they are there with you or have called in for a visit. I believe this now as I stand here looking at my son's address book after an exhausting day of trying to track down people he knows. This shipment from UPS had been lost and they did not think they would find it and then, at the right moment when I needed to have good news, here it is.

I work with renewed fervor, afraid I will run out of time. I have used every avenue possible to trace his life back to its beginning and find those individuals who are part of his memories. Each day when I open my computer to view emails I would see names from his past and it fills me with joy knowing that I am getting it right. I am doing what I need to do for my son and those who touched his life will have an opportunity to say their goodbye.

In the beginning it is hard to work through the memories that flood my mind with each connection made. It is like every highlight of Erik's life replays itself as if it is happening right now, and it hurts at first because these memories now have an ending.

But gradually I let myself enjoy reliving these pieces of his life. Slowly I learn how to walk through the pain. I focus on the life of my son and the joy he brought to us. That helps because I know I am the only one who can really feel what I am feeling and although family and friends are there for me, their children are still alive, putting me in an isolated existence.

I've been here before with Erik being a little person and no one else sharing that experience. Then the medical issues set me aside again, but they also were a turning point because then I realized from seeing other parents with their children at the hospital, that I was not experiencing anything more devastating than they were. It was then that I began to realize that a child is a child and a child who suffers from any illness affects the parents in the same way.

I learn that there are a lot of things that people will try to say to comfort me and these words can be very painful. Time doesn't heal anything, it is what you do with the time that helps you through. That and knowing that I am not the only person who loved him keeps me trying to be strong so that I can offer comfort to others who are feeling his loss.

The fact that Erik was a grown man and on his own when this happened in a way makes it easier because at first I can pretend he is still just a phone call away. Later I can believe that there was nothing I could do to prevent this from happening. Nothing!

My final preparation is to call Erik's father and his Aunt, Dorothea and fill them in on the date, time and discuss the arrangements for the service. I want to give them plenty of time to arrange their travel from California. This will also be the first time I have seen Erik's father since our divorce.

CHAPTER 11: THE MEMORIAL SERVICE

(OCTOBER 30, 2010)

On the eve of the service I have a chaotic dream. In it my son, Erik and I are on our way home from church. When we arrive home Erik says he left his Bible at the church so I tell him not to worry that I will go back and get his Bible for him. As I pull the car out of the garage, I take the same route as before but something happens and I stop the car, at a point that should be a short distance from my destination.

I look out the window and I notice that the road is now a sandy path, dry and vacant of vegetation as if I am in the desert and not on the paved, tree lined streets I know. Scared, but determine I start the car and continue on my way and soon I see the church in the distance. I drive up to the front of the church and park the car. I get out of my car and make my way up the staircase to enter through the front door. Once inside I search for Erik's Bible. I am having no luck when a woman approaches me.

"Can I help you," she says.

"Yes, I am looking for my son, Erik's Bible."

We look together from pew to pew and then I find it.

"That can't be his Bible," she says. "Erik can't read."

This upsets me and I wonder why is she saying that it's not Erik's Bible and why does she think he can't read. I unzip the casing and look inside, but instead of a Bible it is a Stephen King novel. I quickly zip the casing and tell the woman it is his Bible and turn quickly and head toward the door. Before I can reach my destination a little boy comes up to me and says, "Here, you can leave through this door."

"No," I say, "I need to leave through the door I entered or I will get lost."

I move quickly until I find the door where I had entered and leave the church. Gratefully, I wake up.

The dream scares me because it makes no sense beyond the fact that I am dreadfully afraid of getting lost and always have been. I write it all down so I won't forget. I have other things I need to think about now.

###

I am as ready as I can be. On Friday evening, October 29, Harold, Erik's father and his Aunt Dorothea come to the house and we meet for the first time in many years. We go over the service details. At first I think it will be awkward, but because we love Erik and we are united for him, it isn't difficult at all. Even introducing them to my husband, Mark, goes smoothly. I think that our common reason for being here and the passing of time has changed us all. We are not the same person that each of us knew before. Sure there is bits and pieces of who we were, but they have united into the 'new us' and we all feel it.

We meet up again early Saturday morning to join them for coffee at their hotel on East Ridge Road. Again I am surprised how well this goes for all of us. Harold and I have been divorced since November of 1989 and shortly after the divorce he moved to California. I have not had any contact with him since then, but Dorothea has talked with both Mark and myself. Now as we sit together, it is not uncomfortable and it feels right for us to be together. Mark and I invite them to the house after the service and they accept. We then leave to get ready.

All I can think about is the memorial service that is to be held at one o'clock at our church, the Irondequoit United Church of Christ. The Rev. Janice Lee Fitzgerald would officiate for the family and friends in attendance.

It is as though time is on a new cycle as it passes by so very quickly. When it is time, we make our way to the church and I can't help thinking of the poem I have chosen to say goodbye to my son and so glad I have found that picture.

"Someone hurt you deeply and a cure could not be. So God put his arms around you, and whispered, "Come To Me." With tearful eyes we heard the news, too late to hold you near. God broke our hearts to prove to us He only takes those dear."

I had tried hard to make sure I did it right. That Erik would be put to rest, but not forgotten by those who loved him. I sincerely hope that I would succeed. Now as we made our way into the church and move down the aisles to the front, I keep my eyes forward. It is the only way I can keep the tears from flowing. I have already said my goodbyes over and over again, but this seems more final. As I walk into the aisle of our seats, I allow myself to look over the sea of faces, marveling at how many people I have reached and how many have come to say goodbye.

These people today are friends and family members, some I haven't seen in years, but yet underneath the signs of aging I can still see the person as I use to know them. Only recognition is not enough. Age has taken away my ability to remember each one of their names, but age has not blanketed how much a part they played in my life and that of Erik.

In order to keep my feelings from overflowing I think about what is good in all of this. I tell myself that in many ways I am lucky because they already have the murderer in custody and she has confessed. There are many cases where the murderer is still at large when their loved one is memorialized. There are too, many who have not been given the chance to see their loved ones for the last time. I try and try to think of my 'blessings' to help me make it through this final time to say goodbye.

The service begins right on time with Jill Harbin and Laurel Fuller singing 'Here I Am, Lord' accompanied by organist, Carol Cowan. When the last chord ends, The Rev. Janice Lee Fitzgerald gives the Call To Worship

Rev Fitzgerald: "I am the resurrection and the life", says the Lord. "Those who believe in me shall live, even though they die, and whoever lives and believes in me shall never die."

People: God is our refuge and strength, a very present help in trouble. Therefore we will not fear.

Rev Fitzgerald: Jesus said, "Come to me, all you that are weary and are carrying heavy burdens, and I will give you rest.

People: We believe that Jesus died and rose again; and so it will be for those who have died in Christ. God will raise them to be with the Lord forever. Let us comfort one another with these words.

At the conclusion we stand and sing, 'Now Thank We All Our God' and when we finish, we bow our heads in prayer.

Erik's Aunt is introduced and she reads, "The Broken Chain." By Author: Ron Tranmer.

We little knew that day, God was going to call your name. In life we loved you dearly, In death, we do the same. It broke our hearts to lose you. You did not go alone. For part of us went with you, The day God called you home.   You left us beautiful memories, Your love is still our guide. And although we cannot see you, You are always at our side. Our family chain is broken, And nothing seems the same, But as God calls us one by one, The chain will link again.

From the first time Erik met Peter Bouley at the Rotary Sunshine Camp, they became inseparable friends. Now, it will be Peter who presents his memories of Erik and he is the one who has suggested that we allow time for those present to share an experience or thought of Erik.   When Peter maneuvers his wheelchair up to the front of the church and begins to speak, his voice, his pure and his memories of Erik hold everyone in its grasp.

"Let's travel back into time....the date is 1974 and the place is Rotary Sunshine Camp not too far from here. Imagine me, a fresh-faced 4-year old in his wheel chair at my first day at camp. I remember this other kid coming up to me with a funny laugh and he is actually shorter than me. This is where Erik eventually coined the term "Brothers in Shortness" as a private joke between us. He said, "Catch me if you can...." and took off--that's all it took. In the cabins, the pool, Camp crafts, or other activities, Erik and I chased each other around camp for 17 consecutive years after that. Each and every year he'd sneak up behind me when I got there and would say very simply, "Hey Shorty-catch me if you can" and soon we'd be getting yelled at for either him to stop running or me for going too fast.

Soon it is a clan of chasers and chasees that included Sandra Barnard, Renee Barnard, Bonnie Murray, Jason Steitler, Heather

Lynch and Freddy Dove. Each year the group reunited feeling as though they has never been apart as they have a private bond that will never be severed.

Here Erik could excel and his arm-wrestling matches are infamous over the years. With the partial paralysis on his left side, Erik worked hard at getting that motion back and while doing it, he built up the power on his right."

Our two favorite counselors Roosevelt Murray and Jean Penner (now Grover) earned their keep with this group."

Peter has added the humor and lightness that we need to remember fondly how much Erik meant to each of us.

Erik's cousin Dennis Walker reads Mathew 5: 1-12a and then we all sing 'Just a Closer Walk With Thee'.

Erik's cousin Anu Chathampally reads Revelation 21: 1-5a, 6b-7 and she is followed by his aunt, Mary Walker reading Heaven's Special Child

A meeting was held quite far from earth, "It's time again for another birth." Said the Angels to the Lord above, "This special child will need much love." His progress may seem very slow, Accomplishments he may not show; And he'll require extra care From the folks he meets down there. He may not run or laugh or play. His thoughts may seem quite far away. In many ways he won't adapt, And he'll be known as handicapped. So let's be careful where he's sent; We want his life to be content. Please, Lord, find the Parents who Will do a special job for You. They will not realize it right away The leading role they're asked to play. But with this child sent from above Comes stronger faith and richer love. And soon they'll know the privilege given In caring for this gift from heaven. Their precious charge, so meek and mild Is Heaven's Very Special Child.

We say the Lord's Prayer together and then sing 'Amazing Grace' verses 1,3,4,5

Rev. Fitzgerald then performs the Benediction followed by the Song Of Hope, 'You'll Never Walk Alone' song by Erik's aunt, Barbara Sartin.

It has been a wonderful service and I have made it through with tears of joy.

With the final song sung and the final prayer said, it is time for us, the family to move to the front of the church and receive the blessings of those present. This is indeed hard. So many familiar faces keep drawing me back to the times of joy. The children who blessed our home with their presence to play with Erik are here and I can still see the child face in each of these now adults as they smile through glistening eyes. I hope that God has allowed Erik to see and feel the love of those he left behind.

Erik's body has been cremated in Oklahoma and the ashes have not arrived in Rochester in time for the service, yet I know he is here with us.

There is a video presentation with many pictures of Erik at the ages most have known him as well as photo albums to look through. These are set up in the Fellowship room of the church where now everyone is invited to enjoy the wonderful spread that the church has prepared.

One of my close friends and neighbor during Erik's childhood comes up to me and tells me she saw that I have continued with my tradition and she loved it. At first I am unsure what she means but then I remember. For most of the special moments in Erik's life I have always written a poem so I placed a final one at the end of the program.

You sent a lovely card, or sat quietly in a chair; Perhaps you sent a floral piece, expressing your despair. Perhaps you prayed a sincere prayer, or came to share your love. Perhaps it was an email, or Facebook message filled with love. Perhaps you spoke the kindest words or didn't know what to say. Perhaps a donation or food expressed you are with us each day. Whatever you did to console our hearts, by word or deed or touch, whatever was the kindly part, we thank you , oh, so very much.

Mark and I have invited people to come to our house so we stay for a short time then head home to greet our guests.

There is much conversation that evening with catching up with those I haven't seen in a while and reliving those precious moments spent watching our children grow up. There is also time to talk with family members and thank them for being a part of the day.

AN UNFAIR ADVANTAGE　　　　BY: JUANITA TISCHENDORF

The evening goes by fast and I know we can all feel that it has been hard on each one of us. Yet, it is still hard to say goodbye but each guest finally does and when everyone has left, together, Mark and I go about straightening up the room and then we both fall into bed exhausted.

###

That night when I finally fall asleep I again dream. I dream I am falling. I am freezing as I look around to try and get my bearings and there is nothing, nothing but whiteness and no one or anything. I hug myself against the cold and then I wake.

There is no way I can sleep so I lay there wondering. I wonder if Erik called out to me for help. I wonder what did he feel. What did he hear in those last moments.

I ask, were you aware of the ones who came to save you. Did you know it was the end or feel that it would be all right now that you were found. Did you feel the life leave your body. Did you hear the savior say that you will be all right. Did you think about the good times in your life. Did images of those precious moments go through your mind. Did you suffer and if so for how long. I knew each moment of your life and now one of the most important, I did not know a moment, not a moment of what it was like.

Did you sense danger or was it unbeknownst to you at the time. Did you get a chance to protect yourself or feel that this was just not really happening to you. Were you scared. Could you admit it to yourself or was it shock that ruled the moment. Did you want to strike out but knew that you couldn't and was it helplessness you felt.

I know this manner of thinking will do me no good, but I need to speak of it in my head just the same. If I had been there I would have protected him and told him to not be afraid. Now the tears flow chokingly free and I don't even try to stop them.

###

I am no better the next morning as I walk around in a daze from lack of sleep and the feeling that this is not real. I know at that moment every time someone talks about their children, I will remember that I was a mother too. I know what it feels like to have a baby.   I know that each time someone's child graduates from college, I know that I experienced that too.   And when that special day comes when someone's child is getting married, I will remember that day when It was Erik's turn and I was the mother of the groom.

As the days, months and years pass I find that I no longer cry so hard that my throat hurts, or my heart starts pumping out of my chest so that I feel I can't breathe.   I no longer feel as though I want to scream each time I remind myself that he is dead.

I continue to feel all the rage and anger, all the loneliness and hopelessness, all the sadness and emptiness in the world inhabiting my heart each day and that is what helps me to move forward and keep on top of what is going on in Oklahoma City.   None of these feelings will abate until I have full closure.

Life is not always fair and Erik knew this.   But none of to us could imagine his journey ending as it did.   On September 16, 2010 in the emergency room of Integris Southwest Medical Center in Oklahoma City, Oklahoma Erik had passed away.   It would not be a seizure or a medical issue that would take his life.   Instead, Erik would die at the hands of a woman I never knew and who would not begin to realize what her actions would cause in the hearts of so many.

CHAPTER 12: THE AUTOPSY REPORT

(SEPTEMBER 27, 2010)

An autopsy—also known as a post-mortem examination, is a highly specialized surgical procedure that consists of a thorough examination of the body in order to determine the cause and manner of death and to evaluate any disease or injury that may be present. It is usually performed by a specialized medical doctor called a pathologist.

This includes an external examination of the body as well as an internal examination.   When a coroner receives a body, he or she must first review the circumstances of the death and all evidence, then decide what type of autopsy should be performed if any.

Autopsies are performed for either legal or medical purposes. For example, a forensic autopsy is carried out when the cause of death may be a criminal matter, while a clinical or academic autopsy is performed to find the medical cause of death and is used in cases of unknown or uncertain death, or for research purposes.

###

The autopsy was performed on September 17, 2010, at 9:25 a.m. with the Autopsy report being completed on September 27, 2010. The Report of Autopsy showed the Decedent as Erik Scott Saxton, and Type of Death as Violent, unusual or unnatural. Along with Chai's Choi, M.D, Chief Medical Examiner was Jason Snider.

The details would include that Erik Scott Saxton was a male 41 years of age and was born on April 10, 1969. He would be identified by his toe tag. The Case No. was assigned as 1003720.

The details reported are blunt force injury of the head Subscalpular contusion over the left frontotemporal region with subgaleal hemorrhages, including left temple muscle and two subscalpular contusions over the left parietal region near the midline. Subdural hematoma, right (approximately 220 mL in aggregate) with multifocal subarachnoid hemorrhages Cerebral edema with focal cortical contusions (weight 1480 gm). Status post craniotomy, right (11 cm in diameter) for tumor resection (10 years old) Subcortical fibroglial scar of the right temporal region, including basal ganglia (thalamus) Cranio-peritoneal shunt, intact. Neck injury, blunt force Cutaneous contusions and abrasions, back of neck at the base. Perithyroidal and retropharyngeal hematoma and right sternomastoid muscle contusion, mainly on the right.

Acute pulmonary congestion with edema (combined weight 1080 gm). Aspiration of blood in the trachea and bronchi with focal agonal aspirations. Petechial contusion over the right back of shoulder, contusions of back of right forearm and dorsum of the right hand, and abrasions over the left back and the dorsum of the left hand and left second toe

Cause of death is subdural hematoma due to: blunt force head trauma. He has a neck injury, dwarfism with left upper extremity. Hemiparesis, status post craniotomy with Cranio-peritoneal shunt and Manner of death is a homicide

Erik is 53 inches tall, weighs 62 kg. His eyes are brown and the right pupil is R7 mm, the left 6 mm. His hair is black with gray. He does not have a beard but has a mustache. He is circumcised.

Rigor is complete (jaw, neck. back. legs, arm, chest. Abdomen is. Complete and livor (color, anterior. posterior. Lateral, regional) is purple, posterior. The body heat is cool.

A hospital bag containing Driver License, shorts, gray "Hanes L" with contents of $1.21, one 7 -11 receipt, and a piece of glass in the pocket; a pair of tennis shoes, white with black and blue "Nike 7 V2 "; underwear, black with gray stripes "Fruit of the Loom" that is underneath the body. The shorts and underwear have been previously cut. There are brown paper bags enclosing each hand separately, sealed by plastic tape.

The medical application include endotracheal tube through mouth, intravenous needle placement over the right subclavian region, needle placement over the left subclavian region, bilateral chest tube in place, needle puncture mark with tape over the dorsum of the right hand identification band around the right wrist, intravenous needle placement over the right tibia, two electrode pads over the chest and abdomen, six monitor pads attached over the chest, arm, and abdomen

Injuries are reported as Over the left eyelid, there is a diffuse purplish contusion with edema. Just above the eyebrow, there is an ill-defined purplish red contusion measuring approximately 4.5 x 10 cm. At the lateral angle of the eyebrow, there are two vertical red abrasions that measure 1.3 x 0.3 cm and 0.5 cm in diameter. There are focal purple right eyelids. On the back of the neck region, there are several superficial linear abrasions measuring between 0.5-1.7 cm, along with somewhat curvilinear red contusion measuring 3 x 2 cm located at the base of the neck on the right. It shows small cutaneous hemorrhages. Underneath the abrasions, the skin shows subcutaneous hemorrhages measuring approximately 2 x 1.2 cm.

There are purplish contusions over the back of the right forearm and the dorsum of the right hand that measure 4 x 1.2 cm and 3 x 3 cm, respectively. On the back of the right shoulder, there is a fine petechial contusion that measures 4.5 x 5 cm that shows extensive subcutaneous hemorrhages. Over the left back, there is a somewhat V -shaped horizontal linear red abrasion that measures 7.5 and 6 cm. Over the dorsum of the left hand there are fine linear red horizontal abrasions that measure overall 3 x 3 cm. Just lateral to it, there is a vertical 1.3 cm linear red abrasion.   Body Marks are shown as none.

The external body marks state that the body is that of a relatively well developed, well nourished, black male with short limbs approximately 15 inches from the shoulder to fingertips and 24 inches long from hip to heel (dwarfism). The head is normocephalic, other than large in size, having previous craniotomy over the right temporal region with a shunt. The scalp hair is tightly curled and 1,1/2 inch long. The conjunctivae are white and show no petechiae. There is blood in the nose and left ear canals. The nose is concave in the bridge (saddle nose). The inside of mouth is in fair condition. The neck is unremarkable. The chest is of normal contour and unremarkable. The abdomen is flat and shows a linear scar over the right epigastrium measuring 3 cm.

The genitalia are those of a circumcised normal adult male. The extremities are symmetric, other than short limbs described above. There are numerous gray striae over the hip region. There is a brownish mole, approximately 0.3 cm, over the right forearm and right lower leg. Overall, the legs are hairy. There is a 1 cm scar over the inner aspect of the right arm. The left hand is somewhat deformed. There is a vertical linear scar over the back of the left ankle that measures 6.5 cm. The back is unremarkable, other than blackish fine nodular skin measuring overall 7.5 x 4 cm over the middle back. There are numerous gray striae over the buttock region, bilateral.

For the internal examination the body is opened through the customary "Y" shaped incision. Subcutaneous fat is normally distributed, moist, and bright yellow. The musculature through the chest and abdomen is rubbery, maroon, and shows no gross abnormality. The sternum is removed in the customary fashion. The sternum is normal with substernal focal hemorrhages. The organs of the chest and abdomen are in normal position and relationship. The liver edge extends 0 cm below the right costal margin at the midclavicular line. The diaphragms are intact bilaterally. The parietal pleura:is smooth, glistening membrane without associated adhesions or abnormal effusions. The pericardium is a smooth, glistening, intact membrane, and the pericardial cavity, itself, contains the normal amount of clear, straw-colored fluid. The peritoneum is smooth, glistening membrane in both the abdominal and pelvic cavities. The peritoneal cavity contains multifocal dense fibrous adhesions in the ileocecal region, in which there is a cannula tip located, being surrounded by dense fibrous tissue. The shunt cannula is located through the back of the neck through the right chest region down to the peritoneal cavity. The cannula is surrounded by dense fibrous tissue. The lumen is intact.

The heart weighs 280 gm. It has a normal configuration and location. There are no adhesions between the parietal and visceral pericardium, and the latter is a smooth, glistening, fat laden characteristic membrane. The coronary arteries arise and distribute normally with no significant atherosclerosis. The coronary ostia are normally located and widely patent. The chambers and atrial appendages are unremarkable. The valves are normally formed and measure as follows: tricuspid 13 em, pulmonic 7.S cm, mitral 9.S cm, and aortic 6 cm, The endocardium is a smooth, gray, glistening, translucent membrane uniformly. The myocardium is intact, rubbery, and red-tan, with the left ventricle measuring 1.2 cm, the septum measuring 1.3 cm, and the right ventricle measuring 0.3 cm. The papillary muscles and chordae tendineae are intact and unremarkable. The arch of the aorta is classically formed with mild atherosclerosis. Other great vessels also arise and distribute normally and are widely patent.

Neck organs have extensive hemorrhages surrounding the right side of the thyroid gland and the right side of the retropharyngeal region down to the right sternomastoid muscle. The tongue is intact and normally papillated, without evidence of tumor or hemorrhage. The hyoid bone is intact. The thyroid cartilage is intact and shows midline periosteal hemorrhages that measure 2 x 1 cm. The hemorrhages extend to the right side of the thyroid, as well as the retropharyngeal region. The hemorrhages of the right retropharyngeal hemorrhages measures 7 x 4 cm. The perithyroidal hemorrhages measure 2.8 cm. The thyroid gland is symmetric, rubbery, light tan to maroon, and in its normal position without evidence of neoplasm. The epiglottis is a characteristic plate-like structure which shows no evidence of edema, trauma, or other gross pathology. The larynx is comprised of unremarkable vocal cords and folds, is widely patent without foreign material, and is lined by a smooth, glistening membrane. There are no petechiae of the epiglottis, laryngeal mucosa, or thyroid capsule. No significant tissue is identified grossly in the thymus.

The right lung weighs 590 gm, and the left weighs 490 gm. Visceral pleurae are smooth, glistening, and intact with minimal anthracosis and no bleb formation. The overall configuration is normal. The trachea contains an excessive amount of bloody fluid in the lumen. Likewise, the major bronchi and bronchioles bilaterally contain similar bloody fluid. The pulmonary arterial tree is free of emboli or thrombi. The lung parenchyma is mostly purplish at the lower lobes and posterior segment of the upper lobes with pale pinkish red remaining upper lobe and exudes a large amount of bloody and a small amount of frothy edema fluid from its cut surfaces. There is no evidence of granulomatous or neoplastic disease. Hilar lymph nodes are within normal limits with relation to size, color, and consistency.

The G.I. Tract report is that the esophagus shows an unremarkable mucosa, a patent lumen, and no evidence of gross pathology. The esophagogastric junction is unremarkable. The stomach is of normal configuration, is lined by a smooth, glistening, intact mucosa, has an unremarkable wall and serosa, and contains approximately 120 mL of brownish fluid admixed with several pieces of brownish nut-like food material that has partly passed to the duodenum. The duodenum, itself, is patent, shows an unremarkable mucosa and no evidence of acute or chronic ulceration. Jejunum and ileum are unremarkable and contain soft brown fecal material. There is no Meckel's diverticulum. The ileocecal valve is intact and unremarkable. The appendix is unremarkable. The colon is examined segmentally and shows no evidence of neoplasm or trauma. There are no diverticula. Anus and rectum are unremarkable.

The liver weighs 1160 gm. It IS of normal configuration, rubbery, tan, and intact. Cut surface shows no pathology.

The gallbladder lies in its usual position, contains liquid bile, no calculi, and shows an unremarkable mucosa. The biliary tree is intact and patent without evidence of neoplasm or calculi.

The pancreas lies in its normal position, shows a normal configuration, is pink-tan and characteristically lobulated with no apparent gross pathology.

The spleen weighs 100 gm. The capsule is intact. The organ is rubbery, maroon, and shows characteristic follicular pattern.

The adrenals lie in their usual location, show yellow cortices and tan to gray medullae.

The right kidney weighs 140 gm and the left weighs 150 gm. Both are configured normally with no abnormality. Sections show the organs to be moderately congested with unremarkable cortices, medullae and pelvis. Ureters and blood vessels are patent and unremarkable.

The urinary bladder contains approximately 150 mL of the yellowish brown urine. Its serosa and mucosa are unremarkable.

The prostate is symmetric, rubbery, gray-tan, and of normal size. The prostatic urethra is unremarkable. The testes are bilaterally present and show no evidence of tumor, trauma, or inflammation. The investing membranes are unremarkable as is the epididymis.

The scalp is opened through the customary intermastoid incision and shows multiple subscalpular contusions, mainly over the left frontotemporal region with regional subgaleal hemorrhages and left temple muscle contusion. There are two subscalpular contusions over the parietal region on the left near the midline. There are scattered subgaleal hemorrhages over the craniotomy area on the right. The calvarium is otherwise unremarkable. The craniotomy scar is well-healed and measures approximately 11 cm in diameter. The brain weighs 1480 gm. Dura and leptomeninges show a large, mostly clotted, subdural hematoma approximately 220 mL in aggregate located in the right hemisphere, along with multifocal subarachnoid hemorrhages, mainly right temporal lobe at the lateral superior surface and left temporal lobe at the superolateral surface, along with diffuse subarachnoid hemorrhages over the cerebellum. Cranial nerves and circle of Willis are unremarkable. Externally the brain is diffusely edematous with uncal herniation on the right, approximately 2 cm, with focal hemorrhages of the uncus. Multiple serial sections of cerebral hemispheres, pons, medulla, and cerebellum show approximately 2 cm subcortical yellowish gray firm scar over the right temporal region, along with atrophic yellowish brown thalamus that measures 2.5 x 1 cm and focal hemorrhages of the corpus callosum with malacia.

The ventricular system is obliterated by the hematoma on the right with dilated left lateral ventricle. The base of the skull is intact without osseous abnormality.

The ribs, pelvis and vertebrae remain intact. To the vertebrae is a mild lordosis toward the left. The bone marrow is unremarkable.

For the microscopic examination sections of scalp contusions' over the left frontotemporal region show early neutrophilic leukocytes infiltration in the hemorrhagic area. The left back of the head shows subscalpular contusion in which there is no acute inflammation in the hemorrhagic area. Sections of the right hand contusion shows no acute inflammation in the hemorrhagic area, right forearm contusion shows hemorrhages with early neutrophilic leukocytic cell infiltration. Subcutaneous hemorrhages over the back of the right shoulder shows acute hemorrhages in which there is no acute inflammation. Brain and meninges sections show acute subdural hematoma with no organization. Dura membrane shows multifocal hemorrhages multifocal acute inflammatory cells infiltration in the hemorrhagic area. There are foci of thickened fibrotic arachnoid membrane with multifocal acute subarachnoid hemorrhages and focal acute inflammatory cells infiltration. There are foci of cortical hemorrhages.

Brain shows diffuse interstitial edema and focal old fibroglial scars in the cortex and basal ganglia. Sections of the heart, liver, and kidney show no significant pathology. Sections of the lungs show acute vascular congestion with multifocal intraalveolar hemorrhages. There is blood cell elements collected in segmental bronchus. The perithyroidal hemorrhages show acute hemorrhages in which there is no acute inflammation.

The decedent is a 41-year-old black male who lives with his girlfriend. It was stated that the decedent had been drinking vodka all day long yesterday and has a history of seizures due to his drinking. Around 1800 hours, the decedent was found to have been allegedly beaten. Today at 0800 hours, it was stated that the girlfriend checked on him and he was okay. When she checked on him later, she found him unresponsive. 911 was called and he was transported to southwest Medical Center where he was pronounced dead.

Complete autopsy showed a blunt force injury of the head with a large subdural hematoma with multifocal subarachnoid hemorrhages, along with cerebral edema with focal cortical contusions. In addition, there was a previous craniotomy with subcortical adhesive fibrogJial scar formation of the right temporal region and cranioperitoneal shunt placement. There are blunt force neck injuries with hemorrhages, mainly perithyroidal front neck muscle contusions. The decedent is to be dwarfism and has a history of left upper extremity hemiparesis for a brain tumor operated on at the age of 10 years old. It is felt that cause of death is a large subdural hematoma due to blunt force head trauma. The neck injuries and the underlying natural disease of dwarfism with left upper extremity hemiparesis would be participating factors to his death. The manner of death is ruled a homicide. Postmortem toxicological studies were negative for ethanol and drugs.

Though the report is not easy for a layman to read, the findings are an important part of the case. Two factors are easy to translate and that is there is an error on determining this was his girlfriend and that as she reported, he was not drug or did he have any drugs in his system.

CHAPTER 13: EVIDENCE COLLECTING CONTINUES

It is one of the primary duties of police officers, detectives and crime scene processors to obtain, preserve and properly package evidence found at the scene. This involves expertise, using the correct tools and applying true diligence. Since evidence at crime scenes can be easily destroyed or ruined, police officers must take care when handling it. Also, if it isn't handled properly while in transit or when it reaches the laboratory, the evidence could be ruined and the case never solved.

In a criminal case, evidence is anything that proves one of the elements of a crime. It can also be something that alone seems innocent, such as a store receipt, but which proves intent, motive, or some other aspect of a crime the prosecutor must prove.

###

Once leaving the homicide division on September 16, 2010, Officer Chris Click returned to the CSU office. He carefully reviews the photos he has to make sure that they are clear and show what needs to be seen for evidence. When he is satisfied, he uploads all 44 digital photographs into the CSU computer under Case #10-77977.

With this done, Officer Click next turns to the single brown paper sack that contains the evidence collected by Detective Vorel and signed over to him for processing. This contains Clara A Blocker's clothing that Detective Vorel has documented as containing one black sleeveless shit, a brown tank top, flip flops, black jeans, black leather belt, boxer shorts and a blue and white bandana. These are noted as collected at OCPD Homicide Office on September 16, 2010.

Officer Click removes the clothing and carefully looks for trace evidence. This is tedious work as trace evidence can sometimes be minute and can be difficult to detect and he doesn't want to miss a hair, fiber, grass, glass, soil, blood flecks or skin. After the inspection of each piece, he notes that he is unable to locate anything of evidentiary value. He secures the items of evidence in the CSU lab because the evidence room is not available 24 hours a day. He then calls it a day and goes home.

On September 17, 2010 Officer Chris Click returns to work and in the CSU lab he diligently gathers the articles he has left overnight in the secure CSU lab and seals the evidence inside the brown paper sack. Officer Click then makes sure that the items are packaged, labeled, and/or documented in accordance with departmental requirements. When he is confidence it has all been done properly, he takes one last look around and then leave the lab. What happens to the items between the time they are seized and the time they are entered into the property room is essential to maintaining a proper chain of custody. Officer Click makes a copy of the evidence label.

There is only one thing left to do and Officer Click makes his way to the property room. He hands his evidence bag over and waits as the technician checks to be sure protocol has been met. When he feels confident, he has Officer Click sign in the property and it is given Item #14 under Case #10-77977. Officer Click request a copy of the signed property sheet.

This job done, Officer Click locates Sergeant Curtis Ferguson and gives him the copy of the evidence label and signed property sheet.

Along with the evidence filed on September 16, 2010 other photographs of the victim are processed by Officer Everett Baxter. He takes overall, mid-range and close-up photographs of the body. He photographed the injuries both with and without a scale. He will upload his results into the CSU computer and file them under Case #10-77977 Next Officer Everett Baxter is called to the crime scene and photographs the area and the items collected at the crime scene. This will serve as back up for the locations of items collected within the crime scene apartment.

Officer Everett Baxter will provide the property room with the items he has collected and photographed on September 16, 2010. They will be filed under Case #10-77977. This will include: Item #1, a "Sungate" DVD Player (S/N – SU20265K05823) and found on the living room floor, 1 foot, 3 inches north of south living room wall. Item #2, numerous pieces of broken glass and possible hair fibers found on the floor and bed in the bedroom, Item #3, one bottle of 'Tvarscki 100" vodka found on floor of living room, 8 feet, 4 inches north of south living room wall. Item #4, one green bathroom rug found on the floor of the bedroom at foot of bed, 5 feet, 9 inches north of south bedroom wall. Item #5, one red S/S 'Structure' shirt, size small, one white bath towel, one bluish green hand towel, and one white bed sheet, found in laundry basket in bathroom, 4 feet, 5 inches north/south bathroom wall and 6 feet, 4 inches east of west bathroom wall. Item #6, one green 'Cherokee' t-shirt (bloody), found on top of DVD player in living room, 1 foot north of south living room wall. Item #7, one set of wet swabs from a red stain believed to be blood found on bedroom floor near bed. Item #8, one set of wet swabs from a red stain believed to be blood found on living room floor 5 feet, 7 inches north of south living room wall. Item #9, one set of wet swabs from a red stain believed to be blood found on west living room wall, 4 feet 1: Item #10, one set of wet swabs from a red stain believed to be blood found on floor of threshold of bedroom, 11 feet, 9 inches south of north bedroom wall. Item #11, one set of wet swabs from a red stain believed to be blood found on the side of the seat cushion on a chair in the living room (chair facing north), 4 feet, 8 inches north of south living room wall. Item #12, one set of wet swabs from a red stain on top of the DVD player (Item #1) collected at the OCPD CSU Office on September 17, 2010. Item #13 one reddish colored bath towel found draped over the back of the desk chair in the living room, 11 feet, 5 inches north of south living room wall.

Officer Everett Baxter will have Sergeant Ferguson sign for Items #2, 4-13. They will be filed under Case #10-77977 and will later be logged into Serology. Once the testing is complete Sergeant Ferguson will log these items into the property room

Dr. C. Choi, M.D, will provide the property room with the items he has collected on September 17, 2010. They will be filed under Case #10-77977. This will include: Item #15, one pair of black and gray underwear briefs (soiled), from the victim's clothing collected at the morgue. Item #16, one pair of grey

'Hanes' shorts with draw string (soiled), from the victims clothing at the morgue. Item #17, one pair of gray and white 'Nike' shoes (size 7 ½), from the victims clothing collected at the morgue. Item #18, one 7-11 receipt and an Oklahoma State Driver's License, found in right front pants pocket of victim's clothing, and collected at the morgue. Item #19, $1.21 in cash, found in right front pants pocket of victim's clothing and collected at morgue. Item #20, right hand bag, collected from victim at the morgue. Item #21, left hand bag, collected from victim at the morgue. Item #22, right hand fingernails, collected from victim at the morgue. Item #23, left hand fingernails collected from victim at the morgue, Item #24, pubic hair collected from victim at the morgue. Item #25, scalp hair collected from victim at the morgue. Item #26, DNA Blood card, collected from victim at the morgue, and Item #27, morgue prints, collected from victim at the morgue.

Dr. C. Choi, M.D. will submit Item #27 to Sergeant Ferguson to be sent to the Automated Fingerprint Identification System (AFIS). Item #27 will be filed under Case #10-77977 and will later be logged into the property room

Dr. C. Choi, M.D, will have Sergeant Curtis Ferguson sign for Items #17, 20-26 and Item 28. They will be filed under Case #10-77977 and will later be logged into Serology. Once the testing is complete Sergeant Ferguson will log these items into the property room

Determination of the type and characteristics of blood, blood testing, bloodstain examination, and preparation of testimony or presentations at trial are the main job functions of a forensic serologist, who also analyzes semen, saliva, other body fluids and may or may not be involved with DNA typing. Since blood evidence associated with a crime can provide information that may solve the case, it is essential to correctly document, collect, and preserve this type of evidence. For this reason, all serology fluids collected are signed over to Sergeant C. Ferguson before it goes to the property room.

###

Jason Snider of the Board of Medicolegal Investigations submitted blood, vitreous, urine, liver, brain, and gastric hospital specimens to the Office of the Chief Medical Examiner for Laboratory Analysis. The material was submitted on September 20, 2010 and completed by September 30, 2010. Tests performed were Blood alkaline drugs, Blood EIA – Amphetamine, Methamphetamine, Fentanyl, Cocaine, Opiates, PCP, Barbiturates, and Benzodiazepines. Results were 'none detected'.

###

On October 21, 2010, the forensic DNA Analysis unit receives the evidence to test.

The following evidence was transferred by Sergeant M. Spencer on March 9, 2011, received from Crime Scene Unit Sergeant C. Ferguson, one tape sealed EE (Evidence Envelope) containing the following. The items obtained from Erik Saxton: One, blood stain card, scalp hair, public hair, fingernail clippings from left and right hand, one tape sealed BPS stained to contain grey ''Hanes' shirt, not examined, one tape sealed BPS stated to contain underwear, briefs, not examined, one tape sealed BPS stated to contain one pair grey/white 'NIKE' shoes, not examined and one tape sealed BPS stated to contain one left hand bag and one right hand bag not examined.

The following evidence was transferred by Sergeant M. Spencer on March 9, 2011, received from Crime Scene Unit, Sergeant C. Ferguson obtained from 3042 SW 89th Street, Apartment #E, Oklahoma City, OK. The one taped sealed EE (Evidence Envelope) contained: One tape sealed manila coin envelope stated to contain two swabs from bedroom floor (near bed), not examined. One tape sealed manila coin envelope stated to contain two swabs from living room wall, not examined. One tape sealed manila coin envelope stated to contain two swaps from threshold bedroom floor, not examined. One tape sealed manila coin envelope stated to contain two swabs from chair in living room, not examined. One tape sealed manila coin envelope stated to contain two swabs from DVD player. One tape sealed BPS stated to contain green bath rug, not examined. One tape sealed BPS stated to contain one bath towel, one hand towel, red shirt, and a white bed sheet, not examined. One tape sealed BPS stated to contain reddish towel, not examined. One tape sealed BPS stated to contain numerous pieces of broken glass and possible hair, not examined.

The following evidence was transferred by Sergeant M. Spencer on March 9, 2011, received from Oklahoma City Police Department evidence storage facility, one tape sealed BPS stated as collected from Clara Ann Blocker and contain the following. One black sleeveless shirt 'American Honey', not examined. One brown tank top 'Old Navy' not examined, one pair brown flip-flops 'OP' not examined. One pair black denim jean shorts, 'Faded Glory', not examined. One black leather belt, not examined. One pair boxers, plaid purple and green 'Fruit Of The Loom' not examined and on blue/white bandana, not examined.

The following evidence was transferred by Sergeant M. Spencer on June 9, 2011, received from Detective Sergeant K. Whitebird in one tape sealed EE (Evidence Envelope) containing four buccal swabs.

The requested analysis is to attempt to develop a DNA profile form the swabs collected from the DVD at the crime scene. Based on these results, the DNA profile obtain from the DVD player swab appears to be a mixture. The source of the one blood stain card obtained from Erik Saxton and the four buccal swabs from Clara Ann Blocker cannot be excluded as potential contributors to this mixture. The probability of selecting unrelated individuals at random from the population who could also be potential contributors to this mixture is approximately 1 in 25,600,000 in Caucasians and 1 in 43,500,000 in African Americans and 1 in 97,660,000 in Southwest Hispanics.

On August 1, 2011, the remaining bulk evidence was returned to the Oklahoma City Police Department evidence storage facility. The remaining swabs and morgue evidence were retained in the Serology freezer. The remaining DNA extras were retained in the Oklahoma City Police Department DNA freezer. This was the report given by Elaine M. Taylor, Forensic, Scientist III. She would distribute copies to OCPD Homicide Unit, Detective Sergeant K. Whitebird and Cleveland County District Attorney's Office, A.D. A. Jennifer Austin.

###

While I worried that nothing was happening on my son's case, information was coming over the wires in response to request made to the NCIC, a computerized index of criminal justice information that includes criminal record history information, fugitives, stolen properties, and missing persons. The NCIC operates 24 hours a day, 365 days a year and the information collected is available to Federal, state, and local law enforcement and other criminal justice agencies. The information center was set up for the purpose of providing a ready access computerized database for criminal justice agencies who inquire. The reports are for prompt disclosure of information in the system from other criminal justice agencies about crimes and criminals. This information assists authorized agencies in criminal justice and related law enforcement objectives, such as apprehending fugitives, locating missing persons, locating and returning stolen property, as well as in the protection of the law enforcement officers encountering the individuals described in the system. Information is not released to unauthorized personnel but is restricted to those with a need to know to perform their official duties.

###

On October 21, 2010, Detective Sergeant K. Whitebird received a response to his requests for reports from the National Crime Information Center (NCIC) Interstate Identification Index.

'Concerning Erik Scott Saxton: Based on the information provided, you are advised that the subject has no criminal history. Information in the files of the OSBI for Erik Saxton, DOB: 04/10/1969, Race: Black, Sex: Male.'

'Concerning Clara Ann Blocker, DOB: 1/17/1972, Race: White, Sex: Female, Eyes: Blue, Hair: Blonde, Birth Place: Missouri, Height: 5" 10", Weight: 150 lbs. On her body was chest tattoos of a Lisa Marie, Tear drop, Freedom wing. On her finger was the letters H, R, and M plus pooh and tigger kissing. On her hand was the word hardword. On her legs were gay dancing word fag, and puppy with wings. On her shoulder was freedom wings, tribal art, pooh bear and back 2 girls kissing. On her wrist was 2 female sex symbols. She also had pierced ears. The report lists her fingerprint class. The criminal history record is maintained and available from the following: Kansas, Missouri, Oklahoma and Texas. Arrest: Conviction on 5/17/2002 for Robbery 1 in Oklahoma, Conviction on 10/09/2012 for Distribution of Ccs. Conviction on 10/09/2012 of Possession of CD (Meth) Afcf in Garvin.'

CHAPTER 14: ERIK SCOTT SAXTON

Being a mother is the most rewarding and the most frustrating experience I have ever had. We are biologically programmed to connect with our babies but this does not mean that a mother's love is straightforward or uncomplicated. It is just worth the effort. Parenting is an exhausting endeavor for each of us, but parenting a special needs child takes things to another level. Hospital and doctors' visits are not just a few times a year, they may be a few times a month. Therapies may be daily. Paperwork and bills pile up, spare time is spent researching new treatments, and advocating for him in the medical and educational system. But at the end there is that reward of knowing that he loved us both and that we had the chance to love him too.

###

Erik Scott Saxton was born on April 10, 1969 in Rochester, New York at the Genesee Hospital. His father Harold and I, his mother tried to do our best in preparing him for the world though we had little to go on. We are able to explain the prejudice he may face being black, but the rest of it at first, was wat above our heads. He is to be our first and only child and we dote all our attention upon him.

After his birth, we are referred to Dr. Bridget Boettrich to be his pediatrician and after his second visit to his pediatrician, Erik is in the hospital again on July 14, 1969 for exploratory surgery. He is released and re admitted on September 19, 1969 for further testing. The report from these two hospitalizations come in February of 1970. Erik is found to be an Achondroplasia dwarf.

"What is achondroplasia? "'I've never heard of this," I ask.

"Achondroplasia is a genetic disease, but a rare one with approximately 1 in every 25,000 births being affected by this disease. It is the disease causing dwarfism and in male patients with the affliction their height will be around 4 feet 3 and half inches."

"Okay, so what do we do?"

"Just what you are doing. Giving us time to examine him. Erik has an enlarged head which is why he is being hospitalized and tested. This could be a symptom of his dwarfism, but it might be related to something else entirely."

Here we are just experiencing being parents and now we are being forced to deal with so much more. My next question is, "Can this kill him?"

The doctor replies. "Yes, it could. Most children diagnosed with achondroplasia die within the first 10 years, but we are learning more each day about what to expect with this genetic disease. You need to be patient, watch him and report any concerns you have, no matter how small they may seem."

Erik is back in the hospital again on March 2, 1970 for further exploratory testing and again on March 10, 1970 when he is finally diagnosed as being hydrocephalic. This discovery is important since the symptom of an enlarged skull could have been overlooked as a symptom of his dwarfism.

Again I am clueless and again the doctor explains it to me. He tells us that Hydrocephalus is a condition where there is an abnormal buildup of CSF (cerebrospinal fluid) in the cavities (ventricles) of the brain. There are three types of hydrocephalus: Congenital hydrocephalus is present at birth. Acquired hydrocephalus develops after birth, usually after a stroke, brain tumor or as a result of a serious head injury and Normal pressure hydrocephalus which only affects people aged 50 years or more.

The fluid buildup is often caused by an obstruction that prevents proper fluid drainage. The fluid buildup can cause intracranial pressure inside the skull and compress surrounding brain tissue which can lead to progressive enlargement of the head, convulsions, and brain damage.

Hydrocephalus can be fatal if left untreated so Hydrocephalus requires urgent treatment to alleviate intracranial pressure or otherwise there is a serious risk of damage to the brainstem.

Again I am taken aback. It's like a marathon training as each new diagnoses is introduced. It seems so unfair for all of this to be happening to one baby boy.

On January 6, 1971 surgery for the correction of hydrocephalus is performed by Dr. William Cotanch. This surgical procedure is the insertion of a shunt. The shunt insertion acts as a drainage system and is like a catheter (a thin tube with a valve) that is placed in the brain to drain away excess fluid into another part of the body, such as the abdomen or a chamber in the heart. One end is placed in one of the brain's ventricles; it is tunneled under the skin to another part of the body which is better able to absorb the fluid.

Sometimes shunt repair surgery may be needed if it gets blocked or infected. Erik may need to have a shunt system in place for the rest of his live and since he is a child, additional surgeries may be required to insert longer tubing as he grows. The shunt in Erik is connected to his abdominal cavity.

The message I get clearly is that I need to report any changes in Erik and I do just that. When Erik begins rubbing his head constantly, I diagnose that as a headache and call the pediatrician immediately. Dr. Boettrich checks Erik over and agrees with me that he needs to see his neurosurgeon and she calls him. On February 10, 1972, Erik has surgery for removal of a shunt obstruction.

The most common problem with shunt systems is that they can become obstructed (clogged). The likelihood of a shunt obstruction is thought to be about 50% for most patients.

We follow the same routine again, later that year when Erik shows signs of having a headache, only this time, after going through the exploratory surgery for an obstruction, none is found.

But Erik still has headaches. I become frantic worrying what is happening and want I can do to help my son, but again the doctors come through. It is his pediatrician who decides that we should take him to see an ophthalmologist. She refers us to Dr. Hobart Lerner and he diagnosed Erik with having strabismus, a deviation of his eye which he cannot overcome without surgery. The exact cause of pediatric strabismus is not fully understood. It can occur in healthy children without any known health problems. However, strabismus is common among children with disorders affecting the brain, such as hydrocephalus.

Surgery is performed on October 12, 1973 by Dr. Hobart Lerner. The surgery is to change the position of his eye muscles to adjust the position of the eye. After surgery, both eyes will be able to focus on the same point at the same time. In Erik's case, a resection procedure is used to strengthen his eye muscle to correct misalignment as he has inwardly turned eyes (esotropia). The surgeon strengthens the lateral rectus muscles that is located on the side of each eye, toward the ear by reattaching the muscle in a different location (resection). In this way, the lateral rectus muscles are relatively strengthened and they can turn the eyes farther outward. This results in better eye alignment. After this surgery, Erik wears glasses with prisms to help correct his eyes.

Everything settles down and the year of 1974 passes medically uneventful, but on the home site it is a year of enjoying being a family. Erik enters kindergarten at the Parkland Elementary School on English Road and the only problem that surfaces is the girls in the school want to baby Erik because he appears so much younger than he is. This doesn't bother Erik at all.

We have been quite lucky that our insurance has handled most of the medical expenses, but we decide we need to beef up our income. I have been a secretary for most of my career, but I take a promotion at Dollinger Corporation that increases my income and my responsibilities. Harold does the same, he attends night school while working as a salesman for Nabisco during the day. One he completes his schooling he will be an electrician.

Outside of school we try to do as many family things as we can. It is like a gift to have time when we are able to care for Erik and not the doctors and nurses so we take full advantage of it. Who knows when it will be taken away again.

It is seven o'clock on a Thursday evening in October, 1975 while Erik and I are alone watching his favorite television show, 'The Jeffersons'. Having not experienced it before, I did not know at the time I was witnessing Erik having a convulsion. I went to the phone and called Dr. Cotanch at home. When he answered the phone it was he who told me Erik was having a convulsion and to take Erik to the emergency department. It would be one in the morning before Erik is stable enough to transfer to pediatrics.

After a battery of tests, with no conclusions found, Erik is put on Dilantin medication for his seizure. On December 8, Erik returns home.

Then, on the morning of December 15, Erik wakes up experiencing weakness in his left arm and left leg. Erik is admitted at Genesee Hospital and from December 15 until December 19, he is put through a series of tests but nothing shows up that explains Erik's headaches or this weakness on his left side. At a loss, Dr. Cotanch has us schedule an appointment at the Millard Fillmore Hospital in Buffalo for a CATT scan.

An article printed in the Buffalo News on Tuesday December 16, 1975 introduces me to this new technology that is said to revolutionize treatment and was received at the Dent Neurologic Institute of the Millard Fillmore Hospital on December, 1973. The Millard Fillmore Hospital was receiving requests for the use of the machine from more than 24 hospitals as far away as Puerto Rico and Las Vegas.

We have an appointment for December 23, 1975 for the CATT scan and the results are to be sent to Dr. Cotanch. My hopes are up since reading the article and learning that the CATT machine had a phenomenal success rate.

What amazes me is that my son has not once complained about the weakness on his left side. Here was a little boy that was able to walk, run and kick a ball without a problem, yet now his movements were limited and he accepted that. What was it about him that he could overcome so much so easily?

***

On December 23, 1975 Dr. Cotanch shares the results with us on the CATT scan. On January 5, 1976, Erik is back in the hospital.

The CAT machine has revealed a large mass in the right cerebellar hemisphere. The cerebellum relays movements, and the mass was located in this vital area. The cerebellum rests against the brainstem, which is the most important part of the brain as far as vital processes are concerned. This explains why Erik has experienced a weakness of the left side, and why he has the headaches and the resultant convulsions. On January 9, 1976 Erik undergoes exploratory surgery. We know from past experience that when a specific diagnosis is not possible using noninvasive or simple biopsy techniques, it might be necessary to surgically explore the area in question. It is revealed that Erik has a very large cyst in this area of his brain. The cyst is opened and made to freely communicate with the ventricles and the shunt to the peritoneum, the peritoneum being the serous membrane that forms the lining of the abdominal cavity. In simple language, the cyst is being drained through the shunt that Erik has had since he was less than a year old.

It is after this surgery that Erik, for the first time, goes to ICU and remains there struggling for his life for ten days. It is frightening whenever Erik is in the hospital but it is more frightening to have Erik be admitted to the pediatric intensive care unit (PICU). I am aware Erik is seriously ill and needs intensive care and obviously his medical needs can't be met on the hospital's main medical floor. This is the first time I verbalize the feeling that I might lose him. I have trusted his doctors explicitly and believed they would save Erik during each of his hospital stays, but now it is harder because Erik looks to be acutely ill. It doesn't help to hear that following major surgery like Erik has undergone it happens often that the child will be sent to PICU for a single day, a week or even months.

Finally on January 19, after several episodes where they struggle to save his life, Erik is sent back to pediatrics. On February 7, 1976 he is finally released and my faith in his medical team is renewed.

Things change drastically after this surgery. Erik is fitted for a leg brace to help him walk and though he is not pleased with having to wear it, he adjust knowing that it is the only way he will be able to walk. He has a therapist and a tutor coming daily to work with him and though he improves, he does not gain 100% mobility back. As for his studies, he completes the lessons assigned.

Erik is growing up with doctors and nurses as his parental figures—the ones who look after his well-being—while my husband and I have to push our way in for a moment of mothering and fathering. How would Erik learn what a normal relationship between parents and a child is like when there has been so much intervention? Still there would be more.

On February 20, 1977 Erik needs to have his tendon stretch on his left leg He is in and out of the hospital by February 22. This time he has a cast and he has it filled with signatures. To Erik this is great, he tells me, because a cast is something that lots of children have at one time or another. To Erik's dismay, the cast is removed on March 19, 1977 and it is back to the leg brace again.

There are several adjustments made to the leg brace but it is always handled as an outpatient, but there is something else that needs addressing.

It becomes quite obvious that Erik has allergies or something is causing him to have trouble breathing. His pediatrician refers us to an Ear, Nose and Throat Doctor (Otolaryngologist) and we take him for allergy testing on April 1 and then again on April 15;.1977. The test used to determine what Erik is allergic to is called the intracutaneous test. The allergen is diluted and then injected into, but not through, the epidermis. It is similar to the scratch test method where there is a test site and a control site area. The allergen is injected into the test site area and only diluent is injected into the control site areas. After ten minutes, both sites are checked for a reaction. Areas of positive reactions will have a whelp and redness.

Erik's back is used as the testing ground, and each injection is circled until every inch of his back is covered. Once the results have been tabulated, Erik is found to be allergic to everything that walks, crawls or blows in the breeze. As a consequence, Erik is to receive injections of a special serum for desensitization. The theory of desensitization is that the more Erik is exposed to the allergen, the more he will be able to develop what is called a blocking antibody. During the visit with the Ear, Nose & Throat doctor (ENT) we are warned that sinus problems may result from allergies. The doctor also points out that Erik, who does not have a nasal bridge, may require reconstructive surgery on his nose at a later date.

Like Scarlett O'Hara, my reaction was to say that I'd deal with it when I had to, but I was not going to subject myself to having to think about it now.

On December 14, 1978 it's time to deal with it again when Erik is having breathing problems. I take him to his ENT doctor and he examines Erik and later explains that Erik has what is called a perennial rhinitis. Perennial rhinitis can be allergic in origin, but in some people the cause is not known. He points out the indentation on Erik's right nostril, then blocks the left nostril so that he is forced to breathe through the right one. I watch as Erik tries to breathe but can't. When the left nostril is released, Erik is able to breathe again.

The doctor explains that he will first prescribe medication to try and correct the problem. He gives me a prescription for Keflex, an antibiotic used to treat many different types of bacterial infections. For a period of ten days Erik is to take 250 mg of Keflex four times daily; he will then have to return to the allergy clinic on December 28, 1978, to see if the Keflex has indeed cleared up the infection. If not, further x-rays will be required. It is not better and the ENT puts him on Koteldrin. The matter is closed for the time being, but not for long.

On February 13, 1979 there is not much improvement and once he re-examines Erik and looks at the x-rays the ENT doctor consults with Erik's other doctors. It is determined that Erik has what is medically termed a marked hypertrophy of the right inferior turbinate, meaning the turbinate had become enlarged. Turbinates, also called nasal conchae or turbinal bones, are thin, curled, leaf-like bones within the nose that serve to enlarge the surface area of the nasal cavity. Along with this Erik also has a depression of the nasal dorsum, which means that the back part of his nose has sunk below its surroundings—the surgeon referred to this as a developmental phenomenon. Erik's obstruction is believed to be due to intermittent edema of the turbinates, which would account for the fact that the blockage alternates between the right and left nostril. Intermittent edema is the coming and going of the swelling of the turbinates.

On May 10, 1979, I take Erik back to the ENT doctor, who agrees with the surgeon's report and I am given a steroid aerosol called Decadron turbinaire, to give Erik two sprays in each nostril twice a day for the next seven days. Erik is also to continue his bi-weekly hypo-sensitization shots, and his medication is changed to 8 mg of Teldrin twice a day. The results—ineffective so surgery is performed to relieve sinus blockage and increase the nasal airway.

Erik is admitted as an inpatient at Strong Hospital, where the surgery is performed with scopes through the nose. The removal of nasal polyps and the operation result in a marked improvement. However, the surgery only relieves the symptoms associated with the blocked sinus and did not improve his allergies.

So, on the heels of this surgery, Erik undergoes a surgical procedure to remove his adenoids. In Erik's case, removal of the adenoids was necessary because they were too big: they blocked the back of his nose and forced him to breathe through his mouth. The procedure takes only fifteen minutes to complete.

In March of 1979 Erik's dentist mentions that Erik will eventually need braces to correct his overbite, so it really doesn't come as a surprise when in 1981, just before his twelfth birthday, Erik is fitted with braces.

Dr. King, his dentist, explains that the teeth could slowly be moved and shifted into the proper position by applying pressure in certain directions through the use of bands, wires and elastic placed on the teeth. He explains that the change would take place slowly and carefully over an extended period of time. When I ask how long, he said that shifting teeth back into a functional position can take months to years. But that wouldn't be the end of it, since once the braces are removed Erik will most likely need a retainer to hold the teeth in their new position until they are stable.

So, my son's beautiful wide smile is now compromised by a flash of steel. Though it didn't discourage him from smiling as often as he used to there is indeed a significant change in his bedtime and morning rituals.

Since the paralysis, and even after gaining some of the use of his left side, Erik has worked very hard at being self-sufficient, which means that he takes longer than most kids to get ready for bed or school each morning. I use to offer to help, but he wouldn't have it. He insists he can manage on his own, and he does, given an adequate amount of time.

    ***

During the latter part of 1982, Erik is able to stop wearing his glasses, as his eyes have been corrected. Around the same time, his braces are taken off; and before the middle of 1983, he no longer needs his retainer. He also no longer requires allergy injections and, finding that he has outgrown his allergies, the oral medication is stopped as well. Then follows a slow weaning-off of his seizure medication, which he has stopped taking altogether by the time he is 15 years of age in 1994.

Since the end of 1982 it has been a quiet time when all three of us are enjoying a breather from medical issues and doctors. This is a time when we are able to concentrate on each other and this is good, but, it is also bad. With all that has filled our lives, Harold and I have had little time for ourselves. The one thing that we still have in common is Erik desperately needs his parents and we stay married to each other, and try to love each other. Erik's future depends on it. As we go through these different life experiences, we are affected and changed by them, each generating different feelings and reactions in us. Change is inevitable in life and each experience throws a different light on how each of us experience life and who we become. So, no wonder we are confused and dismayed by the many emotional changes we have gone through during the course of our marriage. No wonder we are afraid for our future together! No matter how hard we try we lost our love for each other.

    ###

In June of 1988 there are many changes coming into play. First, Erik's father, who has been a member of the Electrical Union Local 86 since the later part of the 70s, finds himself on the bench. When an offer for a job laying cable lines in New York City comes his way, he takes it, leaving right after Erik's graduation from high school.

The joy of seeing Erik walk across that stage and accept his diploma from the Rush-Henrietta High School is such a time of mixed emotions. My life has been so intertwined with his that it is like seeing a piece of me separating. Yet I am so happy for him. This is an end to a chapter in our lives that will close forever. Erik is now an adult. As a graduation gift he will soon leave for California and at this moment I wish I hadn't agreed to this.

On June 26, 1988, Erik leaves for Mission Viejo, California, and at 4:00 a.m. the next day I receive the call from Erik's Aunt in California, bringing the past back into full focus again. It begins with a frantic call from his Aunt explaining what has transpired. From her description I know that Erik is having convulsions and they seem to be continuous.

It could be seizures which involve abnormal or rapid neuronal activity of the brain, but I think it is convulsions which is abnormal or involuntary muscle contractions or jerky muscle movements. Besides I have learned from doctors and a convulsion is often the first diagnosis given to a patient until the time that a seizure disorder has been established.

Between his Aunt making calls locally and I contacting his doctors in Rochester, everyone is soon on the same page. A doctor is assigned to Erik at the hospital in California who has all the information needed from Erik's doctors in Rochester and what starts out as a medical emergency is soon under control. By the evening of the June 29, Erik is listed in satisfactory condition, and he is transferred to a regular hospital room where he soon begins responding coherently to questions asked of him. He is released on June 30, 1988 and the rest of his trip goes smoothly.

I find myself recalling his pre-adolescent years when for Erik it is much easier as the size differences between himself and his peers are not as noticeable and easily accepted. Yet through the years Erik learns how to 'fit in'. I remember when the kids in the neighborhood started riding bikes and Erik was unable to master this. They would ride him on the handlebars or decide to walk to the mall instead. Then when it came to the junior and senior prom, he was not left out, but instead had a date and joined his friends, riding in the limo together. Erik, I realize, has discovered what it takes to be accepted and what it takes to adjust to those around him and have them adjust to him. Where did he learn this!

After graduating from high school, college became an ongoing project as Erik sought to find the field that would accept him and his disabilities. He attended Monroe Community College and then Rochester Business Institute, studying in the field of computer science. From my point of view I wanted him to remain in Rochester, New York where he has friends and family as a base to spring forward.

It might sound simple, but it's not easy for Harold and I to make the decision to end a marriage of twenty-one years. We did spend a long time trying to solve problems before deciding to divorce. But sometimes you just can't fix the problems. So after much discussion, Erik's father and I divorce in 1990.

Erik remains in California for two years and after our divorce, Harold moves there. Only Erik finds that after attending the University, he is still unable to find a job. His next move surprises me, though I understand it.

In California he is still being influenced by a parent and this along with unsuccessful job interviews takes him to Oklahoma City. There he plans to attend the University of Oklahoma, in the state where his father hails. Even though Erik collects Social Security Disability Insurance, it is not enough for him to give up his need to earn a living. So he will continue his efforts to find a field where his size and handicap will not affect him being hired. Erik will study drafting, airline and cable technician and architectural design. For each field he will go on interviews and when nothing materializes, he will start all over again in the next field of training.

In 1995 I remarry and my husband, Mark, and Erik develop a good relationship. We visit Erik in Oklahoma City and see him at the yearly family reunions that are first held at our home in Rochester, New York, then later moved to Sanford, Tennessee when my mother relocates there to live with my sister.

On Thanksgiving Day, November 2000, Erik has a surprise. He brings Heather Goodban to dinner to meet us. We have no information or details to prepare us for this visit and I admit both

Mark and I wonder. Mark tells me that it is only a girlfriend so not to get all nervous about it. So I try not to. On the day of her arrival we go to the airport to pick her up and the minute I see her, I feel more relaxed. She is a dwarf as well and because of her extremely small hands and feet, I think she is a Turner Syndrome Dwarf. She has a 'sturdiness' is the word that comes to mine, about her. As she walks toward me I can feel her need to force people to look the other way and not stare at her and I'm sure, like Erik she has had her share of stares. Like Erik too, she is an only child and as the days progress I find I like her and I like the way the two of them interact with each other. When Thanksgiving arrives and with family around us, Erik announces that he has asked Heather to marry him and she has accepted.

How did I know this. I have always been in tune to my son's feelings and what he plans to do, but I had no hint of this being so serious a relationship. I have not even noticed that she is wearing an engagement ring until she raises her hand up to show everyone.

She was unknown to me until Erik called to say he was bringing her to Thanksgiving Dinner. Now I learn that they have known each other for about a year or two, having met at several LPA (Little People of America) conventions and this was the reason that he made his decision to move to Oklahoma City, in the first place. He wanted to be near her.

After that day, we make trips to Oklahoma City to meet Heather's parents, who are in a same-sex relationship and two of the most loving individuals I have ever had a chance to meet. We meet and talk about the wedding plans which turns out to be a big wedding with all the pomp and circumstances, right down to a horse-drawn carriage to take them to the hotel for the night. All of this happens on May 25, 2001, when Erik marries Heather Goodban in Oklahoma City, Oklahoma. Erik's step father becomes his best man and his cousins become his groomsman.

Within two years after their marriage, with help from the us and her parents, Erik and Heather purchase their first home. Now on our visits to Oklahoma we spend most of it doing repairs along with Heather's parents. It all seems very comfortable. So much so that it does come as a surprise when after eight years of marriage, a rift opens and Heather and Erik divorce.

No one knows what goes on between a couple even when you feel close to them. I divorced his father because we were growing in opposite directions and unable to find a common interest between us once Erik was out on his own. This we did not discuss with Erik, though I am sure he knew.

So whatever has happened between Heather and Erik it is their life and their decision. So in 2009, Erik moves out of the house and strikes out on his own. He moves twice in Oklahoma City to various apartments before finally settling in the residential area apartments known as the Hunt apartments.

###

This is my son Erik Scott Saxton and how he lived his life to the fullest, not asking anyone for anything and trying his best to fit into the world around him. He did not complain or wish for an easier life. Instead he embraced the one he was given.

Erik did not have any tattoos which was most likely because he had plenty of needles and pain during his lifetime to not go out of his way to seek more.. He didn't take drugs, except prescriptions given to him by his doctor for his seizure disorder.

Erik has never been accused or incarcerated for any crimes as he strived to be an upstanding member of society. He would have a beer now and then, but nothing stronger. In his apartment and in his home before with his ex-wife Heather, there was no liquor, except when expecting guest they may purchase some wine or beer. As for drugs, Erik would always say how he hated taking the meds he required to eliminate having a seizure because he didn't like taking drugs of any kind. He also didn't smoke cigarettes or weed.

Erik knew what it was like to fight hard for what he wanted. He knew what rejection felt like and how cruel people can be so he could sympathize with those in need. If that meant giving someone money, or the shirt off his back, he would do it willingly.

I have been challenged and pushed beyond my limits in raising my son. I've grown tremendously as a person, and developed a soft heart and empathy for others in a way I never would have without him. But I'm just like the next mom in some ways because I am in love with my son. I love how cute he was as a child and how handsome he became as an adult. I love how he can be funny and make me laugh. I love how he has accepted who he is so that others did not focus on his disabilities, but on his abilities. And over the years I love how he gave me bragging rights for school and life accomplishments.

I loved him—I loved him just as he was. I enjoyed the fact that I needed to make his clothes so that they fit his exact proportions. I even enjoyed the need to go up to bat for his rights and needs.

Erik did look like a dwarf and that was most apparent to me when we went to the LPA national conference in Orlando, Florida and I saw so many achondroplasia dwarfs and fell in love with each of them because they allowed me to see Erik at all stages of his growth.

So the question remains, what placed these two individuals in the same place. One is a gay female and the other is a straight male, one has a criminal record and the other has none. One has a history of drug abuse and the other does not. One drinks to access and the other drinks little and infrequently. Here are two individuals from two different walks of like and different views.

Chapter 15: Clara Ann Blocker

"Every unpunished murder takes away something from the security of every man's life." Daniel Webster.

In the recent past, one highly regarded homicide investigator stated, "if you want to understand the art, you must understand the artist". What he meant by this is that in order to understand the act of murder, you need to understand the murderer. What compels a seemingly normal person to disregard a fundamental societal principle and commit murder?

Trying to understand what happens in the mind of a murderer has traditionally been a question for psychologists. But now other scientists are beginning to explore processes and changes in the brain itself that may explain why some people are more likely to kill than others. The first explanation centers on the belief that many killers were abused and taunted as children and that these experiences lead them to commit violent acts as adults. Many believe that social circumstances are the root cause. Others may believe that there are genetic mental issues that lead to criminal behavior. Poverty and social class have a lot to do with many crimes. Of course there are some criminals who are simply looking for an easy way to make money and survive, however, there are plenty of criminals that simply wish to harm others.

Most people who commit murder don't feel strong but feel week and ashamed. Many murderers feel little or no remorse for the crimes they have committed. This seems impossible for the normal mind to comprehend that lack of emotion, but trying to understand it is the key to solving such crimes. In some cases, the murderer is truly convinced that what they did was right or necessary.

There are plenty of debates about what causes criminal behavior. Crimes that are committed for a specific financial gain are fairly easy to understand. However, many crimes are committed without any obvious purpose.

In trying to understand why Clara Blocker did what she did, I first asked her, but she did not respond. But the need to know why continues to baffle me so I tried a different approach. I studied what I did know about her and what others say about murderers.

###

Located on the Missouri-Kansas border on the Missouri River in the state of Missouri in Clay County is Gladstone. Clay County was settled primarily from migrants from the Upper Southern states of Kentucky, Tennessee, and Virginia. They brought slaves and slaveholding traditions with them, and this was one of several counties settled mostly by Southerners to the north and south of the Missouri River. Given their culture and traditions, this area became known as Little Dixie.

Gladstone is a city with a median income of $52,600 and a median home value of $133,500. Here there are around 11,600 housing units in all of Gladstone and though most are owner-occupied, 30% are rentals. The economy in Gladstone is struggling with less than 5 percent of the population working at the general medical and surgical hospitals and other residences are employed by supermarkets and other grocery. The city is surrounded by Kansas City and falls within Tornado alley averaging 40 or more tornadoes per year.

This is where Robert and Linda Blocker would settle and raise three children at their home on N Agnes Ave in, Gladstone, Missouri and would live in this house from 1969 to 2007. The house that Clara grew up in was an average split level home with 3 beds and 2 baths, built in 1967. Clara would have attended one of three elementary schools in the area, one of two middle schools and the only high school which is the Oak Park High School. The area averages seven crimes per month that covers aggregated assault with firearms, possession of drugs, sex intimidations, and theft. This would be the only home that Clara would live in with her family.

There is no indication that her upbringing was anything but normal as her siblings, both younger did not follow her path of crime.

###

Some hereditary factors that contribute to personality development do so as a result of interactions with the particular social environment in which people live. For instance, Clara's genetically inherited physical and mental capabilities have an impact on how others see her, and how she sees herself. Characteristics such as skin color, gender, and sexual orientation are likely to have a major impact on how she perceived herself. Whether Clara is accepted by others as being normal or abnormal would lead her to think and act in a socially acceptable or even deviant way.

Clara did have a secret and it was that she was a Lesbian. Born January 17, 1972, gay life style in the 80's was very much a time of conflict and contradiction for many gay woman and men. There was little acceptance of gay people and as a result one could be very much affected by all of this and refused to accept being gay. Even for those who were out, many were very careful about whom they came out to.

There were few, if any, legal protections back then. In fact, in 1986, the United States Supreme Court upheld the constitutionality of a Georgia law that made consensual sodomy a crime. It was not until 2003 that the Supreme Court overturned the earlier decision and ruled that it was an unconstitutional invasion of the right to privacy to make private, consensual sex a crime.

Gay marriage was not even on the radar screen as something remotely possible. Back in 1990, homosexuality had taken a huge step back in liberation because of AIDS which became an extremely socially sensitive subject and the epidemic was blamed on gay people in the early 80's, Towards the end of the 90's the gay disease rumor had begun to subside and being gay, particularly in western society, became a lot more acceptable.

Clara may have tried to hide or not admit it to herself the fact she was a Lesbian which could lead to much confusion, but by 1980 being gay was arguably more acceptable than in 1990. It wasn't until 2000 that everything was back on track and huge progress had been made in the acceptance of gay individuals. At that point I believe from pictures seen, Clara developed an open stereotype portraying masculine traits. She cut her hair short, even shaving her head at one point, and definitely had lots of tattoos.

It may have been a slow acceptance of who she was as a result of society frowning on Lesbians that lead her to drinking and drugs.

Clara did drink. She may have first chose drinking to give her confidence and help her relax when around others. Only her drinking did not stop at social, but leaned toward abusive. In time alcohol would not work for her and this may be why she turned to drugs. People generally take drugs because they want to change something about their lives. It may be that Clara wanted to fit in or just wanted to escape her life which differed from what she knew as 'normal'. But Clara became a drug addict and drugs can affect the mind. They can distort the user's perception of what is happening around him or her and as a result, the person's actions may be odd, irrational, inappropriate and even destructive.

From abusing substances, Clara became unable to control her anger or frustration. When confronted with feelings of disappointment, frustration and anger she would strike out and her actions soon ended in violence. Of course, the criminal justice system would have to determine the specific about why some individuals act on their violent thoughts whereas others do not. Clara's lack of self-control, in my estimation is the result of her abusing substances and feeling uncomfortable with whom, she is.

By the time of the murder, Clara had chosen to be open about her sexual preference as she would say to the police that she has a girlfriend. She further announces her lifestyle by the tattoos she has which mostly have gay undertones.

So all of this could have led to Murder? It is said that murder is unlawfully killing another human being with what is referred to as "malice aforethought," or killing deliberately and intentionally. In either case the end results is the taking of a life and that is not acceptable.

There are a lot of factors that trigger a person to want to kill somebody. An example is drug addiction. There have been numerous murders related to drug usage. Illegal drugs have negative effects on the user's behavior due to the fact that they mess up a person's mind causing paranoia, hallucinations, jealousy, and much more. Drugs also provide a feeling of invincibility and looser inhibitions that definitely strengthen a person's intentions to kill.

Since viewing the interview tapes of Clara and the fiddling with her money, it may have been for money that she murdered Erik. Killing because of money is not something new. Since the inception of civilization, money has caused bloodshed, regardless of gender, age or race. It may in part have been an issue, but not wholeheartedly since Erik would have given her the money if she asked.

So this is a view of the person named, Clara A Blocker who would be incarcerated several times only to move closer to committing the ultimate crime--Murder.

###

Clara Blocker would move frequently after leaving home. She would live in Columbia, Missouri in 1992, move to Lebanon, Missouri in 1994, then in 1999 she would move to Riverside, Missouri, then Moore, Oklahoma which is approximately eleven miles from Oklahoma City. This move to Moore, Oklahoma I believe was to fulfill an order of the court to enroll in a drug abuse program in 1998.

In 2003 Clara would move again only this time to Albuquerque, New Mexico which for someone with a drug habit, Albuquerque is the place to go. Albuquerque is the most populous city in the U.S. New Mexico is situated in the central part of the state, straddling the Rio Grande. The Albuquerque Police Department executes stings involving multiple pounds of product and tens of thousands of dollars roughly once a month. Meth stings happen in Albuquerque far more often than stings for cocaine or any other drug

There may have been other residencies for Clara Blocker but since she tended to live with someone else or give a false address it is hard to verify.

###

The contents of the record report for Clara Ann Blocker would be quite extensive. The report would show her date of birth as January 17, 1972 and her age as 43. Her aliases would be shown as Clara Blocker, C. Blocker, Clara A. Blocker and Tigger. Previous addresses would be 924 Penn Ln Moore, OK, 4937 NW Gateway Ave Riverside, MO, 306 W 7th St Kansas City, MO, N Hickory Cir Kansas City, MO, W 5th St Lebanon, MO, and 1000 Maxine Street, Albuquerque, NM.

Clara's criminal record is telling of the type of person she had become. Clara would first be arrested on May 23, 1990 in while living at 6503 N. Agnes Street in Gladstone, MO. The Case Number 7CV190003877 shows her crime as AC Misc. Associate Civil. The record would show she was unemployed and a transient with no residence filed. The case was never settled as Clara moved before the disposition date for sentencing on June 25, 1990.

Her next offense took place in Kansas City where she was arrested for Passing A Bad Check a criminal infraction and set by the 13th Judicial Circuit as a Misdemeanor Class A level offense on Case Number 13R019233878. She entered a Guilty Plea and was sentenced on April 22, 1992. She would be given a Court Sentence of Jail, minimum of 60 days.

Clara would again be before the courts on March 21, 1995, Case Number: 14R059200375, in Missouri for the 14th Judicial Circuit court for Burglary in the 2nd degree, a Felony charge. Court recommended defendant placement in institutional treatment center and requested report and recommendation of Department of corrections. Sentence set at six years, to be completed by September 13, 1995.

Her next offense was during this institutional treatment. Clara was sentenced on May 16, 1995, Case Number CR0592000375F. She was arrested in So Randolph County, Huntsville, Missouri, the crime was handled by the Department Of Correction and the offense was Burglary in the 2nd degree. Clara was given a 3 year term sentence.

Clara would again be sentenced on August 18, 1998, Case Number: M-40-DR-9800070. She would be arrested in Tucumcaria Magistrate in New Mexico and it would be a non-jury conviction for a petite, misdemeanor that included the offenses of Speeding (26-30 Over Limit), Reckless Driving (1st Offense), Consume Possess Open Container Of Alcoholic Bev, Driving Under Influence Of Liquor Or Drugs (1st). She pleaded Guilty. There is no record of any sentence given.

Clara A Blocker was arrested again in 1999, Douglas County Sheriff's Office, the charge was placing body fluids on a government employee,. It was filed as a Misdemeanor Assault. The case was Dismissed.

Clara was next convicted on Case no CF-2001-2626 (Criminal Felony) on, May 17, 2002 in the State Of Oklahoma, for Robbery With A Dangerous Weapon. She entered a Guilty plea for Assault And Battery with a Deadly Weapon and the charges were dismissed. Clara would have served a 5 year term for this charge that was dismissed. This crime was not one she did alone. There were two accomplices, a Penny Renee Bratcher, And Nathaniel Lee Rowe.

She would next be convicted on Case No. CM-2006-3693 (Criminal Misdemeanor) on August 29, 2006 in the State of Oklahoma. The charge was filed on October 23, 2006 as LMFR, Larceny Of Merchandise From A Retailer. She would have an accomplice. Clara was convicted on November 8, 2006 and pleaded Guilty to the charge. Her accomplice, Teresa Rene Stanfield received the same charge. Clara listed her place of residence as 2000 Mustang RD APT 4101 Yukon, Oklahoma.

Clara would again be in court for conviction on Case Number 07-260 in Garver County, Oklahoma. She would face charges for Possession of CDS (METH) AFCF and plead guilty. She would receive a sentence of ten years plus 1 day. The sentence would start on January 18, 2008 and she would be incarcerated until May 5, 2009 when the sentence was suspended.

Clara would next be in front of the courts to be convicted on Case No. CF-2009-5336 (Criminal Felony) and convicted on February 22, 2010 for Distribution Of A Controlled Dangerous Substance //Cocaine Base//SCHD II(ODO). She would plead Guilty and Sentenced to a Count1 Felony. The offense took place on September 14, 2009 and the case was closed on February 22,

2010. Clara was given a 12 year suspended sentence where she would be supervised.

###

Looking over her case history it is hard to comprehend that a person who continued to commit criminal acts would not be required to serve her full sentence. I needed to understand this and so I took a look at the Oklahoma Laws.

I found that in Section 5 of Oklahoma Statutes Title 21 it states that a felony is a crime which is, or may be, punishable with death, or by imprisonment in the penitentiary. A Misdemeanor is stated in Section 6 as every other crime. In most cases, Clara has been convicted of a felony.

Felonies are broken into different punishments according to the circumstances of the crime or crimes. Each felony is measured by a specific degree under each individual crime. These categories define the crimes as violations, misdemeanors, or felonies and places each into differing required sentences. All felony offense punishments are to be served in state prison facilities instead of county or local jails as these are reserved for lesser crimes and lesser punishments. However there are a few exceptions.

Murder in the first degree can be punished by death as Oklahoma has capital punishment. First-degree murder is also punishable by life in prison without the chance of parole or life in prison with the opportunity to be paroled. The severity of the sentence depends on the severity of the crime as well as any prior offenses or additional offenses.

In checking further I learned that though capital punishment is legal in Oklahoma it is not a choice at the time of my son's murder. On December 16, 2010, Oklahoma became the first American state to use pentobarbital in the execution of John David Duty In 2014, Oklahoma had put scheduled executions on hold until the Department of Corrections implemented 11 proposed improvements in protocols governing capital punishment. The review of the lethal injection administration process resulted from an Oklahoma inmate's April execution case in which a doctor and a paramedic failed nearly a dozen times to administer an IV with lethal drugs. Executions would resume on January 15, 2015 with the execution of Charles Warner by lethal injection.

Murder in the second degree is punishable by confinement of no less than ten years but no more than a single term of life in prison. Second-degree murder cases can have varying consequences if an individual pleads nolo contender or pleads guilty to the offense. At times the punishment can be lesser and sometimes the punishment can be more severe.

Misdemeanors are never punishable via death, but instead always via a fine or a jail sentence. These jail sentences rarely exceed more than a year. The fines for misdemeanors do not exceed five hundred dollars. Like felonies, a person may be convicted and sentences to both a jail sentence and a fine. These convictions are much lower than any other state.

The charges for misdemeanors are wide and encompass many different kinds of crimes. Alcohol related charges include driving under the influence and driving while intoxicated in vary degrees and of multiple offenses as well as public drunkenness and transportation of an open container. Drug charges include possession of different substances and marijuana along with trafficking and possession with the intent to distribute.

Clara is a habitual offender, a person who is convicted of a new crime, who was previously convicted of a crime(s). Three Strikes legislation has been enacted by many states as a way to target repeat offenders. This law states that after three separate felony convictions, convicts could send you to jail for life. Many Three Strikes laws count only violent or serious crimes for the first two strikes, but have a much lower threshold for the third. Title 21-13.1 of Oklahoma law requires service of minimum percentage of sentence for persons convicted of crimes in the following areas that Clara has been convicted.

The three-strikes law in Oklahoma under Title 21 Crimes and Punishments mandates a life sentence when two convictions for any drug felony are followed by a drug-trafficking conviction. Oklahoma courts may oblige first-time offenders to participate in addiction treatment and rehabilitation programs. When individuals successfully complete these required programs, their charges may be dismissed and their records may be expunged. As for drug purchasing, the Oklahoma drug possession law in Oklahoma sees drugs as a gateway to other more violent crime. The vast majority of other controlled substances are classified as either Schedule I or II drugs. These include things like: cocaine, heroin, and methamphetamines. They are penalized more severely than pot.

A first offense possession of a Schedule I or II substance carries felony charges and 2 to 5 years in prison with $5,000 in fines. If this is the second possession charge, you can face 4 to 20 years in prison and $10,000 in fines. Other drugs, including some more popular prescription drugs, are classified as Schedule III, IV, or even V substance. A first offense possession charge of these substances, like marijuana, carries up to one year in jail and fines reaching $1,000. A second or subsequent offense, however, carries felony charges along with 2 to 10 years in prison and fines reaching $5,000.

All states regulate and control the possession of (CDS), though each differs in its exact definition of CDS and the penalties for possession. Oklahoma classifies not only well-known drugs like marijuana, heroin, and cocaine as CDS, controlled dangerous substances, but also the compounds used to manufacture them. Oklahoma divides CDS into five "Schedules." Schedule I lists the most dangerous drugs, which have a high probability of abuse and addiction, and no recognized medical value. Schedules II, III, IV, and V decrease in dangerousness and probability of abuse, and increase in recognized medical uses. For Schedule I or II CDS, Penalties for a first offense include a fine of up to $5,000, at least two (and up five) years in prison, or both. Second and subsequent offenses incur a fine of up to $10,000, at least four (and up to 20) years in prison, or both. Schedule III, IV or V CDS carry Penalties for a first offense include a fine of up to $1,000, up to one year in jail, or both. Second and subsequent offenses incur a fine of up to $5,000, at least two (and up to ten) years in prison, or both.

Clara was also convicted for burglary. Title 21-1436 addresses burglaries and states that Burglary is a felony punishable by imprisonment in the State Penitentiary as follows: Burglary in the first degree for any term not less than seven (7) years nor more than twenty (20) years; and Burglary in the second degree not exceeding seven (7) years and not less than two (2) years.

All of this and then murder. As defined in Section 701.7 of this title of Oklahoma law it states that First degree murder includes; Second degree murder as defined by Section 701.8 of this title; Manslaughter in the first degree as defined by Section 711 of this title; Assault with intent to kill as provided for in Section 653 of this title; Robbery with a dangerous weapon as defined in Section 801 of this title; First degree robbery as defined in Section 797 of this title; and First degree burglary as provided for in Section 1436 of this title. For each of these offenses it states the person is required to serve not less than eighty-five percent (85%) of any sentence of imprisonment imposed by the judicial system prior to becoming eligible for consideration for parole. Persons convicted of these offenses shall not be eligible for earned credits or any other type of credits which have the effect of reducing the length of the sentence to less than eighty-five percent (85%) of the sentence imposed.

Then in Title 21-701.7 it clarifies that a person commits murder in the first degree when that person unlawfully and with malice aforethought causes the death of another human being. Malice is that deliberate intention unlawfully to take away the life of a human being, which is manifested by external circumstances capable of proof.

###

Some murder cases are so shocking and heinous they capture the minds of the general public and won't let go until the killer is brought to justice, but this is not always the conclusion. When the accuse goes free the public never really gets that feeling that justice has been served, and that feeling is felt by many a family who have to face the fact they may never see justice for the murder of their loved one. That has happened in recent cases. Amanda Knox, the American student charged with murder after British college student Meredith Kercher was found dead in November 2007, her throat slashed in an Italian villa she shared with Knox. Casey Anthony mother of Caylee Marie Anthony, a toddler that disappeared in June 2008 and whose remains were later discovered. Jodi Arias was charged with first-degree murder for her ex-boyfriend, salesman Travis Alexander's murder.

What has led to the accused never going to prison is what scares each family who faces the death of a family member at the hands of another. It is what leads to the research and 'hands on' approach throughout the proceedings.

CHAPTER 16: STAYING INVOLVED

I am determined to be well educated and on top of everything concerning my son's murder on September 16, 2010 by Clara Ann Blocker even though the processes in a criminal case can be confusing and that causes doubt as to how to act.

In this case it begins with a "911" call, which acts as the Central Dispatch for all police calls. An officer was then dispatched to handle the case as all crimes must be investigated by a police agency.   The investigation by police include: interviews of witnesses, and suspects; visiting, viewing, measuring and photographing the crime scene; collecting physical evidence such as clothing, fingerprints, or blood samples which may have to be sent to a crime laboratory for analysis; identifying suspects through crime scene analysis and witness statements. This takes days because a thorough investigation is necessary to a successful prosecution.

They arrest a suspect on the spot without an arrest warrant. The officer then submitted a warrant request to the prosecuting attorney, suggesting potential charges to be authorized.   After submitting a warrant request to the prosecuting attorney, the officer submits a police report containing all the information obtained about the incident. The report included witness' statements, pictures, driving record and the criminal history record of the suspect.

This is the first time that the prosecutor's office is involved in the case. At this stage, the prosecuting attorney determined whether a person should be charged with a crime and, if so, what the crime should be. The prosecutor thoroughly reviews all reports and records concerning the case.

The prosecuting attorney issued a charge that "probable cause" exists that the suspect committed the offense. The prosecutor determines that a charge should be brought and a complaint and warrant is prepared. The complaining witness, the police officer, testified before the district court magistrate that the information for the complaint and warrant is true. The magistrate heard the testimony of the complaining witness, and made an independent determination for the charge to be brought. The suspect (now called the "defendant") is arrested.

Once the complaint and warrant have been issued and the defendant is in custody, the magistrate in this being a murder case, refuses to set any bond, which meant that the defendant remains incarcerated until the case is decided.

The Pretrial procedures are the first in-court appearance for the offense. The Examination Conference is when the defendant is appointed an attorney The Preliminary Examination,   an evidentiary hearing is scheduled before the District Court judge within 14 days of the District Court arraignment, but is adjourned to a later date. When held the prosecutor questions witnesses to convince the judge that there is at least probable cause to believe that a crime was committed and the defendant committed it. Because the burden of proof is much less at the preliminary examination than at trial, the prosecutor does not call all potential witnesses to testify at this hearing. The defendant's attorney, cross-examines the witness. Probable cause is established, the judge orders that the defendant is "bound over" (meaning "sent") to Circuit Court for trial.

After the case was sent to Circuit Court, the defendant is again arraigned on the charge(s) that were the result of being bound over. Again, the defendant is given formal notice of the charges against her and the maximum penalty in a document called an "Information." The defendant is given the opportunity to enter one of four pleas at this time: guilty, no contest, not guilty or stand mute. A plea of guilty or no contest means the defendant is convicted of the offense without a trial and is subject to being sentenced by the court. The defendant pleads not guilty or stands mute, the case is scheduled so it is set for a pretrial conference where a meeting between an assistant prosecuting attorney and the defendant's attorney is set to determine whether the case will go to trial or be resolved with a plea. A member of the court staff is also involved to facilitate the meeting that focuses on resolving the case short of going to trial. Testimony is not taken at this time. Plea bargains are discussed at this meeting.

Many other events occur prior to trial. There are pretrial hearings on confessions, searches, identification, etc. The issues are presented to the court through written "motions" (e.g., Motion to Suppress Evidence). The judge determines whether evidence will be admitted or suppressed at the defendant's trial, whether there is some legal reason why the defendant should not be tried, and decides other ground rules for trial. Based on the judge's rulings, efforts are made to resolve the case through a plea bargain. And that is where we are now.

###

In an effort to stay informed I may have become a pest, but if I did, my Oklahoma contacts never let on. Instead I find they are willing to help in any way they can.

There is Kerrin Jones, the Victim Witness Coordinator of the District Attorney's Office, Jennifer Pointer Austin, Associate District Attorney, Lyndell Easley, Detective, Homicide Unit in Oklahoma City, and Jane Cannon, OKNews. These are the ones who would explain in laymen's terms what is happening now and what has transpired before.

I am given the case number CF-2010-1390 assigned to my son's case. Kerrin explains how to log into the Oklahoma City State Network (ocsn.net) where I can see a listing of what is happening and documentation on each step taken in my son's case. It will be Kerrin who lets me know when to come to Oklahoma so that I don't make unnecessary trips.

Jennifer will fill me in on how to get copies of the preliminary hearing proceedings. These help translate what the case still needs and what has been already obtained. Because it will be of no benefit to be personally in the court room during the preliminary hearings, this is a way to know each word that is said and who says it and to personally determine if I should be present at the next hearing or not.

Detective Easley will send many detailed emails that answer my questions and give me a feeling as though I am doing what I set out to do—be active in my son's case. He can verify that Clara

Blocker is still in jail as no one paid her bail. He can also give me the details that he can share early on, on what he personally saw at the site of the murder and can give me the confidence that they will have enough to convict Clara.

Jane is informational and very personable in sharing even her life experiences to help me realize she did know how I felt. Her articles are tasteful and her interest seems genuine. Each article she writes she will send me in an email or alert me that it is out on the internet.

With the help of all these individuals I am able to stay informed on happenings in the case.

###

Each day I log on to oscn.net and see if anything has taken place. If there are documents available, I download them to read and file. Each time a preliminary hearing is held I immediately contact Jacinda Dye-Johnson, CSR, the official court reporter and obtain a copy of the Hearing. The cost seems minimal as it allows me to read what happened as though I am sitting in the court, but it has an additional one advantage. The Preliminary Hearing Report shows the name of the speaker, followed by what they say.

I feel confident for a while. By October of 2010 the documents do not carry much information and I see forms with a check mark for Reason for continuance as 'further negotiation'. Then the forms state they are looking for additional discovery, Not sure what 'discovery' refers to I look it up on the internet and learn that it is used to describe the formal process that a lawyer uses to obtain information from the opposing side before trial which usually involves the opposing side answering interrogatory questions under oath.

I continue going online to the ocsn.net to see the postings as quickly as they are made. Along the way I learn that the 'CF' in front of the case number stands for Criminal Felony and that the case is listed as State of Oklahoma v. Blocker, Clara Ann. Clara Ann Blocker is the Defendant, the Oklahoma City Police Department , is listed as the Arresting Agency and the State Of Oklahoma is the Plaintiff.

By December, 2010, David Smith is appointed as the defendant's attorney after a series of six preliminary hearing conferences (PHC).

The plea and sentencing document, dated September 23, 2010 supplied all details concerning Clara Ann Blocker and the charge as Murder in the first degree.

Inspector Ken Whitebird the Affiant reported that the facts known to him were that a criminal offense had been committed by the Defendant on September 16, 2010 and that Detective Lyndell Easley was assigned to conduct the Homicide Investigation at Erik's apartment. It was noted that the officers found the defendant at the scene and she was transported to the Oklahoma City Police Department, Homicide Unit and during the course of an interview, she would give numerous stories which were inconsistent. Inspector Ken Whitebird would mirandize Blocker and she confessed to getting into an altercation with Erik. She would report that she hit him in the back of the head and on the side of the head with items from the apartment on September 16. She would then call 911 after she found he was deceased on the morning of September 17, 2010. .

The Inspector would then speak with Sherry Nunziato of the State medical examiner's office and she would advise him that Erik had a laceration on the back of his head and a large contusion on the side of his face. These injuries were consistent with how Blocker advised that the murder had occurred.

Based upon the information, Inspector Ken Whitebird believed there was probable cause to arrest Blocker for the charge of Murder in the first degree.

On September 23, 2010, the defendant Clara Ann Blocker appeared in person at her arraignment in the Cleveland County Court and entered a plea of "Not Guilty". To the Crime of Murder 1 as charged in the information presented against the defendant. Bond was denied and the defendant was committed to the Cleveland County jail. The first Public Hearing (PHC) was scheduled for October 5, 2010 where she would be represented by an attorney.

The court denied bond because of the seriousness of the crime (Murder 1), the apparent likelihood of conviction (confession), the fact that this was a capital offense and that Clara Ann Blocker had a criminal record.

###

Looking at her description I knew Erik would not have stood a chance against her. Clara Ann Blocker was described as being born on January 17, 1972, a white female; standing 5 ft. 10 in. tall; and weighing150 pounds. This woman could have taken whatever she wanted from Erik and walked away. Why didn't she?

###

The record would state: "Clara Ann Blocker, with malice aforethought killed Erik Saxton, a human being, by causing blunt force trauma to the head, inflicting mortal wounds on the body of Erik Saxton which caused his death between the 15th day of September 2010 and the 16th day of September 2010, contrary to the form of the Statutes in such cases made and provided and against the peace and dignity of the State of Oklahoma."

The witnesses included the Oklahoma State Medical Examiner's Office, Lyndell Easley, Sergeant Curtis Ferguson, Dennis Bueno, Jay Coffee, Ken Whitebird and A. Pointdexter of the OCPD. Greg Mashburn also included an enhancement page that stated, "*I, Greg Mashburn, the undersigned District Attorney of said county, in the name and by the authority of the State of Oklahoma, and in addition to the original information filed herein, further inform the court That the aforementioned offense was committed subsequent to the time that the defendant was convicted of, or pled guilty to, the offense of Distribution of Controlled dangerous substance on the 22nd day of February 2010 in the District Court of Oklahoma county, State of Oklahoma, Case No. CF-09-5336 and was sentenced. Further, that the aforementioned defense was committed subsequent to the time that the defendant was convicted of, or pled guilty to, the office of Count 1: Robbery with a dangerous weapon on the 17th day of May, 2002 in the District Court of Oklahoma county, State of Oklahoma, Case No. CF-01-2626 and was sentenced. Further, that the aforementioned offense was committed subsequent to the time that the defendant was convicted of, or pled guilty to, the offense of Possession of a Controlled dangerous substance on the 18th day of January, 2008 in the district court of Garvin county, State of Oklahoma, Case No. CF-07-260 and was sentenced."*

Following this report on the same date a 'Probable Cause Affidavit was filed for the Arrested person, Clara Ann Blocker, being arrested on September 16, 2010. For the charge of Murder in the first degree 21-701.7. "I, Inspector Ken Whitebird, the affiant being first duly sworn upon oath, depose and say: That the facts known to the Affiant which establish probable cause to believe that a criminal offense was committed and that the offense was committed by the above named person, are the following: On September 16, 2010, Your Affiant and Detective Lyndell Easley were assigned to conduct a Homicide Investigation at 3042 SW 89th Street, Apt. E, Oklahoma City, Cleveland County. On arrival officers located the arrested person at the scene. She was transported to the Oklahoma City Police Department's Homicide Unit. During the course of an interview, arrested subject gave numerous stories which were inconsistent. Your Affiant mirandized the arrested subject. She confessed to getting into an altercation with the victim. She hit the victim in the back of the head and on the side of the head with items from the apartment. The arrested subject advised she called 911 after she found the subject deceased the morning of the 16th. Your affiant spoke with Sherry Nunziato with the State medical examiner's office. She advised the victim had a laceration on the back of his head and a large contusion on the side of his face. The injuries were consistent with how the arrested subject advised the murder occurred. The incident occurred in Oklahoma city, Cleveland county, Oklahoma. Based upon the information provided, your affiant believes there is probable cause to arrest the above listed defendant for the charge of murder in the first degree."

On September 24, 2010, Oklahoma County Information System (OCIS) has automatically assigned Judge Lori Walkley to the Case. At this time a court appointed attorney, David Smith was assigned to represent the defendant and waive his fee. The fee was waived as the defendant had been declared an indigent.

On October 5, Blocker appeared before Judge Walkley with her attorney, David Smith and with Jennifer Austin, the Assistant District Attorney, representing Erik at the Preliminary Hearing Conference. It was set to continue for further negotiations on October 19. On October 19, the case was set to continue on October 26, 2010; again for further negotiation. Then on October 26, the case was set to continue on November 16, 2010 at the State's request for additional discovery.

##

I don't get it. Why so many PHC when they have the defendant in custody and she has stated she is guilty of the murder. They must have the evidence, I would assume. I need more information so I send an email to several individuals in Oklahoma and on November 18, 2010, I receive an email from Detective Lyndell Easley.

Mrs. Tischendorf,

Your concerns are not at all unusual and I can't say I understand, having not had the terrible experience you are going through, but I can empathize from the many cases I have investigated. Unlike the cases I worked when I was assigned to the Robbery Unit, the cases I work now have no victim to which I can explain the judicial process, and it falls to the family. Again, I empathize and hope I can help you.

Clara Blocker was arrested on 09-16-10, and was booked into the Oklahoma County Jail on the charge of Murder, in the First Degree. This is policy for my department. Although the crime actually occurred in Cleveland County, the Oklahoma County Jail is a joint city/county facility where arrestees are held until formal arraignment in front of a judge (usually a video arraignment). At this time the arrestee is transferred to the county in which the crime occurred. Blocker was transferred to the Cleveland County Detention center on 09-22-10, and she is still in their custody.

Defendants (which she is now, after having been formally charged) are held in the county jail until after the case is adjudicated. At this point, assuming the defendant is found guilty, they are transferred to the custody of either the Oklahoma Department of Corrections or the Federal Bureau of Prisons, depending on which court heard the case. In your son's case, it will be state court, and the Cleveland County District Attorney's Office. This is the reason you can't find that she has been incarcerated. The Cleveland County Detention Center has a website, but it does not include an "inmate lookup" feature.

The reason I know Blocker is still sitting in jail awaiting trial is because bond was denied in her case. This is a rarity in Cleveland County, usually bond is set at one million dollars, which prevents defendants from bonding out in most cases. Typically, six months will pass between arrest and the preliminary hearing. In between will be one or more preliminary conferences, which are usually held between the prosecutor and defense attorney. Often, the defendant is not present in these conferences, and they are conducted in the judge's chambers. The purpose for the conferences is to provide discovery items to the defense, set terms for the hearings, etc. Occasionally the prosecutor will offer a plea deal, but usually this waits until after the preliminary hearing, which has not yet been set.

The preliminary hearing is to determine if probable cause exists to bind the defendant over for a jury trial. There is no jury present in the prelim, and the judge listens to the prosecutor's witnesses, making his or her determination from this. The defendant is usually present in the courtroom, which is their right, however they are dressed in orange coveralls and not cleaned up as they would be if they were in front of a jury. Once the defendant is bound over for jury trial, we wait again, and for another six months, give or take. In the meantime, prosecution and defense will most times try to negotiate a plea agreement. Keep in mind, I am speaking "typically", and homicides are anything but typical. I am a witness in a homicide in Cleveland County that occurred over two years ago, but has yet to go to even prelim, due to motions filed by the defense to have their client psychologically evaluated, etc. Any number of things can delay the final adjudication.

Pleas used to give me severe issues, I felt as though a jury should decide a defendant's fate as opposed to a plea deal. The reality is the court system is overloaded, and all cases can't be brought to trial. If justice is served by a plea agreement, I no longer have issues with it, provided the family is in agreement. Another facet to the plea agreement is that it is impossible predict what a jury will do, and I have seen cases that appeared to be a slam-dunk take a bad turn with just one juror who can't or won't sentence a defendant. A plea is no longer undesirable, in my opinion, and they get a defendant in prison where a jury might fail to do this.

You can track the progression online through OSCN.net. use this for your web address, or Oklahoma State Courts Network for the search title (I have had difficulty with typing the web address directly on occasion). Once you get the page opened, there is a menu bar at the top, you will need to click on "Legal Research". A menu on the left side of the page will give a number of options, at the bottom is "Docket Search". When you click on this, it will take you to a page giving you, among others, the option of "Search by name". Type in the name "Blocker" and "Clara" and then hit return. This will take you to all cases involving this individual in Oklahoma, Erik's case in is Cleveland County under case number CF2010-1390. Click on this and you will see what has been done to this point, and also scheduled events in the future. Cleveland County is pretty good at updating their information in a timely manner, and also good at scanning in documents that can be reviewed.

Mrs. Tischendorf, my partner and I have investigated 15 homicides this year alone, which is huge for a city that sees between 50 and 60 homicides each year. I have been in Homicide for two years, my partner for ten. We each have over 20 years of experience in this department. I say all this to hopefully ease your mind, at least a little. Most cases will have days, months, or even years elapse between the murder and the arrest. This one was a matter of hours, thanks in part to the interrogation skills my partner has developed. I have not heard of anything else the prosecution feels is important for this case, and the Assistant DA is not shy about asking for more investigation to be done. I can't predict the future, but we have a great feeling about this case.

Most homicides we investigate have some degree of culpability on the part of the victim, through criminal activity, gang affiliation, or other choices made. Erik does not fall into this category, he was a true victim by every definition, and guilty of nothing more than helping someone who was in need. I am so very sorry for your loss.

Then, on the heels of that email, I receive one from Susan Witt whom I had found on line.

Dear Mrs. Tischendorf,

I am so sorry for the loss of your son and your frustration in learning information about this murder case. I work in the Tulsa County District Attorney's office and this murder case is filed in Cleveland County – which is across the state.

But I can give you some information and tell you where to call for more.

The case is CF-10-1390 in Cleveland County. If you go to OSCN.NET you can follow the court docket on the case. Near the top of the page, where it says select database, click on the arrow to the right and select Cleveland County Next type in Case Number CF-10-1390 or the name Blocker, Clara .

You should call the Cleveland County District Attorney's Office and ask to speak to a Victim's Advocate. They should help you. The number for the Cleveland County District attorney is (405)321-8268.

If you still are not able to get someone to help you, please get back with me and I will try to see if I can get someone from that office to call you.

God bless you and heal you in the loss of your son.

I had found a way to stay informed and I used it. Detective Lyndell Easley would email me with contact information and a bit of history that I took to mean he wanted to let me know I needed to be patient.

Just know that a murder case is kind of a marathon and usually takes about a year to get to trial. In Oklahoma, we have preliminary hearings, where the prosecutor presents evidence to a lower level judge. At this hearing, all the prosecutor has to establish is that the crime was committed and there is probable cause to believe the defendant did it. If prosecutors meet this burden the judge orders the defendant to stand trial in District Court before another judge. Of course, at any time the defendant can choose to plead guilty. If the defendant plans to plead guilty the prosecutor should contact you and let you know this in advance.

On November 11, 2010 Susan Witt sends a follow up email.

Let's pray that there is a satisfactory outcome in this case. It's true that our caseloads are staggering and there seems to be more to do in a day than we can get done. But this is our job, and we try to remember that we are dealing with people and making decisions that are important to them as well as to the public in general. I am a mother, too, and I cannot imagine the anxiety of not knowing what is going on with this case.

Please try to connect with a victim advocate in Cleveland County. They are hired for the purpose of serving as a liaison between the prosecutor and the victim's family. They should be keeping you informed. You even have a victims' bill of rights: http://www.da.tulsacounty.org/BillOfRights.aspx

You (or other survivors) also are entitled to file for victim compensation to help pay for funeral expenses, etc. Save any bills. A victim advocate should help you with the paperwork. You can find information about this on our website.

Please feel free to contact me again if you need further assistance. If I can be of assistance further, you can contact me directly at 405-316-4815.

Then the Cleveland County office sends an email.

I received your correspondence earlier today. The State of Oklahoma will be represented by the District Attorney of Cleveland County, Oklahoma, or one of his assistants. The district attorney's contact information is as follows: Greg Mashburn, District Attorney, 300 County Building, 201 S. Jones Ave., Norman, Oklahoma 73069, 1-405-321-8268.

Mr. Mashburn's office should be able to help you. According to your information, District Judge Lori Walkley has been assigned to this case. It is not proper for anyone to contact the judge. I wish you well.

Even in my current state of impatience, I am aware I am getting wonderful support from Oklahoma, but I am distraught and so ignorant of what to do and so afraid that what should be done is not being done. I have watched so many forensic and crime shows to know the routines and what it they didn't do what was necessary to seal the case. They knew who did it, but from those shows I knew it would not be enough. They still needed to gather the evidence. This was my son who was murdered and I wanted justice.

I was at my wits end trying to understand what was taking so long. In a desperate measure I send out emails again. On December 8, 2011 Susan Witt, the Tulsa County District Attorney, Community Outreach Director responds.

"Hello. I am so sorry that you are not being kept up to date on this case. You have a right to know what is going on. This is my best guess at translating the minute from OSCN: I am thinking that they started the preliminary hearing on January 25 and were not able to finish the testimony that day, so they set it to continue on March 9th. Apparently the judge is saying that if they don't get all the witnesses finished on the 9th, he/she will not allow another continuance, they will keep coming to court day after day until it is completed. At the completion of the preliminary hearing, if the judge determines that there is sufficient evidence that a crime was committed and probable cause to believe the defendant committed it, the judge will order her Bound Over to District Court for trial. Then the proceedings move to the next higher level of court, and she will appear before a (higher) District Judge for arraignment – and eventually for trial – unless she pleads guilty. A court reporter transcribes the proceedings and after the hearing the DAs office and the defense attorney have to order and purchase a transcript from the court reporter. (expensive) Not allowed to copy and share, but there will probably be one in the official court file when it is eventually transcribed.

If I were you, I would contact the victim advocate and/or prosecutor by phone and email and ask them to call you and brief you on what happened and will happen at the preliminary hearing. You have a right to know. Also- you might wish to contact this reporter at the Daily Oklahoman, who has written about this case and ask her if she can fill you in or point you to someone who will. Reporter is Jane Glenn Cannon; email is jcannon@opubco.com Of course you don't want to say anything to her that would jeopardize the court case, but you can certainly talk about your son and how this has affected you – and your difficulties in keeping up with the courthouse from so far away.

If you do not get the answers you need, do not hesitate to contact me again and I will see if I can shake the bushes for you from this end.

I will tell you that Oklahoma is still digging out from a horrible winter blizzard, with more snow on the way tonight. We do not have the equipment to handle 20 inches of snow. Our courthouse in Tulsa was closed Tuesday – Friday last week and may be closed tomorrow. As you can imagine, we are scrambling to catch up, and it is probably a similar situation in Cleveland County. So that might add to the time you need to allow for an answer, but the squeaky wheel does get the grease! Good Luck to you and I hope all goes well with your knee surgery!   Susan"

On December 3, the information requested was received and the CCDC custody case was set for December 21 at 1:00 p.m. On December 21, the preliminary hearing was set for January 4, 2011 for further negotiations and for the Defendant to consider record.

###

I have been cheerful through Thanksgiving with the family and now it looks like I will need to do the same for Christmas.

CHAPTER 17: PRELIMINARY HEARINGS

Within Oklahoma criminal justice systems, a preliminary hearing, preliminary examination, evidentiary hearing or probable cause hearing is a proceeding, after a criminal complaint has been filed by the prosecutor, to determine whether there is enough evidence to require a trial. Usually held soon after arraignment, a preliminary hearing is a "trial before the trial" where a judge decides, not whether the defendant is "guilty" or "not guilty," but whether there is enough evidence to hold a trial. In making this determination, the judge uses the "probable cause" legal standard, deciding whether the government has produced enough evidence to convince a reasonable jury that the defendant committed the crime charged.

###

I scrutinize the documents on the website again starting with the September 23, 2010 document that stated there was no bond. On closer review I realized that the plea then is "not guilty" to the crime of Murder 1. I also notice that the PHC scheduled for October 5, 2010, says they require further negotiation and thus the rescheduling, over and over again.

So it began that the PHC report that the parties appearing are for the State, Austin and Pratt and for the Defendant, David Smith. There is one witness sworn for the Medical Examiner report which was admitted as Exhibit 1 without objection. The Defendant is to remain in jail for the trial. The case set for formal arraignment before Judge Walkley on May 19, 2011 at 8:30 a.m.

On January 4, 2011 the preliminary hearing is again reset for January 18. On January 18 the preliminary hearing is scheduled for January 25 for further negotiations. Ten reschedules later, it is a go on March 9, 2011 @ 1:30PM. The attorneys estimate 3 hours of court time.

Judge Walkley states the preliminary hearing will not be reset, and it will continue until completed day to day if necessary. All witnesses under subpoena who appear will remain until excused by a judge

The report that accompanied this declaration was a subpoena from the State of Oklahoma, County of Cleveland to Detective Ken Whitebird. Stating you are hereby commended to appear before the District Court of Cleveland County in the City of Norman on the 9th day of March, 2011 at 1:30 p.m. Then and there to testify on behalf of the State of Oklahoma as a witness in the above entitled case wherein the State of Oklahoma prosecutes the said Clara Ann Blocker and you will remain in attendance and on call of said court from day to day and term to term until lawfully discharged. If you are a law enforcement officer, you are hereby commanded to provide all reports and/or statements in your control to the district attorney's office at least ten (10) days prior to the above date. This you shall in no way omit under penalty of law. Witness my hand and seal this 11th day of February, 2011. The document was signed by the Authorized subpoena clerk.

Here we were 175 days or 5 months, 22 days since Erik had been murdered and the person who had murdered him had already confessed and been placed in jail. It had taken 20 days to sentence the murderer, Clara Blocker and now, 9 preliminary hearings had passed for one reason or another until finally on March 9, 2011 the PHC was convened. After talking with the D.A. and others, it is clear that my presence is not needed or would benefit in any way.

###

I am in pain that has nothing to do with what is happening in Oklahoma. It is my knee. At first I try to ignore it, but finally go to see an orthopedic surgeon, who tells me that I need a total knee replacement (TKR).

I try to research information online, but I know he is right because it hurts and is getting worse, the longer I wait so I set the date. On February 16, 2011, I am scheduled for the surgery.

I have to admit I am scared but I am willing to have this done since I cannot walk or exercise the way I want or need to. I have no idea what I am in for even though I read up on the procedure and discuss it with my orthopedic surgeon. It's not that I am ignorant; it's just that my ability to absorb details and concentrate on information has been challenged beyond its limits. So, the fact that I need to be one hundred percent for Erik is what serves as my reason to go forward.

My mind made up, my doctor chosen and having attended the required class, I am prepared. My doctor is a surgeon at the Unity Hospital so that is where my surgery will take place. On the appointed day, Mark drives me to the hospital and we take care of the paperwork before I am taken back to be readied and then whisked away to surgery. I remember getting undressed and having an IV put in. I remember being told they were giving me some pain medication and then everything went black.

When I wake up after my TKR surgery, my knee is encapsulated by a device called a continuous passive motion (CPM) machine. This was explained during the pre-surgery seminar so it is not a surprise. The machine gently and slowly bends and straightens my knee while I am lying in bed. I sort of like the idea that the machine is doing all the work, while I lay there, medicated and feeling quite comfortable. It's the best. I can sleep at will and still do the exercises. But that doesn't last long.

The day of my knee replacement surgery is mostly a day to recover but it is not just about rest. Since I have my surgery in the morning, I am waken by the physical therapy nurse who says, "We need to get you up and into the chair."

This is the last thing I want to do, but I know she will have her way so I let her help me into a sitting position on the side of the bed and before I can say anything, she says, "Just sit for a bit. We will take it slow."

I feel dizzy and incapable of getting on my feet, so I do take it slow and when I feel ready, I lift my butt off the bed and with the nurses help we manage a wobbly trip to the nearby lounge chair, which later I realize is on wheels and will be used like a wheelchair.

When the nurse asks if I am okay, I truthfully say, "Yes, this is easier than I thought."

During the procedure and immediately afterward, I receive pain medication intravenously. The oxycodone is delivered through the IV catheter and helps tremendously in alleviating the pain, or so I am told, because I don't feel any pain. I am just tired.

The next day after surgery I am wheeled up to the PT room of the hospital along with all the other knee and hip replacement patients. Here we are shown what they call simple exercises including ankle pumps, leg lifts, and heel slides. I am surprised at how hard these exercises are to do, but I give it my best. Most of us survive simply because we are given sufficient pain medication to allow us to participate.

Each day now starts with a trip to the PT room where I am expected to sit in a wheelchair, and with assistance stand up and walk. It is the goal to get me mobile before my release and once they start on me, I am oh so ready to get well enough to go home. When ask if I have stairs at home like an idiot I say, yes. I realize my mistake when she tells me that I will need to be able to navigate those stairs, and she will help me master this task.

And so it begins. I take my first steps after surgery with the aid of a walker and because I will need to do stairs, there is a set of stairs in the PT room that I must master going up and coming back down. They even have a fake car that I practice getting in and out and being able to operate the gas and brake pedals. Even as I suffer through these exercises I am told that I am not to actually operate a vehicle until I am off oxycodone.

The PT nurse reviews my work history and says that she feels that I should be able to do the computer classes in about 4-6 weeks, but as for the upholstery jobs, that will take longer. I listen and agree because that is fine with me. I have given long turnaround times for recent upholstery jobs and as for the classes; they were cancelled as soon as I received my surgery date.

After three days in the hospital, I have improved my functional mobility and I am discharged. At first I am glad, but after the major struggle to get into our car I have some doubt. It had been so easy in that fake car in PT, but the real thing is a lot different. I slide into the passenger seat fairly easily, I can even lift my legs, but bend them so that my feet are on the floor? It takes several tries and several seat adjustments to finally get all of me inside.

I am exhausted when we drive off and before we arrive home, my knee begins to ache. This is the first time I have really felt pain since the surgery. I sit beside Mark with my eyes watery from the sheer agony and my breathing comes out in sharp, shallow rasps. I can feel sweat drip down the side of my face and cover my forehead in a thin sheen. I have one objective and that is to take my meds. But there is a problem with that and Mark points it out,.

"Nita, do you want me to stop and drop off your pain prescription now or should I take you right home."

Good question. Dropping off the prescription means I have to sit a bit longer, but not to drop it off and have Mark leave and have to wait for it could take a lot longer. I really don't have a choice. "Let's drop it off now."

Mark pulls into the drugstore parking lot and gets out. I watch as he goes in and for the first time that I can recall, I understand how a person addicted to drugs may feel. All they want is that next fix.

By the time Mark returns to the car, I am at my wits end trying to keep calm and not start bawling like a baby. It hurts so much.

By the time we pull into the drive way my knee hurts so badly I can't even concentrate. I focus on watching Mark as he gets out the walker and snaps it into shape. I let him practically lift me off the seat by himself and then I barely manage to move forward with the help of the walker.

By the time we reach the steps at the side door, I want to give up. It is just too hard. Mark either senses my predicament or can read the pain on my face. "Rest a bit before we go up the stairs," he says.

I would like nothing more than to hurry up the stairs, get into the house and lay down, but that's not going to happen. Instead I lean all my weight on the left leg to try and relax the right one. It does help some.

"I'm ready," I say and Mark helps me with my walker to get up the three steps that will take me into the house. It's slow going, but we make it and once inside, he has a surprise.

Mark has taken the spare bedroom bed and brought it downstairs to the library. Now he leads me into the room and I am so full of thanks. I could have lain on the couch, but this is so much better.

With his help, we manage to get me undressed and into a nightgown. I sit down on the edge of the bed and Mark carefully helps me get my legs up onto the extra pillow he has arranged at the bottom of the bed. With that done, he leaves me saying, "Let me get the ice bags."

Mark puts the ice bags over my knee, the same ones that I had in the hospital and for the first time I truly believe in cold relieving pain. Mark asks if he can get me anything else and I tell him, no. All I want to do is sleep.

I don't remember drifting off, but I do and when I wake, Mark is back and shaking me so that he can give me my pills. Then I'm off to dream land again.

The next day my PT nurse arrives and begins my first session of helping me gain more range of motion and strength as well as maneuvering stairs. She starts out explaining that when my post-op pain is controlled, my pain and stress is minimized and my body's energies will focus on healing. Taking my meds properly I will be able to perform physical therapy and home exercises with minimal discomfort. So it is important that I manage pain because not to will actually hinder recovery. She doesn't have to worry about me not taking my meds.

For the next two weeks I have two session of physical therapy each day, preceded by two oxycodone pills with a non-steroidal anti-inflammatory drug (NSAID) in this case ibuprofen. The oxycodone pills will control pain and the ibuprofen will help reduce swelling and soreness. It's hard, especially because all I want to do is sleep so each day after she leaves that is just what I do.

It is around this time the PT nurse tells me that generally she will look at a patient's ability to ambulate properly with the rolling walker and if that individual is using the proper foot sequencing and posture, she sees it as time to move to the cane. It is her hope to begin the process of converting me to a single point cane now, two weeks from the day of surgery. She feels I am ready.

When I am first told I will need to use the walker, I shun the ideal, but all it takes is that first time, standing to know that this walker is my friend. So, now as I am encouraged to let go and try using a cane, I think they are crazy. I need that walker.

I tell myself, I can fight this and end up hurting myself, or I can give in and use the cane. So I practice endlessly at home until I feel comfortable that I won't fall down and embarrass myself.

Then comes the day when it is time to remove the staples. When the nurse replaced the bandage coverage on my knee I had a chance to see the knee. I counted sixteen staples, real staples in the knee and now I am not looking forward to having them removed. This is going to hurt.

I've done what I can and that is taking my meds before she begins. I watch as she unwraps the band aid, looks it over, mumbling something about it looking real good and definitely ready to have the staples taken out. I've seen it and there is nothing appealing about having sixteen silver staples up the front of your leg, over the knee, holding together a lengthy incision.

"This won't hurt," she says.

I am pretty sure it will hurt just like the scar tissue massage and mobilization does. Just like she says when she begins this massage exercise, it won't hurt, it did. I know it is necessary that she do this to improve the mobility of my incision so as I cringe. I tell myself it is necessary because it will help the skin and other tissues around my knee move better and more freely. Not that I can tell, exactly, but I do trust her.

Now as she leans over my leg, she takes out the medine skin staple remover tool and says, "You'll feel a little pinch."

By now my meds have kicked in and I barely feel anything. She works diligently and when she is about half through she puts tape stripes over the area she has completed and then continues on. It isn't until she reaches the knee area that I can feel the pinch, but I keep quiet and keep still so that that she doesn't have to stop, or god forbid, tear the cut. Somehow I make it through. "That's it," she says.

Thankfully we are done for the day and she doesn't ask me to do any PT with her but I am to do my exercises from the sheet she has given me, before the end of the day. Right, like that's going to happen.

And it is still not over. I am being weaned off my oxycodone. What happened to the idea of the drugs helping me to recover? I try to console myself in knowing that I am still to take the ibuprofen, though I doubt it will help much.

If I thought it hurt before, I know now what real pain is. The dose is lowered each time Mark has the prescription filled and I am to take the pain pills less often now so that I can drive to the physical therapy facility down the street from my home. With the control on this narcotic, there is no way to fight it and I am forced to subsist on less and less.

From the third week after surgery until the end of the sixth week, I go twice a week to PT at the Physical Therapy Center, just down the street from where I live. That first time behind the wheel is scary as I feel insecure, trying to press down on the accelerator and again when I need to apply the brake, but I manage.

After the first week of outside PT, it is time to see the orthopedic surgeon and I am in for a surprise. While I am feeling pretty good as I look at the other people in the waiting room who are still using their walkers, I should have been paying attention to myself. Not continuing the exercises beyond the sessions has not been enough and now the doctor tells me that I am not bending my knee to the degree expected.

I can't be shocked because I know the truth. Why should I have expected this to go any other way? Each time after my PT I am told to repeat the exercises of the day at least twice more. Did I do that? No. I slept instead thinking it is their job to get me mobile, not mine. How stupid of me. My punishment for doing this is to have to have my knee stretched.

The orthopedic surgeon explains that my knee flexibility is not satisfactory and that is because of developing scar tissue so he recommends manipulation of the knee under general anesthetic. He explains the procedure will be performed at the Surgery Center as an out-patient.

###

People say they have too much on their plate and what it means is that they have too much going on at the moment, making it impossible to concentrate on anything else. This is what happens to me. Until this point, I have been drugged and so engrossed in my recovery I have not thought much about the case in Oklahoma. Now, with a clear head and almost back to my regular routines, I try to catch up on three months of activity.

###

On February 11, 2011, a subpoena is sent to Detective Ken Whitebird of OCPD to appear before the District Court of Cleveland County in the City of Norman on the ninth day of March, 2011 at 1:30 p.m. to testify on behalf of the State of Oklahoma as a witness in the Clara Ann Blocker versus the State of Oklahoma.

On March 9, 2011 Clara Blocker, along with her lawyer, David Smith appeared before Judge Steven L. Stice with Jennifer Pointer Austin and Clinton W. Pratt both serving as Assistant District Attorney, Cleveland County Courthouse. One witness is sworn in and the State Exhibit 1, the Medical Examiners Report is admitted without objection. The case is set for trial and formal arraignment before Judge Walkley on May 19, 2011 at 8:30 a.m.

###

Preliminary Hearing Transcript

On March 9, 2011 at the District Court in the State of Oklahoma for Cleveland County, The State of Oklahoma represented Erik Saxton in the Case No. CF-2010-1390. The Honorable Steven L. Stice presided. In appearances were Ms. Jennifer Pointer Austin, Assistant District Attorney, Mr. Clinton W. Pratt, Assistant District Attorney, all appearing for the State of Oklahoma. And, representing the defendant was Mr. David D. Smith, Attorney at Law.

The state witnesses included Detective Tim Ken Whitebird.

The Transcript

The Court: All right. Let's go on the record in CF-2010-1390, State of Oklahoma versus Clara Ann Blocker. The State is present through Assistant District Attorneys Jennifer Austin and

Clint Pratt. The defendant is present and in person with her attorney, David Smith, and the defendant is in custody.

Ms. Austin, has the State complied with LaFortune[3] discovery?

Ms. Austin: Yes, your Honor.

The Court: Mr. Smith, would you concur with that as best you can?

Mr. Smith: Yes, Sir.

The Court: All right. Obviously, due to the nature of this case, it's very rare that negotiations may or may not have taken place, but I think the law requires me to at least ask, Ms. Austin, if there has been an offer extended in this case.

Ms. Austin: And that's a difficult question to answer, Judge. We have talked about certain options and whether or not the defendant would be willing for those options and whether or not we need to actually extend it, if it would be accepted as – we've had discussions about it, but no concrete offers have been made or accepted.

Mr. Smith: I think that's correct, Judge. Most of our discussions about the nature of plea negotiations have been hypothetical in nature.

The Court: All right. Then are there any matters form the State we need to deal with before we take evidence?

Ms. Austin: Not that I can think of, no.

The Court: From the defendant?

Mr. Smith: No, your Honor.

We call for the rule of Sequestration[4].

---

[3] This is a new Discovery Code set by William D. LaFORTUNE, District Attorney, Tulsa County, Oklahoma in 1998 that provides that motions for discovery or disclosure of evidence by both parties in a criminal case cannot be made until after the preliminary hearing. The Legislature has thus established the time period and method for defendants to discover and obtain materials and information contained in the State's files. The only exception is requests for police reports may be made.

The Court: All right. The Rule of Sequestration has been invoked, meaning anyone called or endorsed to testify must remain outside the presence of the courtroom, not discuss your testimony with anyone other than the lawyers in this case. I would ask that the lawyers assist the Court with enforcing that Rule.

And at this time the State may call its first witness.

Ms. Austin: Thank you. State calls Inspector Ken Whitebird.

The Court: Detective, just have a seat in the Witness stand, and I'll swear you in from there. Raise your right hand. "Do you swear to tell the truth, the whole truth and nothing but the truth, so help you?"[5]

The Court: All right, sir. If you'll have a seat. Pull yourself up as close as you can to that microphone. And if you will state your full name for the record and spell it for us, please, sir.

The Witness: Tim Ken Whitebird, W-h-i-t-e-b-i-r-d.

The Court: All right. Ms. Austin, you may inquire.

Ms. Austin: Thank you.

Ms. Austin: Can you tell us how you're employed, sir.

Mr. Ken Whitebird: I am a police officer with the City of Oklahoma City.

Ms. Austin: And how long have you been with the Oklahoma City Police Department?

Mr. Ken Whitebird: I've been with Oklahoma City now 21 years. I was a police officer here in Norman for five years prior to that.

---

[4] The Rule of Sequestration is a common law rule that could be invoked by parties to a legal proceeding to exclude non-party witnesses from listening in on what other witnesses testified to.

[5] The act of swearing in a witness is done in the hopes of avoiding perjury, which is the act of a witness lying during his or her testimony. After a witness is under oath, perjuring can then be prosecuted to the full extent of the law. Some groups have taken issue with the phrase "so help you God" at the end of swearing in a witness. In the event that a witness has no religious affiliation, that phrase is simply removed, and is then referred to as an "affirmation." In most cases the Bible is not used during the swearing in.

AN UNFAIR ADVANTAGE   BY: JUANITA TISCHENDORF

Ms. Austin: And who are you currently assigned with in OCPD?

Mr. Ken Whitebird: I am assigned to the homicide unit.

Ms. Austin: And how long have you been in the homicide unit?

Mr. Ken Whitebird: Eleven Years.

Ms. Austin: Being assigned to the homicide unit, what are your duties?

Mr. Ken Whitebird: We investigate suicide by gunfire, suspicious deaths, any homicide, any officer-involved—any officer-involved incident period, put used to be it was any officer-involved shootings, but it's expanded.

Ms. Austin: And how do you receive those cases?

Mr. Ken Whitebird: They're assigned to us when we're on call.

Ms. Austin: And are you on call all the time or is it a rotation?

Mr. Ken Whitebird: It's a rotation.

Ms. Austin: And do you have partners you work with, or do you work solo?

Mr. Ken Whitebird: No, we work with a partner.

Ms. Austin: And who is your partner?

Mr. Ken Whitebird: Detective Lyndell Easley.

Ms. Austin: I'm going to talk to you about September 15 or 16, 2010. Were you working on that day as a homicide detective?

Mr. Ken Whitebird: Yes, ma'am.

Ms. Austin: And were you assigned to work a case or did you get called out regarding the death of an individual on that day?

Mr. Ken Whitebird: We were actually working a case up around Memorial Road and Western. It was an officer-involved death. We were about to clear from that, and I received a phone call that we had a suspicious death on the south side.

My partner was at the headquarters office, which is located downtown, at 701 Colcord, and I was 20, 30 minutes to the north. He said he would go to the scene and see what was going on and – if I would come downtown and do the interviews when I was done at the officer – scene.

Ms. Austin: Is that common for you to do with your partner?:

Mr. Ken Whitebird: Yes.

Ms. Austin: And sometimes do you separate and stay in different areas and some go back to headquarters and do interviews?

Mr. Ken Whitebird: That's correct. That's how it usually functions. One's assigned to the scene, and one's assigned to do interviews.

Ms. Austin: And you say do interviews. You don't just do interviews out at the scene of witnesses there, do you?

Mr. Ken Whitebird: Not necessarily. Sometimes you do, sometimes you don't. It just depends on what we have going on.

Ms. Austin: Most of the time you try to take them back down to the police department and do interviews there in interview rooms?

Mr. Ken Whitebird: Yes.

Ms. Austin: And are usually those interviews recorded, if possible?

Mr. Ken Whitebird: Yes

Ms. Austin: And in this situation, did you only go to the department to do interviews of witnesses, or did you go to the scene at some point?

Mr. Ken Whitebird: I never made it to the scene. I went straight to the police department and waited on the interviews.

Ms. Austin: Okay. And how were people brought there for interviews?:

Mr. Ken Whitebird: Usually they were given a ride by either a scout car or a detective car.

Ms. Austin: And that goes for eyewitnesses, anyone who might have heard anything at the scene or people who even called in crimes?

Mr. Ken Whitebird: That's correct.

Ms. Austin: And they are given a ride as a courtesy and then given a ride back to their –wherever—well, actually wherever they want to go?

Mr. Ken Whitebird: That's correct.

Mrs. Austin: In this particular case, what information did you receive in regards to who was deceased?

Mr. Ken Whitebird: Well, we had information that a – he hadn't arrived at the scene yet, but when he initially called me, he said, "It's a weird deal. We don't know what we got yet. We're heading down there to find out." He said, "the individual has been transported to the hospital already, but we're going to go down to the scene because," he said, "the officers at the scene don't feel like something's right."

Mrs. Austin: And is that common in your cases?

Mr. Ken Whitebird: Yes. With patrol officers. The younger patrol officers will heed on the safe side and call us out, which I have no problem with at all.

Mrs. Austin: Okay. And what time of day or night was this?

Mr. Ken Whitebird: It was around noon.

Mrs. Austin: And is this on a weekday or weekend, if you recall?

Mr. Ken Whitebird: I believe it was a weekday.

Mrs. Austin: And you said that the person – was the person at the scene deceased or were they transported to a hospital?

Mr. Ken Whitebird: The person at the scene that they were detaining, to bring downtown to talk to us, was the calling party. The person that was transported to the hospital was the victim.

Ms. Austin: Okay, and was the victim still alive when he was transported?

Mr. Ken Whitebird: To the best of my knowledge.

Ms. Austin: Okay. And pronounced dead at the hospital?

Mr. Ken Whitebird: Correct.

Ms. Austin: And so you said that the calling party was being transported to the police department. What do you mean by the calling party?

Mr. Ken Whitebird: The person who called 911.

Ms. Austin: And did you make contact with the calling party?

Mr. Ken Whitebird: Yes.

Ms. Austin: And who was that?

Mr. Ken Whitebird: Clara Blocker.

Ms. Austin: And do you see Clara Blocker in the courtroom today?

Mr. Ken Whitebird: I do.

Ms. Austin: Can you please tell the Court where she's seated and what she's wearing.?

Mr. Ken Whitebird: Clara's sitting on the opposite side of this gentleman, wearing orange coveralls, I guess.

Ms. Austin: The record reflect identification of the defendant, Clara Blocker?

The Court: The record will reflect identification of the defendant.

Ms. Austin: And at that point, the – well, let me ask you, normally do you have people identified as suspects at the scene, or sometimes do they become suspects later, or is it always very clear from the beginning?

Mr. Ken Whitebird: It's never clear from the beginning, unfortunately.

Ms. Austin: But at the time this – you were involved in this investigation and people are being transported to the police department for interviews, do you have a suspect yet?

Mr. Ken Whitebird: We have no suspect.

Ms. Austin: And so Ms. Blocker is transported as just the reporting party?

Mr. Ken Whitebird: As the calling party, yes.

Ms. Austin: Okay. And do you make contact with her when she arrives at the police department?

Mr. Ken Whitebird: I do.

Ms. Austin: And where do you make contact with her?

Mr. Ken Whitebird: In the hallway outside the homicide office.

Ms. Austin: And does she appear to be upset?

Mr. Ken Whitebird: Not at that time. I thanked her for coming down and cooperating. We were just trying to find out what was going on. She was very polite.

Ms. Austin: At that point do you have any information as to what has caused this individual to be deceased?

Mr. Ken Whitebird: Not as of yet.

Ms. Austin: Do you even know, in fact, if it's a homicide yet?

Mr. Ken Whitebird: No.

Ms. Austin: And so when you're talking to Ms. Blocker, is she in any way a suspect in anything at that time?

Mr. Ken Whitebird: No, not at all.

Ms. Austin: And information – when you are interviewing a person in an interview are you still receiving information throughout that interview sometimes?

Mr. Ken Whitebird: Yes, ma'am.

Ms. Austin: And how do you do that?:

Mr. Ken Whitebird: We send detectives out, like, to the hospital, and then we'll send – of course, the guys that are at the scene will call the office and let us know what they've got out there. The officer that – or Detective Miller, I believe it was, that went to the hospital, will call back and relay what information he's able to gain from the hospital, what preliminary information he could gather.

Ms. Austin: And they feed that information back to you –

Mr. Ken Whitebird: Correct.

Ms. Austin: --with the witnesses?

Mr. Ken Whitebird: Correct.

Ms. Austin: Do you sometimes use that information to incorporate into your interviews with witnesses?

Mr. Ken Whitebird: Yes.

Ms. Austin: The interview with Ms. Blocker, did that take place in an interview room that has the capability of recording?

Mr. Ken Whitebird: Yes, it did.

Ms. Austin: And was that interview recorded?

Mr. Ken Whitebird: Yes, ma'am.

Ms. Austin: How was it recorded?

Mr. Ken Whitebird: On a DVR.

Ms. Austin: Audio and video?

Mr. Ken Whitebird: Yes.

Ms. Austin: And who else was present in the interview besides yourself and the defendant?

Mr. Ken Whitebird: Just myself and the defendant.

Ms. Austin: Is there a capability at the Oklahoma City Police Department of being able to view what's going on in the interview room by a closed circuit?

Mr. Ken Whitebird: There is.

Ms. Austin: And where is that other monitor located that would be able to see what's going on in the interview room?

Mr. Ken Whitebird: There are actually two. One is in the lieutenant's office, which is just north of the interview rooms; and then the back of the homicide office, there's a room that's sectioned off where the recording devices are, and you can view it there.

Ms. Austin: And why is that?

Mr. Ken Whitebird: So the detectives can assist in viewing the interview.

Ms. Austin: And during this interview that you're having with Ms. Blocker, is there anyone observing that interview?

Mr. Ken Whitebird: Numerous people, yes.

Ms. Austin: And is that common?

Mr. Ken Whitebird: Yes, very common. On a slow day, especially.

Ms. Austin: And sometimes do those other detectives help you and feed you information and maybe pick up on things you might miss while you're in the interview?

Mr. Ken Whitebird: Oh, Yes. All the time.

Ms. Austin: And do you do that, in turn, for other detectives sometimes?

Mr. Ken Whitebird: Yes.

Ms. Austin: When you go in and meet with Ms. Blocker, I think we covered already, she's just the calling party at that point, she's not a suspect in anything?

Mr. Ken Whitebird: That's correct.

Ms. Austin: What is your purpose for talking to her?

Mr. Ken Whitebird: Just to try to establish what occurred and – to the victim and what had happened the night before, how she found him; and if she was, in fact, the person that called 911.

Ms. Austin: Okay. So when you go in and talk with her, she's not in custody?

Mr. Ken Whitebird: No.

Ms. Austin: And when you're talking with her, what does she tell you?

Mr. Ken Whitebird: Initially, when we start off the conversation, she explains to me that she's been living with Mr. Saxton; the victim, for about a month. She'd known him for about a year. Was introduced to him by a mutual friend by the name of Charles.

I asked her about his medical condition she advised that he was taking the drug called Topamax for seizures. So, again, you know, in my mind, I'm just trying to establish what do we have here.

We continue to talk. I asked her about if he had been – did it appear that he had been beaten up, and initially she said yes, it did appear like he had been beaten up, and then later on in the conversation, she said, but that could have been caused from a fall.

Ms. Austin: Okay. So at that point, you still don't know what you're dealing with?

Mr. Ken Whitebird: No, I still think – I don't know what we got, to be honest with you. And I even – I don't have a clue at this point.

Ms. Austin: Okay. And I believe you said a second ago, Mr. Saxton, the victim. Did you learn the name of the victim in this case?

Mr. Ken Whitebird: Yes, Later on.

Ms. Austin: What is his name?

Mr. Ken Whitebird: Erik Saxton.

Ms. Austin: And you said that the defendant had told you she had been staying with him for about a month?

Mr. Ken Whitebird: That's correct.

Ms. Austin: Where had they been staying?

Mr. Ken Whitebird: The Pine Apartments. I believe the exact address is 3042 Southwest 89th Street.

Ms. Austin: And is that location within Cleveland County?

Mr. Ken Whitebird: Yes, ma'am, it is.

Ms. Austin: And, actually, 89th Street is the cutoff, correct?

Mr. Ken Whitebird: Yes.

Ms. Austin: South side 89th is Cleveland County, and north side is Oklahoma County?

Mr. Ken Whitebird: That's correct.

Ms. Austin: But this was on the south side of 89th Street?

Mr. Ken Whitebird: Yes, ma'am.

Ms. Austin: And that apartment that they had been staying in, do you know whose apartment that was?

Mr. Ken Whitebird: I believe the leasee was Erik Saxton.

Ms. Austin: Now, when you said that you talked to the defendant about whether or not he looked like he got beat up, did she mention that or did you?

Mr. Ken Whitebird: I think I asked her. Or she may have – yes, I believe she initially asked – or told me that it looked like he got beat up. And then during the conversation, I explained to her that he had since died. I think I had gotten word that he had since died and told her. And she was visibly upset, began crying, and when I asked her; I said, "Well, let's go back to the day before and let's start from there. Let's try to figure out what's going on here." And then she explained to me what her sequence of the day was.

Ms. Austin: Okay. And at some point, did you, in the beginning, ask her – when she said he looked beat up, did you ask her if she knew who had beat him up?

Mr. Ken Whitebird: Yes, I did.

Ms. Austin: And did she know who?

Mr. Ken Whitebird: No, she didn't know who.

Ms. Austin: And did you ask her if she beat him up?

Mr. Ken Whitebird: I did.

Ms. Austin: And what was her response?

Mr. Ken Whitebird: No. She wouldn't do that. He was a midget. He was just a little person.

Ms. Austin: And do you know that already at that time, that he was a – had dwarfism?

Mr. Ken Whitebird: I did not. I think the first time I was told about it was during one of the breaks I took, and I got a phone call from the hospital. And that was when I learned that he was – had dwarfism.

Ms. Austin: And she, in fact, told you that also, though, in the –

Mr. Ken Whitebird: Yes.

Ms. Austin: -- interview? Did she – what did she tell you had gone on that previous day?

Mr. Ken Whitebird: She had told me that a friend of Erik Saxton, the victim, by the name of Chase had brought over some vodka around afternoon and that Erik – initially, she said told me that Erik drank alone. Later on during the conversation, she told me that, yeah, she had a little bit with Erik; that she and he had drank some Varsity Vodka for most of the day.

She laid down and went to sleep, and then around sixish to 6:30, she realized that she needed some minutes on her telephone and the place that she had to go was called Cricket, and she called a friend of hers by the name of David Elkins, and David came to pick her up, brought her back – or, I'm sorry, took her to Cricket, got some minutes put on her phone, and then brought her back to the apartment.

That's when she told me that she saw the victim had been beaten. And –

Ms. Austin: When she returned?

Mr. Ken Whitebird: When she returned at 7:30, and that's when she initially saw that the victim had been beat up. But she still did not know who it was.

Ms. Austin: Throughout your interview with her, does she tell you that the victim was drinking?

Mr. Ken Whitebird: Yes.

Ms. Austin: I'm sorry, drinking alcohol?

Mr. Ken Whitebird: Yes.

Ms. Austin: And does she – she admits that she had been drinking alcohol at some point also?

Mr. Ken Whitebird: Initially, she said she didn't because – she didn't. and then later on in the conversation, she said, "Yeah. Okay. Yeah. I did drink some with him."

Ms. Austin: And throughout the interview with her, at some point do you start noticing inconsistencies in what she's telling you?

Mr. Ken Whitebird: Yes.

Ms. Austin: And do you leave the room and – do you leave the room at all throughout this interview?:

Mr. Ken Whitebird: Yes, I left the room shortly after she told me the first story. I went out. She had mentioned this David Elkins, and she gave me a telephone number to call him and verify that he was the one to take her to Cricket, and I also wanted to know what we had at the scene. I still was unsure what was going on. So I --

Mrs. Austin: And I'm going to stop you for one second. Had she told you before she left the room when she had discovered – or when she called 911 and why she called 911?

Mr. Ken Whitebird: Yes. She had discovered – she had told me that usually the victim gets up around 6:00, but on this day he apparently had slept in. It was around 8:00 is when she found him, and that's when she called 911.

Ms. Austin: Okay. And you're talking to her around noon; is that right?

Mr. Ken Whitebird: Yes.

Ms. Austin: That doesn't mean that's when she called 911; correct?

Mr. Ken Whitebird: No, no, that's –

Ms. Austin: Did the call come in earlier than that?

Mr. Ken Whitebird: I have not seen the CAD sheet. I apologize, I couldn't tell you what exactly – but I would think it was a lot earlier than that.

Ms. Austin: Because it sometimes take a while for you guys to respond and interview witnesses?

Mr. Ken Whitebird: Right.

Ms. Austin: And does she tell you why she called 911?

Mr. Ken Whitebird: Because she had found the victim not breathing.

Ms. Austin: Unresponsive?

Mr. Ken Whitebird: Unresponsive, yes.

Ms. Austin: If the police department records reflect that the 911 call came in around 9:47 a.m.;, do you have any reason to disagree with that?

Mr. Ken Whitebird: No, not at all.

Ms. Austin: Okay. And you said that at some point you leave the room. And does she make a phone call when you leave the room?

Mr. Ken Whitebird: Yes, she did.

Ms. Austin: Okay. Before she made the phone call, did you make a phone call to do anything to verify what she'd been telling you?

Mr. Ken Whitebird: Yes. I called David Elkins on the telephone number she had given me, and he explained to me he had come over and taken her to Cricket.

Ms. Austin: So he did confirm what she had told you?

Mr. Ken Whitebird: He confirmed, yes.

Ms. Austin: Okay. Based on – and you don't have to tell me what Mr. Elkins said, but is there anything Mr. Elkins said that caused you concern to make you want to go back in and talk to her some more about some things?

Mr. Ken Whitebird: Yes.

Ms. Austin: Okay. Before you go back in the room, does she make a phone call?

Mr. Ken Whitebird: Yes.

Ms. Austin: And do you overhear or see her on the monitor making a phone call?

Mr. Ken Whitebird: Yes.

Ms. Austin: And what was the nature of that call?

Mr. Ken Whitebird: She was talking to – after I had hung up with him, she was talking to David Elkins, that the police had her downtown; they were talking to her about the victim; she was short on money she didn't know where she was going to stay tonight as soon as we released her. She was asking him if he was out of town or if he could come pick her up once we were done with her.

Ms. Austin: So she was worried about where she was going to go when she left the police department?

Mr. Ken Whitebird: Yes.

Ms. Austin: And does she tell the person she's talking to on the phone, that you believed to be David Elkins, that Erik Saxton is dead?

Mr. Ken Whitebird: Yes.

Ms. Austin: Does she say at that point what has happened to Erik Saxton?

Mr. Ken Whitebird: No. I just think she told the individual, Elkins, that he was dead and it just didn't add up. It just didn't add up; she didn't know why he was dead.

Ms. Austin: And did you go back into the room and talk to her some more?

Mr. Ken Whitebird: Yes, I did.

Ms. Austin: And when you go back into the room to talk to her, do you have any further information yet on the condition or the injuries to Mr. Saxton?

Mr. Ken Whitebird: At that point I had talked to my partner before I went back in the room, and he said, "Honestly, I don't know what we got." He goes, "We got a mess. There's some bodily fluids here that don't make any sense." He said. "there's some blood on the towels." He goes, "I just don't know what we got, and it could be a fall. I don't even know what we got." So that's where I was at that point.

Ms. Austin: Okay. So when you go back in and talk to her, do you talk to her about some of the things you learned from the scene --.

Mr. Ken Whitebird: Yes.

Ms. Austin: --from the – from your partner about what was at the scene?

Mr. Ken Whitebird: Right.

Ms. Austin: Okay. What do you go back in and talk to her about?

Mr. Ken Whitebird: I initially asked her about what Mr. Elkins had told me. He had told me that she had been drinking, and I asked her about that again. And she did admit, "Yeah, I had been drinking with him."

Ms. Austin: Did you ask her about making a strange statement to Mr. Elkins about the victim?

Mr. Ken Whitebird: Yes.

Ms. Austin: And what did you ask her about?

Mr. Ken Whitebird: Mr. Elkins had told me when he brought her back to the apartment complex, she made a statement to him that Erik might not let me back in the apartment. And I asked her what that was about. And she said, "well, I always tell Erik to lock the doors," and she was real big on this locking the door thing. And she was afraid that Erik wouldn't be able – wouldn't answer the door, wouldn't let her back in.

Ms. Austin: Had she told you earlier in your conversation with her that the door had been unlocked when she came back and maybe that's when he got beat up?

Mr. Ken Whitebird: Yes.

Ms. Austin: So was that – did that contradict what she had told you earlier?

Mr. Ken Whitebird: Correct.

Ms. Austin: Did you ask her about anything that your partner had found at the scene?

Mr. Ken Whitebird: I believe at this point I did ask her about the towels.

Ms. Austin: What did you ask her?

Mr. Ken Whitebird: If she had cleaned the victim up, and she said she had and placed them in the bathroom.

Ms. Austin: Okay. And at that point, cleaned him up from what? Did she tell you what she had cleaned him up from?

Mr. Ken Whitebird: I don't believe I specifically asked that. But I had mentioned that there was blood on the towels in the bathroom and if she cleaned him up, and she said, "Yeah, I did."

Ms. Austin: So she told you she had cleaned blood off of the victim at some point with some towels?

Mr. Ken Whitebird: Yes.

Ms. Austin: And those were located in the bathroom?

Mr. Ken Whitebird: Yes.

Ms. Austin: And at that point, does she give you another story about what happened?

Mr. Ken Whitebird: Yes, she did.

Ms. Austin: What did she tell you?

Mr. Ken Whitebird: I just told her, I said, "Clara, there's some inconsistencies in the stories you're telling me. I mean, I'm just – we're getting one thing and now I'm getting another, and it's just not adding up here." I said, "why don't you just tell me the truth."

And she said, "Okay. C did it."

And I said, "who is C?"

And C was a guy, supposedly, that had lived with Erik in the past. He was supposed to be a black male, gang-banger type.

But I never got an actual name on the guy. She had explained to me initially that C came in and she ran him off. And then later on in the conversation, she explained to me that C was trying to rob them and she ran him off and saw his girlfriend in the car, and that she got angry with Erik about not locking the doors.

Ms. Austin: And is that who she tells you then beat Erik up?

Mr. Ken Whitebird: I don't think she actually just said, "C beat Erik up," but she implicated that's who it was, that's what she had been hiding from me. She never actually said she saw C beat Erik up, but she was implicating that to me during the conversation.

The Court: Ms. Austin, how are you spelling "C"?

Ms. Austin: The letter C?

Mr. Ken Whitebird: That's just how I spelled it.

The Court: The letter C?

Mr. Ken Whitebird: Yes, sir.

The Court: All right. Thank you.

Ms. Austin: But she didn't ever spell it for you. That's just what you --.

Mr. Ken Whitebird: That's just what I put down, "C."

Ms. Austin: Okay. And at some point, does she tell you that Erik Saxton had a seizure or something medically had gone wrong with him?

Mr. Ken Whitebird: Yes. She did tell me that she – Erik had a seizure, but it wasn't a bad enough seizure that she needed to call anybody.

Ms. Austin: So she didn't indicate that he had a seizure where he hurt himself or any type of injuries occurred from that?

Mr. Ken Whitebird: No. No.

Ms. Austin: Okay. At that point, are you thinking that something is not right?

Mr. Ken Whitebird: Yes. I really don't know what to think because I don't know what I got at the scene. I don't know what we're working here. Are we working a medical emergency? Are we working a domestic? You know, I didn't think a domestic, per se, but – so I left the room again, and I told her before I left the room, you know, "all I want is the truth." I mean, "We're going to take this to the next level if, you know, you don't tell me the truth and quit lying to me." And I left her in there, in the interview room.

Ms. Austin: And you said you didn't think it was a domestic, per se. She didn't tell you they were in any type of relationship, did she?

Mr. Ken Whitebird: No, she did not. Just friends.

Ms. Austin: And he was allowing her to stay there with him?

Mr. Ken Whitebird: That's correct.

Ms. Austin: Did you learn through her or through your investigation that the victim had some physical limitations other than having the condition of the dwarfism?

Mr. Ken Whitebird: During the investigation, we did.

Ms. Austin: And what was that condition?

Mr. Ken Whitebird: That he was paralyzed on his left side.

Ms. Austin: Not to where he couldn't walk, though, right?

Mr. Ken Whitebird: Well, I mean, depending on who you talked to, initially it sounded a lot worse. But we did learn later that, yeah, he was able to walk and function a little bit.

Ms. Austin: He wasn't wheelchair bound or anything of that nature?

Mr. Ken Whitebird: No. And that's what we were initially thinking had happened. But it wasn't.

Ms. Austin: But he – normally, he lived by himself at least at some point and was able to care for himself and didn't require other people to take care of him?

Mr. Ken Whitebird: That's correct.

Ms. Austin: When you left the room the second time, did the defendant make another phone call?

Mr. Ken Whitebird: She did.

Ms. Austin: And were you able to overhear her making this phone call?

Mr. Ken Whitebird: No. Initially, I had gone back out and was walking back to the room, and I called my partner again, and he's still confused about what we got. He hasn't heard anything from the hospital. And I did walk back there and observe her in the room, and she did make a phone call.

Ms. Austin: Okay. And could you tell who she was talking to at that time?

Mr. Ken Whitebird: I heard a name, but I didn't know who she was talking to, no.

Ms. Austin: Okay. And what was she talking to that person about?

Mr. Ken Whitebird: Well, she was just confused on what was going on. She didn't know, you know, why the police were talking to her and she explained that I was getting upset.

She said, "they may just end up putting me in jail. I don't know." And then she transferred the phone to a guy named Vaughan, and that's when she made the statement, "Fight or no fight, it just ain't adding up."

Ms. Austin: At some point, did she say to the person she was talking to on the phone that they were talking to you about an accidental homicide?

Mr. Ken Whitebird: I don't recall that. I'm sorry, I don't recall that one.

Ms. Austin: And the – you said she said, "fight or no fight. It just doesn't add up."

Mr. Ken Whitebird: That's what I recall.

Ms. Austin: And when she's talking to Vaughan, does she also – or the person you say that she said was Vaughan, did she state that she never laid hands on him?

Mr. Ken Whitebird: I don't recall her ever saying that either. I'm sorry.

Ms. Austin: And, I'm sorry, did you prepare a report in –

Mr. Ken Whitebird: I did.

Ms. Austin: -- conjunction with this?

Mr. Ken Whitebird: If I can refer back to it?

Ms. Austin: And I'm looking at the bottom of Page 4.

Mr. Ken Whitebird: Yes, she did. I apologize. She did admit she was "fucked up," but she never laid hands on him.

Ms. Austin: And at that point does that change – when you hear her make those statements, does that change your focus of this interview?

Mr. Ken Whitebird: It did. It began to make me more suspicious of what might have occurred, especially that they were the only two in the apartment together. So I called over – I had noticed previously that she had some injuries on her person, so I called one of our CSI units over to photograph the injuries.

Ms. Austin: And did they come in and do that?

Mr. Ken Whitebird: Yes.

Ms. Austin: And what injuries did you note on her person?

Mr. Ken Whitebird: On her knees, there were what appeared to be carpet burns. And I had them come over and take photographs of those.

Ms. Austin: And something – you said the investigation changed some. So before all of this, before you hear this phone call things aren't quite adding up, but is she a suspect of anything at that point?

Mr. Ken Whitebird: No. Because, I mean, I still don't know what we got up to that point.

Ms. Austin: But once you hear her make that phone call, does it change the way that you're going to conduct your interview with her?

Mr. Ken Whitebird: It does. It does.

Ms. Austin: And do you go back in and talk to her again?

Mr. Ken Whitebird: Yes, I do.

Ms. Austin: And when you come back and talk to her, do you do something before you start talking to her?

Mr. Ken Whitebird: I did.

Ms. Austin: What do you do?

Mr. Ken Whitebird: I explained her rights to her,

Ms. Austin: And why did you do that at that time?

Mr. Ken Whitebird: Because I was going to start asking her – I was going to start pressing her more, asking her questions that would incriminate her if she answered them truthfully.

Ms. Austin: And she almost moved over into a suspect in your mind –

Mr. Ken Whitebird: Yes –

Ms. Austin: --would that be safe to say?

Mr. Ken Whitebird: --she has,

Ms. Austin: But you do not place her into custody or tell her she's under arrest or anything like that?

Mr. Ken Whitebird: No.

Ms. Austin: --Do you read her, her right from a card?

Mr. Ken Whitebird: No.

Ms. Austin: -- a form, or from memory?

Mr. Ken Whitebird: Just from memory.

Ms. Austin: And this entire interview with her, the phone calls, the photographs, being taken, reading her rights, is that all preserved on a video recording --.

Mr. Ken Whitebird: It is.

Ms. Austin: -- and audio also?

Mr. Ken Whitebird: Yes.

Ms. Austin: When you tell her, her rights, does she appear to understand those rights?

Mr. Ken Whitebird: She did.

Ms. Austin: Now, you've been with her for a period of time now. Would that be safe to say?

Mr. Ken Whitebird: That's correct.

Ms. Austin: Do you know about how long it was before this point?

Mr. Ken Whitebird: Maybe an hour, hour and a half.

Ms. Austin: And at any point does she express to you that she's done talking and she wants to leave?

Mr. Ken Whitebird: No.

Ms. Austin: Okay. In your experience as a law enforcement officer, in your 21-plus years, have you come into contact with persons under the influence of alcohol or drugs?

Mr. Ken Whitebird: Oh, yes. Yes.

Ms. Austin: Did you believe she was under the influence when you were speaking to her in that room?

Mr. Ken Whitebird: No, not at all.

Ms. Austin: Did she – the entire time you were talking with her, did you have the opportunity to assess her level of understanding of what was going on and the questions you were asking her?

Mr. Ken Whitebird: Yes.

Ms. Austin: And did she always appear to be appropriate for what the conversation was and the questions that were being asked?

Mr. Ken Whitebird: Yes.

Ms. Austin: And did she appear to understand her rights as you told them to her?

Mr. Ken Whitebird: Yes.

Ms. Austin: And when you told her, her rights, did she have any questions about those?

Mr. Ken Whitebird: No.

Ms. Austin: And when you – after you explained her rights to her including the right for an attorney, did she request an attorney or request to stop the questioning at any time?

Mr. Ken Whitebird: No, she didn't.

Ms. Austin: And after you explained her rights to her, did she continue talking with you?

Mr. Ken Whitebird: She did.

Ms. Austin: And when she was talking with you, at any point in time after reading her, her rights, did she want to stop talking with you?

Mr. Ken Whitebird: No. She never stopped talking to me.

Ms. Austin: In fact, when the interview was finally concluded, who stopped the interview, you or her?

Mr. Ken Whitebird: I did.

Ms. Austin: And was she ever placed into custody?

Mr. Ken Whitebird: Yes. After the interview was terminated.

Ms. Austin: At the very end of the interview?

Mr. Ken Whitebird: Yes.

Ms. Austin: And is that – did you tell her she was under arrest at that time?

Mr. Ken Whitebird: Yes.

Ms. Austin: Okay. But was there any conversation about that before then?

Mr. Ken Whitebird: No.

Ms. Austin: In fact, when she had made one –

Mr. Ken Whitebird: Ma'am?

Ms. Austin: Yes.

Mr. Ken Whitebird: I did before I left – before I left the room the second time I told her that we were going to – if she continued to lie to me, we were going to take it to the next level and that would be reading her rights and taking her into custody.

Ms. Austin: Okay. And that was before you left the room the last time?

Mr. Ken Whitebird: Yes.

Ms. Austin: And then when you came in, you did read her, her rights?

Mr. Ken Whitebird: Yes.

Ms. Austin: And then she spoke with you and continued to speak with you and agreed to speak with you?

Mr. Ken Whitebird: Correct.

Ms. Austin: After you had explained her rights and she was speaking with you, what did she say?

Mr. Ken Whitebird: Well, after I was talking to her, she goes, "I've already told you everything I know. I've already told you that." And just based upon my experience, sometimes – I decided at that point I would raise my voice to her and try to elicit some sort of emotional response and try to anger her. So I did,

I said, "why are you lying to me?" in a loud manner.

And she said, "I'm not lying to you."

And I said, "Yes, Clara, you are lying to me."

And she ducked her head, and she said, "Okay. I got into a fight with him, but I didn't hit him with my fist."

And at that point, I knew that the conversation had changed from somebody else doing it to her.

Ms. Austin: And so you raised your voice to her, an interview technique?

Mr. Ken Whitebird: Yes.

Ms. Austin: And it obviously worked?

Mr. Ken Whitebird: Yes.

Ms. Austin: Okay. So then she says that she got into an altercation with him, but she says she didn't use her hands; is that correct?

Mr. Ken Whitebird: Correct.

Ms. Austin: What does she tell you?

Mr. Ken Whitebird: She told me that she – initially, they had gotten into an argument over his locking the door. She had to put herself in check because she knew she was getting angry. And at some point they ended up in the bedroom where she hit him in the head with a crystal ball, is what she described it as.

And then she told me that she couldn't remember exactly where she hit him the second time, but it was with a DVD player and she thought it was in the living room.

Ms. Austin: Okay. Did she say what part of his body she hit him on?

Mr. Ken Whitebird: In the head.

Ms. Austin: And – but she couldn't remember what room it occurred in?

Mr. Ken Whitebird: She was pretty sure that the crystal ball was in the bedroom, but thought – she wasn't positive. She said she does black out – but thought that the DVR was in the living room.

Ms. Austin: Okay. And the injuries that he had received, she doesn't then say anyone else had come over or anyone else had – there was no other person coming in and beating him up at that point, was there?

Mr. Ken Whitebird: That's correct.

Ms. Austin: Do you – are you able to establish a time frame that she is there with the victim?

Mr. Ken Whitebird: It's established on her testimony that Elkin or – David Elkins – I'm sorry, Elkins – had brought her back around 7:30, and then I believe she had told me they woke up around 8:00 the next morning, and then, of course, the 911 call.

Ms. Austin: And does she tell you that anybody else was ever there at the house from that time frame when she got home from Mr. Elkins until she calls 911?

Mr. Ken Whitebird: No, nobody else was there.

Ms. Austin: And does she tell you what happens after she hit him with the DVD player and the crystal ball?

Mr. Ken Whitebird: Yeah. She said that after the fight, they went to 7-Eleven, got a cherry pop and some cigarettes and came back home, and he went to sleep by the couch, and I believe she went to sleep by the door.

Ms. Austin: Was there a bedroom in the house?

Mr. Ken Whitebird: There was.

Ms. Austin: And was it his bedroom?

Mr. Ken Whitebird: Yes.

Ms. Austin: But she doesn't say he goes to sleep in his bed; he sleeps on the floor?:

Mr. Ken Whitebird: He ends up sleeping on the floor.

Ms. Austin: And based on the crime scene itself, does it appear that's where he had been laying when she discovered him?

Mr. Ken Whitebird: Yes.

Mr. Smith: Objection, your Honor. I don't think he's entered the proper foundation to render that opinion.

The Court: It will be sustained.

Ms. Austin: Have you observed the crime scene photos?

Mr. Ken Whitebird: Yes.

Ms. Austin: And from what she told you, were you able to corroborate any of the things that she told you from the crime scene photos?

Mr. Ken Whitebird: There were bodily fluids in the area where she said he was asleep.

Ms. Austin: And this crystal ball that she talks about, was there anything consistent with that that was found at the scene?

Mr. Ken Whitebird: Yes, broken glass.

Ms. Austin: And what room was that found in?

Mr. Ken Whitebird: In the bedroom.

Ms. Austin: And that's where she told you that she had hit him with the crystal ball –

Mr. Ken Whitebird: That's correct.

Ms. Austin: --in the bedroom? Does she tell you where on the person she hit him with the crystal ball?

Mr. Ken Whitebird: On the back of the head.

Ms. Austin: And you said also that she told you that she hit him with the DVD player. Was that located at the crime scene?

Mr. Ken Whitebird: Yes, it was.

Ms. Austin: And was it taken into custody, into evidence?

Mr. Ken Whitebird: Yes.

Ms. Austin: And was it damaged in any way?

Mr. Ken Whitebird: Yes.

Ms. Austin: How?

Mr. Ken Whitebird: It was on the top – or the portion over the top looked like it had a slight dent in it.

Ms. Austin: Does she indicate while she's talking with you at any point in time that Mr. Saxton ever struck her or hit her?

Mr. Ken Whitebird: No, uh-uh.

Ms. Austin: Were you able to, based on your contact and descriptors that you got from the defendant, determine how tall she was – or she is? I'm sorry.

Mr. Ken Whitebird: Just based upon the information that I had looked up as far as her name, I believe she was well over six foot.

Ms. Austin: And you sat across from her and interviewed her for a period of time.

Mr. Ken Whitebird: Oh, yeah.

Ms. Austin: Did she appear to be six foot –

Mr. Ken Whitebird: Yeah –

Ms. Austin: --tall?

Mr. Ken Whitebird: Yeah, yeah.

Ms. Austin: Okay. And did you learn how tall the victim was approximately?

Mr. Ken Whitebird: I did not. I just knew that he was a dwarf.

Ms. Austin: Okay. Did she want to make a point while she was talking to you that she did not hit him with her hands?

Mr. Ken Whitebird: That's correct.

Ms. Austin: And did she say that one time or more than one time?

Mr. Ken Whitebird: More than once. I believe it was about two to three times.

Ms. Austin: And did that appear, when you were talking to her, that was important for her to tell you?

Mr. Ken Whitebird: Yes.

Ms. Austin: Did you find that unusual?

Mrs. Smith: Objection, Judge, the opinion about whether it's unusual or not.

Ms. Austin: And I'll rephrase my question.

The Court: Objection will be sustained. Please rephrase your question.

Ms. Austin: During your conversation with her, did that appear to be a main focus for her to tell you?

Mr. Ken Whitebird: Yes.

Ms. Austin: And did you learn from leaving the room and talking with other people that he had any injuries that could be visible? And if so, did you talk to her about those?

Mr. Ken Whitebird: I learned later, but I didn't talk to her about those.

Ms. Austin: And in your report – I'm sorry. In your interview, do you remember asking her how he got a black eye?

Mr. Ken Whitebird: Yes, I do. And I think she stated that it appeared like he got beat up.

Ms. Austin: Okay. And at some point, do you tell him – do you tell her that he's got a black eye, and she says, "Yes. But that didn't kill him"?

Mr. Ken Whitebird: Yes. Yes, she did say that.

Ms. Austin: And is that when she tells you she got in an altercation with him?

\ Mr. Ken Whitebird: Yes.

Ms. Austin: Now, I know you've told us – you've said she hit him with a DVD player and a crystal ball. Does she say how many times she hit him?

Mr. Ken Whitebird: Just once. I believe.

Ms. Austin: During your investigation, either while you're interviewing her or later, do you learn that this individual died from a head wound?

Mr. Smith: Objection, Judge. That's hearsay.

The Court: It will be sustained.

Ms. Austin: Do you learn during the interview with her what he died from?

Mr. Ken Whitebird: Yes – no. With the interview with her?

Ms. Austin: Yes.

Mr. Ken Whitebird: No. I mean, she didn't tell me what he died from. I'm sorry if I'm understanding the question (sic).

Ms. Austin: I'm sorry, that was a poorly worded question.

Did you learn from talking with other people while you're in your interview with her what he died from? Or is it later that you learn that?

Mr. Ken Whitebird: I think it's later. It's later in the day.

Ms. Austin: Okay. But during your interview with her, she tells you she hit him over the head at least twice?

Mr. Ken Whitebird: Yes.

Ms. Austin: Okay. And does she tell you when that happened in regards to the time that they're alone together?

Mr. Ken Whitebird: It was after 7:30, but I don't think she gave me a specific time. And I really didn't press that issue. I wish I would have, but I didn't.

Ms. Austin: But it's sometime after she returns from Cricket?

Mr. Ken Whitebird: Yeah. After she gets the minutes added.

Ms. Austin: Which was 7:30 the night before she calls 911?

Mr. Ken Whitebird: Yeah. I'm actually anxious to get back out of the room at that point to call the crime scene and tell them, :"This is what we got. Look for this." So I probably ended the interview a little quickly.

Ms. Austin: And you say you're anxious to get out so you want to talk to them about things she's telling you?

Mr. Ken Whitebird: Yeah.

Ms. Austin: Like the DVD player and the –

Mr. Ken Whitebird: Yeah. The evidence at the scene.

Ms. Austin: Because is that something you normally look for at crime scenes is DVD players or things that normally belong in a home?

Mr. Ken Whitebird: No, I mean, of course, with blunt-force trauma, you look for any type of weapon that could cause that. But, I got to be honest with you, I wouldn't have thought of that. I wouldn't have thought of a DVD player because there's so many wires on them.

Ms. Austin: Did you talk to her about calling 911? Or did she admit that to you? Or what was that conversation about with 911?

Mr. Ken Whitebird: I think she just told me that she was the one that called 911 –

Ms. Austin: Did she –

Mr. Ken Whitebird: -- initially.

Ms. Austin: I'm sorry. Did she tell you why she called 911?

Mr. Ken Whitebird: Because the victim was unresponsive and not breathing.

Ms. Austin: And did she tell you what room in the house she finds him unresponsive and not breathing?

Mr. Ken Whitebird: I believe she told me it was the living room.

Ms. Austin: And that's also where she told you that he laid down?

Mr. Ken Whitebird: Correct.

Ms. Austin: Okay. And I believe earlier – and I want to make sure that you were clear when you testified. You said that from viewing the crime scene photos, there was an area of bodily fluids. Was that in the living room?

Mr. Ken Whitebird: Yes. By the couch.

Ms. Austin: Which is where she told you he laid down?

Mr. Ken Whitebird: Yes.

Ms. Austin: Okay. Was this a one-bedroom apartment or a two-bedroom apartment?

Mr. Ken Whitebird: I believe it was one. Or maybe what they call an efficiency. But I think it's a one-bedroom apartment.

Ms. Austin: Okay. So at any point in time in your interview, does she tell you that anyone other than herself is responsible for injuries that he might have incurred during that time once you've read her Miranda?

Mr. Ken Whitebird: No.

Ms. Austin: Before she did, but then after you read her Miranda, she –

Mr. Ken Whitebird: Correct.

Ms. Austin: All of those other stories about C and when she came back, those are not what she told you anymore?

Mr. Ken Whitebird: That's correct.

Ms. Austin: If I could have just one second, your Honor?

The Court: Yes. (Brief pause.)

Ms. Austin: After she tells you that she has gotten into this altercation with the victim, do you go back over with her at all or do you talk with her again about the bloody towels?

Mr. Ken Whitebird: I don't believe I did. Again, I was – honestly, I made a mistake. I was so anxious to get out of the room and call the crime scene and tell them, "This is what you need to look for," that I didn't go back over the story with her again.

Ms. Austin: But there's nothing she told that third time you went in that told you there would have been anything else that occurred for her to need to clean blood up other than this altercation?

Mr. Ken Whitebird: That's correct.

Ms. Austin: Okay. Thank you.

Ms. Austin: Pass the witness.

The Court: Cross-examination.

Mr. Smith: Afternoon, Detective.

Mr. Ken Whitebird: Afternoon, sir.

Mr. Smith: Am I correct in assuming that pretty much all you did in this investigation was interview Ms. Blocker?

Mr. Ken Whitebird: That's correct.

Mr. Smith: Okay. If there was any other investigation in this case, it was done by people other than you?

Mr. Ken Whitebird: That's correct. Now, sir, are you referring to the crime scene and stuff, yes, sir.

Mr. Smith: Well, other than interviewing Ms. Blocker, did you do anything else in this investigation?

Mr. Ken Whitebird: No, sir.

Mr. Smith: I mean, I realize you've looked at crime scene photos, that kind of thing, but as far as the actual investigation, this is pretty much all you did?

Mr. Ken Whitebird: That's correct.

Mr. Smith: This interview happened on the afternoon of the 16th; is that right?

Mr. Ken Whitebird: Yes, sir.

Mr. Smith: Now, at some point you remarked about some injuries to her knees.

Mr. Ken Whitebird: Correct.

Mr. Smith: Okay. How far into the interview was that?

Mr. Ken Whitebird: Maybe 30 minutes.

Mr. Smith: So if the interview started about 12:30, we're talking about 1:00 in the afternoon?

Mr. Ken Whitebird: Right.

Mr. Smith: And did you note, sir, that those injuries had not begun to heal yet?

Mr. Ken Whitebird: They had not begun to scab over.

Mr. Smith: They hadn't scabbed over?

Mr. Ken Whitebird: No.

Mr. Smith: They were fresh, right?

Mr. Ken Whitebird: Correct.

Mr. Smith: Okay. So you may or may not feel qualified to answer this, but you could assume that they didn't happen, for example, the night before?

Mr. Ken Whitebird: I'm not qualified to answer how long it takes a scab, but –

Mr. Smith: Sure.

Mr. Ken Whitebird: -- they looked fresh to me.

Mr. Smith: All right. At some time during the time that you were out of the room, she made a couple of phone calls?

Mr. Ken Whitebird: Yes, sir.

Mr. Smith: And is it your understanding she called – one of the phone calls was with David "Elrich"?

Mr. Ken Whitebird: Elkins.

Mr. Smith: Elkins. Okay. And then she called somebody else?

Mr. Ken Whitebird: Correct, sir.

Mr. Smith: Okay. You did – do know that OCPD did talk to Mr. Elkins?

Mr. Ken Whitebird: Yes, I did.

Mr. Smith: You yourself did?

Mr. Ken Whitebird: I believe – yes, I did. I'm sorry.

Mr. Smith: Did you yourself talk to anybody else that she had called while you were out of the room?

Mr. Ken Whitebird: Never did, no, sir. Couldn't track down who Tory – or Lori and Vaughan were.

Mr. Smith: Lori and Vaughan?

Mr. Ken Whitebird: Lori and Vaughan were the names she used.

Mr. Smith: Okay. She was arrested at the end of the interview, right?

Mr. Ken Whitebird: Yes.

Mr. Smith: And all of her personal property was seized –

Mr. Ken Whitebird: Yes.

Mr. Smith: --taken? Including her cell phone; right?

Mr. Ken Whitebird: I believe we did, yes.

Mr. Smith: I mean, you're not going to let her take here cell phone into the cell; right?

Mr. Ken Whitebird: That's correct.

Mr. Smith: That's not why they call it a cell phone, is it?

Mr. Ken Whitebird: That's correct.

Mr. Smith: Okay. So the average cell phone, based on your experience, has a feature on it that records the numbers that have been called?

Mr. Ken Whitebird: That's correct.

Mr. Smith: Okay. Do you know if anybody looked at those numbers and tried to contact the people she talked to?

Mr. Ken Whitebird: I did not.

Mr. Smith: Do you know if anyone else did?

Mr. Ken Whitebird: I do not, sir.

Mr. Smith: Okay. As I understand your testimony, and if I understand it correctly, you're saying that after you read her the Miranda warnings and after you confronted her and elevated your voice to try and get an emotional response from her, she did tell you that they had had a fight and that she'd struck him twice?

Mr. Ken Whitebird: Yes.

Mr. Smith: Okay. Is it true, sir, she also told you that she didn't intend to kill him?

Mr. Ken Whitebird: I think eventually in the conversation that she didn't ever say that she didn't intend to kill him, she just didn't understand how he could die from the way she hit him. She just – and then she was in tears. She just – "I just don't understand how he could have died."

Mr. Smith: You got the impression from her demeanor and the tone of voice and her body language that she was sincere when she said that?

Mr. Ken Whitebird: Yeah. Yes, sir, I did.

Mr. Smith: And I say, "said that." I mean, she said that she didn't understand how he could die?

Mr. Ken Whitebird: Correct.

Mr. Smith: Just from her demeanor, did she appear surprised by that?

Mr. Ken Whitebird: That he had died?

Mr. Smith: Yeah.

Mr. Ken Whitebird: Yes. When I initially told her that he had died, she began to cry and was very upset.

Mr. Smith: We were talking about whether she ever told you she didn't mean to kill him. You wrote a report about this, right?

Mr. Ken Whitebird: I did.

Mr. Smith: And you've had a chance to look at it before your testimony?

Mr. Ken Whitebird: Briefly, yes, sir.

Mr. Smith: I mean, you didn't have a chance to memorize it, right?

Mr. Ken Whitebird: No. I just – we had a jury trial going on in Oklahoma County, and I ran down here and I looked at it as –

Mr. Smith: Sure. Do you have it with you?

Mr. Ken Whitebird: Yes, sir.

Mr. Smith: Will you turn to Page 5, please.

Mr. Ken Whitebird: Yes, sir.

Mr. Smith: And it's – let me ask you to look at the third paragraph from the bottom.

Mr. Ken Whitebird: Yes, sir.

Mr. Smith: And read that to yourself and see if that refreshes your memory.

Mr. Ken Whitebird: Okay. It's Page 5, third paragraph?

Mr. Smith: Yes, sir. It's the paragraph that starts – it's the third from the bottom. I'm sorry. It starts with "Blocker and Erik."

Mr. Ken Whitebird: Oh, "Blocker and Erik were arguing"?

Mr. Smith: Yeah.

Mr. Ken Whitebird: Do you want me to read it out loud?

Mr. Smith: Just read that to yourself, please –

Mr. Ken Whitebird: I'm sorry.

Mr. Smith: -- and then see if that refreshes your memory.

Mr. Ken Whitebird: Okay. Yes, sir, it does.

Mr. Smith: She said to you –

Mr. Ken Whitebird: She did say, " I didn't mean to kill him."

Mr. Smith: "Hit him a couple of times, but I didn't mean to kill him"?

Mr. Ken Whitebird: Yes.

Mr. Smith: Okay. She told you that she had gotten mad at him?

Mr. Ken Whitebird: Yes

Mr. Smith: Did she say why?

Mr. Ken Whitebird: For not locking the door.

Mr. Smith: Okay. Now, you said that this interview happened on the afternoon of September 16; right?

Mr. Ken Whitebird: Correct.

Mr. Smith: And at that time she didn't appear to be high or drunk or anything?

Mr. Ken Whitebird: No, she didn't appear at all.

Mr. Smith: You're not able to say whether she was high or drunk the night before?

Mr. Ken Whitebird: No, sir.

Mr. Smith: Okay. Thank you.

Mr. Smith: I pass the witness, your Honor.

The Court: Redirect.

The Court: Thank you, sir.

Ms. Austin: You said that she – you saw some injuries to her knees. Did you ask her about those injuries to her knees?

Mr. Ken Whitebird: Yes, I did.

Ms. Austin: And how did she tell you they occurred

Mr. Ken Whitebird: While having sex.

Ms. Austin: And did you try to talk with her a little more about that?

Mr. Ken Whitebird: I kind of backed off after that. I mean, I didn't –

Ms. Austin: She didn't want to give up with who or anything like that, so you –

Mr. Ken Whitebird: I didn't ask. I'll be honest with you, I just – I said, "Well, they're injuries and it's something I need to look at," but I didn't push the sex issue.

Ms. Austin: Okay. And you said that you interviewed David Elkins over the phone. Did you talk to him again later?

Mr. Ken Whitebird: Yes, I did.

Ms. Austin: Okay. So you actually interviewed another witness besides her?

Mr. Ken Whitebird: Correct. And, I apologize, I had forgotten about that.

Ms. Austin: And your partner had some involvement in this case also and did other things?

Mr. Ken Whitebird: Correct. He did the crime scene.

Ms. Austin: And CSI unit or TI unit responded to the house and did some investigation there?

Mr. Ken Whitebird: Correct.

Ms. Austin: And you weren't involved in that?

Mr. Ken Whitebird: No, ma'am.

Ms. Austin: Okay. And that's not common in – or not uncommon in homicides in Oklahoma City, is it, to have a lot of different division or departments dealing with things?

Mr. Ken Whitebird: Not on that day it wasn't uncommon at all. We were running left and right. That was the second of three.

Ms. Austin: On that day?

Mr. Ken Whitebird: On that day.

Ms. Austin: You were asked about the statement, about she didn't intend to kill him. Before she says that, though, she said she hit him a couple of times; is that right?

Mr. Ken Whitebird: That's correct.

Ms. Austin: And she's told you at least two items that she hit him with; correct?

Mr. Ken Whitebird: Correct.

Ms. Austin: And from what she told you, it was never with her hands?

Mr. Ken Whitebird: No. She was adamant she never hit him with her hands.

Ms. Austin: You said that she appeared kind of shocked he was dead, but that she kept saying she didn't understand how he could have died.

Mr. Ken Whitebird: Correct.

Ms. Austin: Did you explain to her any of his injuries or anything like that at that time or just tell her that he was – that he had passed on?

Mr. Ken Whitebird: Initially, at the first of the interview, I just told her that he had died. And, now, later on – later, when I told her she was under arrest, I explained to her, "Hitting somebody in the head can cause injuries that can cause death."

Ms. Austin: Did she appear to understand better when you told her that?

Mr. Ken Whitebird: Yeah.

Ms. Austin: Thank you.

Ms. Austin: Pass the witness.

The Court: Cross.

Mr. Smith: Nothing further from the defendant. Thank you.

The Court: All right. May this witness be excused?

Ms. Austin: Yes, sir.

The Court: All right. Detective, you may step down. Come and go as you wish, sir.

The Court: State may call its next witness.

Ms. Austin: Your Honor, at this time the State has no further witnesses. The state would, however, move to introduce State's Exhibit 1, which is a certified copy of the Medical Examiner's report in this particular case, showing the victim to be Erik Saxton; date of death, September 16, 2010. The location of death to be at the hospital, but to be transported from the location that we have heard previous testimony on. The Medical Examiner's report showing the findings of death, probable cause of death to be a subdural hematoma due to blunt force head trauma and showing that there are – the blunt force head trauma, two different areas – two different areas to the head, and that the manner of death in this particular case was homicide.

The Court: Mr. Smith?

Mr. Smith: Judge, I don't know if we got notice of the intent to use the report. However, I think in view of the fact that our only remedy for that would be to adjourn the hearing until the notice period has passed, I don't have any objection to the –

Ms. Austin: And, your Honor –

Mr. Smith: --introduction of the report other than I think we'll address the probative value of that in argument, but –

Ms. Austin: Judge – I'm sorry. I'm so sorry.

Mr. Smith: That's okay.

Ms. Austin: I don't believe the statute requires that we show notice, under 751. She said we'd have to require – to show a copy of it. I do know and I don't think Mr. Smith has seen the amended copy, where it changed the address from – the address of the injury exchanged --.

Mr. Smith: I have not seen the amended part, Judge, but, frankly, I don't know that that's – well, I have, Judge. Thank you I do have that, and I will say I did get this well in advance of the hearing, so – and, again, our only remedy would be to a brief continuance of the hearing, so I don't see the point in objecting, frankly.

The Court: Then I will show State's Exhibit 1 admitted without objection for preliminary hearing purposes only.

Ms. Austin: And I will tell the Court that the amended – the Page 1 that I'm introducing may not be the same Page 1 that he has. It is just showing that the home address of the victim was amended, as was the address of injury, because they were listed incorrectly originally on the reports.

Mr. Smith: Judge, I think what – she's referring to Page 1 of State's Exhibit 1, which is titled "Amendment to Report of Investigation." I don't think I have that, but, again, the amendment is to the home address which is the same as the address of the decedent listed in the police report. So I don't object.

The Court: So do you feel comfortable that that is the only amendment that we have as far as there's nothing substantive as far as the medical evidence is concerned?

Mr. Smith: Again, this is all I've seen. The only amendment that Page 1 of State's 1 shows is the address. I don't know of any substantive amendments that would affect the probative value of the report.

Ms. Austin: And this amendment, I will tell the Court also, was done on October 7, 2010. And the report that I believe the defense has been provided was provided subsequent to that date. We've only ever had the amended copy as far as I'm aware.

The Court: All right. So State's Exhibit 1 will be admitted without an objection. And I am concerned for future hearings, this will be State's Exhibit 1. All right. Then it will be admitted.

And with that –

Ms. Austin: Can I have just – sorry, Judge, let me look at my information to make sure.

Your Honor, there being no amendments to the information, the State would rest.

The Court: All right. State has announced rest.

Mr. Smith?

Mr. Smith: Your Honor, the defense comes now and demurs[6] generally to the State's evidence in this case. Specifically, we demur to the charge of first-degree murder. Murder in the first degree is defined as "Willful and with malice aforethought causing the death of another human being," and that is Title 21, Section 701.7A. the other sections of that statute pertain to things like child abuse, murder, felony murder, that sort of thing.

"Malice is that deliberate intention unlawfully to take away the life of a human being, manifested by external circumstances."

In this case, Judge, the only evidence before the Court is that she admitted to hitting him twice and stated that she didn't intend to kill him.

And, again, because this is under Subsection A, it's not – State hasn't shown any evidence of any of the enumerated underlying felonies that would give rise to a felony murder charge which are set forth in Subsection B of that section.

I understand for purposes of the demurer, your Honor, the evidence is considered in the light most favorable to the non-

---

[6] A demurrer is a pleading in a lawsuit that objects to or challenges a pleading filed by an opposing party. The word demur means "to object"; a demurrer is the document that makes the objection. Lawyers informally define a demurrer as a defendant saying, "So what?" to the pleading. Typically, the defendant in a case will demur to the complaint, but it is also possible for plaintiff to demur to an answer. The demurrer challenges the legal sufficiency of a cause of action in a complaint or of an affirmative defense in an answer. If a cause of action in a complaint does not state a cognizable claim (for example, the claim is nonsense) or if it does not state all the required elements, then the challenged cause of action or possibly the entire complaint can be essentially thrown out (informally speaking) at the demurrer stage as not legally sufficient. A demurrer is typically filed near the beginning of a case, in response to the plaintiff filing a complaint or the defendant answering the complaint.

moving party. In this case, it's not so much a question of the interpretation or the weight given the evidence, but rather whether there's any at all: "Without evidence of malice aforethought or deliverable intent to kill." They haven't shown that the crime of first-degree murder was committed.

If the Court considers a bindover, I'd ask the Court for a bindover on murder in the second-degree or first-degree manslaughter.

The Court: Ms. Austin?

Ms. Austin: Your Honor, I think that the evidence has shown in this case that this defendant said that she hit this victim over the head with a DVD player and a crystal ball. The intent to kill can be formed in and instant. Just because she said she didn't intend to kill him, that's obviously what she's telling the detective after she's been telling him several other things that occurred. The evidence that we have is from the medical examiner's report is this man was 4 foot 5 inches tall. The defendant is six feet tall. What else are you trying to do when you hit him over the head with a DVD player? From that evidence that's been presented, that she hit this small man over the head with a DVD player, I think that can show her intent to deliberately take the life of this man and that the evidence is sufficient.

The Court: Mr. Smith?

Mr. Smith: Stand on my argument.

The Court: All right. The demurrer will be overruled.

The Court: Any evidence on behalf of the defendant?

Mr. Smith: Not at this time, your Honor. We re-urge our demurer, move to dismiss, and we'd rest.

The Court: All right. I want to take just a moment, and I'll do that here, to review the ME's report. (Brief pause.)

The Court: All right. Having reviewed State's Exhibit 1, the Court finds that at this point there is probable cause to believe that the crime was committed and that this defendant committed the crime; therefore, she's bound over for trial. This case will be set for formal arraignment before Judge Walkley on a date and time that the lawyers will get through Judge Walkley's bailiff.

I will return State's Exhibit 1 to the State and ask that they keep it in its form as admitted here at this hearing. I noted in the record that the defendant is being held without bond. Is that correct, Mr. Smith?

Mr. Smith: Yes, sir.

The Court: And I believe Judge Tupper is the judge that entered that order; is that correct?

Mr. Smith: I don't know, your Honor.

The Court: All right. Well, is there anything else from the State?

Ms. Austin: As far as bond goes?

The Court: No. I'm not addressing bond. I just noted that she was being held without bond. I was going to ask the defendant if he had anything else, and so if he was going to request bond or ask that I set a bond, obviously I was going to determine which judge and now at what point in the case that would be a proper judge to take that to. So that's why I asked that question. I kind of anticipated it, so to speak.

But as far as this hearing is concerned, is there anything else from the State?

Ms. Austin: No, your Honor.

The Court: Anything else, Mr. Smith?

Mr. Smith: No, sir. Thank you.

And, for the record, Judge, the reason we haven't addressed the issue of bond is, as you know, this is an OIDS case. Ms. Blocker's been declared indigent, and it's, in my view, extremely unlikely that we could obtain a modification of bond that would be meaningful to her in any way.

The Court: And I didn't mean to intimate, Ms. Blocker, anything by that comment, other than it is very routine in these types of cases that a lawyer might make that request and there are certain court rules that require that request to be made before a certain judge.

And so I was kind of making a pre-emptive question under that situation. And to be honest with you, I had just – flipping through the file now while reading, I had just seen that you were being held without bond, and so that's why I asked the question. I didn't mean to intimate there was anything improper by the fact that he didn't ask. Do you understand?

The Defendant: Yes, your Honor.

The Court: All right. Then there being nothing else from either party, we'll be adjourned on this matter.

\#\#\#

So, the preliminary hearing is finally held and now it is over. I had so many questions still as I wondered why there was only one witness and one exhibit presented. At the arraignment on September 23, 2010 there were many witnesses. Knowing that an arraignment is usually the first part of the criminal procedure that occurs in a courtroom before a judge and its purpose is to provide the defendant with a reading of the crime with which he or she has been charged, I could see this being done with only one witness. But a preliminary hearing is a "trial before the trial". It is when the judge decides, not whether the defendant is "guilty" or "not guilty," but whether there is enough evidence to force the defendant to stand trial. At the preliminary hearing the judge decides whether the government has produced enough evidence to convince a reasonable jury that the defendant committed the crime(s) charged. To me, more witnesses and more evidence should have been produced.

The plea and sentencing of Clara Ann Blocker took place on Tuesday, October 5, 2010 at 1:00 PM in front of Judge Lori Walkley—20 days following her arrest on September 16. They knew by the end of that day they had the evidence and her confession that she committed the crime. I didn't understand if they had her in custody, had gathered all the evidence and had her confession, why wasn't it a slam dunk. Instead, a new PHC is scheduled for October 19 for further negotiations

\#\#\#

From April, 2011, the emails sent by me and those received were, I must admit, excessive, but being at a distance and not able to get all my answers, I became a major pest. It probably didn't help that I had a knee replacement and was on medication for pain. But, no matter what I asked or how often I sent my emails, somehow the Detective, DA and Court Reporter were able to put up with me and share what they could. One request made early on though, was denied.

An email I sent to Detective Lyndell Easley was responded to on April 19. He would say, "Not a problem at all, with the exception of releasing the police reports. I know there would be no ill intent from you concerning the reports, but releasing them in some cases could hamper an investigation, and possibly the prosecution later. This is the reason the bulk of the reports do not get released, and if we did it for you, we would have to for everyone. I am sure you understand."

I did understand. I knew when I request that he send me his interview records and details written about the crime scene that it would probably be denied, but it was worth a shot.

As to my request concerning the preliminary hearing. I was given the following details to help me understand the Preliminary Hearing Conference (PHC). Detective Easley would respond in an email.

Clara Blocker called 911 requesting an ambulance the morning of Erik's death. Uniformed officers were dispatched to the call as well, and asked Clara what had occurred. Her story seemed inconsistent, and Assaults detectives were called to the scene. Prior to beginning their investigation, Erik passed away, and my partner and I were called to investigate the homicide. Clara was transported to the Homicide Office for an interview with my partner, and initially claimed Erik had been assaulted by an unknown suspect while she was out of the apartment. At the time it was unclear if she was a suspect. The interview progressed to an interrogation, and Clara finally confessed to having hit Erik over the head with a water-filled crystal ball, and then a DVD player. My partner relayed this information to me as I conducted the scene investigation, and the evidence matched her story. I wasn't needed for the preliminary hearing, which was fortunate as I had a jury trial in a different case in Oklahoma County as the pre-lim was being held in Cleveland County. My partner did testify, and said Clara seemed confident at first, but he could tell she was VERY concerned after she was bound over for trial. I had heard a rumor a plea offer of a life sentence was made, but I have not confirmed this. As I expressed before, a plea agreement is a sure thing, and gets her in prison where a jury might fail to do so. There is also the possibility a jury could find her guilty of a lesser crime such as Murder 2, or even manslaughter. The last thing we want is for her to walk or get off with a lenient sentence. I just checked and found a trial date has not been set. Feel free to contact me if you need additional information."

On May 4, I sent another email to Detective Easley asking what he knew about Clara Blocker. He would reply that same day saying, *"Sorry, I can't answer much of that. Here is a link to her criminal convictions, if I have done this correctly. It looks like three felony convictions and one misdemeanor. The rest I don't know about.* "

Worried about the constant delay on the preliminary hearings, I again sent an email to Detective Lyndell Easley. On May 26, he responded

"I can't remember ever seeing one go on the first scheduled date without being continued. There is a first time for everything, I suppose, and Cleveland County seems more efficient than Oklahoma County if for no other reason than the caseload is lighter. I have only testified there a few times, most crimes we investigate are tried in Oklahoma County because the largest percentage of OKC limits are in Oklahoma County. So far as the plea, it is either guilty, not guilty, or no contest. The insanity is explained to a jury in an effort to find the defendant not guilty. That rarely works here, we just had one this week in OK County and the jury didn't buy it because the prosecutor was able to show they knew right from wrong, which is all that needs to be done. Remember, Clara told my partner she hit Erik, but she didn't think it was hard enough to kill him. I wouldn't worry a bit about an insanity defense, I would more expect an offer of a plea. Also remember what I explained about a plea, I think it is a good deal if it is something we can live with. I could easily see a jury reducing this to a murder 2, or even a manslaughter if they believe she didn't mean to kill Erik. Let's let this run its course and see what they will offer to plea to and do prior to making any decisions. I just re-read that last line and tried to think of a way to soften it a bit. The reality is, I have never had to go through the Hell you must be experiencing, thank God, and I can't say I know your anxiety. My relationship with this case is professional instead of personal, and I can be objective and emotionless. Doesn't mean at all that I don't care what happens, and I do worry a jury would reduce it. Think about it, the girl was intoxicated and in a fight with Erik, possibly not fully aware of what she was doing. In the heat of battle, she picked up a DVD player and struck him with it. Premeditation has no set time frame, and by law, the definition says it can be formed instantly. Nonetheless, I would guess a lot of people have had experiences in which they acted in a similar manner, but they were lucky enough no one died. We will see how it plays out.

    ###

Even after the preliminary hearing finally is held, I still have questions and more waiting. I find myself wondering if I was doing all I could. Maybe I should fight the courts in the media, I thought. Erik's case had in fact captured public attention because it had on a small scale received major coverage. So as I searched the NET and made contact with the Detective, the DA and the court reporter, it became clear to me what I should do. In Erik's case, I needed to keep the case tried in the courts because I could see no reason not to continue to believe in the way the Cleveland County, Oklahoma City, court was handling the case. I have been kept well informed and have individuals who are allowing me to contact them. I have also been told that once the case is finalized, all the records and information will be shared with me.

Yet, I need some assurance so I decide to educate myself on DA's. I found that District Attorneys are elected officials, responsible for prosecuting crimes in a designated county or district, and in order to do their job they require the cooperation of law enforcement. They also manage the office of the prosecutor, consider the facts of a case against an individual to determine if there is enough evidence to file criminal charges, and gather evidence to bring before a Grand Jury. Because of the nature of the job, the district attorney needs to have administrative as well as prosecutor skills. The criminal prosecution process is not glamorous; it entails a lot of backbreaking and often frustrating investigations, cross-checking and evidence analysis. Aside from prosecuting cases, DAs also have to manage a staff of other lawyers, called assistant district attorneys who have to be monitored in putting cases together, field investigators, researchers and legal assistants. They rely on their ADA (Assistant District Attorney) who becomes an ADA according to how much one has participated in a courtroom, preferably as the lead attorney. It is possible to become a DA without going through the ADA route, but it requires an impressive resume as a trial attorney.

Jennifer Austin, the ADA handling Erik's case is young, born in 1972. She is very familiar with the area as she lives in Oklahoma City , before that, she lived in Norman , OK from 2002 to 2006. Jennifer Austin attended Norman High School in Norman, OK and graduated with the class of 1990. I learned that she has voted in person except only once she voted by absentee election. She has a spotless record, is married and has children. From our personal connections, I am pleased with her ability and her people skills.

I then needed to know more about the public defender. I found that the Public Defender's Office provides competent, quality legal representation to indigents in Oklahoma County who are charged with all types of criminal offenses, including misdemeanors, felonies, and capital crimes. So Clara's attorney is court appointed.

David D. Smith is Representing, Clara Blocker. He is considered to be a talented trial lawyer and is a fighter for his clients. He is also noted to be caring and attentive toward his clients. I learn that David D. Smith is always a gentleman and very dedicated and thorough in his work. He has been an attorney for over 20 years. His law office is on Eufaula Street in Norman, OK and it is a privately held firm with an annual revenue of less than $500,000 and employs a staff of less than 4.

Not much, but enough to make me feel comfortable. So it is now a waiting game until August 29, 2011.
###

On May 5, 2011, Mark takes me to the Surgery Center where I am put to sleep for about five minutes so that the Surgeon can gently manipulate my knee to break down the developing scar tissue.

I did learn my lesson after that. I become a full participant in my recovery. Each day at the facility, my PT begins with them using a neuromuscular electrical stimulation (NMES). This is to help improve the muscular activation of my quadriceps by contracting my quadriceps muscle for me until I am able to do it on my own. After the surgery and a week more of the basic knee work in PT, I begin riding the stationary bicycle. I anticipate this will be a breeze since I ride bikes all the time. It is not. I am unable to pedal all the way around when I first start on the bike and it hurts so bad I want to stop trying, but I am determined to put in the effort and gradually I work the pedals forward and backwards, until I can fully pedal the bike.

None of this is easy especially because the pain is great. I am told to use the heat packs to relax the tight muscles and relax the tissues. This will decrease the pain as a result of muscle tension or spasms. It also causes vasodilatation of the blood vessels which increases circulation to the area and will help with the muscle strains, spasms, and the arthritis. I am to follow this with cold packs which will treat areas of pain and inflammation. Like they do in PT, I am to wrap the cold packs in a wet towel and apply it directly to the knee area, or I can use the ice pack holders given to me by the hospital. The cold temperature will cause vasoconstriction of the blood vessels in the area to decreases the inflammation.

I have little confidence in hot and cold doing the same for me as the meds, but I have no choice but to give it a chance. It takes a while, but it does seem to work with a little help from Ibuprofen.

I don't know how, but they have managed to get me off the medications and feeling very little pain when they tell me that I should continue my PT on my own. Since I belong to Planet Fitness they go over the equipment I use there and tell me how much I can do on each machine. I feel good and ready for this final move in my recovery.

###

At the May 19, 2011 hearing a summary of the formal arraignment appears on the website stating that the requested information had been received by the defendant and the defendant enters a plea of not guilty. The matter is set for further proceedings on the next Felony Jury Call docket on August 29, 2011 at 9:00 a.m. The states motion for Discovery is granted.

The request for discovery is to require the defendant to disclose all of the material and information within the defense attorney's possession. It state the request includes the names and addresses of any witnesses which the defense intends to call at trial, together with their relevant written or recorded statement, if any, or if none, significant summaries of any oral statement. Any witness who will be called to show that the defendant was not present at the time and place specified in the information and finally any witness the defendant will call, for testimony relating to any mental disease, mental defect, or other condition bearing upon her mental state at the time the offense was allegedly committed.

The State also requests access to inspect any and all types of info the defendant intends to offer in evidence and a report or statement as to a physical or mental examination or scientific test or experiment made in connection with this case. All of this is required to be completed at least 10 days prior to trial.

###

On August 29 is posted a Waiver of Right To Jury Trial filed by the Defendant and signed on August 26, 2011. It states that she desires to waive and give up permanently her right to have a Jury Trial in this case and to exercise the constitutional and other rights related. She states she is not under the influence of any drug or alcohol at this time and not now under the care of a mental health professional and knows of no reason why she is not completely competent to enter this waiver. She has discussed this with her lawyer and he has conferred with her and believes without reservation that she understands the right to a Jury Trial and the other rights that attach thereto, and that she is competent to waive Jury Trial unconditionally and understanding that this waiver is final. The State waives for purposes of plea only.

###

I know that Clara Blocker is entitled to a trial by jury where the jury, not the judge of the court, will determine whether the defendant is guilty or not guilty of the charged crime. I can't help but wonder why she has deferred having a jury trial and have her fate decided by the judge. I find out that there has been a lot of negative publicity and this is being called a heinous crime. Then there is her criminal record. It may be that she feels and at the advice of her lawyer, knows that the criminal issues of the trial are so terrible that they'll influence the jurors into seeking punishment regardless of the evidence.

###

On August 29 the Clara Ann Blocker case is set for September 16, 2011 at 8:30 a.m. It is noted that the parties have waived jury trial and have been instructed to obtain a date for a Disposition Hearing. Since she has waived the jury trial the Disposition Hearing is the sentencing stage of the proceedings, and its purpose is to provide a program of treatment, training, and rehabilitation. Judge Instanter is notified and the Disposition Hearing is set for October 27, 2011 at 2:00 p.m.

Then it starts getting confusing again when on September 28, it is noted that David D. Smith is Clara Blockers lawyer, though he, I thought was her attorney all along. The signature though on previous records appears to be David L. Smith.

So out on the internet I go and search for an attorney, David L. Smith in Oklahoma City. I find one so now I know that Clara has either fired him or he has decided not to try her case. From this point on, David D. Smith appears as her attorney.

Then, on the heels of this document comes one on October 27, 2011 stating that the Disposition Hearing is stricken in lieu of a competency to be filed. It gets me wondering if this has something to do with the attorney reassignment, but I cannot get answers to that question. In any case, the Disposition Hearing is moved to November 10, 2011 at 2:00 p.m. The Notice of Application for Determination of Competency is filed on October 31, 2011

I am confused, because I am unsure if what is happening in the background. At this point it seems that Clara Blocker is trying to find a way to beat the charge of murder. Can she do it? Is there any way she can end up not serving a life sentence. I need answers so I send emails.

###

From: Me on Thursday, May 19, 2011 6:46 AM To: Jane Glenn Cannon

Just a reminder that the arraignment for Clara Ann Blocker is scheduled for 5/19/2011 at 8:30 a.m. your time. Will be interested in hearing your version of how it goes.

From: Jane Cannon on Date: Wed, 1 Jun 2011

Apparently, Clara Blocker's arraignment was reset until 9 a.m. Aug. 29. I'm sorry I was so slow getting back to you about it. I've had a bunch to do and kept forgetting to check on when it was reset.

From Me: Thursday, July 14, 2011 5:43 AM To: Jane Glenn Cannon

Hi Jane, I am planning on being there at the arraignment in August and hope I get a chance to meet you. I don't know if you are aware that I am a writer and so this will be my next book. Only, I will have a hard time with the research from my location and would like to ask you if you would like to co-author this book with me. I previously wrote a book about Erik's life that was released at the Little People of America's annual convention and would want to include them again in promotionals as I have always supported the organization. I want Erik to be remembered and I want to "write" what has happened to him out of my head. Recording it will allow only the good memories to remain since this event will be recorded. If this is of interest to you, I would love to collaborate. Let me know your thoughts on this.

From: Jane Glenn Cannon on Wednesday, July 20, 2011 11:08 AM

Sorry I took so long to answer. It's been kind of a busy summer. I may be on vacation when Erik is arraigned. I haven't checked the date for sure, but I will be gone from Aug. 4 through Aug. 11. I honestly don't think I have time to co-author a book, but I would be glad to meet with you and talk about it, or give you any help I can. I'm a good editor, so maybe I can help you in that respect. Or, I might like to co-author, depending on the time frame. We can get together when you're here unless it is while I'm on vacation. Let me know the dates you'll be here. Jane

From Me: Wednesday, July 20, 2011 2:16 PM   To: Jane Glenn Cannon

Thanks for getting back to me. We will be in Oklahoma from the 27th through the 30th. If there is time during that time period or a day or two before or after, we can extend the time. I definitely would love to meet you and see if we can work together on this as I want to be sure to get all the facts straight. With email it is easy to send the manuscript back and forth for either editing or co-authoring. I think it can work. Nita From: Jane Glenn Cannon on Wednesday, July 20, 2011 4:47 PM

Sounds great. I'll be here those dates, so I'm sure we will have time to meet. From Me: Tuesday, August 30, 2011 1:14 PM To: Jones, Kerrin

Yesterday was the Jury Trial sounding docket. Can you tell me what happened. I went to the case file online and there is nothing out there. Nita

From: Jones, Kerrin on Tuesday, August 30, 2011 6:31 PM

It was set for the 27th of October for plea. Jennifer Austin is going to call and fill you in. The defendant has decided to no longer fight the charges and admit to what she did. I will be flying you and Erik's father here to speak at the sentencing. That day will probably not be the same as the plea date, they will do it in 2 different hearings as far as I know. I will check on all of that and remind Jennifer tomorrow to call you.

From: Me on Thursday, September 01, 2011 5:22 AM To: Jones, Kerrin

I stayed in all day waiting for the call from Jennifer Austin but it never came yesterday (Aug 31). On August 13 you wrote you should be receiving a copy of the PH transcript within the next few weeks, and will make me a copy as soon as you get it. I am still waiting for this information and was wondering if I could do anything to speed this up. I know you are busy and I understand that, but it's hard for me to keep waiting and not knowing. Please see what you can do on these matters. I also sent an email to verify that you are including both the plea date of October 27 and the sentencing which we don't have a date yet in bringing us there. We want to be there for both of these. Nita

From: Jones, Kerrin on Thursday, September 01, 2011 5:14 PM

I'm sorry she has not called you yet, I will make contact with her again. Please talk to Jennifer about the PH transcript as well. I have not had a copy to copy to send to you and she can explain why. If the plea and sentencing are on separate days, the State of Oklahoma will only allow me to fly you in for the sentencing. Jennifer will be able to explain this further when you speak with her.

From: Jones, Kerrin on Friday, September 02, 2011 12:40 PM

Jennifer said she will have time on Wednesday a 10:30 am (our time) to block off to talk with you. Will that work for you? Also, when I told you that we would be able to make you a copy of the transcript, we were under the belief that we would need it for a jury trial. Now that the defendant is pleading guilty we no longer require it, so therefore the State will not pay for a copy. I will find out how much it is and get back with you so that you may decide whether or not you would like to purchase yourself a copy.

###

On Wednesday, September 7, 2011 I received a call from Jennifer Austin of the DA office. She informs me it seems that Clara's lawyer says that she has given up which means she is willing to not go to trial and accept life for sure, but maybe not life without parole. If she takes life she must serve 85% of a life sentence which would be 45 years total and means 38 years served. Since she is 39 she would be 77 or more when she got out. Because the taped interview with Inspector Ken Whitebird was not thorough in that he did not get Clara to say why, when, how she did it, there is nothing to fight with against her statement. To that add the fact that she called 911 and sounded remorseful and that the jury in Oklahoma can include anyone with a license, so she may get manslaughter. Manslaughter would be only 20 years.

Clara wants to give a statement which is thought will be an apology for the murder and this is an exception because most murderers do not do this. Two things in the tape interviews that are odd, one is that she keeps saying she didn't use her hands and the other is that she didn't mean to kill him.

Since she is entering a plea, she can't get an appeal. If it goes to manslaughter she can keep appealing over and over again. Murderers do a post-conviction thing whereby they give reasons why they should be released.

I ask her to explain what she means by a plea and Jennifer replies that the defendant Clara entered a 'not guilty' plea so the plea bargain was negotiated between the defendant and the prosecutor's office to get her to plead guilty. Of course in order to change her plea she expects something in return from us. This means for us that the defendant will plead guilty to murder and in return she wants life with parole instead of life without parole.

I ask why the competency hearing.

Jennifer says that the competency hearing will determine whether the defendant is competent to stand trial and competent to enter a plea. A person must meet certain requirements for competency in order to be able to aid in their defense, and if a person is declared incompetent, they cannot enter a plea to a criminal charge or be tried for it so this must be done.

Now what should I do? I have no idea what is the right thing to do. I have been told I will be informed of everything; what jail she is in, anything that happens to her, if she dies, etc. for the rest of her life. I want her to pay for what she did, of that I am sure.

I reached out again. Jane Cannon would reply: "I will try to find out. I didn't go. I was off. My son had a medical emergency. I'll be able to find out sometime this week. "

I would email Jane later, "Yes, I got an email finally on this. I was also told that it may take two pleas before it is settled, but right now they will make arrangements for me to fly down. I was scheduled to have a second knee replacement done on Oct 14 but I cancelled and will reschedule once I have found the closure I am hoping this will bring to me. How is your son? Did everything to well?".

Jane would come back again, "Yes, thanks for asking. He had a seizure over the weekend and cracked his skull, but it is healing now and he's on better medicine than before. I hope to meet you when you're here. And I hope they are not too lenient on her. Judge Walkley is pretty strict when it comes to violent crime, so that should help."

The disposition date is set for October 27 at 2 p.m. Detective Lyndell Easley would report back to me saying, "I was not at the hearing, but looking on OSCN, it seems a plea deal has been met. There is a document showing she waived her right to a jury trial, and a hearing is set for 10/27. I have not heard what the recommendation is for time to serve, but as I have stated before, a plea ensures prison time and you never know what a jury will do."

###

Then it is cleared and I understand. I understand why the plea bargain and I understand why not taking the case to trial is a good idea. Right now with her willingness to accept life with parole, we are getting the best possible sentence without fear of having it overturned in court. Before the phone call I was feeling as though Erik was not getting justice, that anyone hearing the case would give her death or life in prison. I would have been wrong.

I begin researching what I can find in the Oklahoma Laws. I begin a search on my own. I first try to determine what is a life sentence and find that in Oklahoma a life sentence means you must serve life, or 99 years whichever comes first. You can get parole after 1/3rd of your sentence has been served unless parole was specifically denied, or other factors that are too in depth to follow so I just briefed through the Oklahoma Statute 57-332.7. Yet in further research I am unsure of that 1/3rd since Jennifer has said 85% of sentence must be served. This doesn't pan out and I assume I have written the figures she shared in our conversation incorrectly.

I find a .pdf file entitled, "The Service Of Sentences And Credit Applicable To Offenders In Custody Of The Oklahoma Department Of Corrections. This told of credits given in certain cases. The part of interest to me was the section on Life Sentences:

"Life Sentence No deductions will be credited to any inmate serving a sentence of Life imprisonment; however, per 57 O.S. 138, a complete record of the inmate's participation in work, school, vocational training, or other approved programs is maintained. If a Life sentence is ever commuted or modified to a determinate sentence, the recorded credit would apply as a reduction."

"Offenses Required to Serve 85% of Sentence Effective March 1, 2000, 21 O.S. 13.1 provides that offenders who commit certain crimes on or after such date, must serve 85% of their sentence of imprisonment before becoming eligible for parole consideration, earned credits, or any type of credit that might reduce the length of the sentence to less than 85%. The crimes are Murder I, Robbery with a Dangerous Weapon, Rape I, Arson I, Burglary I, Bombs and Explosives Violations, Child Abuse, Forcible Sodomy, Child Pornography, Parental Consent to Child Pornography, Child Prostitution, and Lewd Molestation of a Child. Effective July 1, 2001, 21 O.S. 13.1 was amended to include the following crimes: Murder II, Manslaughter I, Poisoning with Intent to Kill, Shooting with Intent to Kill, Assault and Battery with a Deadly Weapon, Use of a Vehicle to Facilitate Use of a Firearm/Crossbow/Weapon, Assault with Intent to Kill, Conjoint Robbery, Robbery I. Effective July 1, 2001, 63 O.S. 2-401 was amended to provide that offenders convicted of the crime of Aggravated Manufacture of CDS must serve 85% of their sentence of imprisonment before becoming eligible for parole consideration, earned credits, or any type of credit that might reduce the length of the sentence to less than 85%. Effective March 8, 2002, 21 O.S. 13.1 was amended to include the crime of Abuse, Neglect, or Financial Exploitation by Caretaker of a Vulnerable Adult who is a resident of a nursing facility. Effective November 1, 2007, 21 O.S. 13.1 was amended to include the crime of Aggravated Trafficking, 63 O.S. 2-415. Effective November 1, 2011, 21 O.S., Section 13.1 was amended to include aggravated assault and battery upon any person defending another person from assault and battery. "

It can become quite confusing which way to go, but I am determine to understand. In my search I come across a case that took place in May 2011.

###

"Self-Defense or Murder? Oklahoma Case Sparks Debate May 30, 2011

By Clayton Sandell, Sabrina Parise And Katie Kindelan

Pharmacist Claims Self Defense

A story of crime and punishment that is dividing an Oklahoma community has now entered the online world, raising questions about what is self-defense and first-degree murder.

The debate stems from the life sentence an Oklahoma City, Okla., jury handed down to pharmacist Jerome Ersland on May 26 for a first-degree murder conviction in the killing of 16 year-old Antwun Parker.

Ersland's attorneys told jurors throughout the murder trial that their client had acted in self-defense when he shot Parker six times during an attempted robbery at his Oklahoma City pharmacy. Prosecutors, meanwhile, argued Ersland went too far.

"This defendant was absolutely not defending himself or anyone else," Assistant District Attorney Jennifer Chance told jurors during closing arguments Thursday.

Defense attorney Irven Box asked jurors to close their eyes and imagine what they would do in the same situation.

"He eliminated the armed robber," Box said.

After 3.5 hours of deliberation, the jury — eight women and four men — recommended a life sentence."

###

I next come across the fact that Oklahoma City has the death penalty and I think I remember being told they did not. I see what I can find on this.

"The current death penalty law in Oklahoma was enacted in 1977 by the Oklahoma Legislature. The method to carry out the execution is by lethal injection. The original death penalty law in Oklahoma called for executions to be carried out by electrocution. In 1972 the U.S. Supreme Court ruled unconstitutional the death penalty as it was then administered."

"Oklahoma has executed a total of 191 men and 3 women between 1915 and 2014 at the Oklahoma State Penitentiary. Eighty-two were executed by electrocution, one by hanging (a federal prisoner) and 111 by lethal injection. The last execution by electrocution took place in 1966. The first execution by lethal injection in Oklahoma occurred on September 10, 1990, when Charles Troy Coleman, convicted in 1979 of Murder 1st Degree in Muskogee County was executed.   On December 16, 2010, Oklahoma became the first American state to use pentobarbital in the execution of John David Duty. "

###

One thing leads to another and I review the cases that went to the death penalty in Oklahoma.

###

Wanda Jean Allen in Oklahoma on January 11, 2001- She was sentenced to death in 1989 for killing her lover, Gloria Leathers, in Oklahoma City in 1988. The two women, who had met in prison, had a turbulent relationship. Leathers' death followed a protracted argument between the couple which began at a local shop, continued at their home, and culminated outside a police station. Allen maintained she had acted in self-defense, claiming that Leathers had struck her in the face with a hand rake during the confrontation at the house, and that outside the police station Leathers had again come at her with the rake. Allen shot Leathers. The wound to Allen's face from the rake was still visible when she was photographed in jail. Later in 1995, A psychologist conducted a comprehensive evaluation of Wanda Jean Allen found "clear and convincing evidence of cognitive and sensori-motor deficits and brain dysfunction" possibly linked to an adolescent head injury.

Marilyn Plantz in Oklahoma on May 1, 2001 - Plantz hired her teenage boyfriend Clifford Bryson and his friend William McKimble to kill her husband for about $300,000 in life insurance. Entering his home after work, he was ambushed by Bryson and McKimble and beaten with bats while Plantz and kids were asleep in bed. Plantz got up and instructed them to "burn him" to make it look like an accident. They drove him to deserted location, doused him and his pickup with gasoline and set it on fire. McKimble pled to Life and testified. Plantz and Bryson were tried jointly. Bryson was executed in 2000.

Lois Nadean Smith in Oklahoma on December 2, 2001- Smith was convicted of killing her son's 21- year old ex-girlfriend, Cindy Baillie in July 1982. Baillie was shot nine times and stabbed in the throat. Authorities said Smith and her son, Greg, picked up Baillie the morning of the killing. Smith then confronted her about rumors that she had threatened to have her son killed. Lois Smith's attorneys said she was trying to protect her son and was under the influence of alcohol and drugs at the time.

Prior to the modern era of the U.S. death penalty beginning in 1976, the last female offender executed was Elizabeth Ann Duncan by California on August 8, 1962.

Death sentences and executions for female offenders are rare in comparison to such events for male offenders. Women are more likely to drop out of the death-penalty system the further it progresses: The stats are that women account for about 1 in 10 (10%) murder arrests; women account for only 1 in 50 (2.1%) death sentences imposed at the trial level; * women account for only 1 in 67 (1.8%) persons presently on death row; and women account for only 1 in 100 (.9%) persons actually executed in the modern era.

###

I spend hours each day gathering as much knowledge as I can so that I don't suggest anything that would change the life sentence. The more I learn, the more I realize that even if she was to get a death sentence it would certainly go to trial and a jury may be reluctant to take a life since the information she has withheld is important for a jury to make a decision. I feel more confident in agreeing to life with parole.

###

On October 31, 2011 the defendant's lawyer, David D. Smith filed the following Application for Determination of Competency.

###

In The District Court Of Cleveland County
State Of Oklahoma
State Of Oklahoma

Plaintiff

Vs.

Clara Ann Blocker

Defendant

Comes Now David D. Smith, court-appointed counsel for the above named Defendant, and applies to the Court for a determination of the present competency of the said Defendant, and respectfully shows the Court:

1. The said Defendant advises that she has a long history of mental illness and has from time to time received treatment for the same;

2. The said Defendant is unable to state what diagnoses have been made during those periods of time;

3. The Defendant does not appear to understand the nature of the present proceedings against her. In particular, the Defendant does not appear to comprehend that certain facts urged by her do not constitute a defense to the charge, or the potential consequences of proceeding to trail without a viable defense;

4. At this time there is reason to doubt whether this Defendant is competent to undergo further proceedings,

Wherefore, premises considered, Movant prays the Court to proceed under 22 O.S. §§1175.2 et. Seq. to determine whether the Defendant is competent.

This scares me. I think she is trying to get off by reason of insanity. She had said in the interrogation that she was no stranger to the system. Could this be what she is doing. I go to the internet and looked up the Oklahoma Title 22 law.

"§22-1175.2. Application for determination of competency - Service - Notice - Suspension of criminal proceedings.

A. No person shall be subject to any criminal procedures after the person is determined to be incompetent except as provided in Sections 1175.1 through 1175.8 cf this title. The question of the incompetency of a person may be raised by the person, the attorney for the person whose competency is in question, or the district attorney, by an application for determination of competency. The application for determination of competency shall allege that the person is incompetent to undergo further proceedings, and shall state facts sufficient to raise a doubt as to the competency of the person. The court, at any time, may initiate a competency determination on its own motion, without an application, if the court has a doubt as to the competency of the person.

If the court so initiates such an application, it may appoint the district attorney for the purpose of proceeding with the application. If the district attorney opposes the application of the court, and by reason of a conflict of interest could not represent the court as applicant, then the court shall appoint private counsel. Said private counsel shall be reasonably compensated by the court fund.

B. A copy of the application for determination of competency and a notice, as hereinafter described, shall be served personally at least one (1) day before the first hearing on the application for a competency determination. The notice shall contain the following information:

1. The definition provided by Section 1175.1 of this title of competency and incompetency;

2. That, upon request, the hearing on the application may be conducted as a jury trial as provided in Section 1175.4 of this title;

3. That the petitioner and any witnesses identified in the application may offer testimony under oath at the hearings on the petition and that the defendant may not be called to testify against the defendant's will, unless the application is initiated by the defendant;

4. That if the person whose competency is in question does not have an attorney, the court will appoint an attorney for the person who shall represent the person until final disposition of the case;

5. That if the person whose competency is in question is indigent or poor, the court will pay the attorney fees; and

6. That the person whose competency is in question shall be afforded such other rights as are guaranteed by state and federal law and that such rights include a trial by jury, if demanded. The notice shall be served upon the person whose competency is in question, upon the person's father, mother, husband, or wife or, in their absence, someone of the next of kin, of full age, if any said persons are known to be residing within the county, and upon any of said relatives residing outside of the county, and within the state, as may be ordered by the court, and also upon the person with whom the person whose competency is in question may reside, or at whose house the person may be. The person making such service shall make affidavit of the same and file such notice, with proof of service, with the district court. This notice may be served in any part of this state.

C. Any criminal proceedings against a person whose competency is in question shall be suspended pending the determination of the competency of the person.

Added by Laws 1980, c. 336, § 2, emerg. eff. June 25, 1980. Amended by Laws 1983, c. 104, § 1, eff. Nov. 1, 1983; Laws 2000, c. 421, § 3, eff. Nov. 1, 2000."

###

All I can do is wait for the report of the competency that is being done by Shawn Roberson, Ph.D. and hope that Judge Walkley rules she is competent.

It's like a snowball gathering more and more snow. It seems that one thing leads to another. Now I find myself wanting to learn more about The Honorable Judge Lori Walkley. From my contacts in Oklahoma City I hear nothing but good, yet I do a search to see if I can find out more. I do.

Lori Walkley won her appointment with 64.45% of the vote. She was appointed by Governor Brad Henry in 2003, and elected in 2006 and 2010. Walkley received both her bachelor's and J.D.

from the University of Oklahoma Prior to her judicial appointment, and worked as a trial attorney before her election to this post.

In searching further I found this transcript form the Norman Transcript group.

"District Judge Lori M. Walkley has announced that she is seeking re-election to her position as district judge in the 21st Judicial District. The District includes Cleveland, McClain and Garvin counties.

Walkley was appointed district judge by Gov. Brad Henry in 2003 and was elected unopposed in 2006. In 2006 and again in 2009, Walkley was elected chief judge.

"Prior to my service on the court, I was a trial attorney in Norman and Oklahoma City. That legal experience and my subsequent 6 1/2 years on the bench confirm what I have always believed — that there is no substitute for court related experience to ensure that the justice system works for everyone," Walkley said.

Walkley is an instructor for judicial seminars that train judges throughout the state and has been a faculty member of the National Judicial College. She is the education chairman of the Oklahoma Judicial Conference. Walkley served two terms as vice president of the Oklahoma Judicial Conference and is the only trial court member of the Supreme Court Policy Committee.

"My work as a trial judge has been the most challenging yet rewarding aspect of my legal career," Walkley said. "I am acutely aware that each case that comes before me represents an individual or a family. At all times, I strive to apply the law to that individual case evenly and fairly."

Walkley handles approximately 1,400 cases each year in the areas of criminal matters, civil disputes and family law. She is particularly proud of the programs she developed to help cases move through the system more quickly and to help reduce jail overcrowding in Cleveland County.

Receiving her undergraduate degree as well as her law degree from the University of Oklahoma, Walkley is a longtime resident of Norman. She served as president of the Cleveland County Bar Association and has been active in the Oklahoma Bar Association, serving on the Continuing Education Commission and as an editor of the Oklahoma Bar Journal. She is a former member of the Norman Children's Right Commission and a former board member for the Center for Children and Families.

Walkley has been married to her husband, Bryan Walkley, for 17 years. They have three daughters, ages 21, 15 and 8. Judge Walkley stays busy being a "soccer, softball and golf mom." The Walkleys' have participated in Habitat for Humanity and Cleveland County Bar Foundation charitable functions as well as various disaster relief programs, church activities and small groups."

After this, I am confident that this is the best judge for Erik's case.

###

We make it through the holiday season and I pray that before another Thanksgiving or Christmas passes, my son will have justice.

I did everything I could to educate myself and now I wonder about this lengthy time period, or if it was the normal way these proceedings go. I wonder if I should be worried that something isn't right and there are doubts of any kind that are holding the case up. At this point I know there is nothing more I can do except keep on top of what is happening in Oklahoma City by visiting the site and reviewing any documentation.

###

So what do I do. Law & Order I watch with a passion as its format was to have the first half hour be the investigation of a crime (usually murder) and apprehension of a suspect by the Police Department homicide detectives and the second half was the prosecution of the defendant by the District Attorney's Office. Because this show was based on real cases it drew me in. 48 Hours was another one to watch because it presents the stories of real crimes recounted entirely by the victims and people who are friends of the victims of crimes. And I watched Criminal Minds probably because it helped to understand how the mind works and this show provided me with that insight as they profiled the criminals.

Still I needed direct answers from the source as I am afraid she might walk. So, working myself into a panic I start with the emails and phone calls.

I had been told at times when I tried to reach the Detective or the DA, that they were very busy. I checked it out on the internet and found that indeed the police and the courts were keeping busy. The FBI reported crime rates were down across the U.S. in the first half of 2010, but rates in Oklahoma City rose over the same time period in some categories. On the FBI Crime in the U S Report tables, Oklahoma City was dealing with 5, 304 violent crimes and 54 murders in 2010, 5,108 violent crimes and 58 murders in 2011 and later I would learn that these increased to 5,474 violent crimes and 85 murders in 2012.

I thought, I could ease up on them some, but I still needed answers.

###

I began to track some of the cases in Oklahoma and came across one about a missing man.

"Missing Oklahoma man, a Bill Dwayne, It seems that Mr. Shipley withdrew several thousand dollars from his bank account in July as he prepared to leave for Arkansas to paint an Arby's restaurant. He never made it to the job, and the last time anybody reported seeing him was on July 19, 2011. Since his work typically caused him to make frequent trips out of state Shipley wasn't reported missing until Aug. 20 and shortly afterwards the police found one of Shipley's trucks in south Oklahoma City, abandoned in an apartment complex parking lot. Then investigators caught a break viewing a video surveillance tape showing a stocky white man in his 50s or 60s using Shipley's credit cards at several metro-area businesses yet six months since Shipley was last seen, the case came to a standstill. One year later, Bill Shipley's parents are offering a $4,000 reward for information about his whereabouts."

"On Nov. 2, 2010, a woman's badly beaten body was found in a closet in her northwest Oklahoma City home she shared with her husband and child. Julie Mitchell, 34, was found by her stepson. Her 13-month-old daughter was found unharmed in a blood next to her mother's body. Mitchell's body was found around 10:30 p.m. in the master bedroom. The state medical examiner concluded that she died of blunt force trauma to the head and autopsy report showed she had four front teeth missing, a broken rib, a shattered skull a broken nose and jaw and 25 large cuts to her scalp in the attack that ended her life. Her husband, Teddy Mitchell, was traveling to California when the body was discovered and he was called to give testimony before a multicounty grand jury. The members of the state of Oklahoma Grand Jury spent 47 days over 18 months, investigating allegations of criminal conduct. Thousands of subpoenas were issued and hundreds of witnesses were called. Although this case remains unsolved, investigators continue to follow leads. This case was still ongoing.

Through investigation, detectives identified Mr. Dan Lee as a suspect in the murder of Marquis Lewis in Oklahoma City on May 25, 2011 just before midnight at the Willow Cliff apartments in the 5400 block of Willow Cliff Rd. The victim Marquis Lewis was found dead outside on the grounds of the complex.. Patrol officers located Mr. Lee and took him into custody without incident. He was interviewed by Homicide investigators, and subsequently booked into the Oklahoma County Jail on 1 count of Murder I on 5/27/2011. Investigators believe that some type of altercation occurred just before Danny Lee shot the victim. Dan "

###

There were others, but these two stood out because they happened during the same time period that I have been dealing with my son's murder. The difference is that two are unsolved and the other, like my son's case the murderer has not stated why they did it.

There were so many cases and so many would remain unsolved. If I were to be truthful, I found myself thinking that I indeed had been lucky because Erik's murderer had been caught, confessed and was in jail. I should thank this DA, and the detectives for managing to solve this case so quickly, and I was thankful, but I have seen on television, read in the paper and viewed on the internet that even cases with the evidence and the confession, can also lead to an unsatisfactory conviction or, God forbid, a release.

It may sound cruel to find some peace knowing of others sufferings, but it was true. These cases helped me realize that not all murders were solved immediately. Not all cases had a defendant being held for the crime and answering for their loss. I at least had that.

CHAPTER 18: THE PSYCH REVIEW

Psychology is concerned with how people perceive the world around them and how they react to it, how they grow and how they learn, and how they relate to others and function in groups. It is about how people think, feel, and behave. That is the gist of it, but when ordered by a court, a psychological evaluation is much more.

In most cases this is done by a forensic psychologists, who provide a psychological assessment of individuals who are involved, in one way or another, with the legal system. Therefore, a forensic psychologists requires training in law and forensic psychology.

A common standard is whether the person knew what he/she was doing was wrong. "Insanity" is not a psychological term but a legal one. The forensic psychologist has to determine not how the person is functioning at the present moment, but his/her mental state at the time of the crime and in order to do this, a forensic psychologist's work is retrospective and must rely on third-party information, collateral contacts and written communications (e.g., statements made at the time of the crime).

###

To murder someone in cold blood leads to the assumption that there must be something mentally wrong with the person who committed the crime. It is no different in this case and Clara Blocker undergoes a psych evaluation.

January 12, 2012 arrives and the lawyers appear in court for the status conference, but there is not a competency report filed. So the judge orders that in 5 days she is to be in receipt of the competency report and sets the next status conference for February 16, 2012 at 3:30 p.m.

At the Status conference, the competency evaluation is still pending so the matter is again set for yet another status conference on March 15, 2012 at 2:15 p.m.

Finally the competency report is completed on March 6 and filed on April 17. The contents of the report and the research necessary to complete supports the extensive amount of time required before it is finally filed.

###

COMPETENCY REPORT

Oklahoma Department of Mental Health And Substance Abuse Services, Oklahoma Forensic Center

March 6, 2012

The Honorable Lori Walkley, Judge of the District Court, Cleveland County Courthouse   201 S. Jones Avenue Norman, Oklahoma 73069

Re: Blocker, Clara Ann , Case No. CF-2010-1390

Dear Judge Walkley:

Pursuant to your Court Order I have examined Ms. Blocker on an outpatient basis and have arrived at conclusions regarding her adjudicative competency.

METHODS OF EVALUATION:

1. Review of the Order for Competency Examination dated November 10, 2011 from the Cleveland County District Court.

2. Review of the Application for Determination of Competency, filed October 31, 2011 in the Cleveland County District Court.

3. Review of available information regarding the alleged offense, including the criminal complaint information, Enhancement Page regarding prior convictions, and a Probable Cause Affidavit by Inspector K. Ken Whitebird.

4. Review of Ms. Blocker's prior convictions according to the Oklahoma State Courts Network database (www.oscn.net).

5. Review of this examiner's (Dr. Shawn Roberson) prior competency report on Ms. Blocker (Oklahoma County CF-2009-5336) dated December 7, 2009.

6. Records check regarding Ms. Blocker with Griffin Memorial Hospital (Norman, Oklahoma).
7. Records check regarding Ms. Blocker with the Oklahoma Forensic Center.
8. Review of Ms. Blocker's available records from the Oklahoma County Crisis Intervention Center dated July 23, 2009 to July 28,2009.
9. Telephone interview on March 6, 2012 of Cindy Bilyea, R.N., Cleveland County Detention Center (CCDC) medical staff.
10. Evaluation of Ms. Blocker conducted by Shawn Roberson, Ph.D. (and observed by Ravindesjit Singh, M.D.) on March 5, 2012 at CCDC, totaling approximately one hour, thirty-five minutes and including:
- Clinical interview
- Competency examination
- Test of Memory Malingering
- Structured Interview of Reported Symptoms, Second Edition

CRIMINAL ALLEGATIONS AND REASON FOR REFERRAL: According to the criminal complaint information Ms. Blocker is charged with murder in the first degree. On or about or between September 15th and 16th, 2010 she allegedly struck the victim with objects causing blunt force trauma to the head, resulting in his death. According to the Application for Determination of Competency filed by Ms. Blocker's attorney, David Smith, he questioned his client's competency because "The said Defendant advises that she has a long history of mental illness and has from time to time received treatment for the same ... The said Defendant is unable to state what diagnoses have been made during those periods of time ... the Defendant does not appear to comprehend that certain facts urged by her do not constitute a defense to the charge, or the potential consequences of proceeding to trial without a viable defense."

INFORMED CONSENT: Ms. Blocker was informed (in simple language) that she was being evaluated to determine if she was competent for adjudication. Additionally, she was told that the interview was not private and the usual doctor-patient relationship did not exist. She was informed that a report would be prepared and submitted to the referring court. It was also explained that the report would be distributed to both the prosecuting and defense attorneys, and could be used in legal proceedings. Ms. Blocker's responses indicated that she understood the information provided to her.

COLLATERAL INFORMATION:

Criminal history: According to the enhancement page regarding prior convictions, as well as a search of Ms. Blocker's criminal history via the Oklahoma State Courts Network database (www.oscn.net). she has the following convictions:

Oklahoma County:

CF -2009-5336: Distribution of controlled dangerous substance (cocaine).

CF-2001-2626: Robbery with a dangerous weapon.

Garvin County:

CF-2007-260: Possession of a controlled dangerous substance.

CM-2007-589: Unlawful Possession of a Controlled Dangerous Substance

The issue of Ms. Blocker's competency was only raised in her 2009 Oklahoma County case. As will be noted later in this report, I evaluated her in that case and the results indicated she was competent for adjudication. She was subsequently deemed competent by the Court and convicted. In both of her Garvin County cases it was noted that "Defendant raises possible mental health concerns and advised that defendant has not been taking her prescribed medications for several months. By agreement of parties [the preliminary hearing was moved] so that defendant may resume taking her prescribed medications before proceeding further." However, she was never evaluated for adjudicative competency.

Records check: According to the medical records department at Griffin Memorial Hospital Ms. Blocker has no history of treatment or evaluation at their facility. Aside from this examiner's prior competency evaluation of Ms. Blocker in Oklahoma County during 2009, she had no other contact with the Oklahoma Forensic Center or their staff.

Oklahoma County Crisis Intervention Center (OCCIC) records: OCCIC records indicated that Ms. Blocker was brought to OCCIC in July 2009 from St. Anthony's Hospital by police after she claimed she was suicidal with a plan to walk out into traffic. She was admitted for several days of treatment and complained of hallucinations (i.e., sensory experiences in the absence of external stimuli) directing her to harm herself and complained of stress "due to her girlfriend going to prison." She also indicated that she had relapsed into using crack cocaine and heroin and was observed to have signs of physical withdrawal from heroin during her treatment. During her treatment she reportedly threatened to assault her roommate. Following several days her mood reportedly improved and she no longer voiced suicidal ideation or intent. She was discharged with medication and a follow up appointment at Northcare. Her discharge diagnoses included "Mood disorder, NOS [not otherwise specified]," "Polysubstance Dep" [dependence], and "BPD" [borderline personality disorder]. She was judged to have average range intelligence.

Competency report (by Dr. Shawn Roberson) in Oklahoma County, CF-2009-5336: I evaluated Ms. Blocker in December 2009 and opined that she was competent for adjudication. During the examination Ms. Blocker reported a long history of behavioral problems since childhood, mental health treatment as an adult with diagnoses of bipolar disorder and schizophrenia, and significant substance abuse. Ms. Blocker was obviously familiar with mental health terminology and continually suggested she should be transferred to a treatment center as an alternative to incarceration. Ms. Blocker's statements were rational, coherent, and reality-based throughout the evaluation. She displayed no signs of mania or psychosis, but it was noted that based upon her description of anger control problems and past aggression she likely had personality disorder traits and may become aggressive when angry with others. It was opined that Ms. Blocker did not meet the

Oklahoma State statutory criteria for inpatient psychiatric treatment and it appeared uncertain if she even had a genuine underlying mental illness. It should be noted that in 2009 Ms. Blocker provided some information which was highly inconsistent with her reported history during the current evaluation in 2012. For example, in 2009 she claimed she had experienced auditory hallucinations since she was 8 years old; whereas now she reported that these symptoms did not occur until early adulthood. She suggested that she had "two personalities" inside of her, the other of which was named "Tigger"; she claimed no "multiple personalities" during this evaluation. Ms. Blocker suggested that her prior hospitalization at OCCIC occurred because she attempted to "jump out of my girlfriend's car" during a suicide attempt; whereas OCCIC records indicated she only made suicidal threats and had stated her girlfriend was actually in prison at the time.

Cleveland County Detention Center (CCDC) information: Cindy Bilyea, R.N., indicated that Ms. Blocker's behavior was generally appropriate, though she did exhibit emotional volatility at times. Ms. Bilyea stated that on one day Ms. Blocker may appear normal, laughing and joking, and the next day appear depressed and crying. She stated that Ms. Blocker requests to see the jail's psychiatrist every time he is present (he is at the jail only intermittently) and often requests to have her medications changed. Ms. Bilyea stated that Ms. Blocker has not exhibited any odd or strange behavior and showed no signs of confusion or being out of touch with reality. She indicated that Ms. Blocker occasionally expresses self-injurious thoughts and had been placed in March 6, medical for observation, but has not engaged in any self-injurious behavior. Ms. Bilyea conveyed that Ms. Blocker had period of aggression where she had thrown cellmates belongings out of the cell and had been in several physical fights with other inmates, requiring "lock down" at some points. Ms. Bilyea listed Ms. Blocker's current medications as Propanolol (to treat hypertension; 20 mg., twice daily); Risperdal (antipsychotic; 3 mg., twice daily); and Amitriptyline (antidepressant; 300 mg., once daily).

CURRENT MENTAL STATUS AND CLINICAL EVALUATION: Ms. Blocker was evaluated in a contact room at the Cleveland County Detention Center. From the outset of the examination she expressed that "I'm very confused" but "I'll do my best." Ms. Blocker presented as an adequately nourished Caucasian female who appeared approximately her documented age of 40. Her grooming and hygiene were appropriate for her current confinement. Ms. Blocker's motor behavior was free from any tics, tremors, or unusual mannerisms. Her speech had a normal rate and volume. The content remained coherent, rational, and goal-directed throughout the evaluation. Her eye contact was good and her cooperation excellent, though I question her self-reported symptoms and claimed confusion. For example, when directly asked Ms. Blocker listed the current year as "2001," but her later statements clearly supported that she was aware this was not the case. While she accurately identified her date of birth, she suggested she was 38 or 39 instead of 40. She also offered that she was diagnosed with a "learning disability" while in school and was placed in special education for math as a result. As will be noted later, during my previous evaluation of Ms. Blocker she claimed she had been in special education, but specifically noted that her placement was due to behavior problems and not cognitive functioning. Nonetheless, she did not grossly feign cognitive impairment during this interview and her intelligence is judged to be approximately in the average range. She did not evidence any mental status impairments, such as significant problems in attention, concentration, or memory. She reported no history of significant head injury.

Ms. Blocker described her recent mood as "real depressed," but her affect (i.e., observable emotional state) was unimpaired. She denied any recent crying episodes and did not become tearful during the evaluation. Ms. Blocker suggested that she was chronically anxious and "it scares me .. .I don't know if I'll lash out." She stated she had been sleeping excessively and was only awake 7-8 hours each day. She reported she had gained significant weight during her incarceration, but conveyed no impairment in appetite or energy level. Ms. Blocker stated that she felt hopeless "a little bit" but denied any recent suicidal thoughts or plans.

As during the prior evaluation, Ms. Blocker described herself as "manic" in the past and endorsed nearly every symptom of mania posed to her. However, she indicated that these were past symptoms and she was currently depressed and not manic. She evidenced no signs of mania or hypomania. Ms. Blocker also claimed to experience chronic auditory and visual hallucinations which began in early adulthood. Despite receiving psychotropic medication in jail, she suggested that the symptoms were actually "getting worse" and occurred on a daily basis. She stated she often heard her name being called, saw "puddles of blood on the ground," and saw non-existent persons with whom she held conversations. At no point during this evaluation did Ms. Blocker evidence any signs of psychosis, such as distraction by internal stimuli (e.g., hallucinations), impairments in reality testing, delusions (i.e., fixed false beliefs despite evidence to the contrary), or mental confusion.

RELEVANT HISTORY FROM MS. BLOCKER: Ms. Blocker stated she had attempted suicide multiple times, the validity of which is unknown. She stated she had been diagnosed in the past with "Borderline Personality Disorder," "Manic-Depressive," and "Paranoid Schizophrenic." She conveyed she had received mental health treatment beginning in childhood, including placement at the "Spafford Home" in Kansas City, Missouri. Ms. Blocker reported past inpatient psychiatric treatment in Kansas City Missouri at "St. Mary's" and Western Missouri Mental Health Center, in addition to a crisis center (name unknown) in Wichita, Kansas. As during the prior evaluation Ms. Blocker endorsed a long pattern of substance abuse, including the use of alcohol, cannabis, cocaine, methamphetamine, heroin, and huffing paint. She stated she had undergone inpatient substance abuse treatment on numerous occasions.

PSYCHOLOGICAL TESTING:

Test of Memory Malingering (TOMM): Ms. Blocker was administered the TOMM, an assessment measure used to distinguish bona fide memory impairment from feigning. This instrument was designed such that even persons with severe cognitive impairment, including dementia and traumatic brain injury, perform very well. Ms. Blocker's scores (out of 50 possible points) were as follows in comparison to reference groups:

Reference Group	Trial 1	Trial 2	Retention Trial
No cognitive impairment	47.9	50	50
Aphasia[7]	46.3	49.3	49.8
Traumatic Brain Injury	45.9	49.4	49.6
Cognitive Impairment	43.9	48.6	49.5
Dementia	41.0	45.7	47
Instructed to malinger	32.5	35.3	30.9
Ms. Blocker	35	46	46

Although Ms. Blocker's score on Trial 1 was very low and similar to the standardization group instructed to malinger, it was not statistically low enough to warrant an interpretation of feigning. Therefore, Trial 2 and the Retention Trial should only then be interpreted. According to the test manual any score lower than 45 on either of those trials should raise concern that the individual is likely malingering. Given that Ms. Blocker's scores did not meet that criterion the appropriate interpretation is that she did not attempt to feign memory impairment on this measure.

Structured Interview of Reported Symptoms, Second Edition (SIRS-2): Based on Ms. Blocker's behavior and the absence of any overt genuine signs of severe mental illness, possible feigning was suspected. She was administered the SIRS-2, an objective test specifically designed to detect feigning of psychological symptoms. The SIRS-2 consists of eight primary scales which are interpreted based upon classification and/or index scales to determine the likelihood an individual is feigning mental illness

---

[7] (is a communication disorder that results from damage or injury to language parts of the brain)

versus providing a genuine presentation. The primary scale scores may fall in four ranges:

Definite range of feigning (Markedly Elevated)

Probable range of feigning (Moderately Elevated)

Indeterminate range (Neither indicative of feigning or honesty)

Genuine range (Suggesting honest responding)

Ms. Blocker's results for the Primary and Classification Scales were as follows:

Primary Scale	Description	Results
Rare Symptoms (RS)	Measures an individual's tendency to endorse symptoms that occur infrequently in psychiatric patients.	Indeterminate Range
Symptom Combinations (SC)	Measure an individual's tendency to endorse pairs of symptoms and other indicators of psychopathology that are seldom observed together.	Indeterminate Range
Improbable or Absurd Symptoms (IA)	Measures an individual's tendency to endorse symptoms of a fantastic or preposterous quality.	Genuine Range
Blatant Symptoms (BL)	Measures over-endorsement of symptoms which are obvious signs of a mental disorder to untrained individuals	Indeterminate Range
Subtle Symptoms (SU)	Measures an individual's tendency to endorse a very	Definite Range

Primary Scale	Description	Results
	high proportion of everyday problems and symptoms that are not always associated with mental illness.	
Selectivity of Symptoms (SEL)	Measures an individual's tendency to indiscriminately endorse a wide range of psychiatric symptoms.	Probable Range
Severity of Symptoms (SEV)	Measures an individual tendency to endorse a high proportion of symptoms of extreme or unbearable severity.	Definite Range
Reported versus Observed Symptoms (RO)	Measures an individual's tendency to repot behavioral symptoms that are not observable during the course of the interview	Genuine Range

Ms. Blocker had several elevated Primary Scale scores, including two in the Definite Range and One in the Probable Range. However, her score on the Classification Scale (RS- Total) did not rise to the level to be classified as feigning. Ms. Blocker' score on the MT Index (of 19) placed her in the "Indeterminate-General category." In the standardization sample, approximately 34% of persons with scores at this level were found to be feigning. However, this score alone does not provide evidence for feigning. With such individuals it may be clinically determined that further evaluation is necessary.

RESPONSES TO COURT ORDERED ITEMS:

1. Is this person able to appreciate the nature of the charges made against such person?

YES

When asked about the charge against her Ms. Blocker at times noted that "I really don't understand." However, when asked to explain she clarified that her version of events did not equate to a murderous act as charged by the prosecution. Ms. Blocker's statements clearly supported that she had a factual and rational understanding of her current situation. She listed her charge as "first degree murder" for "killing Eric [by] blunt force trauma to the head." She understood that her liberty was in jeopardy and she was motivated to avoid incarceration, voicing "I've been told by my attorney I could get life without. .. meaning I could spend the rest of my life in prison." It is the opinion of this examiner that Ms. Blocker can appreciate the nature of the charge against her.

2. Is this person able to consult with the lawyer and rationally assist in the preparation of the defense of such person?

YES

Consistent with her prior experiences in the criminal justice system, Ms. Blocker demonstrated sufficient knowledge of basic legal terminology and processes. She accurately described the purpose of a trial, all key legal roles (e.g., judge, jury, prosecutor, defense attorney, and witnesses), her primary available pleas (guilty, not guilty, not guilty by reason of insanity, etc.), and the process of plea bargaining. She understood that defendants typically accept plea bargains "because they're guilty and their usually a good deal so you don't have to go to trial," whereas the prosecution obtained "a conviction." She stated that she was offered a plea bargain of "45 years" in her case, which she agreed to, but then "changed my mind and wrote the judge and [her attorney]." She understood that if she proceeded to trial and lost she could "get life without," but she maintained she was innocent of the alleged offense and was willing to take the risk. While her decision making may not achieve results in her best interests, it is not impaired by mental illness or cognitive deficits. Ms. Blocker did not voice any paranoid ideations or delusions about the criminal justice system, though she believed that she was not being treated fairly based upon the facts at hand in the case.

Ms. Blocker identified her attorney as "David Smith" and she estimated they had met "four times in 18 months." She stated she essentially had no opinion of Mr. Smith, describing him as "Just another attorney. I've been in trouble before, just not quite this serious." She stated she had no specific reason to mistrust him and outlined one possible alternative she hoped he could achieve in this case, though it appeared unrealistic, She indicated she had informed him of her version of the alleged offense and "He believes me." However, she also noted that he disagreed with how she wanted to proceed in the case for a defense, voicing "I sent a letter to him asking him to withdraw from the case and wrote a letter to Judge Walkley saying my attorney didn't have my best interests and asked her to appoint another attorney." Ms. Blocker indicated that her request was not granted.

Ms. Blocker outlined her version of what occurred prior to, during, and following the alleged offense. The information she provided was coherent, rational, plausible, and goal-directed. She recognized that her alleged statements to police might be used to incriminate her, as well as "the autopsy" of the victim which she stated indicated he suffered a "brain aneurysm." Ms. Blocker outlined an extensive number of facts that she believed were exculpatory and/or mitigating. Thought the effectiveness of that information for a defense is highly questionable, none of the information she provided was bizarre or irrelevant to the case at hand. Ms. Blocker had an appropriate appreciation for the strength of the evidence against her in this case.

Ms. Blocker knew how a defendant was expected to behave in court and she stated that if she believed an opposing witness was dishonest she would "talk to my lawyer." She has the capacity to behave appropriately during proceedings, as she did throughout this evaluation. However, as noted earlier, given her personality traits she may choose to react inappropriately if angered. Ms. Blocker stated that she was unaware of her Fifth Amendment right to avoid testimony, or that she could be cross-examined should she testify. She was educated about these facts and easily understood.

Based upon her ability to discuss her version of events in a rational and coherent manner, it is the opinion of this examiner that she could appropriately testify in her defense should she decide to do so.

In summary, Ms. Blocker evidenced no cognitive impairment or signs of mental illness interfering with competency related abilities. Though she may be unrealistic about her proposed defense or the outcome she expects her attorney to achieve, this is not the result of a mental illness. Her personality traits may pose a substantial challenge in her legal representation and she could make very poor decisions in her case. Nonetheless, Ms. Blocker has the capacity to consult with her attorney to rationally assist in her defense, should she choose to do so.

3. If the person is unable to appreciate the nature of the charges or to consult and rationally assist in the preparation of the defense, whether the person can attain competency within a reasonable period of time as defined in Section 1175.1 of this title if provided with a course of treatment, therapy, or training?

NOT APPLICABLE.

4. Is the person a person requiring treatment as defined by section 1-103 of Title 43A of the Oklahoma Statutes?

NO

As noted earlier, Ms. Blocker endorses extensive symptoms of mental illness, but exhibits no signs of such. She is currently receiving psychotropic medication in the detention center. Therefore, it is unclear if her symptoms are appropriately controlled, or if she actually has no underlying severe mental illness. As during this examiner's previous evaluation, Ms. Blocker appears very well aware of mental health terminology and appears to be exaggerating problems at the very least. She does not meet the Oklahoma State statutory criteria for inpatient psychiatric treatment at the present time. It should be noted that Ms. Blocker reported past diagnosis with Borderline Personality Disorder and she has a history of assaultive behavior when angered. The Diagnostic and Statistical Manual of Mental Disorder-Fourth Edition-Text Revision describes Borderline Personality Disorder as characterized by: a pervasive pattern of instability of interpersonal relationships, self-image, and emotions, and marked impulsivity that begins by early adulthood and is present in a variety of contexts; such individuals are hypersensitive to environmental circumstances and have a pattern of unstable and intense relationships with others; they are prone to sudden shifts in their opinions about others and their own self-image; they display impulsivity in areas of life that are potentially self-damaging (i.e., substance abuse, careless spending, etc.); they have a marked reactivity in mood and may display periods of anger, panic, or despair; they frequently express inappropriate, intense anger or have difficulty controlling their anger; and they may display extreme sarcasm, enduring bitterness, or verbal outbursts. It is the opinion of this examiner that Mr. Blocker was not experiencing symptoms of Bipolar Disorder (i.e., mania) or a psychotic disorder (i.e., Schizophrenia) during this evaluation. However, such diagnoses are often misapplied to individuals with Borderline Personality Disorder due to their proneness for volatile behavior.

     5. If the person is incompetent because the person is mentally retarded as defined in Section 1408 of Title 10 of the Oklahoma Statutes?

NOT APPLICABLE.

     6. If the answers to questions 4 and 5 are no, why is the defendant incompetent?

NOT APPLICABLE.

     6. If the person were released, whether such person would presently be dangerous as defined in Section 1175.1 of this title.

NO.

Ms. Blocker claimed past suicidal behavior, the validity of which is unknown. She has not reportedly engaged in any such behavior during her incarceration, though she has voiced suicidal thoughts. During the current evaluation she denied any recent or current thoughts/plans to harm herself. Ms. Blocker has a history of assaultive behavior towards others and prior conviction for a violent offense. The current charge of murder is also a violent offense, though she remains innocent until convicted. CCDC staff indicated that she has been aggressive towards other inmates during her current incarceration. Her behavior was very well controlled during this evaluation and she did not meet the criteria for inpatient psychiatric treatment in my opinion. Therefore, based on all of the available data it is the opinion of this examiner that Ms. Blocker would not presently meet the statutory criteria for dangerousness if released, It should be noted that this is not a formal assessment of her level of dangerousness in the future, which is beyond the scope of the Court ordered question. If she became intoxicated with alcohol, illicit drugs, inhalants, or prescription medication it could raise her assessed level of risk significantly. **This opinion obviously does not factor in the possibility that Ms. Blocker poses a danger to others due to antisocial behavior, which is not the same as being a danger to others secondary to a mental illness requiring inpatient psychiatric treatment (the criteria for the current statutory question). Ms. Blocker's history of violence towards others is clearly a concern and it is strongly recommended that she receive a thorough risk assessment for future dangerousness prior to release.**

REPORT SUMMARY:

It is the opinion of this examiner that Ms. Blocker can appreciate the nature of the charge against her and can consult with her attorney to rationally assist in her defense; though she may be unrealistic about her proposed defense or the outcome she expects her attorney to achieve. Given her personality traits she may pose a substantial challenge in legal representation and she could make very poor decisions in her case. As noted earlier, Ms. Blocker endorses extensive symptoms of mental illness, but exhibits no signs of such. She is currently receiving psychotropic medication in the detention center. Therefore, it is unclear if her symptoms are appropriately controlled, or if she actually has no underlying severe mental illness. As during this examiner's previous evaluation, Ms. Blocker appears very well aware of mental health terminology and appears to be exaggerating problems at the very least. She does not meet the Oklahoma State statutory criteria for inpatient psychiatric treatment at the present time. It should be noted that Ms. Blocker reported past diagnosis with Borderline Personality Disorder and she has a history of assaultive behavior when angered. While she would not presently meet the statutory criteria for dangerousness if released <u>due to a mental illness requiring inpatient psychiatric treatment</u>, she may pose a danger to others due to antisocial behavior. Ms. Blocker's history of violence towards others is clearly a concern and it is strongly recommended that she receive a thorough risk assessment for future dangerousness prior to release.

Respectfully submitted, Shawn Roberson, Ph.D. Forensic Psychologist, Oklahoma Forensic Center Oklahoma Psychology License #: 914

CHAPTER 19: COMPETENCY HEARING

Whether the defendant's mental condition is such that she lacks the capacity to understand the nature of the proceedings against her, it is a sounder practice for the court to consider the nature of the proceedings in which the defendant will be involved, and whether the defendant has a reasonable degree of understanding and additionally, whether the defendant's mental condition is such that she lacks the present ability to consult with her lawyer and assist in her own defense.

###

At the March 15, 2012 status conference the competency report is completed and in the hands of the judge, who sets the post competency hearing for April 11, 2012 at 11:00 a.m.   At the hearing the plea of guilty summary of facts is filed and it shows that additional questions are asked as to whether Clara Blocker is taking any medication and she replies, 'No', but has been prescribed medication for anti-psychotic condition.   It is also learned that in 2008 she was treated for a bipolar condition and medical confinement is reported to have taken place by her lawyer, David Smith.

Judge Walkley rules that Clara Ann Blocker understood the nature of her crime and the consequences of the proceedings. The defendant also admits to being charged formerly for felonies.

It is at this time that the defendant pleads guilty and announces she chooses life with parole. This means she will have to serve 85% of the sentence of imprisonment imposed before being eligible for parole consideration and would not be eligible for any other type of credits that could reduce the length of her sentence to less than 85% of the sentence imposed. With this sentence she would plead guilty to Murder in the first degree.

On March 16, 2012, Jennifer Austin the Assistant District Attorney would send an email to me saying:

"We had the status hearing yesterday on the competency issue. We got the competency report back and she is in fact competent. We have been set for our hearing on the order Wednesday April 11th. Her attorney is having some trouble communicating with her on the results of the report, so he is going to discuss it with her and we should be done with this issue on the 11th and be put on the June trial docket. (She is entitled to a jury trial on the issue of competency, and he has to explain to her that is not the route she wants to go, and get her to agree with the report.) He is still hopeful that he can get her to plead, and is working towards that goal. If not, we should be able to go to trial in June.

This is not an uncommon delay in these types of cases. If we do have to go to trial, it is good that this procedure did happen for appeal purposes, as she had raised a competency issue in one of her past cases also. If her attorney had not done it here, an Appellate Court could later decide that he was ineffective for not pursuing competency, and reverse any conviction and order a retrial, so this was not wasted time (although it took longer than it should have to accomplish it).

The hearing on April 11th is routine and will keep us on track for the June docket. We will get pre-trial hearing dates at that hearing which will ensure all is in line for the trial date. Again, her attorney is hopeful that he can convince her to plead, so he will continue working towards that goal, and we will notify you if we hear anything."

###

After the March 15 status conference hearing, the "Order to Resume Criminal Proceedings report was filed and available on the Oklahoma States Court Network site. It stated:

"That now, on this 11th day of April, 2012, a Wednesday, this matter comes before the court for post-examination competency hearing the defendant is present in person and with her attorney of record. The court, being fully advised in the premises, finds as follows. 1) The defendant waives trial by jury on the matter of competency, 2) The parties stipulate to the competency examination report of the Oklahoma Forensic Center and 3) The defendant is competent to undergo further criminal proceedings in this cause.   It is therefore ordered by the court that criminal proceedings shall resume and proceed forthwith in the above styled and numbered action, CF-10-1390, State of Oklahoma, vs. Clara Ann Blocker. The document was signed by Judge Walkley.

###

I wish I could say that I was sitting patiently back and waiting for the final date, but that would be untrue. Doing my regular calculations I note that from and including: Friday, September 17, 2010 to, Wednesday, April 11, 2012 is a waiting period for me of 573 days, or 1 year, 6 months, 26 days. That is a long time to be patient and understanding.

In Oklahoma City it is the judge of the particular court in which the action is pending who has the final say as to when a case will be tried in the courtroom. The Court Clerk first assigns a number to all cases with a case prefix, a hyphen, and all four digits of the calendar year. Once this is done, the Court Clerk assigns all cases to judges in the various divisions of Court according to their assignments by the Presiding Judge.   Thereafter, the assigned judge will have full charge of the case.

When a case must be prosecuted there is little chance for a speedy or quick recovery. There are motions for continuance of a pretrial, trial or evidentiary hearing that must be signed by the party on whose behalf the motion is made. It is generally accepted that conflicts in scheduling are inevitable, particularly on motion dockets when several are conducted simultaneously.

Then there are psych evaluations and testimony of expert witnesses like physicians, First Responder EMS, or police that will make the case proceed more slowly. Physicians are busy and will generally schedule depositions only on certain days of the month.

All evidence, disclosures and discovery must be in place and nothing overlooked or there will be delays.

###

What plagues me is that Clara Blocker who is in custody and has been since September 16, 2010 admits to what she did. The longer she is incarcerated, the more she plays the system, like the competency order. I am afraid she will find a loophole and get off.

For some reason I decide to look back at my emails and the responses. I came across this one from Detective Lyndell Easley dated January 18, 2012 and I feel reassured.

"Sorry it took me a bit to reply, my partner and I only work one weekend out of seven, and our turn in the barrel is not until this upcoming weekend. Add to this the Monday holiday and the fact I was maxed out on vacation, as I usually stay, and had to take off yesterday, you get the idea, I am sure. Ma'am, this case IS solved, by any definition in the USA. An arrest has been made, and a charge filed, the defendant is held without bond awaiting trial. The Constitution (specifically the Bill of Rights) assures every citizen specific rights concerning arrest, and trial and this even extends to non-citizens, as long as the crime occurs on US soil. I receive telephone calls and emails from families occasionally, making the complaint that criminals have more rights than law-abiding citizens. This is not at all the case, the same rights extend to ALL people, but most people, so long as they obey the laws, never find a need for the provisions in the fourth, fifth, sixth, and eighth amendments. There is nothing a law enforcement agency or prosecutor can do to change this at all, and I would guess anyone who has been charged with a crime would demand the same rights, but they would not have to demand a thing, because it is automatic. I have also had to experience these frustrations, not involving a homicide, but an on-duty shooting that dragged on for six years before my assailants were convicted. This is something we have no choice in, and I had to just accept that fact. Believe me, ma'am, I do understand and empathize. Having said all this, you should know that this case is apace, compared to other homicides. I have seen them take three times this long to reach adjudication, although that has been the extreme end so far. In that particular case, the defense attorney kept postponing things, which again is the right of the accused, it only becomes an issue when the prosecutor continues the case, which denies the right of the accused to a speedy trial by a jury of their peers. The punishment for Murder in the First Degree is Life in Prison, or Life Without Parole. The severity of the punishment requires that we cross all the I's and dot the T's. The last thing any of us want is for the case to be overturned because of a civil rights violation, or improper procedure. I have checked the OSCN website this morning several times, and it seems to be unavailable due to maintenance issues. This is my source for information in a number of pending cases I am working, and the Cleveland County Court Clerk puts more information on cases than do other counties.   I hope this has answered your question ("So what is the problem?") Please believe me when I say I understand the frustration, but these are the rules we have to play by and I ask that you be patient just a bit longer so there is no room for reasonable doubt. What also is in our favor is the fact that the longer Blocker sits, the more agreeable she might be to a plea deal, which we have discussed before. Plea agreements get suspects in prison where a jury might fail to do so. Thank you, Detective Lyndell Easley. "

###

I now felt ameliorate and try to be less critical. I next write an email on March 15, 2012 to all concerned:

"I am writing to let you know that I would like to hear the results of what I believe to be the final competency hearing this afternoon. It is scheduled on the case site for March 15 @ 2:15 p.m. Please email or call to let me know the results. I don't have Jennifer Austin's email address, but if you can let her know too that I am waiting to here, I would appreciate it. Thank you"

Detective Lyndell Easley would reply saying,

"Those are done with just the lawyers, I don't have that information. Sorry I could not reply to the email asking me to friend you, but the city computers block all social media, and I don't use a computer at home. I will let you know when I do hear something."

Later on April 1, I would write asking for details on the plea agreement and Detective Lyndell Easley again responds on 12, "This is great news, and as I told you early on, a plea agreement is a good thing, so long as the time to do is satisfactory for the family of the victim. Have you heard what she agreed to do, or is it a blind plea for the judge to decide?"

I would email back that I didn't know but would try and find out.

CHAPTER 20: IN THE INTERIM

After releasing a book you have only that first year to really get it out to the public and when you have to handle the publicity yourself, it can be a lot of work. I released the book 'The Madman The Marathoner', April of 2010 and since then spent a lot of time promoting the book sending information to newspapers, television stations and even marathons held across the country and in Canada. I would not let myself or Don down on doing all I could to promote this book.

I sent review copies to all the journals and magazines that evaluate books in my genre. I reached out to friends, colleagues, clients who liked the book and ask that they place reviews on Amazon and other online book stores. I offer myself and Don McNelly for interviews on radio stations and TV stations. It isn't surprising that we are given interview dates and booths at events for selling the book since my earlier book on Erik's life had afforded me many contacts. That along with the notoriety of Don McNelly, would keep us busy.

Don McNelly joins me as we are interviewed on all three local networks in Rochester and with the suburban papers including the Brookville Star—the newspaper of Brookville, Ohio where Don McNelly spent his childhood. We did book signings at Barnes & Noble and even at the Seneca Park Zoo, 5K event and though the book isn't a best seller, I know that Don feels like it is and that is what mattered.

While I keep busy with the book promotion, work and everyday life I fill more time keeping in touch with Oklahoma and attending to my personal health.

I had held off from doing the second knee until I knew more about when I would be returning to Oklahoma, because I still didn't feel 100% recovered from the first. It still aches if I don't put it up and ice it often and the thought of flying with even that one knee seems like a painful experience.

Each day that passes with no word of the proceedings even thought to be held anytime soon, I decided to set the date for surgery on my left knee and settle for January 21, 2012. The surgery is performed without a hitch.

I know what to expect this time and what it will take on my part to get mobile as fast as I can. I go through the process, only this time quicker as I take responsibility for my well-being. I do my exercises even more often than told and when instructed to wean myself off the medications, I do it without complaint. I find I am able to drive myself to PT appointments and I do well,. PT stops after two weeks and I am on my way to Planet Fitness to continue my therapy. I am proud of myself and confident I will be ready when Oklahoma calls to say they have a date for the proceedings. Wouldn't you know it, it would be sooner than later.

###

It is like I am two people now; one going about her daily routines and the other caught in the abyss of unknown. I am in constant contact with the DA office and the sheriff's department in Oklahoma, not wanting Erik's case to fall through the cracks, even though I now they won't let that happen. They have Erik's murderer in custody, but I know from my research and information Oklahoma has shared, there are missing elements in the case.

I know there is nothing I can do about the case myself and my knees sing the same tune as I go about trying to keep pace with my normal routines. Most days I am either in the kitchen or at my computer and today is no different. I think about that first birthday of Erik's after his death, I did more grieving than celebrating his birth. I didn't want to do that again. I am a survivor even though I have lived through the worst possible situation that can ever happen to me. The day of his death my life changed in a split second. I went from one moment being someone's mother, to being childless and I could not accept that. But I know I have to, so I am determined that April 10, 2012, will be different.

On April 10, 2012 Erik would turn 43 years old. Just before the day arrived I came across a quote by Walter Anderson, a German Writer that said, *"Bad things do happen; how I respond to them defines my character and the quality of my life. I can choose to sit in perpetual sadness, immobilized by the gravity of my loss, or I can choose to rise from the pain and treasure the most precious gift I have - life itself."*

###

Erik's soul is free, his ashes scattered and carried by the wind to parts unknown, but my heart and memory is where he has always lived. So on April 10, I sat before a picture of me holding Erik and felt his presence and I know that he wants me to remember him, but remember him as he lived, not as he died. It was the most rewarding moments of my life.

CHAPTER 21: THE CALL

When a deal is worked out between all interested parties, the prosecution and defense will arrange a court hearing and inform the judge about the agreement. Assuming the judge accepts the deal or suggests changes that are satisfactory to both sides, the judge will hear the guilty or no contest plea in open court so that it becomes part of the record. This is called a plea hearing when the defendant goes before the judge and says, I plead guilty to the crime I am charged with. When this occurs there is no need for a trial. If the crime is a misdemeanor, the defendant will be sentenced at the plea hearing. If the crime is a felony, it will be scheduled for a sentencing date.

In-custody defendants may be brought to court soon after the agreement is reached for a special hearing in which the judge takes the plea. Otherwise, the taking of the plea (and sometimes sentencing) will occur at the next scheduled hearing.

\#\#\#

One day later, on April 11, 2012 at 1:39 pm EST I receive a call from Kerrin Jones of the Cleveland County District Attorney's office. When the call comes I am in the kitchen putting together a lasagna for dinner, but as soon as she identifies herself, I stop what I am doing and say, "Just a moment, please". Without putting down the phone, I grab two ice bags and go into the family room where I sit on the couch and put my legs up on the ottoman, then put an ice bag on each knee.

It has only been a few seconds that have passed, but I wonder if Kerrin knows part of what I am up to and that is to get my laptop, open up a word document and type what she says. As soon as I am situated I say, "I'm ready".

"I heard from Clara's lawyer today. It seems that Clara has told him she wants to have the hearing and the case presented today. She wants it to be over and she is willing to plead guilty".

"Is this a trick?"

"No, She wants to get out of county jail and go to prison and start her sentence."

I tell her, "This has really affected me on so many levels, but at the end no matter how I look at it in different views it always comes out the same. I want this to be over but I want justice."

Kerrin replies, "The defense has the right to decide whether a case will be tried by a judge or jury. Clara is afraid what will happen at a jury trial and you should be too. For her, since she wants life with parole, and for you because there is no guarantee that a jury will give her life."

She's right. Then it dawns on me what she said earlier. "Kerrin, I can't make it there today."

"Don't worry, that has been handled. The proceedings are scheduled for Tuesday, April 17,2012, at 8:30 a.m."

The rest of the conversation covers the details of our trip to Oklahoma City. Kerrin says she will handle all the arrangements and send an email when they have been confirmed.

###

It has only been two months and 16 days since my second knee replacement. My knees hurt when my legs are down too long. I need ice and heat on a regular basis to help regulate the pain. How am I going to fly 2 hours, 44 minutes with my legs down. That is the question. We are asked if it is possible, could we plan on leaving on Tuesday, April 16 and without hesitation I had said 'Yes', knowing that whatever I decide, Mark will be flexible for me, but will I be physically flexible so I step up my workouts at Planet Fitness.

I check my email constantly that day and then I see something from the University American Travel. I open it. It is a note from Kerrin saying; *"Here is the tentative itinerary...I will be out of the office in a few minutes. I will call you about it first thing in the morning."* The email below her message is from the University American Travel, dated Wednesday, April 11, 2012 at 4:16 p.m.

I will be flying American Airlines Flight: 4143 on Monday, April 16, 2012, leaving Buffalo at 1:30 p.m. and arriving in Chicago O'Hare at 2:15 p.m. From Chicago I am scheduled for

American Airlines Flight 3780 that will leave Chicago O'Hare at 4:40 p.m., arriving in Oklahoma City at 6:40 p.m.

My return trip is scheduled for April 17, 2012 on American Airlines Flight 3681 leaving Oklahoma City at 2:15 p.m. and arriving in Chicago O'Hare at 4:20 p.m. Then in Chicago I am on American Airlines Flight 4014 leaving Chicago O'Hare at 5:00 p.m. and arriving in Buffalo at 7:35 p.m.

My seat assignments have also been arranged.

Kerrin has said they will only be covering my travel expense so I waste no time going online to make the arrangements for Mark on the same flights with me and hopefully get our seats together, but at least be on the same planes. I am in luck and we will be flying together with two seat assignments not together. One seat assignment is across the aisle from each other and another one has a person between us.

Earlier I sent Mark an email explaining that we are a 'go' for Proceedings in Oklahoma and give him the details Kerrin has shared. He emails me back that he has made the arrangements for time off at work.

That evening when Mark arrives home, we stand in the kitchen putting together our dinner and I fill him in on the flight arrangements I have made for him. As we carry our plates into the family room, he tells me about his day, then we go over our calendars to make sure there is nothing we need to cancel before we leave.

Mark asks, "Are you going to let his aunt and his father know?"

"Yes. I plan on sending them an email right away, now that we know it is a 'go'."

That evening we watch a little television and then turn in feeling much better than we have in days. It is finally going to happen. I know Mark has been as anxious as me to have closure on this matter. Now it is about to happen. Clara is days away from facing her fate.

On Thursday morning, April 12, 2012 Kerrin sends me my tickets and on this same day, I send out an email.

"Since Thursday, September 16, 2010 until today, Thursday, April 12, 2012; we have waited for the day when we would finally have closure. Erik Saxton is finally having his day in court, though not before a jury. His murderer has finally decided to enter a guilty plea. This news alone lessens the pain in my heart knowing that she will pay for what she has done. The plea case is open to the public and statements are allowed. I will finally face Clara Blocker and she will know that she took the life of a wonderful and loved child; my child. Justice will be done."

"This will take place on Tuesday morning, April 17, 2012 at 8:30 a.m. at the Cleveland County District Court, 200 S. Peters, Norman, OK 73069. For verification of the court room you can call (405) 321-6402. Friends or family who want to attend are very welcomed. We are being flown out on Monday, April 16 and will return to Rochester on Tuesday, April 17."

I followed this with an email to Jane Cannon and Detective Lyndell Easley, more because I want to see them, than notify them of the hearing.

"Since Thursday, September 16, 2010 until today, Thursday, April 12, 2012; 1 year, 6 months and 27 days later, we are finally having closure. Erik Saxton is finally having his day in court, though not before a jury. His murderer has finally decided to enter a guilty plea. This news alone lessens the pain in my heart knowing that she will pay for what she has done. The plea case is open to the public and statements are allowed. I will finally face Clara Blocker and she will know that she took the life of a wonderful and loved child; my child. Justice will be done."

I would send an email to Detective Lyndell in response to an earlier question he raised.

"I believe that what Kerrin of the DA Office said was Clara wants to get it over with and plead guilty. That's the reason for the rush to do it before she changes her mind. I don't know if it is a blind plea(don't know what that is) I just hope the sentence matches the crime".

Detective Lyndell would reply, "A blind plea is throwing yourself on the mercy of the court. It is telling the judge you are guilty and letting the judge set the sentence without a prior plea agreement with the District Attorney. And I agree, let's "git 'er done!"

That is what we are doing, we are getting it done! Finally.

###

I begin to wonder. Could not having a jury trial prove to be a mistake. I understand the reasoning, but I don't know the law enough to feel totally comfortable with this decision. There is the fact that she hasn't admitted why she murdered Erik and that needs to be considered too. I do another search on the internet and when I finish I feel more confident with this decision.

I come across instances where a minor infraction of the law could shorten or even allow the guilty party to go free.

###

Fomby, Charles Clifton v. State, Court Of Criminal Appeals Case No. F-2005-855_(August 14, 2006) **The Crime**: Charles C. Fomby Jr. was tried by jury and convicted in Comanche County District Court Case No. CF-2004-595 of Count I: Second Degree Burglary, After Former Conviction of Two or More Felonies; Count 11: Possession of a Controlled Substance (methamphetamine); Count IV: Second Degree Burglary, After Former Conviction of Two or More Felonies; and Count V: Knowingly Concealing Stolen Property. In accordance with the jury's recommendation, the Honorable Mark R. Smith sentenced Fomby to sixty (60) years' imprisonment on Counts I and IV, two (2) years' imprisonment on Count 11, and ten (10) years' imprisonment on Count V. Judge Smith ordered the sentences to be served consecutively **The Repeal:** After thoroughly considering the entire record before us on appeal, including the original record, transcripts, briefs, and parties' exhibits, we affirm Fomby's conviction but find that his sentence must be modified. We find in Proposition I that the trial court erred in modifying OUJI-CR 10-21 to include the amount of time Fomby served on his prior convictions. We find in Proposition II that the prosecutor improperly commented on Fomby's presumption of innocence. We also find that the combination of the errors in Propositions I and II compel our modification of Fomby's sentences on Counts I and IV from sixty (60) years' imprisonment on each count, to be served consecutively, to thirty (30) years' imprisonment on each Count, to be served concurrently. We find in Proposition III that there was no error in admitting the "other crimes" evidence. We find that Proposition IV is moot due to the relief recommended in Proposition I. We find in Proposition V that Fomby waived preliminary hearing on the new charges in the Information by entering his plea at arraignment. We find in Proposition VI that the evidence was sufficient to establish that Fomby knowingly possessed stolen property. We find in Proposition VII that the evidence was sufficient to establish that Fomby knowingly possessed methamphetamines. We find in Proposition VIII that trial counsel was not ineffective. We find Proposition IX that there was no double jeopardy violation as Fomby consented to the mistrial.

The Decision The Judgments of the District Court are AFFIRMED and the Sentences for Counts I1 and V are AFFIRMED. The Sentences for Counts I and IV are MODIFIED to thirty (30) years imprisonment for each Count and all Counts are ordered to be served concurrently. Pursuant to Rule 3.15, Rules of the Oklahoma Court of Criminal Appeals, Title 22, Ch.18, App. (2006), the MANDATE is ORDERED issued upon the delivery and filing of this decision.

Gatewood, Clarence Andre v. State, Court Of Criminal Appeals Case No. F-2005-829 (November 17, 2006) **The Crime**: Appellant, Clarence Andre Gatewood, was tried by jury for the crime of First Degree Murder in the District court of Tulsa County, Case No. CF-2004-3607. The jury found Appellant guilty of the lesser offense of Second Degree Murder and recommended a sentence of life imprisonment. On August 23, 2005, the Honorable Rebecca Nightingale, District Judge sentenced Appellant in accordance with the jury's recommendation and appellant timely lodged this appeal. **The Appeal:** The Appellant raises the following propositions of error: 1.The trial court failed to notify defense counsel of a jury note, contrary to statutory mandate; 2, the trial court erred by denying the requested sentencing instruction. 3. The 85% instruction requirement of Anderson v State should be applied to appellant's case, 4. admission of an involuntary confession was error. 5. Appellant's sentence is excessive. After thorough consideration of the propositions, and the entire record before us on appeal, including the original record, transcripts, and briefs of the parties, we affirm Appellant's conviction, but remand for resentencing. Appellant claims his statement to police, implicating himself in the fatal assault on the victim, was involuntarily made, and that its admission into evidence denied him a fair trial. We Disagree. The record shows that Appellant was advised of his rights before the interview, that he was sober and coherent, and that he spoke to police with full knowledge of the attendant consequences, free of any threat or promise. The trial court's conclusion that appellant's statement was voluntary made is soundly supported by the evidence and is denied. However, we find merit and this court held that juries should be instructed, where applicable on statutory restrictions of parole eligibility. Appellant contends he is entitled to the same relief granted because he timely raised the same issue below and on appeal during deliberations, the jury sent a note inquiring into the meaning of a "life" sentence with the possibility of parole and the Appellant's case was pending on direct review at the time. **The Decision**: Accordingly Appellant's conviction for Second Degree Murder is affirmed, but his sentence is vacated and the case is remanded for resentencing. Our resolution of Propositions 2 and thee renders proposition 5 moot..

Hudson, Zachary Michael v. State, Court Of Criminal Appeals Case No. F-2005-440 (August 15, 2006) **The Case**: Appellant, Zachary Michael Hudson, was tried by a jury in Tulsa County District Court, Case No. CF-2004-5, for the crime of First Degree Murder. The jury found him guilty of the lesser related offense of First Degree Manslaughter and recommended punishment of twenty years imprisonment and a $10,000 fine. On April 28, 2005, the Honorable Jesse S. Harris, District Judge, sentenced Appellant in accordance with the jury's recommendation, and Appellant timely lodged this appeal. **The Appeal**: Appellant raises the following propositions of error: 1. Appellant was denied a fair trial when the court took an impermissibly proactive role in the trial of the case. 2. The evidence was insufficient to support a conviction for First Degree Manslaughter. 3. The trial court committed fundamental error in instructing the jury on the lesser offense of First Degree Manslaughter. 4. The trial court erred in refusing to instruct the jury about the mandatory service of 85% of a sentence for murder or manslaughter, and erred in refusing to correctly answer the jury's question about parole. After thorough consideration of the propositions, and the entire record before us on appeal, including the original record, transcripts, and briefs of the parties, we affirm Appellant's conviction, but modify the sentence. As to Proposition 1, the trial court's participation during the examination of witnesses was not improper. The court took an active role in ensuring that witnesses understood the questions asked. Appellant's claim that the court was partial to the State is simply not supported by the record. We find no evidence of judicial bias. Proposition 1 is denied. As to Propositions 2 and 3, the trial court did not err in granting the State's request to instruct the jury on First Degree Manslaughter as a lesser related offense to First Degree Murder. Appellant was not surprised by this alternative, and the evidence reasonably supported it. The evidence shows that Appellant fought with the deceased, left the scene, then returned a short time later in his motor vehicle, fought with him again, and then ran over the deceased in the middle of the street. A rational juror could have rejected Appellant's claim of accident and found, beyond a reasonable doubt, that he was acting in a heat of passion when he hit the deceased with his car.. Propositions 2 and 3 are denied. Finally, as to Proposition 4, Appellant timely requested an instruction on the "85% Rule," but his request was denied by the trial court. During the deliberations, the jury sent a note to the court asking about parole eligibility. We find the circumstances warrant modification of Appellant's sentence from twenty years imprisonment and a $10,000 fine, to fifteen years imprisonment and a $10,000 fine. **The Decision**: The Judgment of the district court is Affirmed. The Sentence is Modified to fifteen years imprisonment and a $10,000 fine.

Lindsay, Charles Earl v. State, Court Of Criminal Appeals Case No. F-2005-252_(August 30, 2006) **The Case**: Appellant,

Charles Earl Lindsay, was tried by jury in the District Court of Cleveland County, Case Number CF-2004-493, and convicted of Robbery with an Imitation Firearm, in violation of 2 1 0.S.200 1, 5 80 1, after former conviction of two or more felonies. The jury set punishment at forty (40) years imprisonment. The trial judge sentenced Appellant in accordance with the jury's determination. Appellant now appeals his conviction and sentence. Appellant raises the following propositions of error in this appeal: **The Appeal**: The State introduced insufficient evidence as a matter of law to sustain its burden of proof and the district court clearly erred in denying Appellant's demurrer to the State's evidence; 11. The State improperly bolstered the complaining witness's testimony by introducing testimony from a police officer that she identified Appellant in a photographic lineup; 111. Appellant received constitutionally ineffective assistance of counsel as a result of counsel's failure to suppress the videotaped interview of Appellant with Officer Uselton; IV. Appellant was denied a fundamentally fair trial when deputies brought him into the courtroom in handcuffs; V. Appellant received constitutionally ineffective counsel when trial counsel failed to request jury instructions on lesser included degrees of robbery; VI. Prosecutorial misconduct during closing arguments resulted in a fundamentally unfair trial; VII. The sentence imposed is excessive and must be modified; and VIII. The accumulation of errors resulted in a fundamentally unfair trial. After thoroughly considering these propositions and the entire record before us, we find modification is required. With respect to proposition one, we find Appellant's claim has merit. The State sufficiently proved the first seven elements necessary for a conviction. However, the State failed to meet its burden of proof on the eighth element, i.e., "through use of an imitation firearm capable of raising in the mind of the person threatened with such device a fear that it is a real firearm." Unquestionably, the imitation firearm was capable of convincing someone that it was a real firearm. However, the victim was never "threatened with such device." The record reflects the victim never saw the imitation weapon, even though it was smashed against her head and knocked her unconscious. She was never made aware of the weapon in any way until after the crime was completed. This is insufficient under the statutory language. Therefore relief in the form of modification is required. Reviewing the information filed in this case and the elements of robbery, which necessarily include the use of force or fear, we find it appropriate under these specific facts to modify Appellant's conviction to First Degree Robbery. Appellant caused "serious bodily injury" to the victim by breaking her finger and striking her in the head with a weapon so hard as to render her unconscious. His actions also intentionally put the victim in fear of serious bodily injury, as she attempted to flee in vain. Modification of Appellant's sentence is also warranted for reasons set forth below. With respect to proposition two, we find this Court has condemned the practice of having third parties testify about extra-judicial identifications made by others in several cases. Here, we find any such error was harmless, if error at all, as the defense strategy was clearly to attack the identification procedures, which resulted in one misidentification and one with conflicts. Indeed, defense counsel himself cross-examined the police officer vigorously concerning the lineup and procedures used. With respect to proposition three, we find defense counsel's performance in this case, including the issue of the admissibility of Appellant's statement, did not rise to the level of constitutionally-ineffective assistance. The motion to supplement the record and application for evidentiary hearing are hereby Denied.. With respect to proposition four, we find error occurred when Appellant was brought into court and escorted out of court in handcuffs in the presence of jurors.. Even though this was not a capital case and the incidents occurred only during sentencing, these events may have impacted the sentence by affecting negatively the jury's perception of Appellant. We take this in consideration with respect to the modification of Appellant's sentence. With respect to proposition five, we find lesser-included offense instructions were not warranted as Appellant's defense was innocence. With respect to proposition six, we find no prosecutorial misconduct warranting relief. With respect to proposition seven, we find, consistent with contemporaneous cases before this Court, that the jury should have been instructed on the applicability of the 85% rule. We take this into account with respect to the modification of Appellant's sentence.~ And finally, we find proposition eight, cumulative error, to be moot, considering the relief granted. **The Decision**: Appellant's conviction is hereby Reversed and Modified to the crime of First-Degree Robbery, and to correct each of the errors discussed, Appellant's sentence is hereby Modified to twenty (20) years imprisonment. The case is Remanded to the District Court of Cleveland County with instructions to enter a corrected Judgment and Sentence in conformity with this opinion. Ordered issued upon the delivery and filing of this decision.

There were many more appeal cases out there for review and knowing that an appeal court does not re-evaluate the evidence or testimonials that were available in the previous court decision, but instead inspects the process revolving around the decision, it is scary. If an error was made in regards to the judicial process, the appeal will be awarded to the defendant. The appeal court will effectively eliminate the case and any punishments attached to the previous charge.

As for a jury, there is considerable power vested in a body of ordinary men and women, who are charged with deciding matters of fact and delivering a verdict of guilt or innocence based on the evidence in a case, or better yet, how they translate the evidence. I firmly believe that a jury takes this responsibility seriously enough to hesitate when the charge is murder and something is missing from the evidence pool. It could then go either way.

CHAPTER 22: THE TORNADO

No one can forget the "The Wizard of Oz". In this charming film based on the popular L. Frank Baum stories, Dorothy and her dog Toto are caught in a tornado's path and somehow end up in the land of Oz. But a real tornado is not so charming, especially along Tornado Alley. Tornado Alley is not an official weather term but the borders of Tornado Alley start in central Texas and goes north through Oklahoma, central Kansas, Nebraska and eastern South Dakota.

###

On Friday, April 13, 2012, a tornado is seen near the University of Oklahoma campus in Norman just after 4 p.m. local time. The tornado ripped roofs from buildings, downed power lines and uprooted trees across Norman, a town just 20 miles south of Oklahoma City. City Hall was among the structures damaged. On the news it is said that residents of Oklahoma, Nebraska and Kansas brace for a major tornado outbreak predicted for Saturday, and officials in Oklahoma City said a small twister had already touched down.

I keep the news on listening and hoping this would not cancel our trip to Oklahoma or stall the plea and sentencing hearing. I check online and find an article from Oklahoma City

"Friday tornado could be first taste of a tornado outbreak expected Saturday

By Juliana Keeping And Jane Glenn Cannon

Officials are warning of a high risk for tornadoes and other severe weather in Oklahoma on Saturday. The Oklahoma City metro is included in an area deemed at the highest risk.

NORMAN — A tornado that cut through the heart of Norman on Friday could be the first taste of a major outbreak expected Saturday in Oklahoma.

The Friday tornado cut a roughly eight-mile path, dropping down about 4 p.m. near southwest Norman at Interstate 35 and W

Lindsey Street. It hop-scotched through the center of town, tossing telephone poles, shredding trees, ripping the roofs off buildings and raking a park near the city's municipal complex before fading out in the northeast side of the city.

At least 10 people were taken to Norman Regional Hospital with minor injuries like scrapes and bruises, said Kelly Wells, hospital spokeswoman.

Deputy Fire Chief Jim Bailey said three individuals were taken to the hospital via ambulance, including two who were in a vehicle when the tornado hit and another person hit by debris.

"It is surprising you don't have more injured with the time of day, about 4:02," Bailey said. "Norman is a busy town. There were a lot of people out driving around, and we had very little notification."

Later this article is revised to include the following additional information.

"On alert

Atmospheric conditions Saturday will be ripe for tornadoes and other severe weather, according to the National Weather Service.

The bottom line is, be ready for it. It may happen in one place, or it may happen across a huge part of the state, but it only takes one tornado and one storm," said Rick Smith, a National Weather Service meteorologist.

Severe thunderstorms are possible throughout the state Saturday, but the Oklahoma City area and most of the middle third of the state are in an area deemed at the highest risk.

Storms are expected to form in the late afternoon or early evening and track across the state, forecasters said. Tornadoes, damaging straight-line winds, lightning, hail and flooding rain are possible.

"If everything comes together like it could, it could be a serious situation for parts of Oklahoma," Smith said."

###

This can't be happening. Why is this happening now? I can't help but worry that everything will be cancelled. Mark tries his darndest to keep me calm. He tells me that I know they have tornadoes all the time in Oklahoma and it doesn't mean anything. I try to believe him, but sit on pins and needles for the rest of the day and go to bed to toss and turn until morning. Anxiously I turn on the television to see if I can catch any updates but there is not much more coming out of Oklahoma. I search the internet for news on Tornadoes predicted for Saturday, April 14. I find several that say basically the same thing.

###

"Three girls among Oklahoma tornado dead; clean-up underway

Oklahoma City | By Steve Olafson

Clean-up efforts were underway across the Midwest on Sunday after dozens of tornadoes ripped across the region, killing five people in one Oklahoma town, three of them young girls, after storm sirens failed to sound and houses were reduced to rubble.

Storms skipped through what is often called "Tornado Alley" in the U.S. Central and Southern Plains on Saturday and into Sunday, but the high winds and dozens of tornadoes mostly struck rural areas, sparing the region from worse damage.

The storms left thousands without power in Kansas, hit an aircraft fuselage production facility, and damaged up to 90 percent of homes and buildings in a small Iowa town. The governors of Kansas and Oklahoma declared states of emergency.

The stormy weekend wasn't over for the Midwest. The National Weather Service declared tornado watches in Arkansas through Missouri and into a corner of Illinois, as well as in parts of Iowa, Minnesota and Wisconsin. But the likelihood of the most destructive tornadoes was low.

Damaging thunderstorms were also predicted from Minnesota south to Texas into Sunday night, according to AccuWeather.com.

A twister struck the northwest Oklahoma city of Woodward after midnight on Sunday, catching many in the town of 12,000 people unaware when storm sirens failed to sound after lightning apparently disabled the warning system, Mayor Roscoe Hill said.

"This thing took us by surprise," Hill said. "It's kind of overwhelming."

The Woodward tornado killed three young girls and two adults, according to Amy Elliott of the Oklahoma Medical Examiner's Office. Two girls, ages 5 and 7, died along with a man thought to be their father in a mobile home park.

A 10-year-old girl and a man were also killed in the small community of Tangiers, just outside the Woodward city limits."

###

On Friday, April 13, it is reported that no injuries were reported from the tornado in southwest Oklahoma City. One home had major roof damage, and trees, power lines and fences were down, but it wasn't over. Severe thunderstorms and tornadoes were expected Saturday afternoon and evening in north central Oklahoma, and the weather service called it a "potentially very dangerous situation". An operator at the University of Oklahoma said people had been warned to get to a basement or low floor.

I read on the internet that at least four tornadoes were reported near Dodge City, in southwestern Kansas approximately 256 miles from Oklahoma City. Two were reported in Rush County , 323 miles from Oklahoma City.

I keep searching and find another article that says an EF1 tornado with winds estimated at 100 mph tracked through downtown Norman, causing widespread damage. Many homes endured varying degrees of damage. A paint store was destroyed by the tornado and many trees and power lines were downed. An apartment complex lost its roof as well. Twenty people were injured by the tornado, though only one required hospitalization. Late in the evening, a potentially violent tornado tracked across a long ribbon of south-central Kansas and into Wichita, 161 miles from Oklahoma City, around 10:15 pm CDT.

###

By the weekend it is not surprising I am unable to get any communication from Kerrin Jones or Jennifer Austin, but I try anyway. Worried, I send out an email, hoping by chance they check from home.

I have been watching the news and was shocked to see tornadoes had hit Norman. I hope everyone is all right. As you are aware, we are due there on Monday, April 16, 2012 for the

Tuesday court sentencing of Clara Blocker. It looks as though the storms have passed and hopefully did not damage or cause any harm to you, your loved ones and friends. Hopefully we will see you soon.

The agony of not knowing is too much to handle. I pray that everyone is fine. I pray that getting so close to finally realizing my goal, it won't be pulled away. I selfishly think of myself first and their safety after because I have waited too long for this day to have it snatched away. I feel like I must do something, but there is nothing I can do except wait and pray.

I am not thinking rationally and it is Mark who speaks the obvious. The storm hit on Friday and it is now the weekend. No one would be in the office until Monday and I would not be able to reach them until then. He's right. I know he is, but it is still hard to wait.

"Stop focusing on the storm. That is out of your control," he adds.

So I stop. I stop flipping through news reports and searching for coverage on the internet. I keep busy doing anything and everything I can think to do and the rest of the weekend passes as one big blur.

When Monday finally arrives, I have to control myself. From the minute I open my eyes I want to make that call to Oklahoma City, but I force myself to get out of the bed, brush my teeth and hair and then go back to the bedroom and wake Mark.

I stick to our usual Monday morning format as I put on my exercise clothes and meet Mark downstairs. I wait patiently as he puts on his sneakers and ties the laces, but inside I want to scream.

I can't just go on with my life, my routines. But I have been doing this all along. I have been performing my duties and life patterns since all of this began so it is nothing new. I manage to smile at Mark as I gather our water bottles and carry them out the door with me. I open the door and slide into the passenger seat of my PT Cruiser and wait while Mark gets into the driver's seat. It is now 4:20 a.m. as we pull out of the driveway and head for Planet Fitness.

It is a short, quiet ride which is not unusual on these early morning drives. Mark concentrates on making sure there are no deer waiting to dash out in front of our car and I keep quiet out of respect for him. He is not one to fall out of bed and immediately carry on a conversation like I am. By the time we reach the gym, I am over my pity party and ready to workout.

Mark and I work out for 90 minutes, moving from one machine to the next. As I normally do I stop to chat with friends between sets. It's easy here to act normally because it is like a 'special' environment where our lives are strangers to each of us and what we say and do here is separate from our real lives.

At five of six a.m. it is time to go. I wait at the door while Mark goes into the men's locker room to put on his spare shirt and gather his belongings. When he reappears, Mark sees me at the door and smiles as he walks over to join me. We exit the building together, climb into the car and soon we are making the five minute ride back home. We talk now, but not about anything important. I know that Mark is aware of my impatience to make that call to Oklahoma. No way he doesn't because he knows me well.

At home Mark starts his morning rituals as he gets ready for work. I go into my office and sit down to sign on to the computer and while it opens, I go into the kitchen to get a cup of coffee.

I carry my coffee to my home office and start going through the email hoping on the off chance that I will see something from Oklahoma in the inbox. I know it is wishful thinking but I need to hope. There is nothing there from Oklahoma City.

I want to contact the detective or Jane Cannon, but that seems so insensitive as they may be dealing with the aftermath of the storm, so I settle on going through the other emails despondently. For those requiring a response, I send one off immediately and the others I read and make any notes required. When done, I close my email and go upstairs to take a shower. I get dressed for the day and go back downstairs.

In the kitchen I find Mark standing at the counter and watching SportsCenter. I go about the rooms opening the blinds in the office, the library and then open the curtains in the great room.

I turn out the back yard light before going over to the kitchen pass through to sit on the stool across from Mark.

Mark looks up and smiles, but doesn't say anything. I can tell he is engrossed in the program so I sit quietly sipping my coffee until he turns to me and asks, "How are you doing?"

"Fine," I lie.

Then it's on to small talk about what he will need to do at Kodak so he can be ready for our trip. From there he asks what should he take and I tell him that I will pack for him too. Then it is time for him to go and I walk to the door, kiss him goodbye and tell him to have a wonderful day. He says the same to me.

I busy myself in the office. I work from home most days, having to go out if I get a call for system support or when I have to go to the schools to teach a computer class. There are no classes pending so I am pretty much on my own to write or take care of any upholstery jobs that are in the shop. I decide to fill my head with details for finishing the sofa project that I need to get done before we go.

I take a landline phone and make sure that I have my cell as well. I fill my water bottle and then head to my upholstery shop in the basement. At the bottom of the stairs I pause wondering if I should first start a load of laundry, but looking at the laundry bin I see there isn't much there so I head directly in to the upholstery room.

It is cool down here, just like I like it. I go over and turn on the television set that is always on Channel 56, HGTV, and then pull out my upholstery tools. In no time my mind is at ease as I become engrossed in the project. And then the phone rings.

At first the sound of the phone ringing startles me, but then my mind rewinds to remind me it could be Oklahoma calling. In my hand is a strip of upholstery tacks that I have been applying along the seams of the sofa. Carefully I release the strip, trying not to disconnect it from the others and step cautiously across the upholstery room floor, trying not to step on the cording that hangs down one side, just before the last place I have applied the decorative tacks.

It seems like it takes me forever to get to the phone, but it is only a few seconds when I pick up the receiver and say, "Hello?"

"Hello, Ms. Tischendorf, this is Kerrin Jones."

"Oh my god, Kerrin, I have been so worried. Are you alright?"

"Yes, I am fine."

"What about Jennifer? Did the tornado do much damage at your building and Cleveland County?"

"It did.." She goes on to say that on April 13 at around 4:00 pm CDT time, the tornado entered the southwest side of Norman, and crossed Interstate Highway 35 (I-35) north of west Lindsey Street. It was rated an EF-1 tornado. The tornado finally lifted near the intersection NE 12th Avenue and Robinson Street at around 4:15 pm CDT. The winds were estimated at 100 mph as they tracked through downtown Norman, causing widespread damage. Many homes sustained varying degrees of damage and a paint store was destroyed by the tornado with many trees and power lines downed. That's the damage apparent here in Cleveland County. There have been reports of an apartment complex in the area losing its roof as well. In total twenty people were injured by the tornado, though only one required hospitalization. Central Oklahoma, which includes Cleveland County was hardest hit with large hail. It caused minor damage in Norman, Oklahoma, where there were unofficial reports of injuries.

I listen intently as she mentions details that I wasn't able to find on line or hear in any news report.

"Did you sustain any damage to your home. Did Jennifer."

"Neither one of us did. Thanks for asking."

"So what is going on now," I ask

"There's been a lot of damage to power lines, gas lines, and electrical systems, throughout the region and according to Oklahoma Gas and Electric Co., more than 800 Norman residents remained without power Sunday evening. OG&E's crews worked Sunday along 24th Avenue SW, between Boyd Street and State Highway 9, where numerous power lines and utility poles were damaged. Just after the storm passed, about 4,000 of OG&E's

Norman customers were affected. I noticed that where your hotel is situated there are tarps on the roofs but they remain open."

"So it hit before the end of the day? What did you do?"

"On Friday, April 13, we were sequestered to the basement at the County office building. We were not allowed to go home or able to receive or make calls. It was really scary, but we are pretty much use to this as it is not uncommon to have tornadoes in April."

"Are we still on?"

"They are in the midst of clean-up in the area, but it should be pretty much done by the time you come. As far as we are concerned, it is still on."

When I hang up the phone I am feeling much better knowing the proceedings have not been cancelled. I go back to the upholstery job. I finish what I need to do and then by early afternoon I am back upstairs. I check my email and find one from Kerrin. I open it up. It has the final instructions for our trip.

###

When we arrive in Oklahoma City we need to go to the baggage claim level and then cross the street where our hotel transportation will be waiting for us. They will transport us by Air Express to our hotel and the bill is going to be sent directly to the DA's office. We will be staying at Country Inn and Suites in Norman, Oklahoma. When checking in at the hotel we are to give them our name and let them know that the bill should be directed to the DA's office.

As for our meals we must pay for them and turn in our receipts to the DA's office. Any long distance calls or movies are at our own expense.

On the day of the court appearance, April 16, 1012 we will be picked up at our hotel at around 7:45 a.m. by an employee of the DA's office. We should pack light and take our bags with us as we will not be returning to the hotel. The hearing is set for April 17, 2012 at 8:30 a.m. so we should eat an early breakfast at the hotel.

From the courthouse we will be transported back to the airport after the court appearance by either the Airport Express shuttle service or by an employee with the DA's office. We are reminded to have our cell phones with us in case there is a need to contact us, and because we will be at the courthouse for a while, it might be advisable to bring a book or something to read.

The day I have been anticipating has arrived and I feel timorous. I can't understand this feeling because there seems to be no reason for it. Yet, that is how I feel. And there is another feeling that I deal with and that is a clearer sense of death. Yes, Erik has been gone all this time, but for some reason it now seems factual. I tick off and total the time from Thursday, September 16, 2010 to Tuesday, April 17, 2012. It is 580 days or 1 year, 7 months, 2 days that will pass to get us to this day. That is one day more since 2012 is a leap year and one more day that I will remember for the rest of my life.

CHAPTER 23: RETURN TO OKLAHOMA

Somewhere on the internet I found that the average length of time between a conviction to sentencing in a murder case where the sentence is Life With Parole is 732 days or 2 years, Life Without Parole is 887 days or 2 ½ years and a sentence of Death is 1,107 days or 3 ¼ years. The figures were based on average estimates of court processing time (from initial filing dates to sentencing) and the number of court hearings, order, and motions. I did this search to find out if the time I was spending waiting for justice was normal or what.

And why is this important? Unless you have been in my shoes, you won't understand that need to determine every facet of existence during the anticipation of closure.   It won't be clear why it is a special type of closure that awaits me because there is not a word in the English language to describe a mother who has lost a child. I was a mother to my son but I cannot claim that title anymore. I have lost one of my identities and there is no word to replace no longer being a mom.

I think of the saying by Lao Tzu, "If you are depressed, you are living in the past. If you are anxious, you are living in the future. If you are at peace you are living in the present". I want to embrace the feeling of peace.

###

On April 15, 2012, Kansas Governor Sam Brownback declared a state of emergency for the entire state due to the tornadoes, straight-line winds, hail and flash flooding. Oklahoma Governor Mary Fallin declared a state of emergency the following day on April 16 for twelve Oklahoma counties that includes Cleveland County but I have been assured that everything would be proceeding as scheduled. .

Here in Rochester we experience a weather phenomenon with temperatures reaching around 80 degrees. For us the weather in April will usually be around 45 degrees so this is unexpected, but appreciated. This means that for our upcoming trip I can eliminate the need for coats and sweaters, making it much easier to pack lightly.

I am able to pack everything in our two carryon bags each which means that we won't have to bother with baggage claim. The thought of standing there with the other passengers, watching the carousel go round and round and feeling the tension mount each time I do not see my bag amongst those that pass, is stress I do not need. In my state of mind, finding I forgot our pills or even our toothbrush would mount a panic attack so I need to really concentrate on packing for even this one day trip.

So for my own peace of mind, I start early, making a list that I hook on the cork board in my office so that each time I think of something to take, I can write it on the list. I ask Mark to do the same. By the time I need to physically pack, I am pretty sure there is nothing we have missed.

As the time grows closer, I go to the airline site and print out a copy of our e-Tickets, and boarding passes. Just doing this makes it seem validated that this is really happening.

Then there is the instruction sheet sent to me in an email from Kerrin. This is important as it has the details to follow while we are in Oklahoma. Without this we would probably be okay, but that is too chancy. I print out a copy.

I then search through the emails for the one from the University American Travel and find it. I look at the trip itinerary information and then send it to the printer. I sit there staring at the computer screen thinking hard, making sure I have everything I need. No, I say to myself, you need to get your contact sheet printed. I exit the email program and open up Excel. I search through the spreadsheet names until I see the one saved as Oklahoma Contacts. I open it up.

This sheet has the name, address and phone number of the important people I have been in contact with since all of this took place. I know I won't have a lot of time, but I would like to know I have the information if I need to reach them. I print a copy of the excel sheet.

I go over and take the papers off the printer. I put Marks e-ticket and my e-ticket side by side on the desk in front of me. I put his boarding pass on top of his e-ticket and then mine I place on my e-ticket. I put the copy of the itinerary on top of my e-ticket and then stop. Before I even know what I plan to do, my hand reaches out and picks up the itinerary and the instruction sheet from Kerrin. I carry them to the copier and put them in the auto feed tray and push the button. I make another set of each of these and put them on the two piles I have made.

Satisfied that I have everything copied now, I take the pile of my documents and go over and place them directly in my purse. I pick up the other pile and go upstairs and put them in the front pocket of Mark's carryon.

I go back downstairs and mentally review what I have done and when I feel confident, I go to the cork board, find the list I have made and check off these items as completed.

Back in the office I get my purse and bring it to my desk. I open it and pull out my wallet. I check that I have my ID, credit cards and cash. I do. I sometimes will slip them into my phone case and forget to put them back in my wallet. Knowing they are where they now belong, I check these items off the list under my name; leaving Mark's blank so that he can verify he has his ID, credit cards and cash for the trip.

It is finally time to start packing. The size restrictions of packaging make it an art form these days. There are so many items that need to be checked to verify they meet the size for liquid requirements, then the search to identify what is considered to be a liquid. Finally you can feel confident as you place the proper items in that quart zip lock bag; a feat that is in itself a magic trick.

Taking my list with me, I go upstairs and I get out my contact lens case and solution, plus a pair of glasses. I go through my makeup and choose just the items that are necessary. Then it is on to our travel toothbrush and toothpaste, mouth wash, razors, shampoo, conditioner, lotion, shower gel, face scrub, hair brush, comb, and soap. It may be only a day, but the hygiene and personal care items are necessary and they take up a lot of space. I double check each liquid container to make sure they meet the size requirements before checking them off the list.

In the midst of doing this I think of something else and rush back downstairs. I search in the kitchen cabinets for a smaller holder for our pills and I find what I am looking for. Carefully I transfer morning and evening pills for both of us into the container and carry it back upstairs with me.

I start to place the liquids in two, one-quart bags so they'll make it through airport security. Even with the smaller sizes, it takes some flair to get all the items in the bag and then seal it, but I manage. I place them on the bed beside the pills.

I get out the clothes we will wear on the plane and lay them out on the settee at the foot of our bed. And now comes the hard part. What to wear to court.

This takes some thought since I have never had to dress for such an occasion, I don't know what to choose. We're not witnesses or even considered to be a part of the proceedings. We are there for no other purpose than for Erik. Yet I want us to look appropriate and I have a feeling that means I do not need to wear a dress, but a pair of slacks, no jeans and a nice top, no t-shirt and no sneakers and definitely no flip-flops. I settle on nice sandals. I write all of this down and carry the paper with me as I gather Mark's attire and then my own.

Thinking I am done, I start to put the quart bags in our carryons, but stop, and review the list again. I find I forgot to pack underwear and Mark's, socks. Not only that, I almost forgot to pack our night clothes and slippers.

I sit on the edge of the bed, feeling sorry for myself. This is hard enough without having to think about such mundane things. I start crying and feel so stupid, but I can't help it so I just let it take control. I know I should be happy that I am near the end of all this, but somehow those days of dealing with the case made me feel closer to Erik. Will I lose that feeling now?

When I finally get over my pity party, I look at the list and make sure everything has been checked. I confidently then, put in the quart bags, but leave the cases open for those last minute items we may need to add.

I can hear Mark downstairs in the kitchen as I pass the stairs on my way to the bathroom to wash my face so that I don't look like I've been crying. I take a mirror check and then go downstairs to join Mark.

"I have us packed," I say. "You might want to check your bags to see if I forgot anything, though."

"Okay, I will later."

I then ask for his cell phone. I take mine and his into the office to put on the chargers. This will be the means of communicating with Kerrin and anyone else who needs to reach us so I want to be sure they are charged before we leave.

Mark has been working in the garden while I have been packing. He decides to call it a day and goes back outside to put his stuff away. When he returns I watch as he goes by me and up the stairs.

I envy him. He loves to spend time working on the yard, while I like spending time inside. I'm sure he thinks about the same things I am thinking about, but in a different way. Erik was grown when Mark and I married in 1995 so even though they are close, there is no biological bond that obligates his relationship, though he has chosen to have one with my son. Erik was 26 when we married and he was there at our wedding just like we were there at Erik's wedding. They have known each other for 15 years, including THAT day so I know they have a genuine love and concern for each other, though I can't help thinking that the biological bond is stronger.

When Mark comes back downstairs, he says, "Everything is packed. I can't think of anything you missed." He gives me a kiss and then we make our evening meal together. This takes my mind off of the trip as I gather the ingredients for his famous tuna noodle casserole and put them on the counter. While he cuts up the vegetables, I put the frying pan on the burner and set it at low. I then fill a pan with water and set it on the stove to boil. By the time I complete these tasks, he is already putting the vegetables into the frying pan. Soon the kitchen is engulfed with the smell of onions and garlic which always makes me hungry.

When the noodles are ready, I take them over and pour them into the strainer, while Mark adds the mushroom soup to the vegetables and follows that with a can of tuna. I remember it so well, probably because the steps have been repeated many times during our marriage. Right now, that is how I keep myself in the present.

We fix our plates and carry them into the family room. Mark sits in his chair and I sit on the couch. We eat our dinner and watch a television show together. When I finish eating, I carry my dish to the kitchen and through the pass through I say, "Don't forget to check you have your ID, credit cards and cash in your wallet."

Mark smiles and says, "I will." Which means that he knows I know that these items are always on his person.

While Mark enjoys a second plate of food, my mind drifts back to the matter at hand. I wonder what will happen in court. I have prepared what I wish to say, but I don't know if I will be able to actually say anything. I am facing this woman who murdered my son for the first time and I wonder what good it will do to 'preach' to her. She won't care what I have to say and what if I say something to make her change her mind and want to take her chances in court. Could that happen? I ponder the question.

I force myself to stop thinking about this and hear Mark say, "If we want to visit with mom in Williamsville before going to the airport we should plan on getting to Buffalo at around ten in the morning. This means we need to be on the road by at least eighty-thirty."

I nod my head in reply and then try to concentrate on the television program. At a little after ten o'clock I go about closing the shades and curtains. As I pass through the kitchen I take my evening pills and say, "Don't forget to take your pills".

Mark says he already has taken his so I tell him I am going upstairs. Mark replies, "I'm right behind you."

I climb the stairs and go into the bathroom to brush my teeth and hair and wash my face. When I enter the bedroom Mark is already there and we change places.

I hear Mark as he gets ready for bed and I start removing the pillows and put them on my jewelry case since the settee has our clothes on it. By the time I turn down the covers, Mark is back in the room and goes to his side of the bed to climb in and grab the remote. Soon the room is filled with the sound of the television, but after I climb in the bed, make one adjustment on my pillows, I am asleep.

###

Monday, April 16, 2012 and the temperature is to be a balmy 86 degrees. We take our time getting ready. With his bags in tow, Mark gathers his clothes and goes to the downstairs bathroom to take his shower. He will have two carryons; the one I packed and the other that he has reading material and other items he needs to review.

Alone upstairs, I make the bed, then gather the clothes I intend to wear on the trip and put them on the bed. I then take off my night shirt and go into the bathroom where I turn on the shower, pin up my hair and after a quick test of the water, climb in.

The water is soothing and I feel as though I could just stay in there forever, but we have places to go today so I allow myself only five minutes before stepping out and drying myself. Now, as I prepare myself for the day ahead, I do a mental recording of my steps from putting on the deodorant, lotion and facial products. I then go into the bedroom and repeat the steps in my head as I look at the quart bag and other products in my carryon. I feel confident I haven't missed a thing.

In no time I am dressed and go about zipping up my carryon and grabbing my purse to take downstairs with me. Of course, this is not my everyday purse. This is much larger so that I can put the personal items and other things inside without too much trouble.

Downstairs we eat breakfast in the Great room, while listening to the news channel to see if there is any weather problems going on that could interfere with our trip. The weather reports are saying that today, Monday, April 16, the temperature in Rochester is 56 degrees currently and will go to 87 degrees later in the day. No showers reported. The temperature in Buffalo will start at 54 degrees and go to a high of 82 degrees with no chance of showers while Chicago is at 48 degrees with the temperature rising to around 77 degrees with no chance of rain. Finally, Oklahoma City is reported to be starting out with a low of 48 degrees and a high of 72 with no chance of showers. There is thankfully, nothing being reported to interfere with our travel.

While Mark cleans up the breakfast dishes, I go and unplug the phone chargers and take them, along with our cells into the kitchen where I put the chargers in our carryon, hand Mark his cell and place mine in my purse. Mark grabs a hat out of the closet and soon we climb into the car. We are finally on our way at a little before 8:30 a.m.

Mark drives from our home to Ridgeway Avenue where he gets on I-490 West that will take us to the New York State Thruway (I-90). Interstate 490 in New York is the major east-west thoroughfare in the Rochester metropolitan area. It connects to Interstate 90 (New York State Thruway) at both ends. For a distance, Interstate 490 follows the path of the old Erie Canal but there is not much to see from the highway. With the traffic surprisingly light for a workday, I relax and just look at the houses and the treed landscape that we pass by until I feel the car slow down. I look in front and see we are already at the entrance to the thruway.

Mark stops at the toll booth and takes the ticket being handed to him. He passes it to me and I put it in the little alcove in front of the gear selector. Soon we are on our way again.

It is a beautiful Monday morning, the temperature warm enough to open the windows, though Mark likes to keep them closed to preserve gas. That's okay with me since with the window down we hear the acceleration of trucks and cars passing each other. Then there is the occasional trucker blowing their horns, but more importantly is the constant enhanced sound and movement of the wind as it stampedes into the windows, making it impossible to hear music or each other talking.

There is not much to see out the window now so I ask Mark if he wants to listen to the book again and he says, yes.

Today we are listening to the third of the six disc Bill O'Reilly's 'Killing Lincoln'. The first words you hear on disc one is, "The story you are about to read is true and truly shocking", grapping my attention from the onset though admittedly I am not a fan of CD books, but they do serve a purpose when driving and this is a very interesting story that we both enjoy. I can't say that O'Reilly is my favorite person or writer, but the topic is most interesting. By November of 2011 the book made Amazon's best seller list and number two on the New York Times list of best-selling non-fiction with nearly a million copies sold.

The book tells the story of the events surrounding the assassination of Abraham Lincoln in details I have never heard before, but that make the event tangible. The CD entertains us as we make our way to Williamsville, a suburb of Buffalo.

We are making good time with hardly any traffic to contend with. We exit the thruway at Transit Road, pay our toll and I turn off the CD. "To continue, another time," I say to Mark.

Transit Road, as usual is heavily congested as we make our way to the first left turn to get off this major artery. Being from Williamsville, Mark deftly turns on one side street after another until finally we are pulling into Canterbury Woods where my mother-in-law lives. From our front door to Mark's mom, Rita's it has been an hour and twenty-three minutes.

We find a parking spot and climb out of the car, this time not needing to take any baggage with us. Together we walk up the driveway and stop at the sidewalk to enjoy the flowers. The center circle between the roadway that runs in front of her apartment door is abloom with a field of lilies and along the white picket fence in front of us are more lilies and spring blooms.

I love coming here, especially because I love and get along well with Rita. She lives in Canterbury Woods which is an English Tudor building style, Continuing Care Retirement Community. These are elegant, maintenance-free apartments with resort-style amenities.

When the Episcopal Church Home and Affiliates opened Canterbury Woods in the summer of 1999, Mark's mom and dad were one of the first to become residents. They would have a 1000 sq. ft. apartment with two bedrooms and two bathrooms, walk-in closets, a spacious living room and dining room combined, a laundry room and a full kitchen. When Jim, Mark's dad passed, Mom moved to a 560 sq. ft. apartment with one bedroom, one bathroom plus all the same amenities. Here Mark and I would sleep on a pull out sofa whenever we stayed overnight.

We continue up the walkway that leads to Mom's door and as usual, when she is expecting us, it is unlocked and we walk in.

The smell of tomato soup reaches our nostrils and we see Rita, busily preparing lunch. Careful not to stun her, we walk slowly over to the pass through of the kitchen and say, "I Mom." Rita turns away from the stove and says, "Hi." We enter the kitchen and help her with the rest of the lunch preparations.

It's fun to hear of the happenings in the building since we have been coming here so often. Each person she speaks of we have met and enjoy being caught up on what they are doing. At one time, Mark made a stool for one of the residents, and I have upholstered many items for several of her friends. Then, too, this is one of the places that has always welcomed me to present my latest book. In a way, this is like a second home to us.

We talk and eat a hearty lunch of tomato soup and turkey sandwiches. When we are able to stay longer, we would sometimes go down to the dining room and eat lunch there, but this is a faster alternative since we won't be staying long.

By the time we finish eating and clear the table it is eleven o'clock. We go for a walk around to the front entrance to see the new plants that the new ground keepers have put in. Mom has told us that they were disappointed with the previous ground keepers and she likes what the new ones are doing. "It looks great," I say and Mark agrees.

Before going back to the apartment, we go over to look at the pond and listen as Mom tells us how the geese are outsmarting them. No matter what they do, the geese still keep coming and they are running out of things to try. It's not that they don't like the geese, it's that it's hard to dodge the goose poop when going for a walk.

Mark checks his watch and says we need to get back, so we turn around and go down the sidewalk and back into the building.

We retrace our steps back to Mom's apartment, stopping several times to say 'hello' to her friends along the way.

We say our goodbyes and head out the door. We walk back to the car and climb in. The time is ten of twelve as we pull out of our parking space and head for the airport.

Little over five miles and thirteen minutes later we arrive at the Buffalo Niagara International Airport, located in the suburb of Cheektowaga. We pull into the FastTrack Parking Lot that is just minutes away from the airport. While waiting for the shuttle service to take us to the airport we gather our luggage from the back of the car and Mark presses the button to lock the doors. In less than five minutes the shuttle arrives. We climb on board and are on our way to the airport. When we are in front of the American Airlines entrance, we gather our carry-ons and disembark the shuttle. It is now 12:13 p.m.

Inside the airport is pulsating with passengers checking in and others returning from their destination. Since we have our boarding passes, we head directly to the security check-in area and enter the access control gates along with the other passengers standing in line ahead of us.

The line moves slowly as some passengers have to dig for their ID and boarding passes, required before entering the access control gates. Finally we are able to place our items in the bins provided and put them on the conveyor belt that will carry them pass the x-ray machine. When I hear security say, "Step Through, Please" I move ahead to enter the metal detectors, that does not 'sound off' because of my knee replacements. If it had, I would have to go through the puffer machine, which would slow us down even more. Mark follows without any problems.

As we step out of the metal detectors our carry-ons have made it through the x-ray machine and are waiting for us on the other side of the conveyor belt. We gather our luggage and enter the airside area of the airport. Now we look about and find a flight board to check our flight to see which gate it will be loading at and if it is on time. We see that it is on time and will be leaving at 1:30

p.m. from Terminal 3 which is four terminals down from where we are.

We start walking to the departure gate for our American Airline flight 4143 and arrive in less than 10 minutes. It is now almost 12:30 p.m. We take turns going to the rest rooms. In the waiting area before our gate, the area is packed so we stand, waiting for our zone area to be called so that we can get in the line to board the plane. As soon as we hear our zone, we squeeze into the line and get our boarding passes out. The line moves slowly up to the entrance to the plane, but finally we are next in line and hand our boarding passes to the flight attendant near the entrance who checks our boarding passes. Finally we are on our way down the jetway to the airplane.

There is a buildup of passengers on the jetway after the boarding pass check, so we have to wait in line again before boarding the plane. I look at the other passengers, some who have heavy luggage to struggle with and feel sorry for them. They will have trouble making it down those narrow aisles to their seats, let alone trying to handle the weight.

Finally we cross the threshold and enter the plane. As we move slowly down the aisle, we check for our row number and our seat assignment, constantly stopping as others stow their carry-on items. When we locate our seats, we place our bag on our seats, and Mark looks for available space in the overhead bins for our larger carryons. This isn't the easiest task, but finally he does find space. When we're finally able to get in our seats, we place our smaller carry-ons under the seat in front of us and fasten our seat belts.

I watch the other passengers as they wait to be seated, or struggle with their luggage in the overhead bins. That occupies me for a bit before I think about the time. We are leaving at 1:30 p.m. EST but are heading to Chicago, CDT. That means they are one hour behind us. So actually when we leave it is 12:30 p.m. in Chicago. So when we land at 2:15 p.m. it is really 3:15 p.m. EST, our time. After a few more silly thoughts, the plane starts moving backwards from the gate. I watch the airport workers scurrying about below us until we switch from reverse to forward travel, heading toward the runway.

We are in line, waiting for the air traffic control to give us the okay to take off. While we remain in hold position before the runway, I lean over and get out my kindle to read my book, but feeling that the plane is moving again, I look out the window instead. The pilot says over the intercom, "Ladies and gentlemen, we have received   clearance from Tower Control to takeoff. Stewardess, please perform your pre-flight checks and ready yourself for takeoff."

Soon we are moving down the runway now at takeoff speed so I look out the window and watch the scenery zooming by. I hear the wheels as they fold up and soon we are soaring smoothly through the sky. Since I can almost recite the presentation that the stewardess will now perform, I turn on the kindle and soon I am engrossed in reading my book.

The first leg of the trip goes smoothly without a problem and a tailwind gets us into Chicago O'Hare, a little before 2:15 p.m. CST. Inside the plane you can feel the tension growing as people anxiously wait for the plane to finish taxiing to the gate and then come to a complete stop. At that very second it seems, everyone is in the aisle trying to claim their luggage from the overhead bins or just stand in line to debark.

We sit in our seats on the plane and wait until it is time for our row to enter the aisle so that we don't get in the way of passengers trying to get their belongings out of the overhead bins. My knees are aching from being in the bent position for so long and I need to stand. I manage to stand up, even under the overhead bins, and am thankful I am short enough to do so. While I stand, I reach down and get my bag from under the seat in front of me and put it on my seat. I search around inside and find what I am looking for. Carefully I remove two Aleve tablets and pop them in my mouth. I dry swallow them.

While I do this, Mark manages to squeeze into the aisle and get to the overhead bin where he has stored our other carry-ons. Carefully he takes them out and balances them in front of him so that he can squeeze his way back to our seats.

We have plenty of time before our flight takes off from here so we wait patiently in the row. Finally it is our turn and Mark steps into the aisle again and moves back and lets me step out in front of him. We follow the passengers down the jet bridge and into the terminal. The flight has taken one hour, seventeen minutes

Our connecting flight American Airline Flight 3780 is scheduled to leave O'Hare at 4:40 p.m. so we have a little over two hours before boarding our next flight. I'm not really hungry after having lunch with Mom, but Mark wants to get a little something so I get a coffee.

Since the area is packed, we take our purchase with us as we find and check a flight board and gladly note that we are in terminal three and will be departing from the same terminal. As we make our way toward the departure gate, we pause to look at pictures along the way that have been done by the Chicago elementary school students and now hang on the walkway aisle walls of the airport.

Soon we arrive at the departure gate, which since we are early, we are able to find seats in front of one of the television monitors so we sit down and watch the news. After a bit my eyes drift about the area, noticing passengers sitting on the floor against the wall. On closer observation I see that they are plugged into outlets either charging phones or laptops or just using the juice to operate them.

Other passengers have purchased food and sit eating as they wait and still others that are not talking to someone, have immersed themselves in reading material. I decide to get out my kindle and read, but there is such a bustle of activity everywhere, I don't turn it on.

In the aisles people continue to come and go in all directions and then there are the constant announcements that one can barely decipher. I find it more interesting to watch the patrons as they mill about the airport. I wonder where they are going and try to determine by their facial expressions if it is to a place for business or pleasure. In most cases, it seems to be for pleasure as they have smiles on their faces or are outright laughing. I wonder if others are looking at me and speculating the same thing. I wonder what they finally ascertain.

I have had 578 days, or 1 year and 7 months to adjust to the fact that I will not see my son again. Even though it hurts, I am able to accept it because I know that nothing I do will change what has happened. I have also learned to accept that it was not my fault that this horrible thing happened and that tolerance took the most time.

Sure, he is a grown man. Sure we live in different states. Yet in the beginning I kept feeling as though I am to blame because I didn't know how to talk him into moving back to Rochester. Now I know how silly that sounds, yet it comes from the belief that parents are responsible for their children.

I am pulled out of my reverie when I hear the announcement they will begin loading passengers on Flight 3780. Mark and I gather up our things and go to stand near the end of the line, awaiting our zone to be called. The wait is even longer than in Buffalo with what seems to be double the people waiting to board the plane but finally we hear our zone called and step in line. The Aleve I took has kicked in and my knees feel much better as we move slowly forward.

Following the same procedures we make it to the jet bridge and hurry down to our plane where upon entry, we nod as they say, "Welcome aboard" to each passenger. Then it's down the narrow aisle trying not to hit anyone in the head along the way, until we reach our seat. I allow Mark to take my carryon and put it in the overhead bin while I sit down and hook my seat belt. We leave Chicago right on time. This is a one hour, thirty-five minute flight, just slightly longer than the first leg of our journey.

Even though I haven't done much of anything, I feel tired so I lean back against the headrest and remember nothing more. I sleep soundly, only waking at the announcement of the pilot saying that we will be landing in Oklahoma City in about ten minutes. I pull out my cell and check the time. It is 6:30 p.m. CST. I look at Mark who sits across the aisle from me and he is busily putting his reading material back in his bag.

Fully awake now my knees are screaming at me. The pain is so intense I can barely stand up, so I take two more Aleve and hope it does the trick. I try not to cringe from the pain, knowing I still have to get off the plane and I don't want to worry Mark. I am grateful that those around me are moving slowly because I don't feel as though I can even take one step, let alone several. When Mark asks if I am all right, I say, yes because there is nothing he can do. I am hopeful that once we get off the plane and I can move around a bit, I will feel better.

Slowly I make it off the plane and up the jet bridge trying hard to put one foot in front of the other, ignoring the pain that still persist. I manage pretty will to keep up with Mark as we walk through the Will Rogers Airport in Oklahoma City, Oklahoma. I keep telling myself this is it and soon I will be able to sit with my legs up and ice packs on each of them.

Mark has the instructions from Kerrin in his hand. He takes us to the baggage claim level where we exit the terminal and go across the street where our hotel transportation is to be waiting. He looks up and down and finally locates the Airport Express, the designated transportation the DA has set up.

Mark speaks to the driver to be sure they are expecting us, then motions me to join him. The driver takes charge of our baggage, putting them onboard for us and we climb in and take a seat.

We are finally on our way. The driver carries on a conversation with Mark about the tornado and the damage done in the area, while I stare out the window in amazement. There is definitely signs of the tornado, but they have done a great job of cleaning up. We take Terminal Drive that I notice becomes S. Meridian Avenue as we continue on our way. I remember that the hotel is located right on this road so I ask, "How far is it to the hotel." "It is about three miles or a little more than that," the drive replies. I thank him, glad it's not far to go.

I barely listen to their conversation as I try to find a comfortable position where my knees don't hurt. There is none. Luckily, the driver is right and soon we are pulling up in front of the Country Inn and Suites in Norman, Oklahoma. The driver gets out, opens the door of the van for us and then helps us with our bags. He asks if there is anything more he can do for us. Mark responds that we are fine and gives him a tip. The driver smiles and says, "You two have a good evening".

Mark and I carry our bags inside and go up to the front desk. Since the arrangements have been made ahead of time by the District Attorney's office, we only need to give them our name and we receive our key. We make our way to our room and once inside, I drop by bags and go over to the bed. I sit down on the edge and then turn halfway around so that I end up leaning my head against the head board and finally I am able to put my legs up.

It feels so good to have my legs in this position that I smile. Mark has been through it all with me so he knows. He goes over to my carry on and digs inside until he finds the ice bag holders. Since we had no way of keeping the icepacks cold, we had to leave them behind, but Mark easily improvises. I listen as in the bathroom, he empties our two quart bags of their contents and then returns, saying he will be back shortly. I then watch him as he leaves the room.

He is only gone for a couple of minutes and when he returns the quart bags are filled with ice cubes. He takes the bags and puts them into the ice bag holders, then places one on each knee.

I can feel the coldness as it seeps through the ice bag holders and I lean back and enjoy the sensation. Mark finds the remote and sits down on the other side of the bed. He turns on the television and searches for a station to watch while I just relax. We remain in this position for about an hour, at which time Mark says, "Do you want to go with me to get something to eat or would you like me to bring you something back?"

My first inclination is to say, 'go ahead', but then I decide to join him. Once we return I will have all night to rest myself and my legs. There is no need to unpack so we don't have to worry about doing anything more when we return except get ready for bed. Besides, I have no idea what food is available and I noticed there were several places in the area to check out.

"Give me a minute and I'll come with you."

I manage to get up, slowly, from the bed and find that it isn't too bad now that I had a chance to put my legs up and ice my knees. I go into the bathroom and freshen up a bit before joining Mark. I talk him into taking the elevator down to the lobby instead of the stairs and soon we are on our way out the door.

I find I am hungry too. I thought there were several places around the hotel to pick from, and there are, but most are not in walking distance for me with my knees so we have two choices— IHOP or a place called Jason's Deli. We've been to IHOP, but Jason's is new to us so we settle on this takeout place called Jason's Deli.

Once inside, it looks interesting even though there is only one other couple inside besides us. We look over the menu on the wall behind the servers and place our orders. I order a Spinach Veggie Wrap with Mushrooms, organic spinach, Asiago, guacamole, pico de gallo, in a toasted organic wheat wrap. Served with salsa. For my side dish I take the fresh fruit and baked chips. Mark orders the Zucchini Grillini with Roasted zucchini, Muenster, organic spinach, red onions, Roma tomatoes, kalamata olives, roasted red pepper hummus, toasted on multigrain wheat bread. He has steamed veggies, and organic blue corn chips with salsa for his sides.

While we wait Mark walks around checking out the place. I settle for reading the sign in front of me that says, "At Jason's Deli we're all about healthy food. From sandwiches to salads Jason's Deli offers healthy and delicious food that everyone can feel good about".

In no time we hear our name called and go up and pay for our sandwiches and we leave, taking them with us back to the Hotel. We notice there are tarps over parts of the roof of our hotel and some of the other buildings in the area, but beyond that, the brush and downed trees are mostly gone. I know the area was hit hard, but what a quick clean up job they did.

It is late when we finally return to our hotel room, much later than we normally eat. I sit in my comfortable position on the bed and put the ice bags back on my knees. Mark takes our sandwich bags and opens them. He makes a makeshift crumb collector out of the bag and places my sandwich in it, before placing it on my lap. The hotel has provided bottled water in the room and Mark opens one for each of us. He puts mine on the night stand and then goes to sit in a chair at the table in the room.

With us both seated and comfortable, Mark turns on the television and we watch the evening news broadcast while we eat. The sandwich is delicious and I thoroughly enjoy it. I ask Mark how his is and he says, "Great."

When we are done, Mark cleans up and says, "Why don't you go in the bathroom first and get ready for bed?" That is fine with me. I take my time getting up and then go over to my bag and dig out my night clothes. I carry them into the bathroom with me. Soon I am in the shower, feeling the release of the tension in my body and the pain in my knees as I let the water soothe me. It feels so good it is hard to get out. But I must. I dry off, put on my night gown then go through my evening hygiene rituals. I return to the bedroom feeling like a new person. "Your turn," I say.

I take the clothes I have been in all day and place them next to my bag, which I reach inside and remove the clothes I plan on wearing tomorrow. I then put the dirty ones inside. Next I go over to my purse and pull out my evening pills, plus the bottle of Aleve. I take the pills with the water Mark gave me and then go over to the bed. I fold down the covers and am just about ready to climb in when I notice that Mark has refilled my icebags, "Thank you," I whisper and then pick them up and put them on the end table before climbing in the bed and putting them on my knees.

Mark finishes in the bathroom and joins me on the bed, I remind him to take his evening pills and watch as he gets back up and digs them out of his carryon. Before getting back in the bed, he brings his water to the side of the bed, and plugs in both of our cell phones. That done, Mark grabs the remote and brings it with him to the bed. When he is finally settled, he searches the stations until he finds 'The Big Bang", something that interest us both and funny enough to lighten our mood.

We both get caught up in the show, but both of us are tired so it isn't long before I slide down in the bed and Mark does the same. He leaves the television on as it seems to lull him to sleep.

I expect to drift off immediately, but instead I listen to the voices on the television, not really understanding what they are saying, but glad to have them interfering with the thoughts running through my head.

Tomorrow I will be face to face with my son's murderer. I have seen pictures of her and so I know what she looks like. I wonder if I will be able to get close enough to her so that I can watch her face when I ask why she murdered my son. I know this will not be a regular court proceeding so I should be able to say whatever I want. She is going to be given a chance to say her piece and I hope she is smart enough to just apologize and not lie about what she did and she needs to say why she did it.

My mind keeps racing, wondering what will unfold tomorrow. I take the icebags off my knees and when I get up and head for the bathroom, I glimpse through the crack in the curtains and see it is already day light. I have been awake almost the whole night! I decide I might as well go ahead and take a shower and get myself ready for the day.

In the shower I do not linger and after drying myself off, I stand before the mirror getting ready. I pack each of my toiletry items after I use them and squeeze them back into the quart bag. I pause for a moment and stare into the mirror hoping that the little make up I'm wearing is enough to hide my fear of making a mistake since I don't know what is the right thing to say and do in this situation. Of course I can ask Kerrin or Jennifer, but what if I don't get to talk to them before court.

It won't help to dwell on the negatives and I know that. I finish up in the bathroom and take a look around to make sure I have packed everything I have used in here. Satisfied, I return to the bedroom.

When I return to the bedroom, Mark is already up and like to ships in the night we past in the doorway. He gives me a quick kiss as he goes in to take his shower and get ready. A look at the nightstand clock lets me know that we have time before our designated pick up so I make myself slow down.

In the bedroom I notice Mark has already made the bed so I put my bag on the bed and take out the clothes I plan on wearing to the courthouse. I get dressed and pat my hair back in place, then walk over to take a look at myself in the mirror. On the outside I think I pass the test, but on the inside I feel like a little girl again, having to put my future in the hands of others. I shake the thought away. This is not the time to feel sorry for myself. I need to be strong and forceful when I walk into that court room. I must be, for Erik.

With my back turned towards him, I hear Mark enter the bedroom. I keep my head down as I pack my night clothes into the bag and then put the quart bag that holds my toiletries in after it. I then walk over to my purse and get out my morning pills. I take them with the water left in my bottle and then walk over to Mark, give him a kiss and say. "Don't forget to take your pills."

"You look nice," he says.

"Thank you."

While Mark goes about getting dressed and repacking his bag, I go into the bathroom, checking once again inside the shower and the top of the vanity making sure we haven't forgotten anything. In the bedroom I check to see if the slippers are back in the suitcases and any other items left on the end tables or dressers have been packed. I don't need to check any drawers or the closet since we both didn't utilize that space.

We have secured all our belongings, except for the cell phones. I go over and unplug them both. I pack the chargers in our carry-ons and then put my cell in my purse and carry Mark's over to lay by the side of the items he will be putting in his pockets.

When I stop, Mark says, "sit down and put your feet up. Ice those knees why you can".

"Good idea." I check the ice bags and they are still cool so I sit down and put one on each knee.

Mark has the papers out that tell about what we need to do and reads out loud the sections that concern us at this point.

"You must pay for your meals and be reimbursed by the DA's office. You may not exceed $46.00 per day in meal reimbursements or charges. We will not pay for long distance calls or movies charged to the room. You will be picked up for your court appearance at your hotel at approximately 7:45 am., on 4-16-12, by an employee of the DA's office. Please bring your baggage with you as you will not be returning to the hotel. Hearing is set for 4-17-12 at 8:30 a.m. Eat an early breakfast at the hotel so that you are well prepared for your morning in the courthouse. There are only vending machines at the courthouse. Don't forget your cell phone, so that you may contact us with any questions. Bring a book, as you may have significant waiting times at the courthouse."

There's more, but for now that's all we need to know. I watch as Mark puts the sheet back in the outside pocket of his bag and then turns to me saying, "We have time before they come to pick us up. Want to go down for some breakfast."

I look over at the clock in the room and see that it is six o'clock now. I remember seeing an IHOP on our exploration last night and say, "We could go to the IHOP. It's almost outside the door of the hotel. What do you thing?"

"Sure. We can try. It might be busy, but if it is we can come back here and eat something."

That decided, we both agree to leave the bags in the room and get them when we return. That way I can fill the ice bags again and take them with me to the courthouse.

Soon we are on our way to the lobby and then out the door, making our way the short distance to the IHOP. Even before we get there, we can tell that it isn't busy, at least not yet. There are only three cars in the parking lot, so we stay on course.

Inside the air is filled with the smell of pancakes and coffee. The hostess comes and takes us to a booth and shortly after we are seated she returns with a coffee pot, two cups, and a creamer. She places these on our table, and then leaves again. While I pick up the pot and pour my coffee, Mark is busy putting creamer in his cup. When I finish, I sit the pot down,, turning the handle toward Mark and he pours coffee into his cup.

This time a waitress returns to the table with menus and lays them on the table telling us to signal when we are ready.

We take a minute to look over the menu. I know what I want.

"I want the spinach and tomato omelet and toast."

Mark raises his hand like he is about to answer a question in school and it makes me laugh. He smiles at me and says, "What? How am I supposed to summon the waitress?"

The waitress acknowledges Mark and returns to the table. I give her my order. Mark says, "I'll have a short stack of the buckwheat pancakes."

"Do you want any potatoes or meat?"

We both say 'no'. She leaves to place our orders.

Mark and I talk about safe topics for a bit, trying to keep our minds clear of why we are here. We will be dealing with that soon enough. In a lull in the conversation, I find myself thinking this is taking place seven days after Erik's 43rd birthday.

Shortly, the waitress returns with our order. Some other early risers stand at the front waiting to be seated and she stops to tell them, "Someone will be with you in a minute." Then she hurries over to our table.

We thank her as she places our food in front of us and I force myself to say something, anything to bring my thoughts to the present. "This looks good. I think the spinach is fresh too."

"Looks like it is."

We eat, noticing how fast the place is filling up now. We concentrate on finishing our meal and actually down several cups of coffee, almost emptying the pot before we are done.

Mark takes a look at his cell and says, "I think we better get going,"

We slide out of the booth and Mark puts a tip on the table before we go to the front where the hostess is waiting. She asks, "Was everything all right?"

"Wonderful," I say.

She takes Mark's credit card and runs it through the machine. In a few minutes she places the receipt in front of Mark and hands him a pen. He scribbles his signature and hands the pen and the receipt back to the hostess, who gives him his receipt in return.

Mark takes a minute to look it over and then puts the credit card and the receipt in his wallet. We exit the restaurant and head across the drive to our hotel.

We enter the lobby of our Hotel and take the elevator to our room. While Mark gives the room one last check, I go down the hall and fill the ice bags again. I may get a chance to use them at the courthouse; at least I hope I do. With everything taken care of together we leave the room for the final time, carrying our bags with us. In the hallway, we wait for the elevator that takes us back to the lobby

In the lobby we go up to the front desk and Mark turns in the key, reminding them that they are to bill the DA's office for our stay. He acknowledges the claim and says, "Hope you enjoyed your stay.

Mark looks at his watch and says, "Let's sit outside. It's nice out and our ride should be coming shortly".

I look at my watch and see that he is right. It is almost seven thirty. We go outside and sit on the porch in front of the hotel. It's cute, and not a common thing for a hotel. We sit on this long, covered porch with eight brown pillars, connected by a white picket like fence. There are tables and chairs making it feel as though you are sitting on a porch at a home, not a hotel. Knowing that we will be stuck inside for most of the day, this is a nice treat.

Right on time our ride to the DA's office pulls up in front of the hotel. Instead of a van, it is a private car and we are unsure until he steps out and asks, "Are you Mr. & Mrs. Tischendorf?"

Mark replies, "Yes, we are."

"I'm here to take you to the court house. Are those all your bags?"

Mark responds that they are and helps by taking his bags while the driver takes mine. Together we walk over to the car and the driver opens the back door so that I can climb in.

I am glad that I iced my knees or this would not have been an easy entry in this low car. By the time I am settled, I hear the trunk close and see Mark opening the door on the opposite side of me. I watch as he climbs in and up ahead, the driver follows suit.

Soon we are weaving out on to the highway. The car has a direction indicator above the rearview mirror and it shows that we are going northeast as we travel from Ed Noble Parkway to Ed

Noble Drive. I look out the side window and see that we are turning right now onto West Main Street.

I know I am being paranoid, but how do we know this is the driver sent for us by the DA? We didn't ask for any credentials, not that he would have them, and we really don't know the way to the court house. Calm down, I tell myself. Stop letting that mind get the best of you.

I settle back and just look at the scenery outside my window. We had noticed more of the damage this morning than we did last night but now as we drive through the area, I can see there are trees down, tarps over roofs, and debris pushed to the sides of the road. I think about how many times there were tornadoes being reported during our visits or when Erik lived at the house. He was lucky that he did not have to go through a seriously damaging tornado touching down where he lived.

Soon we are making a right on South Jones Avenue. I remember from our correspondence that this is the street that the Court House is on. I continue to watch out the window as we pull into the drive on our left and proceed to the front of 201 South Jones Avenue. The whole trip takes us around ten minutes.

The property is massive and I have read about it on the internet..

"The Cleveland County Courthouse is in Norman, Oklahoma and as you can see is a striking Art Deco style building. It was built in 1940 constructed of limestone for both the foundation and walls. The building is three stories with a partial above grade basement. If you look up you will see that the roof is flat. Both the windows and doors are constructed of metal. The historic front doors are double, with metal and glass.

There is a small flat roofed, concrete block addition with a double metal door and to the north of this is a flat roofed, two wall shelter constructed in front of a metal, slab, pedestrian door. Off the rear of the courthouse additional office space has been constructed and is attached to the original building through a one-story, concrete and glass, enclosed corridor on the far north corner of the west elevation.

There is a modern, contemporary style, concrete building Cleveland County Jail on the southwest corner of the block with a concrete and chain link fence just east of the jail, surrounding a parking lot located east of the jail and south of the office addition. This I assume is where Clara Blocker has been since that night.

Inside this main entrance area of the building on the third floor is the office of the Assistant District Attorney, Jennifer Pointer, Austin and also the office of Kerrin Jones, the Victim Witness Coordinator. This is quite a mass of connected buildings and somewhere in there is the Cleveland County District Court and also the office of Judge Lori Walkley who is presiding over Erik's case.

Mark and I climb out of the car and follow the driver to the back to get our carryons. He then takes us inside the building and to the elevator and as we stand waiting for it to arrive he tells us that the connecting veins are very disorienting and he himself has gotten lost in the building.

When the elevator arrives, we take it to the third floor and when the doors open, we again follow the driver as he takes us down the hallways for what seems like forever before finally stopping and depositing us in what appears to be a waiting area. There are comfortable seats, a coffee table with magazines and interesting pictures on the walls.

The driver says, "Please have a seat and I will tell Kerrin you are here."

Because Jennifer had mentioned we will be going to the district court, I researched that as well and learned that the District courts have general jurisdiction over most all civil and criminal matters within their area of control. Oklahoma is divided into nine Judicial Administrative Districts and in Oklahoma there are 77 district courts, each having either a single or multiple District Judges with at least one Associate District Judge to administer justice. As for how they operate, a district judge must be a practicing lawyer or judge for the past four years and must live in the district in which they are seeking election and Associate judges must have been a practicing lawyer or judge for the past two years.

It is facts like this that help me feel comfortable with each 'player' in Erik's case.

We do not have to wait long before Kerrin Jones makes an appearance. She is the Victim Witness Coordinator that I have been in close contact with on the phone, but this is the first time we meet. Until all of this happening, I had no clue of how many people become involved and I had never heard of a Victim Witness Coordinate.

In our first conversation she had to explain that victim witness advocates, are provided by the county or state governments to help crime victims navigate the judicial system and to assist with compensation claims and support services. Her job also is to act as liaison between victims and witnesses and the district attorney's office.

Kerrin explains that she will be taking us to the waiting room outside the Court room and that we can leave our suitcases in the DA's office as they will be bringing us back here. We follow her over to the office and she opens the door. She steps back so that we can deposit our bags inside and then she locks the door.

We follow her back down the hallway we came down to get to the office and stop at the elevator door. While we wait, I look at Kerrin, glad to finally be able to put a face to the voice I have heard for the last two years.

From what I can learn on the internet, I believe Kerrin has lived in Noble, Oklahoma all her life. Noble is a city in Cleveland County, Oklahoma, and is part of the Oklahoma City Metropolitan Area so she is very familiar with the area. She is young, maybe around the same age as my son, or younger. .She has medium length blonde hair and good cheekbones. Today she is wearing an expensive suit and nice sensible heels. What I think I like most is when she speaks she looks directly at you and her voice rings of honesty.

When the elevator doors opens, the three of us step in and Kerrin presses the button for the fourth floor. Not much is said on this short ride, one floor up from where we started. When we disembark Kerrin takes the lead and we follow.

Situated in a build of great character, with none of the buildings originally linking together, or even having floors on the same height, this is, I feel going to be an interesting building to walk through.

Kerrin walks with purpose in front of us at first, confident in her carriage, but slows her pace at each point when she feels we are not in alignment. She easily engages us in conversation by a slight turn of her head in our direction, even managing voice control for turns as we traverse the antechambers of this massive building structure.

I am well aware that we are not her only clients and maybe she took a few minutes to brief herself on us, but even if she has, Kerrin asks with familiarity, "Are you doing all right Ms. Tischendorf? I hope your knees aren't bothering you. We are, almost there."

"Thank you Kerrin. Really I'm fine,"

I am lying but for good reason. Some steps back, my knees were sending out warning signals to stop right now, but I ignored them. What could be done, I ask myself, and come to the conclusion-- nothing. Now as I hoof it, I bet they did have a wheel chair or some other mobility device that she would have offered. I bet too that I wouldn't have accepted it anyway. There is nothing that can be done now so there is no need to make Kerrin or Mark worry about me.

Mark grabs my hand and gives it a squeeze as we continue our walk down these never ending halls and just when I think I may not be able to make it any further, Kerrin finally stops, in front of a doorway. She reaches out and opens the door and says, "This is where you will wait."

She steps aside and lets Mark and I enter the room.

Inside the room has plenty of space and a feel of being a place to come and collaborate and be creative together. They kept the political rule book in mind and decided upon a floor space taken up by a massive mahogany conference table, beautifully crafted with a high gloss shine. The chairs situated around it are of a traditional design, made of solid hardwood with comfortable backs and seat cushions as well as upholstered chair arms. I can't help thinking that this is the perfect workspace for lawyers to come and creatively design the most interesting defense.

Mark and I slide two side by side chairs back from the table and sit down while Kerrin enters the room to stand at the end of the table. She says in a sweet voice, "Jennifer should be joining us soon."

It feels good to sit and I try not to let the 'aah' that escapes my mouth, to audibly be heard. Once seated, I pat my foot around the floor under the table until it comes in contact with the legs of the chair on my left. Knowing from the seat I sit in that there is at least a six inch lip of upholstery overhang on the seat, I discreetly work my left leg up until it rest on the chair, just in front of the arms.

"Can I get you anything?" Kerrin asks.

Hearing her voice, startles me at first, but I modestly say, "Yes, please can I have some water?"

"Sure. Can I get you anything Mr. Tischendorf?"

"I'll take a water too."

Kerrin walks over to the far corner of the room. She leans down and opens the black glass door of what until then, appeared to be a cabinet in the credenza sitting against the back wall. She takes out two bottles of water and carries them back, handing one to each of us. In unison we say, "Thank you."

"You are welcomed. If that is all, I will leave you now. Jennifer should join you soon."

We watch as she leaves the room, leaving the door wide open behind her. Alone with just, I take the bottle of water and lay it on my knee. I hold it there for a bit and then decide I need to take some Aleve so I dig in my purse and get out two capsules that I down with a drink of the cold water. Then making sure the cap is on tight, I again use it to soothe my knee.

"Want mine for the other knee," Mark says. I nod my head, 'no'. Actually the right knee isn't as bad.

I feel like I am in a dream. My brain starts again judging me: What if I do something wrong and make Clara change her mind about pleading 'guilty'. This uncertainty, the worry, the anxiety, the not knowing, makes me hesitant. I feel uncertain and anxious about this whole thing.

Now, instead of my knees being the focus of my pain, my chest hurts and my throat feels dry so I take a drink of the water. Already I feel guilty and muddled with regret for something that hasn't happened beyond thoughts in my head. Seated in this room I feel hot and cold at the same time and it is not the bottle on my knee instigating the feeling.

Thank goodness, at the moment when my judgments are about to overcome me, I look up as in walks a tall, silhouette dark haired, well dressed woman with an engaging smile. She is barely in the room when she lifts her hand up. She seems to glide across the floor until she reaches Mark and he shakes her hand. She then steps behind his chair and reaches between our chairs and across the table to grab my extended hand.

Her hands are cool to the touch, matching the mood she brings to the room. Even though she looks professional, there is an air about her that relaxes the atmosphere. She says, "It is nice to finally meet you both. I am Jennifer Austin, the Assistant DA, who is representing Erik.

I have spoken to her on the phone and drawn my own opinion of her. Here she is now and as I see her in person, I feel as though I do know her. In a way I do. I know her to have developed my confidence in her ability to make sure that justice is served for Erik. What more personal an understanding between two individuals could there be.

After shaking our hands, Jennifer walks gracefully to the other side of the table and sits down across from us. She places her hands on the table in front of her and leans forward, drawing us closer to her as she asks about our trip and if everything went smoothly. We tell her that it did go well and thank her.

She continues to make genuine eye contact without staring as she raises a folder from her lap and places it on the table in front of her. Until now I hadn't noticed the folder.

Suddenly I am aware that I have my leg up on the chair to the left side of me. I cautiously move my leg off its prop and down to the floor, careful not to swing it outward and possibly kick Jennifer.

Jennifer tells us, ""As we discussed on the phone, a plea bargaining is a process where the defense attorney, who in this case is Mr. Smith, negotiates with the district attorney, myself, to obtain the best possible plea for his client, Clara Blocker. Because of the seriousness of the crime, the judge, The Honorable Lori Walkley, has been involved in the plea negotiation by speaking to us. The typical result of the plea bargain is an agreement for the defendant, Clara Blocker to plead guilty to a charge of murder in the first degree, in exchange for a 'with parole' sentence."

"Plea bargains are often good, but of course some are not. Clara did not have to accept the offered plea bargain and even after entering the plea, she can make a motion to withdraw the plea and go forward with the defense of her case."

"The taped interview with Inspector Ken Whitebird was not thorough in that he did not get Clara to say why, when, or how she did it, so there is nothing to fight with against her statement. To that add the fact that she called 911 and sounded remorseful. The jury in Oklahoma can be anyone with a license and she may get manslaughter. Manslaughter would be only 20 years. The plea bargain is that she will get life with parole. The alternative is that this charge is better than risk losing at trial".

"In any case, a guilty plea, makes it easier on both sides than if she pleaded not guilty and took the case to trial."

"So you are saying that it is up to the court and not the individual to accept the plea bargain?" I pause, then add, "Not that I disagree, I just was wondering."

"That's okay. To answer your question though, Plea bargaining is essentially a private process, but this is changing now that victims' rights groups are becoming recognized. Under many victim rights statutes, victims have the right to have input into the plea bargaining process. Usually the details of a plea bargain aren't known publicly until announced in court."

"So who initiated it, the plea bargain," I ask.

"Either side may begin negotiations, though obviously both sides have to agree before one comes to pass. Basically the defendant initiated it by agreeing to plead guilty as charged, with the DA office recommending leniency by agreeing to 'life with parole' as presented in the defendant's plea in sentencing. The judge, however, is not bound to follow the prosecution's recommendation. The judge has discretion to decide whether to accept or reject the plea agreement. To make that decision, the judge evaluates whether the punishment is appropriate in light of the seriousness of the charges, the defendant's character, and the defendant's prior criminal record."

"So what do you think. Is this good?" Jennifer, as if reading my mind, reiterates,

"Pleading 'not guilty' at arraignment is always preferable, as it is easily changed to 'guilty' at any time, while changing from 'guilty' to 'not guilty' is generally more difficult. Clara pled 'guilty' at arraignment. "It is now up to the judge to evaluate the proposed plea bargain, the judge must know all the terms of the deal, including any future conditions or unusual aspects. Similarly, the parties will have to inform the judge if there is anything unusual in how she is to complete her sentence. In this case it is self-explanatory."

"So it's a done deal?"

"Well, Clara Blocker has entered her 'guilty' plea but there is a 10 day period where she can back out but she can't do it by just saying, I made a mistake. She would have to plead 'not guilty' at arraignment, or if the defendant was not represented by competent counsel, but in both matters, it is not the case for Clara. Besides, all possible methods would involve financial charges and she is indigent".

Jennifer waits and they asks, "Do you have any further questions or need any clarification on anything?"

"No", I say, "I feel confident we are doing the right thing."

Jennifer looks in Mark's direction. He says, he is fine with my decision to go ahead as planned.

It is at this point Judge Lori Walkley opens the door and steps in. Having had no dealings with her directly, I can't say what I expected. Judge Walkley is wearing high heels but I believe would be tall even without them. Her frame is thin, her shoulder length blonde hair frames her face. She has a set mouth and eyes that seem to penetrate when she looks in my direction. She wears simple pearl earrings and a necklace of a single row of pearls at her neck. From her stance, I sense that she is in a hurry.

"Hello, Mr. & Mrs. Tischendorf, my name is Judge Walkley. I will be presiding over your son's case. I just stopped by to introduce myself and let you know we are ready for you in the court room.

I start to lift up from my chair and Mark does the same. We stop as Jennifer says, "Thank you Judge Walkley."

Jennifer turns to us picks up where she left off.

"Offering the defendant parole favors us. The defendant also has to produce the funds needed in order to consider parole and seeing as she doesn't have any money or support system now, she wouldn't be able to afford a parole hearing which would come up in 37 years. After this proceeding.

"Even though I am anxious to obey the Judge, I ask, "So what happens next?"

"Clara will be transferred to the prison and you will be notified when the transfer is complete. At that point you will be supplied with instructions enabling you to sign up on the site so that you will be notified of her whereabouts, any parole hearing if it ever comes to be in 37 years, plus anything else, such as her health, death, etc. "

"Any more questions."

I marvel at how calm she is, not affected by the request for us to go to the court room. Me on the other hand, am anxious as the judge has asked us to go to the court room and we are still lingering here. I don't want to be late and I really don't want to make the judge angry because we didn't obey her summon. So when Jennifer asks if we have any questions, we both say, "No", and I stand up with Mark following suit.

Jennifer walks toward the door and we follow close behind her. She opens the door and we stand in the hallway, waiting for Jennifer to lead us in the right direction. Jennifer sifts her papers and once she has them settled, she begins walking. A few steps from our starting point she stops, opens one of the double doors in front of her and we enter the court room.

CHAPTER 24: THE PROCEEDINGS

When a defendant has plead guilty, a hearing is set to determine the obligation of the sentence. Sentencing reports are submitted to the judge and then the judge pronounces judgment at the sentencing hearing.   Violent crimes such as assault, battery, arson, murder, rape, and domestic violence carry the most stringent penalties under the criminal justice system and are considered to be felonies. Whether or not a weapon was used, the seriousness of injuries involved, and an offender's criminal record are all factors that can influence how severely a violent crime is punished.

As we made our way Jennifer files us into one of the bench seats up front, near the table where she will sit. She politely says, "Excuse me." We watch as she walks forward and goes through a small entrance way gate in front of her and walks over to what must be the prosecutor table. There she sits down, reaches in her brief case and arranges papers on the table in front of her.

I look around the room and see someone is looking directly at me. The woman gets up and starts heading in our direction and before she gets close I know who this is. "Hi, she says, I'm Jane Cannon."

"Oh, Jane, I'm Nita Tischendorf. I can't tell you how happy I am to meet you. You have been just wonderful to me. I give her a hug."

I lean over and tell Mark that this is the newspaper reporter who has kept me abreast of what was going on in Oklahoma on this case. "She also shared her own article with me and I liked how she handled the details. It was very respectful".

"I'm glad you approve," Jane says. I watch as she returns to her seat.

There are some other faces sitting on this side of the court room, but from previous conversations, I know there is no one here for Clara and this proceeding is not open to the general public so I assume they are either court personnel or media.

My attention shift's to the left side of the courtroom, up front in an area where the jury would normally sit. The silence in that area is disturbed as a door opens and in shuffles a woman.

I have seen many pictures of her and I know this is, Clara A Blocker. The woman wears an ill-fitting orange two piece surgical scrub, oversized for her frame and wrinkled. An officer blocks her from full view as he enters in front of her, but soon she appears behind him, shuffling into view. Her wrists are incased in handcuffs and from the cuffs is a chain that runs down the front of her, connecting to leg manacles . As she moves forward another person is now visible beside her. I am shocked to see she is chained to a male prisoner who is attired in the same orange scrub of loose fitting tops and baggy pants. She keeps her head down and doesn't look at anyone as she clanks across the room.

Finally the two prisoners are seated and now I can see her face as she sits in the jury box. Clara looks nothing like the pictures I have seen of her before. Her hair has grown out and she seems heavier. She wears glasses and her eyes seem dark and merely slits behind them. She has a very long and thick neck below a square jaw and wide chin. Her prison uniform is wrinkled and ill-fitting with her undershirt hanging below the hemline. She looks disheveled. It is as though she doesn't care how she appears.

I can' help staring at her and it is like it has just happened all over again as I experience a range of thoughts, and feelings, all at once and not having much ability to control myself at all. Nothing in life prepares me for the day when a loved one is murdered especially if you live with illusions of immortality for your son who has survived so much before. Having his life taken from him is a shock that paralyzes my being. This woman has cut short a healthy, young life through an act of wanton human cruelty and at that moment I wish she could get the death penalty.

I push back tears of anger and slowly calm down by concentrating on the person chained to her. I look at Mark to see if he knows what is going on. Who is this other person. I am about to lean forward and try and get Jennifer's attention, but I see

Kerrin coming in our direction. I wait until she is seated next to me and then I whisper, "Who is that guy up there?"

Kerrin explains. "That is another prisoner who is here for his case that will follow this one."

This is not as I had seen it on any of the criminal shows I have watched. She was dressed in the prison orange shirt and pants and had chains on her wrist, that trailed down to chains on her ankles. The chain on her ankles then went over to the ankles of the other prisoner. Maybe because this is not a trial, but a proceeding that we are at, the rules differ. No dressing up in finery and appearing normal for the criminal here and that makes me feel good.

I had thought that I would be all caught up in feelings of hatred for this woman only, but it is more complicated than that. I am finding that the grief of murder is more difficult to deal with than loss from a disease because the answer to "why" is always a third party. I am expected to get some solace with what has happened from the justice system, but the only justice at this point would be to have my son back. There is so much denial and shock because the situation is unbelievable, unexpected, tragic and a crime. It is all these things that I must deal with at once.

Yet as I glance at her I can't help thinking it is degrading to have to appear with chains, but even more so to be chained to another prisoner!

As I see this I think that it is as shocking as it had been for me to see Erik cold, lying on a pallet and covered with a cloth that was more like a rag. Seeing him like that instead of on a metal table, or in any way but that would have been easier, I think but I don't know for sure.

My attention is turned away from the jury box area when I hear the bailiff say, "Hear Ye.. Hear Ye..Cleveland County Court is now in session....The Honorable Judge Walkley presiding".

###

On April 17, 2012, at the Cleveland County court house in Norman Oklahoma justice prevailed. In front of Judge Lori Walkley and with the legal staff present, Clara Ann Blocker accepted a plea of guilty to the crime of murdering my son Erik Scott Saxton. She also agreed to the sentence of life with parole, which in Oklahoma means she must serve 37 years before becoming eligible for parole. Mark and I are there in the court room during the proceedings and for the first time see Clara Ann Blocker in person and hear her confess to the crime.

The judge the Honorable Lori Walkley sits behind a raised desk, wearing a plain black robe . On one side is the tables for the plaintiff, where Jennifer Austin, the Assistant District Attorney sits, representing my son, Erik Scott Saxton.

Across from this table is the defendant table where David Smith, Attorney at Law representing Clara A Blocker sits alone.

In the separate area for the jury, Clara A Blocker sits, chained to another prisoner. There is a podium between the two tables where the lawyers may stand when addressing the judge.

Adjacent to the bench is the witness stand and the desks where the court clerk and the court reporter sits. All of this is before the courtroom railing in back of which we sit. It will be a low key procedure without a jury.

Present are Mark, myself, Jane Cannon the crime reporter in Oklahoma, Kerrin Jones the Victim Witness Coordinator, and a couple of other individuals.

###

The Proceedings

Held on April 17, 2012, with Court, Counsel and defendant present.

The Court: This is State of Oklahoma vs. Clara Ann Blocker, Case No. CF 2010-1390. Matter comes on for – I believe disposition is what we talked about last week, correct?

Counsel, I have the Order to Resume the Criminal Proceedings post-competency evaluation, and I have executed that. And are we ready to proceed with the plea at this time?

Mr. Smith: Yes, ma'am.

The Court: Very good.

Ms. Blocker, if you could, as best you can, raise that right hand. It's going to take effort on both your parts.

(Defendant sworn.)

The Court: Jacinda is going to make a record here. And I know it's kind of a pain for you guys. You can put your hand down. If you can stay standing up so she can see you a little better. She kind of loses you over on that corner.

Because we have to have a record, I need verbal responses, not uh-huhs and huh-uhs, because those are very difficult for her to take down. Same thing with head nods and head shakes. Okay?

The Defendant: Okay.

The Court: You are Clara Ann Blocker; is that correct?

The Defendant: That's correct.

The Court: And you are the same person charged in CF 2010-1390 with one single count of murder in the first degree; is that correct?

The Defendant: Yes,

The Court: Counsel, do we have any announcements?

Mr. Smith: Yes, your Honor.

I have visited at length with Ms. Blocker. I have explained her constitutional rights to her. And I believe, as she stands here today, she is competent to undergo further proceedings. It's her desire to enter – to withdraw her not guilty plea and enter a plea of guilty.

The Court: Ms. Blocker, Mr. Smith tells me you want to enter a plea of guilty to that count; is that correct?

The Defendant: Yes.

The Court: I have this form, which is a Plea of Guilty Summary of Facts. Did you read and review that with Mr. Smith?

The Defendant: Yes, I did.

The Court: Did you understand the questions that were asked?

The Defendant: Yes.

The Court: Did you answer them truthfully?

The Defendant: Yes, I did.

The Court: This form tell you about your legal rights, correct?

The Defendant: Correct.

The Court: Did you have an opportunity to talk to Mr. Smith about those legal rights?

The Defendant: Yes, I did.

The Court: Are you confident that you understand them?

The Defendant: Yes, I am.

The Court: Do you have any questions for me about them?

The Defendant: No, I don't.

The Court: Do you understand, by entering a plea today, you are going to give up some of those rights?

The Defendant: Yes.

The Court: You are going to give up your right to a jury trial, correct?

The Defendant: Correct.

The Court: You are going to give up your right to have the State prove these allegations against you beyond a reasonable doubt, correct?

The Defendant: Correct.

The Court: You are going to give up that right not to say anything against yourself, correct?

The Defendant: Correct.

The Court: Because if I accept this plea, you are going to have to admit you did what the State said you did; is that correct?

The Defendant: Yes.

The Court: Do you understand what can happen with regard to punishment in this case?

The Defendant: Yes.

The Court: Do you understand I do not have to accept the recommendation from the State, correct?

The Defendant: Correct.

The Court: If I don't like what I hear, I set it back and let a jury decide it, correct?

The Defendant: Right.

The Court: So what is on the table is life or life without parole, correct? Do you understand that is the possibility, the maximums, that we're talking about?

The Defendant: Yes.

The Court: Do you understand that this is what we call an 85 percent crime?

The Defendant: Yes, I do.

The Court: Meaning you must serve a minimum of 85 percent of the time that you're given before you are eligible for credits and parole, correct?

The Defendant: Correct.

The Court: Did Mr. Smith explain to you what a term of years, life is before you can start gaining credits?

The Defendant: Yes, he did.

The Court: Okay. And what was that?

The Defendant: Thirty-seven years.

The Court: Thirty-seven years before you can gain any credits. Do you understand that?

The Defendant: Yes, I do.

The Court: Do you have any questions about what those possible consequences are?

The Defendant: No.

The Court: All right. Knowing everything you know about this case, what the facts are, what your legal rights are, and what the consequences can be; do you want to enter a plea of guilty today?

The Defendant: Yes, I do.

The Court: Is that your choice?

The Defendant: Yes, it is.

The Court: Is anyone forcing you into that?

The Defendant: No.

The Court: Is anyone promising you anything for it?

The Defendant: No.

The Court: Are you pleading guilty because you, in fact, committed this crime?

The Defendant: Yes.

The Court: Ms. Blocker, on page 6 of this document, there is a signature line there. Is that your signature?

The Defendant: Yes, it is.

The Court: That signature indicates that you and your attorney completed this form, you went over it with him, you understand the content, and you agreed with the answers; is that correct?

The Defendant: Yes.

The Court: Ms. Blocker, based upon your testimony, I do find that your plea is freely and voluntarily given' that you understand the consequences of making it, I, therefore, am going to accept your plea of guilty and find you guilty of the crime with which you have been charged.

Ms. Austin, what is the state's request with regard to punishment?

Ms. Austin: The State's recommendation is life in prison with all costs and VCA associated, and credit for time served.

The Court: Mr. Smith, anything further?

Mr. Smith: Your Honor, that was the bargained for recommendation. We believe under the circumstances that it's fair, and we ask the Court to follow it.

The Court: Ms. Blocker, based on my review of the file, the competency evaluation, the facts as alleged by the State, I do believe that to be a fair and reasonable recommendation, and I will sentence you to serve a time period of life with the possibility of parole, but a life sentence, with a $50 VCA, a $250 OIDS fee, and I will indeed grant you credit for time served.

There will be some costs associated with this action. Technically, you need to be ordered to pay them at some point in the future. What I am going to do is just hold that payment plan until you get out of prison.

When you get out of prison, you need to come back and see our cost administrator, and we will make a determination at that time whether those costs are to be assessed or waived. All right?

So within two weeks of your release from DOC, you need to come back here. If you don't come back, I will have no choice but to issue a bench warrant for you, because we get a list every week. We know when you get out of prison. So you've got to come back and see the cost administrator here at the courthouse. Okay.

The Defendant: Yes, ma'am.

The Court: Ms. Blocker, you have rights as it pertains to your ability to appeal or withdraw your plea towards the back of that form.

Did you and Mr. Smith read that together?

The Defendant: Yes, we did.

The Court: Is that your signature on that page?

The Defendant: Yes.

The Court: That signature tells me you know what those rights are and you know how to use them if you want to; am I correct?

The Defendant: Yes.

The Court: You understand that you may file an application to withdraw your plea within 10 days of today's date; but on the 11th day, that right goes away, correct?

The Defendant: Yes.

The Court: It must be in writing and for good cause, not just because you changed your mind, correct?

The Defendant: Yes.

The Court: And if I say, No, I'm not going to let you withdraw your plea, you can appeal my decision to the Court of Criminal appeals. Do you understand those rights?

The Defendant: Yes.

The Court: Do you wish to remain in the Cleveland County Detention Center for that 10-day waiting period, or do you want to go on to DOC?

The Defendant: I want to go on to DOC.

The Court: All right. I will show that waiver for the record.

Counsel, Do we have anything further on the Blocker matter?

Ms. Austin: Your Honor, just for purposes of the record, the victim in this particular case, Erik Saxton, just to let the Court know, his mother is present, here for the plea. She has traveled from out of state to be here for today. I just wanted the Court to know of her presence here and that she's here in support of the plea.

The Court: And I appreciate your presence here. I now that it is difficult to travel here and get here; but, hopefully, this will afford you some modicum of closure. And I appreciate your support of our system in being here.

Mr. Smith, anything further?

Mr. Smith: No, ma'am. Thank you.

The Court: Very good.

(end of proceedings.)

###

I leaned over and asked Kerrin what DOC stood for and she informs me that it means Department of Correction. The Oklahoma Department of Corrections (DOC or ODOC) is an agency of the state of Oklahoma and the DOC is responsible for the administration of the state prison system.

Somewhere along the line I have made the decision not to read my statement. Clara has responded positively to each of the questions presented. It has been thought that she was going to make a statement to apologize for taking Erik's life, but she doesn't make a statement.

When it is my turn to make my statement, having already over thought the situation I am admittedly scared. Scared because if I say something that she takes offense to, it might cause her to rethink what she has agreed to and renege on her plea. Instead I remain quiet until Jennifer acknowledges my presence to the judge and her condolence send me into a fit of tears that quickly have me out of control and I couldn't have said anything even if I had wanted to.

Somehow I manage to get back in control. I hear the announcement made for the next case so I stand, along with Mark and Kerrin. But as we begin to leave the court room, I excuse myself and go over to speak with Jane Cannon.

Shortly, Kerrin comes over to join me and after excusing herself, says that she needs to get us back to Jennifer's office. I turn to Jane and say, "I will be in touch. It was nice meeting you."

"Same here."

Kerrin takes us back through the many hallways and climbing into the elevator until we reach Jennifer's office. We are about to sit in the waiting room when Jennifer comes out of her office to great us. I walk over to her and give her a hug. "Thank you for handling my son's case. I am pleased."

"You are welcomed and if there is anything else I can do, let me know."

She leads us into her office and we sit on chairs in front of her desk.

"Here," she says. She hands me a thick folder, explaining that it contains copies of all the records that have crossed her desk on this case. There are the personal interviews with witnesses both on paper and on CD, the interview on paper and on CD of the defendant, the medical examiner's reports—everything obtained over the course of the case.

"Thank you so much."

"No problem, no problem at all. As soon as the transcript is ready, from the proceeding, I know you already know to contac: Jacinda Dye-Johnson to purchase a copy. This will be the last one you need to purchase."

Jennifer adds that what has happened today is the fina. outcome is that Defendant Clara Ann Blocker is charged with Count #1, Murder - First Degree in violation of 21 O.S. 701.7 and will have to serve 37 years before she is eligible for parole.

I make note to look up the law and if reading my mind, or seeing what I have jot down, Jennifer goes into her desk and pulls out a sheet of paper. "Here, you can have this."

It is the write up for 21 OS. 701.7.

"A. A person commits murder in the first degree when that person unlawfully and with malice aforethought causes the death of another human being. Malice is that deliberate intention unlawfully to take away the life of a human being, which is manifested by external circumstances capable of proof.

B. A person also commits the crime of murder in the first degree, regardless of malice, when that person or any other person takes the life of a human being during, or if the death of a human being results from, the commission or attempted commission of murder of another person, shooting or discharge of a firearm or crossbow with intent to kill, intentional discharge of a firearm or other deadly weapon into any dwelling or building as provided in Section 1289.17A of this title, forcible rape, robbery with a dangerous weapon, kidnapping, escape from lawful custody, first degree burglary, first degree arson, unlawful distributing or dispensing of controlled dangerous substances, or trafficking in illegal drugs.

C. A person commits murder in the first degree when the death of a child results from the willful or malicious injuring, torturing, maiming or using of unreasonable force by said person or who shall willfully cause, procure or permit any of said acts to be done upon the child pursuant to Section 7115 of Title 10 of the Oklahoma Statutes. It is sufficient for the crime of murder in the first degree that the person either willfully tortured or used unreasonable force upon the child or maliciously injured or maimed the child.

D. A person commits murder in the first degree when that person unlawfully and with malice aforethought solicits another person or persons to cause the death of a human being in furtherance of unlawfully manufacturing, distributing or dispensing controlled dangerous substances, as defined in the Uniform Controlled Dangerous Substances Act, unlawfully possessing with intent to distribute or   dispense controlled dangerous substances, or trafficking in illegal drugs."

I put it inside the folder that Jennifer has given me.

Jennifer asks if there are any other questions we have. I ask about the Order to Resume Criminal Proceedings that has been mentioned in court. She pulls this out of the pile of files and hands it to me so that I can read it for myself.

"Now on this 11th day of April, 2012, this matter comes on before the Court for post-examination competency hearing. The defendant is present in person and with her attorney of record. The Court, being fully advised in the premises finds as follows: 1) The Defendant waives trial by jury on the matter of competency; 2) the parties stipulate to the competency examination report of the Oklahoma Forensic Center; 3) The Defendant is competent to undergo further criminal proceedings in this cause. It is Therefore Ordered by the Court that criminal proceedings shall resume and proceed forthwith in the above styled and numbered action."

The form is signed by Jennifer Austin, Assistant District Attorney, David D. Smith, Attorney for the Defendant and Lori Walkley, Judge of the District Court. Accompanying this form is the 'Plea of Guilty Summary of Facts' which I look over.

I have watched many an episode of Law and Order to be familiar with the concept of plea bargaining but was unaware that plea bargains are far more common than trials. This is why I agree to going this route in the first place.   Research beyond the television shows taught me that approximately 90% of all criminal convictions are obtained through plea bargains and, these arrangements cannot be altered once they are approved by the court.

I know that this form is the result of Clara's decision to plead guilty and this form solidifies that she agrees to waive her right to a trial by pleading guilty to the offense of murder in the first degree. In exchange for her guilty plea, the court has allowed her to be given in exchange a chance for parole after serving 85% of her sentence. This plea bargain is beneficial for both the prosecutor and the defendant, since a jury trial may result in less satisfactory sentencing. Form 13.10 Uniform Plea of Guilty - Summary of Facts is considered legally binding since it has been approved by Judge Walkley.

I hand the package to Jennifer to put back in her file and she says, "There is a copy of both of these in the files I've given you."

"I want to express my heartfelt gratitude and deepest thanks for I am extremely pleased as well as most indebted to you. You accomplished our most desired results and I commend you. I want you to know also that I know it took considerable hard work and am most grateful for what you have achieved on my behalf. I've done much praying during this case and you have answered my prayers."

"Oh, it's okay. It's my job and my pleasure."

Jennifer then asks if she needs to explain anything or if I have any more questions. I tell her, 'no'. I stand and after saying Thank you again and receiving another hug,

Kerrin appears in the doorway and with our luggage back on our shoulders, I tell Kerrin, "I want to compliment you for the excellent service that we received from your office. Every time I called with questions or concerns you went out of your way to take care of the situation. You were always very polite and friendly when you talked to me and never made me feel as though I was a pain. I so appreciate that and your willingness to help me through this ordeal."

"You are so welcomed. If there is anything else you need, do not hesitate to give me a call."

Kerrin then shows us out of the office and takes us to the elevator. The three of us stand in silence, having said all we wanted to say. When the elevator arrives, Kerrin steps to the side and lets us enter first and then steps inside the elevator. When the doors closes she pushes the button for the first floor.

It is a short, silent ride, but the silence is comfortable and not awkward. When the elevator stops, Kerrin steps out and then waits for us to join her. We are now at the front entrance of the Cleveland County Court House. Kerrin doesn't leave us even then, but instead continues to walk with us, ushering us out the front door. "Well, there is your transport to the airport, " she says.

"Thanks again Kerrin." I stick out my hand and she takes it.

"It has been a pleasure to finally meet you and I wish you both the best," she replies.

###

Outside I notice it has become a beautiful day with warmer temperatures but not unpleasantly so. Mark and I walk across the entranceway and climb into the car that is waiting to take us to the airport. This time Mark climbs into the front and I climb into the backseat with our luggage that the driver has deposited on the empty seat beside me. As the car pulls away from the curb, I look out the window and see Kerrin is waving at us. I wave back.

Mark turns around on his seat and smiles at me and under that smile I can read the relief he feels at having put this matter to rest. I smile back at him so that he knows I know and I totally understand the stress I have caused him too.

"How long does it take to get to the airport," I ask. Our driver replies, "About 20 minutes or so. Depends on the traffic."

We ride in silence at first and I settle back in the seat and look out the window as we make our way to Route I-35 North and once he gets on the route, our driver begins a conversation with Mark, telling him about the tornado that hit Norman Oklahoma on April 13.

We've heard it before, but Mark politely lets him tell us all about it. The driver begins saying, "We are right in the area where the tornado hit. It hit during the rush hour, entering the southwest side of the City of Norman around 4:00 p.m. and going across this

409

highway, I-35 just north of west Lindsey Street which is about 2 miles from the courthouse."

He pauses and turns the car to take exit 116A. It has been around ten or twelve minutes since we left the courthouse. He picks up his conversation once he has merged in with the traffic.

"There were 20 injuries reported and damage was done on either side of the interstate highway as the tornado began moving more toward the northeast. It finally lifted near the intersection of NE 12th Avenue and Robinson Street at 4:12 p.m.....

He interrupts himself, "Here we are folks," he says as he maneuvers the car in front of the American Airlines entrance.

"Thank you," we say in unison. Mark gets out of the passenger seat and walks to the door behind the driver's seat to gather our luggage. I open the back door on the opposite side and climb out. I walk behind the car and over to the sidewalk to stand beside Mark and take my two carryons from him.

Mark turns and leads the way into the terminal where we step over to the side so that we can get out our tickets, ID and boarding passes before making our way to the security checkpoint.

Mark checks the time on his watch. It is 12:30 p.m. Our flight leaves at 2:15 p.m. so we have plenty of time. With the proper documents in hand, we head straight for the security checkpoint that already has a line forming right to the end of the corded off area.

We stand at the end of the line, which is five passengers from the entry way and once in the line, we dig into our carryons and get out our little plastic bags.

The line moves efficiently along the turns and in a matter of five, maybe ten minutes we are at the final stage. We soon are taking off our shoes and putting them along with our belongings in the bins provided. We push the bins up the conveyor to the covered entrance, where it begins moving on its own accord.

The line of people waiting in front of us now moves quite impressively forward, only pausing for a bit when there is a security pat down. When it is our turn in the X-ray machine, we pass through one at a time without incident.

Once screen through security, we wait for our luggage and when it comes out of the covered area of the conveyor, we take our possessions out of the bins. In my case it's just a matter of moving to the side and putting on my shoes and then taking my carryons out of the bin and slinging them over my shoulder. Mark needs more time. He has worn his sneakers so he needs to balance his body as he slips them on and then ties the laces.

Realizing he is blocking the other bins, Mark quickly gathers his stuff out of the bins and moves over to the side where he has to put all of the small items back in his pockets before finally slinging his bags onto his shoulder. Finally he is ready and we walk into the secure area together.

The first thing we do is try to find a flight board to see what gate our plane will board. We find one just a few steps away. We stand there studying the board until we see our flight, American Airlines Flight 3681. It is going to be right on time so we head toward the gate.

Thankfully our bags are not heavy. Right after we pass United Airline's gates, we see the rest rooms and take turns standing with the bags while the other goes in. Then we continue down the walkway until finally we start seeing the American Airline gates, all the way at the end of the terminal we finally reach Gate 4 where our flight will be boarding.

As usual, the waiting area for our flight is full with some people sitting on the floor and others standing. We manage to find two seats together and gratefully sit down, putting our bags tightly against the edge of our seats so that we don't block the aisles.

It's warm in here with all the people and the sun shining through the large windows that are all around us at this end of the terminal. Yet, as much as I hate being warm, right now it doesn't bother me. Right now I silently celebrate what has taken one year seven months and one day to obtain. After eighty-two weeks and five days I have obtained some peace of mind. This day has been the successful culmination of a long torturous waiting period and I am joyful in its ending.

Now as I sit there, I pull out my kindle and turn it on, then actually able to concentrate on what I am reading. I am surprised when I hear them calling our flight and it takes me a minute to bring myself back from my story and get up to follow behind Mark as he take us to a spot near the boarding line. When we hear our zone being called, we step into the line with our boarding passes in hand.

I watch at the head of the line as the airline employee takes the ticket and passes it through the machine that spits it out the other end. Soon it is our turn and as soon as we have our regurgitated tickets in hand, we walk down the jetway to the entrance of our plane.

What starts as a fast clip slows down tremendously the closer we get to the airplane door. Finally we are just standing in line and waiting as the passengers move more slowly up in front of us. I know from experience that slowdown is caused by people trying to put their carryons in the overhead bins on the plane and still others are trying to juggle not only luggage but kids as they struggle down the narrow aisle to their seats.

Finally we begin moving ahead again and soon are able to enter the plane taking baby steps down the aisle until finally we move far enough down to enter our seat row. I step into the seat row aisle to get out of the way and place my largest bag on the seat so that Mark can stash it in an overhead bin next to his.

While Mark is busy with the luggage, I move over to sit in my seat. I squeeze my other bag under the seat in front of me and then take Mark's and place it on the floor in front of his seat then try to maneuver it under the seat in front of him. When done, I buckle my seatbelt.

Mark has had to scrounge around to find an open bin. They seem to fill up fast but he finds one a few seats behind us and pushes our bags inside, making sure that the door will be able to close. Confident that it will Mark makes his way to our seat row sits and buckles in.

I feel tired now. I watch as the last of the passengers board the plane, stow their luggage and buckle in. I listen with one ear to the security announcement being made and watch as the airline stewardess take their seats. I peek at my watch and note that it is exactly 2:15 p.m. That is the last thing I remember as long before the wheels of the plane go up and we are airborne I am asleep.

###

I fall asleep almost immediately after taking off and the two hour flight to Chicago O'Hare is concluded when Mark shakes me back to consciousness. "Nita, wake up. We need to get off."

I am disoriented but trying to bring myself fully awake as Mark urgently keeps shaking me before he leaves to retrieve our bags. I have been in a deep sleep and it is hard to bring myself fully awake, let alone able to follow instructions, but I manage. Soon I am standing in the aisle, but then Mark says, "Don't forget your bag under the seat." So I slide back into the seat area and lean down to retrieve my bag.

That's when it hits me. My knees start screaming at me, forcing me to stop what I am doing and give them a chance to catch up. Until now, they have been fine, the Aleve keeping the pain to a dull roar, but now they are letting me know they don't like all this movement. I manage to stand up straight and slide into the aisle in front of Mark. I look at my watch and see it is now 4:30 p.m. I have to walk forward no matter how painful it is and I take advantage of the tops of the seats on either side of me, using them to hang on to as I make my way off the plane.

I take a deep breath and start the ascent into the terminal. The ramp seems steeper than ever as I slowly navigate my way to the door at the end of the ramp. I make it without having to stop though all I want to do is stop and sit down to give my knees a rest.

Inside the terminal I work my way over to a chair so that I can take a seat. Mark comes over and I tell him. "I need to take an Aleve. My knees are aching really bad."

"I'll get you some water."

I open my purse and start digging through the contents until I find the bottle of Aleve. I twist off the cap and shake out a pill in my hand, then stop and think about it for a minute. I shake out another, thinking I still have another flight to go and I may need two of these to make it.

When Mark comes back, he has a bottle of water with him and I take that to down the pills. I rest there trying to wait out the

Aleve, but finally I look up at Mark and say, "We better go." We need to get to the other gate".

Mark says. "We're in luck. We arrived at terminal three and will pick up our connecting flight at terminal three as well. The flight is leaving at five o'clock from this same terminal three."

"Great I say." I stand up and Mark grabs my bags and we make our way over to the other gate just a few steps away.

This is the last leg of the trip and the least amount of time between flights so as soon as we arrive at the gate, they are in the midst of boarding. Mark and I head to the line forming in the aisle and he reaches in his shirt pocket and gets out our boarding passes and tickets. He hands me mine and no sooner have we checked to see the boarding pass zone, we hear it called and get in the boarding line.

It is all moving so fast now as we head into the jetway and hurry onto the plane which for this leg of the trip is much smaller than the one we were on before. That means less people to board.

In no time we are on the plane and weaving our way to our seat. We no sooner take our seats and settle in when American Airlines Flight 4014 is ready for departure.

I am wide awake now and take out my kindle to read. I look over and see that Mark is also reading some of the material he has brought with him. It is a three and a half hour flight that goes by reasonably fast since we know that soon we will be landing in Buffalo and driving back home to Rochester.

It grows dark and even with the overhead lamp on, it is tiring to continue to read from the kindle so I put it aside, lean back and just close my eyes. Only, I do fall asleep but not as deeply as before since it only takes Mark saying 'wake up' once to get me in action.

By the time the plane has taxied to the terminal gate, I am awake. I pull my bag from under the seat in front of me and slip my kindle inside, then wait while Mark gets our other bags out of the overhead. When he has the bags in tow it is our turn to disembark so he stands in the aisle and like each time before lets me get out in front of him.

The aisle is much narrower than the other plane making it hard to keep the bags close to my body and not let them hit anyone. I concentrate on this, glad for the distraction from the pain in my knees. When we are finally in the terminal relief floods my body. For us, it is over. No more planes to catch or gates to find.

It is now 7:40 p.m. and we are in Buffalo, New York so all that remains of our trip is to catch the shuttle to take us to the parking area and get into our car. Just thinking about it, allows me to move quicker and ignore the pain in my knees. I can pacify myself knowing that the next time I have to get out of a transport, it will be into my own house and bed.

When we arrive at the shuttle pick up area, there are several people already waiting, which I take to mean that the next one must be on its way. It is. By the time we step in line, the shuttle pulls up and begins loading. We find a seat near the back and Mark keeps watch out the window even though he knows that the ticket lets the driver know where the passenger cars are parked.

"This is us," Mark says.

We work our way toward the front and when we are in hearing distance, the driver says, "Which car is yours, sir?"

Mark leans in and looks out the front window and directs the driver to our car. When the shuttle comes to a full stop at the rear of our car, the door opens and Mark moves to the side to let me by. I step down to the drive while Mark gives the driver a tip and then is right behind me.

Mark pushes the unlock button and by the time we reach our car we open the hatch and put our luggage inside. Mark arranges the luggage so that it doesn't move about on our trip while I walk to the front, climb into the passenger seat and put on my seatbelt. I take my purse and put it on the floor under my feet so that they are slightly elevated, giving my knees some relief

I watch Mark as he climbs into the driver's seat and asks if I am okay. I shake my head, 'yes' and he starts the car, backs out of the space and we start the journey through the parking lot, exiting on the roadway. It is now after eight o'clock.

Slowly we make our way out of the airport and take Smith Street toward St. Stephens Place where we turn right and follow the signs for the Thruway, which is less than a mile away from our starting point.

The traffic is moderately light as Mark turns onto the thruway and gets his ticket that he hands to me. I put it in the cup holder for safe keeping and then lean back in the seat, feeling better now than I have in quite a while.

"Are you tired," I ask.

"Yes, I am, but I'm hungry too. Do we need to stop at the store before we go home."

I think about it for a minute and then say, "No, I think we have some left over chili you can heat up."

"Great, that'll be fine. "I am exhausted and I have to go to work in the morning. Not having to make a stop suits me just fine."

I ask if he wants me to drive. I know the answer before I ask, but I ask anyway. "No, I'll be fine."

I ask Mark if he wants me to put the next CD in and Mark says yes so I open the pack and put in the third CD in the set. Soon the car is filled with the voice of Bill O'Reilly telling the story of the killing of Lincoln.

I enjoy reading a good book and watching a good movie, but an audio book is not my thing, but it is Mark's. As I watch him now, I think about why I am not so interested.

Audio books are good for people driving cars because they occupy a part but not all of one's attention. But I associate being read to as a time to sleep since my mother read to us at night to put us to sleep and I passed on the tradition by reading to Erik at bedtime when he was little.

As an author I should applaud audio books because they bring in extra income that is hard to turn down. Any publisher will tell you that between 5 and 10 percent of the total book publishing market is the income from audio books.

I guess my problem is that when I read, I collaborate with the book, but audio books are read with the collaboration of the reader setting the pace, timbre and inflection for me. Yes, I think, that is it in a nutshell.

I'm not driving so I can let the reader soothe me to sleep. I settle back in my seat and reach along the right side until I find the lever that will allow me to recline. I don't recline fully, but just enough to relax me and let me pretend I am not in a car, plane or shuttle. Soon I drift off.

"Babe, it's time to get out the money," Mark says.

"Wow, that was fast."

"I guess so when you sleep the whole way."

"Sorry."

"No, that's okay. I had my book to entertain me."

I smile as I get the eighty-five cent toll charge together. Soon we are taking Exit 47 off the thruway and Mark drives to the first open toll booth. I him the ticket and the change and while he rolls down the window, I stop the CD.

We are now on 490 heading toward Rochester. I start the CD again and think, we have driven almost fifty miles and still have about thirty miles to go, but it seems like less now that we are on our own familiar roads.

We continue on to exit 9A and take the ramp on the left to Route 390 N and head toward Greece. Mark continues listening to the Killing of Lincoln as he drives down the highway, weaving in and out of lanes each time he gets behind a slow driver.

There is a slowdown in traffic as we approach the Lake Ontario Parkway, the preferred route that Mark likes to take home, but once we exit onto the Parkway, the traffic thins.

Lake Ontario State Parkway follows the Lake Ontario shore closely into Rochester. The Parkway is a 4-lane highway, but no commercial vehicles are allowed and there is usually little traffic until you get closer to Rochester. During the daylight you can see outstanding lake views, traveling eastward. The scenery includes the shoreline's truncated dunes and bluffs, and coastal wetlands. The area quickly goes to urban and suburban as the Great Lakes Seaway Trail goes around the south end of Irondequoit, which is our destination. As we exit the parkway we cross over Lake Avenue and the Colonel Patrick O'Rourke Bridge that takes us to Thomas Road. Now there is barely a car in sight as we drive up the hill until we are at the light on St. Paul Boulevard. We wait at the light now, knowing we are almost at our destination. When the light changes, Mark turns right and we head down St. Paul until we reach Pine Grove on our left. Mark makes the turn and we continue until we are at List Avenue, then finally we are turning on Thornton Road and pulling into our driveway. We are home.

We have been on the road for an hour and fifteen minutes and more than ready to get out of the car. By the time we are in our driveway, I bring my seat back to the upright position and have my seatbelt off ready to get out.

Mark stops the car and I start to climb out, but my knees need a moment before I can manage this feat. Tentatively I pull myself out of the seat using the door handle and the back of the seat for leverage. I stand there a moment allowing my knees to decide when I should take the next step and while I wait, I cautiously lean over and get my purse off the floor of the car and onto my shoulder.

I start walking toward the side door entrance where Mark is already at my side, carrying my bag with his own. He puts the bags on the step near the door and then goes back to the car and pulls it into the garage.

I manage the steps, holding onto the railing and in no time Mark is back beside me, leaning over and positioning all the bags on his shoulder before opening the door and walking in together.

I want to just drop everything and go to bed, but I force myself to unpack our pills that we keep in the kitchen. I then get a glass of water and take my evening pills and then say to Mark, "Don't forget to take your pills." He replies, "Don't forget to put the ice bags in the freezer before you go up."

"Good Call," I reply. I dig in the side of my bag and pull out the ice bags and put them in the freezer.

I then carry my bags upstairs and into our bedroom where I remove all the contents, taking my cosmetic bag into the bathroom and depositing each item in its proper location.

I wish I could ignore the bags and just put it off until morning, but I just can't. Before I finish, I hear Mark right behind me doing the same. Before marrying me, he would just as soon put off unpacking until the next morning, but now he has the same habit embedded.

Finally I strip off the clothes I have been wearing all day and turn on the shower. While I wait for the water to warm, I pin up my hair and get out a fresh towel, laying it on the stool next to the shower. I then climb into the shower and allow myself to enjoy the warmth of the water as it relaxes my muscles and gives new life to my sore knees. When I finally climb out, I feel much better and I know why.

###

It has been a long time coming but now the case has been closed. Judge Walkley has handed down her verdict and it has gone as we planned. Clara Ann Blocker has pleaded "Guilty" and has accepted a charge of Murder in the First Degree with the chance of parole after serving 85% of her time. By the time she is eligible she will be around 75 years old, a mature woman who hopefully will not be a threat to any other human being. And there is always the chance she will not make parole.

I go into the bedroom and pull out a night shirt and slide it over my head. Mark is already in the bed and has turned the television on and I climb in beside him. We kiss good night and in no time I drift off to sleep.

CHAPTER 25: VERDICT DAY AFTERMATH

This of course is not the end. After that day, April 16, 2012, I kept watching the posting on the OSCN site. I see the postings for April 17, 2012 shortly after our return home for the cost for the conviction and the sentence of Life. It is slow tedious work and in some cases doesn't pan out as I try to decipher all the acronyms appearing in the listing.

After the cost for the conviction comes the notice of the Court Costs on a Felony. Following this posting comes the District Attorney Council Prosecution Assessment for a felony cost, then the Oklahoma Court Information System Revolving Fund costs, the Sheriff's Service Fee for Court House Security, Medical Expense Liability Revolving Fund, Penalty Fee State of Oklahoma Council on Law Enforcement Education and Training Penalty Assessment Fee, PFE7 Law Library Fee, Forensic Science Improvement Assessment, Sheriff's Service Fee On Arrests, Oklahoma State Bureau of Investigation AFIS Fee, C.H.A.B. Statutory Fee, Attorney General Victim Services Unit, Court Appointed Attorney Fee Assessed To Defendant Oklahoma Information District System (OIDS), Victims Compensation Assessment (AC12), and the Court Clerk Administrative Fee On Collections.

###

The sole job of the Oklahoma County Court Clerk's Cost Administration Department is to collect court ordered fines, fees, costs and other assessments in criminal cases. Court ordered criminal assessments are due at or before the time of sentencing, unless Cost Administration provides a defendant with a payment plan as sanctioned by the sentencing Judge, or the Cost Judge. Payment plans are not automatic. Defendants must appear in the Cost Administration Department, as ordered by the sentencing Judge and no appointments are made; Defendants are seen on a first come, first serve basis.

###

There are so many fees, in my calculations $1,305 shown on the Oklahoma Court State Network (OCSN) Case Summary and though this isn't a lot of many, for someone who is indigent it can be a fortune. Then there is the cost of the attorney.

High-quality criminal defense attorneys who boast solid track records tend to charge lots of money for their services. Although most lawyers bill by the hour, it's common for private defense attorneys to quote lump-sum fees for their services. A relatively straightforward murder case that requires the defense counsel to find just one or two witnesses to prove the defendant's innocence is liable to be inexpensive by most lawyers' standards. On the other hand, a more complex case with mountains of discovery and numerous witnesses is liable to cost several times as much.

Individuals who wish to find a competent criminal defense attorney for a first-degree murder charge must be prepared to spend at least $20,000 on their case. First-degree murder is a very serious crime that carries stiff penalties. Defendants who plead "not guilty" and lose their cases during the trial process face the near-certain prospect of a permanent prison sentence. As such, a defendant who lacks faith in his or her lawyer's ability to secure an acquittal should strongly consider pleading "guilty."

###

Finally there is a posted document for the Judgement And Sentence.

The State of Oklahoma, Cleveland County, filed in the office of the County Clerk on May 23, 2012. The plaintiff versus Clara Ann Blocker, the defendant. Attorney for the Defendant, Doug Smith versus the Attorney for the State, Jennifer Austin. On this 17th day of April 2012, this matter comes on before the undersigned Judge for sentencing. The Defendant appears personally and with attorney Doug Smith. The State of Oklahoma is represented by Jennifer Austin.

The Defendant having previously entered a plea of Guilty, with a plea agreement recommendation which the State and Defendant ask the undersigned Judge to accept. To the crime of Murder in the First Degree the Court finds the Defendant has 3 prior felony convictions and the sentences are hereby enhanced after former conviction of two or more felonies. Sentence to a term of LIFE imprisonment with credit for time served. All under the care and custody of Oklahoma Department of Corrections. Probation to be subject to Rules and Conditions of Probation filed. Further, it is ordered adjudged and decreed by the Court that the Defendant is to pay a Victim compensation Assessment and pursuant to Section 979a of the amended Oklahoma Statutes, Title 22 (C. Costs of incarceration shall be a debt of the inmate owed to the municipality, county, or other public entity responsible for the operation of the jail and may be collected as provided by law for collection of any other civil debt or criminal penalty.), Defendant is hereby assessed the cost of her incarceration in the Cleveland County Jail, said costs to be certified by the Sheriff upon the Defendant's release or this date, whichever comes later, said costs to be collected by the clerk of the Court and distributed per statute. The above noted fines, costs and fees shall be paid per Rule 8 (When the Judgment and Sentence of a court, either in whole or in part, imposes a fine and/or costs upon a defendant, a judicial hearing shall be conducted and judicial determination made as to the defendant's ability to immediately satisfy the fine and costs.) agreement with the court cost administrator.

The defendant shall pay a court appointed attorney fee which shall be taxed as costs of the case and payable as designated hereinabove. Further, it is ordered that judgment is hereby entered against the defendant as to the fines, costs and assessments noted and set forth above.

The court further advised the defendant of her rights to appeal to the Court of Criminal Appeals of the State of Oklahoma, and of the necessary steps to be taken by her to perfect such appeal and that if she desired to appeal and was unable to afford counsel and a transcript of the proceedings, that the same would be furnished by the State without costs to her.

In the event the above sentence is for incarceration in the Department of Corrections, the sheriff of Cleveland County, Oklahoma is ordered and directed to deliver the Defendant to the Lexington Assessment and Reception Center at Lexington,

Oklahoma and leave therewith a copy of this Judgement and Sentence to serve as warrant and authority for the imprisonment of the Defendant as provided herein. A second copy of this Judgment and Sentence to be warrant and authority of the Sheriff for the transportation and imprisonment of the Defendant as hereinbefore provided. The Sheriff to make due return to the Clerk of this Court, with his preceding endorsed thereon.

The form is witnessed by Judge L. Walkley and Attested by Deputy Court Clerk Rhonda Hall.

###

Cleveland County Detention Center (CCDC) submits a listing for a no charge item on April 17, 2012. The cost for Judgement & Sentence is $706.00 more added to the defendants bill.

###

The PLEA OF GUILTY - SUMMARY OF FACTS (PGSF) document appears next. This document is like a questionnaire. It carries the same standard information in the header of the Defendant, Case No. and the Judge for the Case. The Part A is the Finding of Fact, Acceptance of Plea and it is at this point I see that what has oddly happened is a misprint or Clara has a change from her original Attorney. The Attorney for the Defendant, Doug Smith was noted in the Judgement for Sentence document, but on this document actually filed on April 17, 2012 the Attorney for the Defendant, is David Smith, but whatever the situation is, this part of the form she verifies her name is Clara Ann Blocker and her Lawyer is David Smith and she does not wish to have a record of the proceedings made by a Court Reporter, her age is 38 years old she has a high school equivalency of 10th grade. She responds that she can read and understand, that she is not currently taking medication but she has been prescribed medication which includes an anti-psychotic medication she takes, and she has been treated by a doctor for mental illness and she has been confined in a hospital for mental illness in 2008 at the Bipolar Disorder Treatment Center in Oklahoma (OK) for Manic Depression and Kansas City, Missouri Mental Health Treatment Center. She then responds that she understands the nature and consequences of this proceedings, and has received a copy of the information and has read its allegations. She responds not applicable to whether she wishes to waive her right to a Preliminary Hearing and that the State does not move to dismiss or amend any case or count. She responds that she does understand the charge of Oklahoma Statutes Citationized Title 21. Crimes and Punishments Chapter 24 Section701.7 - Murder in the First Degree . which reads:

###

Oklahoma Statutes Citationized, Title 21. Crimes and Punishments, Chapter 24, Section 701.7 - Murder in the First Degree

A. A person commits murder in the first degree when that person unlawfully and with malice aforethought causes the death of another human being. Malice is that deliberate intention unlawfully to take away the life of a human being, which is manifested by external circumstances capable of proof. B. A person also commits the crime of murder in the first degree, regardless of malice, when that person or any other person takes the life of a human being during, or if the death of a human being results from, the commission or attempted commission of murder of another person, shooting or discharge of a firearm or crossbow with intent to kill, intentional discharge of a firearm or other deadly weapon into any dwelling or building as provided in Section 1289.17A of this title, forcible rape, robbery with a dangerous weapon, kidnapping, escape from lawful custody, first degree burglary, first degree arson, unlawful distributing or dispensing of controlled dangerous substances, or trafficking in illegal drugs. C. A person commits murder in the first degree when the death of a child results from the willful or malicious injuring, torturing, maiming or using of unreasonable force by said person or who shall willfully cause, procure or permit any of said acts to be done upon the child pursuant to Section 7115 of Title 10 of the Oklahoma Statutes. It is sufficient for the crime of murder in the first degree that the person either willfully tortured or used unreasonable force upon the child or maliciously injured or maimed the child. D. A person commits murder in the first degree when that person unlawfully and with malice aforethought solicits another person or persons to cause the death of a human being in furtherance of unlawfully manufacturing, distributing or dispensing controlled dangerous substances, as defined in the Uniform Controlled Dangerous Substances Act, unlawfully possessing with intent to distribute or dispense controlled dangerous substances, or trafficking in illegal drugs. E. A person commits murder in the first degree when that person intentionally causes the death of a law enforcement officer or correctional officer while the officer is in the performance of official duties.

For Addendum B she states that she does have former conviction charges for a felony and enters the charges of Distribution of CDs, Robbery with charges of weapon and finally possession of CDs. This is followed by her admitting to being now convicted of a felony. Then to respond to the choices given her she checks the applicable item as"85% of the sentence of imprisonment imposed before being eligible for parole consideration and are not eligible for earned or other type of credits which will have the effect of reducing the length of sentence to less than 85% of the sentence imposed." For the charge she enters Murder, First Degree. On Addendum B she responds that she understands the range of punishment for the crime and list that there is no minimum of and that the maximum is Life or Life without Parole. On the following page she reads the following statements:

(1) You have the right to have a lawyer represent you, either one you hire yourself or if you are indigent a court appointed attorney.

(2) You are presumed to be innocent of the charges.

(3) You may remain silent or, if you choose, you may testify on your own behalf.

(4) You have the right to see and hear all witnesses called to testify against you and the right to cross-examine them.

(5) You may have your witnesses ordered to appear in court to testify and present evidence of any defense you have to these charges.

(6) The state is required to prove your guilt beyond a reasonable doubt.

(7) The verdict of guilty or not guilty decided by a jury must be unanimous. However, you can waive a jury trial and, if all parties agree, the case could be tried by a Judge alone who would decide if you were guilty or not guilty and if guilty, the appropriate punishment.

###

She answers that she does understand these rights, and that by entering a plea of guilty she gives up these rights, and she understands that a conviction on a plea of guilty could increase punishment in any future case committed after this plea. She understands and has talked over the charge with her lawyer, advised him regarding any defense she may have to the charges and had his advice. She agrees that she believes her lawyer has effectively assisted her in the case and is satisfied with his advice, that she wishes to change her plea of not guilty to guilty and give up her right to a jury trial and all other previously explained constitutional rights and if there is a plea agreement she is to enter it and she enters Life, with parole. She then states she understands the court is not bound by any agreement or recommendation and if the court does not accept the plea agreement she has the right to withdraw her plea of guilty. She understands if there is no plea agreement the court can sentence her within the range of punishment stated earlier and if she understands the plea of guilty to the charge is after two or more prior felony convictions. And that her plea in these were guilty. That she did commit the acts as charged and enters that for this case the plea of guilty is written by her that she hit Erik Saxton in the head twice and caused his death on September 15, or 16, 2010 in Cleveland County, Oklahoma That she has not been forced abused, mistreated or promised anything by anyone to have this plea entered and that she pleads guilty on her own free will and without any coercion or compulsion of any kind, that she does not want the report that she has the right to a pre-sentence investigation and report which would contain the circumstances of the offense, any criminal record, social history and other background information about her. She does not have any legal reason why she should not be sentenced now and that her attorney completed this form and they have gone over the form and understand its contents and agree with the answers. She signs her name as the Defendant, Judge Lori Walkley Notarizes her signature, her Attorney signs and Jennifer P. Austin, signs as the Assistant District Attorney.

Behind this form is the Court findings which acknowledges the Defendant was sworn and responded to questions under oath, that the defendant understands the nature, purpose and consequences of this proceeding, the defendant pleads guilty, knowingly and voluntarily and the defendant is competent for the purpose of this hearing, that a factual basis exists for the plea and that the Defendant is guilty as charged, that the sentencing shall be imposed. The document is signed on by Judge Lori Walkley

The next form is the "Notice of Right To Appeal, Sentence to Incarceration, suspended or Deferred:"

###

To appeal from this conviction, or order deferring sentence, or your plea of guilty, you must file in the District Court Clerk's Office a written Application to Withdraw your Plea of Guilty with ten (10) days from today's date. You must set forth in detail why you are requesting to withdraw your plea. The trial court must hold a hearing and rule upon your Application with thirty (30) days form the date it is filed. If the trial court denies your Application, you have the right to ask the court of Criminal Appeals to review the district Court's denial by filing a Petition for Writ of Certiorari within ninety (90 Days) from the date of the denial. Within ten (10) from the date the application to withdraw plea of guilty is denied, notice of intent to appeal and designation of record must be filed pursuant to Oklahoma Court of Criminal appeals rule 4.2(1). If you are indigent, you have the right to be represented on appeal by a court, appointed attorney.

She responds that she understands each of these rights to appeal and that she does not want to remain in the county jail ten (10) days before being taken to the place of confinement and that she does fully understand the questions that have been asked and that she does answer freely and voluntarily. She signs the form as the defendant on April 17, 2012. Her attorney signs and the Judge Lori Walkley.

###

After reading through this form I know I need to keep checking to see if she does appeal within the 10 days. I also know that she is now also saying that she does not want to say why she murdered Erik so she will not appeal or have it in any form of writing anywhere. I understand that by what I have read, but I still hope that somewhere along the line she will tell, but then, will it be the truth.

So much to do on this case.

###

The next document is The Order Of The Court - Rule 8 Hearing which states.

You have been sentenced to the custody of the Department of Corrections or the Cleveland County Jail and are thereby ordered to report to the Cost Administrator on the first floor of the building within two weeks of her release form the Department of Corrections, or the next business day after her release form the Cleveland County jail, to make payment arrangements. If she fails to pay, appear in person or report as ordered, a warrant will be issued for her arrest and she may be confined to the Cleveland county jail until the balance is paid in full. She is further ordered to notify the cost administrator immediately upon a change of her mailing address, residential address, and/or telephone number. The form is signed on April 17, 201 by Judge Lori Walkley, David Smith and Clara Blocker.

###

This is followed by the Letter From Oklahoma Department Of Mental Health And Substance Abuse Services, the last posting for April 17, 2015.

It is dated, March 6, 2012 and filed on April 17, 2015. The letter is to the Honorable Lori Walkley, Judge of the District court, Cleveland county courthouse at 201 s. Jones Avenue, Norman, Oklahoma, Re: Blocker, Clara Ann for Case CF-2010-1390.

Dear Judge Walkley, Pursuant to your Court Order I have examined Ms. Blocker on an outpatient basis and have arrived at conclusions regarding her adjudicative competency.

Methods of Evaluation include a review of the order for Competency Examination dated, November 10, 2011 from the Cleveland county district court, Review of the Application for Determination of competency, filed October 3e1, 2011 in the Cleveland County District court, Review of available information regarding the alleged offense, including the criminal complaint information. Enhancement Page regarding prior convictions, and a Probable Cause Affidavit by Inspector K. Whitebird, Review of Ms. Blocker's prior convictions according to the Oklahoma State Courts Network database, Review of this examiner's (Dr. Shawn Roberson) prior competency report on Ms. Blocker (Oklahoma County CF-2009-5336) dated December 7, 2009, Records check regarding Ms. Blocker with Griffin Memorial Hospital (Norman, Oklahoma), Records check regarding Ms. Blocker with the Oklahoma Forensic Center, Review of Ms. Blocker's available records from the Oklahoma County Crisis Intervention Center, dated July 23, 2009 to July 28, 2009, Telephone interview on March 6, 2012 of Cindy Bilyea, R. N. , Cleveland County Detention Center (CCDC) medical staff, Evaluation of Ms. Blocker conducted by Shawn Roberson, Ph.D. (and observed by Ravindesjit Singh, March 5, 2012 at CCDC, totaling approximately one hour thirty-five minutes and including Clinical interview, Competency examination, Test of Memory Malingering, and structured Interview of Reported symptoms, Second Edition.

Under Criminal Allegations and Reason For Referral it states that according to the criminal complaint information, Ms. Blocker is charged with murder in the first degree. On or about or between September 15th and 16th, 2010 she allegedly struck the victim with objects causing blunt force trauma to the head, resulting in his death. According to the Application for Determination of Competency filed by Ms. Blocker's attorney, David smith, he questioned his client's competency because "The said Defendant advises that she has a long history of mental illness and has from time to time received treatment for the same. The said Defendant is unable to state what diagnoses have been made during those periods of time...The Defendant does not appear to comprehend that certain facts urged by her do not constitute a defense to the charge, or the potential consequences of proceeding to trial without a viable defense."

Informed Consent section states Ms. Blocker was informed (in simple language) that she was being evaluated to determine if she was competent for adjudication. Additionally, she was told that the interview was not private and the usual doctor-patient relationship did not exist. She was informed that a report would be prepared and submitted to the referring court. It was also explained that the report would be distributed to both the prosecuting and defense attorneys and could be used in legal proceedings. Ms. Blocker's responses indicated that she understood the information provided to her.

Collateral Information section states Criminal history: According to the enhancement page regarding prior convictions, as well as a search of Ms. Blocker's criminal history via the Oklahoma State Courts Network database (www.oscn.net), she has the following convictions: In Oklahoma county, CF-2009-5336: Distribution of controlled dangerous substance (cocaine)., CF2001-2626: Robbery with a dangerous weapon. In Garvin county: CF-2007-260: Possession of a controlled dangerous substance. CM-2007-289: Unlawful Possession of a Controlled Dangerous Substance.

The issue of Ms. Blocker's competency was only raised in her 2009 Oklahoma County case. As will be noted later in this report, I evaluated her in that case and the results indicated she was competent for adjudication. She was subsequently deemed competent by the Court and convicted. In both of her Garvin county cases it was noted that "Defendant raises possible mental health concerns and advised that defendant has not been taking her prescribed medications for several months. By agreement of parties (the preliminary hearing was moved) so that defendant may resume taking her prescribed medication before proceeding further." However she was never evaluated for adjudicative competency.

Records check section states that according to the medical records department at Griffin Memorial Hospital, Ms. Blocker has no history of treatment or evaluation at their facility. Aside from this examiner's prior competency e valuation of Ms. Blocker in Oklahoma county during 2009, she has no other contact with the Oklahoma Forensic Center or that staff.

Oklahoma County crisis intervention Center(OCCIC) records: (OCCIC) records indicated that Ms. Blocker was brought to (OCCIC) in July 2009 from St. Anthony's Hospital by police after she claimed she was suicidal with a plan to walk out into traffic. She was admitted for several days of treatment and complained of hallucinations (i.e., sensory experiences in the absence of external stimuli) directing her to harm herself and complained of stress: due to her girlfriend going to prison. (she also indicated that she had relapsed into using crack cocaine and heroin and was observed to have signs of physical withdrawal from heroin during her treatment. During her treatment she reportedly threatened to assault her roommate. Following several days her mind reportedly improved and she no longer voiced suicidal ideation's or intent. She was discharged with medication and a follow-up appointment at North care. Her discharge diagnoses included " mood disorder, NOS [not otherwise specified], "polysubstance Dep" [etc. dependence], and "BPD" [borderline personality disorder]. She was judged to have average range intelligence.

Competency report (by Dr. Shawn Roberson in Oklahoma County, CF-2009-5336: I evaluated Ms. Blocker in December 2009 and opined that she was competent for adjudication. During the examination Ms. Blocker reported a long history of behavioral problems since childhood, mental health treatment as an adult with diagnoses of bipolar disorder and schizophrenia and significant substance abuse. Ms. Blocker was obviously familiar with mental health terminology and continually suggested she should be transferred to a treatment center as an alternative to incarceration Ms. Blocker's statements were rational and coherent and reality-based throughout the evaluation. She displayed no signs of mania or psychosis but it was noted that based upon her description of anger control problems and past aggression she likely had personality disorder traits and may become aggressive when angry with others. it was opined that Ms. Blocker did not meet the Oklahoma State statutory criteria for inpatient psychiatric treatment and it appeared uncertain if she even had a genuine underlying mental illness. It should be noted that in 2009 Ms. Blocker provided some information which was highly inconsistent with the reported history during the current evaluation in 2012 for example in 2009 she claimed she had experienced auditory hallucination since she was eight years old whereas now she reported that these symptoms did not occur until early adulthood. She suggested that she had "two personalities" inside of her the other of which was named "Tigger" she claimed no multiple personalities during this evaluation. Ms. Blocker suggested that her prior hospitalization at OCCIC occurred because she attempted to "jump out of my girlfriend's car" during a suicide attempt whereas OCCIC results indicated she only made suicidal threats and had stated her girlfriend was actually in prison at the time

Cleveland County Detention Center (CCDC) information states Cindy Bilyea, R.N. indicated that Ms. Blocker's behavior was generally appropriate; through she did exhibit emotional volatility at times. Ms. Bilyea stated that on one day Ms. Blocker may appear normal, laughing and joking, and the next day appear depressed and crying. She stated that Ms. Blocker requests to see the jail's psychiatrist every time he is present (he is at the jail only intermittently) and often request to have her medications changed. Ms. Bilyea stated that Ms. Blocker has not exhibited any odd or strange behavior and showed no signs of confusion or being out of touch with reality. She indicated that Ms. Blocker occasionally expresses self-injurious behavior. Ms. Bilyea, conveyed that Ms. Blocker had period of aggressions where she had thrown cellmates belongings out of the cell and had been in several physical fights with other inmates, requiring "lock down" at some points. Ms. Bilyea listed Ms. Blocker's current medications as Propanolol (to treat hypertension, 20 mg. twice daily), Risperdal (antipsychotic, 3 mg. twice daily); and Amitriptyline (antidepressant, 300 mg. one daily).

Current Mental Status and Clinical Evaluation states that Ms. Blocker was evaluated in a contact room at the Cleveland county Detention Center. From the outset of the examination she expressed that "I'm very confused" but "I'll do my best." Ms. Blocker presented as an adequately nourished Caucasian female who appeared approximately her documented age of 40. Her grooming and hygiene were appropriate for her current confinement. Ms. Blocker's motor behavior was free from any tics, tremors, or unusual mannerisms. Her speech had a normal rate and volume. The content remained coherent, rational, and goal-directed throughout the evaluation. Her eye contact was good and her cooperation excellent though; I question her self-reported symptoms and claimed confusion. For example, when directly asked, Ms. Blocker listed the current year as "2001" but her later statements clearly supported that she was aware this was not the case. While she accurately identified her date of birth, she suggested she was 38 or 39 instead of 40. She also offered that she was diagnosed with a "learning disability" while in school and was placed in special education for math as a result. As will be noted later, during my previous evaluation of Ms. Blocker she claimed she had problems and not cognitive functioning. Nonetheless she did not grossly feign cognitive impairment during this interview and her intelligence is judged to be approximately in the average range. She did not evidence any mental status impairments such as significant problems in attention, concentration, or memory. She reported no history of significant head injury.

Ms. Blocker described her recent mood as "real depressed," but her affect (i.e. observable emotional state) was unimpaired. She denied any recent crying episodes and did not become tearful during the evaluation. Ms. Blocker suggested that she was chronically anxious and "It scares me. I don't know if I'll lash out." She stated she had been sleeping excessively and was only awake 7-8 hours each day. She reported she had gained significant weight during her incarceration, but conveyed no impairment in appetite or energy level. Ms. Blocker stated that she felt hopeless "a little bit" but denied any recent suicidal thoughts or plans.

As during the prior evaluation, Ms. Blocker described herself as 'manic' in the past and endorsed nearly every symptom of mania posed to her. However, she indicated that these were past symptoms and she was currently depressed and not manic. She evidenced no signs of mania or hypomania. Ms. Blocker also claimed to experience chronic auditory and visual hallucinations which began in early childhood. Despite receiving psychotropic medication in jail, she suggested that the symptoms were actually "getting worse" and occurred on a daily basis. She stated she often heard her name before called, saw "puddles of blood on the ground," and saw non-existent persons with whom she held conversations. At no point during this evaluation did Ms. Blocker evidence any signs of psychosis, such as distraction by internal stimuli (e.g. hallucinations), impairments in reality testing, delusions (i.e. fixed false beliefs despite evidence to the contrary), or mental confusion.

Relevant History from Ms. Blocker includes Ms. Blocker stated she had attempted suicide multiple times, the validity of which is unknown. She stated she had been diagnosed in the past with "borderline Personality disorder, "Manic Depressive," and "Paranoid Schizophrenic." She conveyed she had received mental health treatment beginning in childhood, including placement at the "Spafford Home" in Kansas City, Missouri. Ms. Blocker reported past inpatient psychiatric treatment in Kansas City Missouri at "St. Mary's" and Western Missouri mental Health Center, in addition to a crisis center (name unknown) in Wichita, Kansas. As during the prior evaluation, Ms. Blocker endorsed a long pattern of substance abuse, including the use of alcohol, cannabis, cocaine, methamphetamine, heroin, and huffing paint. She stated she had undergone impatient substance abuse treatment on numerous occasions.

Psychological Testing include Test of Memory Malingering (TOMM) states that Ms. Blocker was administered the TOMM, an assessment measure used to distinguish bona fide memory impairment from feigning. This instrument was designed such that even person with severe cognitive impairment, including dementia and traumatic brain injury, perform very well. Ms. Blocker's scores (out of 50 possible points) were as follows in comparison to reference groups:

Reference Group	Trial 1	Trial 2	Retention Trial
No cognitive impairment	47.9	50	50
Aphasia	46.3	49.3	49.8
Traumatic Brain Injury	45.9	49.4	49.6
Cognitive Impairment	45.9	48.6	49.5
Dementia	41.0	45.7	47
Instructed to malinger	32.5	35.3	30.9
Ms. Blocker	35	46	46

Although Ms. Blocker's score on Trial 1 was very low and similar to the standardization group instructed to malinger, it was not statistically low enough to warrant an interpretation of feigning. Therefore, Trial 2 and the retention Trial should only then be interpreted. According to the test manual any score lower than 45 or either of those trials should raise concern that the individual is likely malingering. Given that Ms. Blocker's scores did not meet that criterion the appropriate interpretation is that she did not attempt to feign memory impairment on this measure.

Structured Interview of Reported Symptoms, Second Edition (SIRS-2) states that based on Ms. Blocker's behavior and the absence of any over genuine signs of severe mental illness, possible feigning was suspected. She was administered the SIRS-2, an objective test specifically designed to detect feigning of psychological symptoms. The SIRS-2 consists of eight primary scales which are interpreted based upon classification and/or index scales to determine the likelihood an individual is feigning mental illness versus providing a genuine presentation. The primary scale scores may fall in four ranges: Definite range of feigning (Markedly Elevated), Probable range of feigning (Moderately

Elevated), Indeterminate range (Neither indicative of feigning or honesty) and Genuine range (Suggesting honest responding.)

Ms. Blocker's results for the Primary and Classifications Scales were as follows.

Primary Scale	Description	Results
Rare Symptoms (RS)	Measures an individual's tendency to endorse symptoms that occur infrequently in psychiatric patients.	Indeterminate Range
Symptom Combinations (SC)	Measures an individual's tendency to endorse pairs of symptoms and other indicators of psychopathology that are seldom observed together.	Indeterminate Range
Improbable or Absurd Symptoms (A)	Measures an individual's tendency to endorse symptoms of a fantastic or preposterous quality.	Genuine range
Blatant Symptoms (BL)	Measures over-endorsement of symptoms which are obvious signs of a mental disorder to untrained individuals.	Indeterminate Range
Subtle Symptoms (SU)	Measures an individual's tendency to endorse a very high proportion of everyday problems and symptoms that are not always	Definite Range

Primary Scale	Description	Results
	associated with mental illness.	
Selectivity of Symptoms (SEL)	Measures an individual's tendency to indiscriminately endorse a wide range of psychiatric symptoms.	Probable Range
Severity of Symptoms (SEV)	Measures an individual's tendency to endorse a high proportion of symptoms of extreme or unbearable severity	Definite Range
Reported versus Observed Symptoms (RO)	Measure an individual's tendency to report behavioral symptoms that are not observable during the course of the interview.	Genuine Range

Ms. Blocker had several elevated Primary Scale scores, including two in the Definite Range and One in the probable Range. However her score on the Classification Scare (RS-Total) did not rise to the level to be classified as feigning. Ms. Blockers' score on the MT Index (of 19) placed her in the "Indeterminate-General category". In the standardization sample, approximately 34% of persons with scores at this level were found to be feigning. However, this score alone does not provide evidence for feigning. With such individuals it may be clinically determined that further evaluation is necessary.

Responses to Court Ordered Items states questions: Is this person able to appreciate the nature of the charges made against such person and the answer is yes. When asked about the charge against her Ms. Blocker at times noted that "I really don't understand." However, when asked to explain she clarified that her version of events did not equate to a murderous act as charged by the prosecution. Ms. Blocker's statements clearly supported that she had a factual and rational understanding of her current situation. She listed her charge as "first degree murder" for "killing Erik [by] blunt force trauma to the head". She understood that her liberty was in jeopardy and she was motivated to avoid incarceration, voicing "I've been told by my attorney I could get life without...meaning I would spend the rest of my life in prison." It is the opinion of this examiner that Ms. Blocker can appreciate the nature of the charge against her.

In answer to the question is this person able to consult with the lawyer and rationally assist in the preparation of the defense of such person, the answer is yes. Consistent with her prior experiences in the criminal justice system, Ms. Blocker demonstrated sufficient knowledge of basic legal terminology and processes. She accurately described the purpose of a trial, all key legal roles (e.g. judge, jury, prosecutor, defense attorney, and witnesses), her primary available pleas (guilty, not guilty, not guilty by reason of insanity, etc.), and the process of plea bargaining. She understood that defendants typically accept plea bargains "because they're guilty and they're usually a good deal so you don't have to go to trial," whereas the prosecution obtained "a conviction." She stated that she was offered a plea bargain of "45 years" in her case, which she agreed to but then "changed my mind and wrote the judge and [her attorney]." She understood that if she proceeded to trial and lost she could "get life without" but she maintained she was innocent of the alleged offense and was willing to take the risk. While her decision making may not achieve results in her best interests, it is not impaired by mental illness or cognitive deficits. Ms. Blocker did not voice any paranoid ideations or delusions about the criminal justice system, though she believed that she was being treated fairly based upon the facts at hand in the case.

Ms. Blocker identified her attorney as "David Smith" and she estimated they had met "four times in 18 months." She stated she essentially had no opinion of Mr. Smith, describing him as "Just another attorney. I've been in trouble before, just not quite this serious." She stated shed had no specific reason to mistrust him and outlined one possible alternative she hoped he would achieve in this case, though it appeared unrealistic. She indicated she had informed him of her version of the alleged offense and "He believes me." However, she also noted that he disagreed with how she wanted to proceed in the case for a defense, voicing, "I sent a letter to him asking him to withdraw from the case and wrote a letter to Judge Walkley saying my attorney didn't have my best interests and asked her to appoint another attorney." Ms. Blocker indicated that her request was not granted.

Ms. Blocker outlined her vision of what occurred prior to, during, and following the alleged offense. The information she provided was coherent, rational, plausible and goal-directed. She recognized that her alleged statements to police might be used to incriminate her, as well as "the autopsy" of the victim which she stated indicated he suffered a "brain aneurysm." Ms. Blocker outlined an extensive number of facts that she believed were exculpatory and/or mitigating. Though the effectiveness of that information for a defense is highly questionable, none of the information she provided was bizarre in irrelevant to the case at hand. Ms. Blocker had an appropriate appreciation for the strength of the evidence against her in this case.

Ms. Blocker knew how a defendant was expected to behave in court and she stated that if she believed an opposing witness was dishonest she would "talk to my lawyer." She has the capacity to behave appropriately during proceedings as she did throughout this evaluation. However, as noted earlier, given her personality traits she may choose to react inappropriately if angered. Ms. Blocker stated she was unaware of her Fifth Amendment right to avoid testimony or that she could be cross-examined should she testify. She was educated about these facts and easily understood. Based upon her ability to discuss her version of events in a rational and coherent manner, it is the opinion of this examiner that she could appropriately testify in her defense should she decided to do so.

In summary, Ms. Blocker evidenced no cognitive impairment or signs of mental illness interfering with competency related abilities. Though she may be unrealistic about her proposed defense or the outcome she expects her attorney to achieve, this is not the result of a mental illness. Her personality traits may pose a substantial challenge in her legal representation and she could make very poor decisions in her case. Nonetheless, Ms. Blocker has the capacity to consult with her attorney to rationally assist in her defense, should she choose to do so.

To the question if the person is unable to appreciate the nature of the changes or to consult and rationally assist in the preparation of the defense, whether the person can attain competency within a reasonable period of time as defined in section 1175.1 of this title if provided with a course of treatment, therapy, or training? The answer was not applicable.

In answer to the question is this person a person requiring treatment as defined by Section 1-103 of Title 43A of the Oklahoma Statues? The answer was No. As noted earlier Ms. Blocker endorses extensive symptoms of mental illness, but exhibits no signs of such. She is currently receiving psychotropic medication in the detention center. Therefore, it is unclear if her symptoms are appropriately controlled, or if she actually has no underlying severe mental illness. As during this examiner's previous evaluation Ms. Blocker appears very well aware of mental health terminology and appears to be exaggerating problems of the very least. She does not meet the Oklahoma state statutory criteria for inpatient psychiatric treatment at the present time. It should be noted that Ms. Blocker reported past diagnosis with Borderline Personality Disorder and she has a history of assaultive behavior when angered. The diagnostic and Statistical Manual of Mental disorder-Fourth Edition Test Revision describes Borderline Personality Disorder as characterized by as pervasive pattern of instability of Interpersonal relationships, self-image, and emotions, and marked impulsivity that begins by early adulthood and is present in a variety of context, such individuals are sensitive to environmental circumstances and have a pattern of unstable and intense relationships with others they are prone to sudden shifts in their opinions about others and their own self-image., they display impulsivity in areas of life that are potentially self-damaging (i.e.

substance abuse, careless spending, etc.) they have a marked reactivity in mood and may display periods of anger, panic or despair, they frequently express inappropriate, intense anger or have difficulty controlling their anger, and they may display extreme sarcasm, enduring bitterness, or verbal outbursts. It is the opinion of this examiner that Ms. Blocker was not experiencing symptoms of bipolar disorder (i.e. mania) or a psychotic disorder (i.e. Schizophrenia) during this evaluation. However, such diagnoses are often misapplied to individuals with borderline Personality disorder due to their proneness for volatile behavior.

To the question of the person is incompetent because the person is mentally retarded as defined in Section 1408 of title 10 of the Oklahoman Statutes, the question response is not applicable.

To the question if the answer to this is no, why is the defendant incompetent must be explained and to this it is not applicable. To the question if the person were released, whether such person would presently be dangerous as defined in Section 1175.1 of this title, the answer was no. Ms. Blocker claimed past suicidal behavior, the validity of which is unknown. She has not reportedly engaged in any such behavior during her incarceration, though she has voiced suicidal thoughts. During the current evaluation she denied any recent or current thoughts/plans to harm herself. Ms. Blocker has a history of assaultive behavior towards others and prior conviction for a violent offense. The current charge of murder is also a violent offense, though she remains innocent until convicted. CCDC staff indicated that she has been aggressive towards other inmates during her current incarceration. Her behavior was very well controlled during this evaluation and she did not meet the criteria for inpatient psychiatric treatment in my opinion. Therefore, based on all of the available data it is the opinion of this examiner that Ms. Blocker would not presently meet the statutory criteria for dangerousness if released. It should be noted that this is not a formal assessment of her level of dangerousness in the future. which is beyond the scope of the Court ordered question. If she became intoxicated with alcohol, illicit drugs, inhalants or prescription medication it could raise her assessed level of risk significantly. This opinion obviously does not factor in the possibility that Ms. Blocker poses a danger to others due to antisocial behavior, which is not the same as being a danger to others secondary to a mental illness requiring inpatient psychiatric treatment (the criteria for the current statutory question). Ms. Blocker's history of violence towards others is clearly a concern and it is strongly recommended that she receive a thorough risk assessment for future dangerousness prior to release.

The Report Summary states that it is in the opinion of this examiner that Ms. Blockier can appreciate the nature of the charge against her and she can consult with her attorney to rationally assist in her defense though she may be unrealistic about her proposed defense or the outcome she expects her attorney to achieve. Given her personality traits she may pose a substantial challenge in legal representation and she could make very poor decisions in her case. As noted earlier, Ms. Blocker endorses extensive symptoms of mental illness, but exhibits no sign of such. She is currently receiving psychotropic medication in the detention center. Therefore it is unclear if her symptoms are appropriately controlled, or if she actually has no underlying severe mental illness. As during this examiner's previous evaluation, Ms. Blocker appears very well aware of mental health terminology and appears to be exaggerating problems at the very least. She does not meet the Oklahoma State statutory criteria for inpatient psychiatric treatment at the present time. It should be noted that Ms. Blocker reported past diagnosis with Borderline Personality disorder and she has a history of assaultive behavior when angered. While she would not presently meet the statutory criteria for dangerousness if released due to a mental illness requiring inpatient psychiatric treatment, she may pose a danger to others due to antisocial behavior. Ms. Blocker's history of violence toward others is clearly a concern and it is strongly recommended that she receive a thorough risk assessment for future dangerousness prior to release.

Submitted by Shawn Roberson, Ph.D., forensic Psychologist, Oklahoma Forensic Center, Oklahoma Psychology License #914.

###

On April 24, 2012 more charges are filed. A charge for Judgement and Sentencing (J&S) and the issuance of the outcome being life in prison with recognition for the period of incarceration prior to sentence. The final posting is the Oklahoma Court Information System Revolving Fund charge and finally the cost realized for transporting Clara Ann Blocker to prison. All of these fees are included in the total mentioned earlier.

##

On May 1, 2012 the Attachment A appeared. This document stated that "The Defendant, Clara Ann Blocker, is ordered by the attached judgment and sentence to repay the court fund of Cleveland County.

The May 23, 2012 document was the Return Judgment & Sentence document. It continued with fees such as the Victim Compensation Assessment, jail fees forthcoming covering her incarceration, and attorney fees. The final paragraph stated:

"In the event the above sentence is for incarceration in the Department of Corrections, the sheriff of Cleveland County, Oklahoma is ordered and directed to deliver the Defendant to the Lexington Assessment and Reception Center at Lexington, Oklahoma, and leave therewith a copy of this Judgment and Sentence to serve as warrant and authority for the imprisonment of the Defendant as provided herein. A second copy of this Judgment and sentence to be warrant and authority of the Sheriff for the transportation and imprisonment of the Defendant as hereinbefore provided. The sheriff to make due return to the Clerk of this Court, with his proceedings endorsed thereon. "

This was signed by Judge Walkley. On May 17 the original transcript of the proceedings was available and I placed my order for a copy. It was received a few weeks later.

On July 12, 2012 the final post was a notice of the Witness fees paid by the District Attorney being added to the costs owed by Clara Ann Blocker. The cost incurred is shown as $189.00.

###

This ended the posting on the Oklahoma States Court Network (OSCN). Now I wait to be notified of the appearance of the information on Clara Ann Blocker at the Oklahoma Department Of

Corrections site. I am sent the web address and immediately log on. Now instead of using the Case Number, Clara has a Oklahoma Department Of Corrections (ODOC) #:423584 with pictures dating back to June 5, 2002. She is listed as a White Female; 5 ft. 10 in. tall; 150 pounds; Brown hair; Blue eyes. All of her tattoos and previous incarcerations in Oklahoma are shown and they total four, starting in 2006. This of course is not the total convictions, just the ones in this state alone.

These days she does have an address and it is the Mabel Bassett Correctional Center, at 29501 Kickapoo Road, McCloud, OK 74851 and she can be reached through Warden, Debbie Aldridge. The site shows that for the Case # 2010-1390 listed in Cleveland County as Murder In The First Degree (85%), Clara was convicted on 04/17/2012   for a LIFE Sentence that begins on 05/09/2012, but has no ending.

The warden, Ms. Aldridge, appears to be around 50 or 60 years of age with short gray hair, oversized glasses and a non-nonsense smirk on her face in the picture posted.

The Mabel Bassett Correctional Center (MBCC) is the only medium-security institution for women in the state of Oklahoma and was originally located in northeast Oklahoma City, adjacent to the Oklahoma Department of Corrections (ODOC) Administration Building. In 1978, the center was changed to a medium-security facility then in 1982, Mabel Bassett was converted to include maximum security with offenders ranging from minimum security to death row.

The institution has a capacity of 1,139 minimum and medium security offenders and 102 offenders in assessment and reception.

The demographics in this facility ranges around 4 percent Hispanic, 12 percent Native American, less than 1 percent Pacific Islanders and 70% Caucasians, with violent offenders being around 18 percent and nonviolent offenders ranging around 82%.

On the outside the facility appear as a big white cement building with a wide glass entranceway, neat landscaping and a deep blue paint trim on the top and lower area of the building. The building is surrounded by a bob wire fence that is curled at the top and has a tall white guard tower situated at the left side of the building.

At the front entrance there is the Oklahoma Department of Corrections Sign at the base of a flag pole before the high wired fencing. For all intents and purposes as you pull up in front of the building, it looks quite nice.

From photos posted of the inside it is a total different viewpoint. The inside is in need of repair with peeling paint on the outside walls of the cell area. The rotunda that sits in the center of the cell housings is a square cement unit surrounded by a circular wall of white bars. At the top of this two story structure is a square box room encased in bars.

A view of the non-contact visitation area has wooden topped stools to sit on in front of the glass paned windows. The floors are alternating brown, yellow and white panels. On the non-contact visitation area there are regular chairs, paneling and a more pleasant decor.

The visitation area has laminate wood like tables with bright orange chairs. There is a viewing area window at the upper end of the wall. The entrance past the administrative building has a limit of 5 people at a time behind a gray vertical metal gate. There are four levels of cells on either side of a very wide hall way on the first floor.

Clara's incarceration at this site started on May 9, 2012 but this was not her first time at this facility. Before this she had been in this same facility for robbery and was in for a 5 year sentence from June 2002 to February 2006. Also she had a conviction and was sentenced to this facility for possession of Meth. That sentence was set for 10 years, starting in January of 2008 and ending in January of 2018, only her sentence had been suspended.

So there were several times that this defendant had an address, being 29501 Kickapoo Road, McCloud, Oklahoma. She was in the Mabel Bassett Correction Center first under Warden Rickey Moham and this time it will be Warden, Debbie Aldridge.

##

I read every word in the psychiatric review in the hopes that Clara gave her reasons why she did what she did, but she still does not say the 'why' for her actions beyond trying to appear as having a lot of mental problems. Are they true? I do not know or wish to know because in my book there is no excuse for killing.

CHAPTER 26: CLOSURE

As I write this I am slowly beginning to accept that Erik's time came and though I could not be there to console him, I was there later to touch him one more time and tell him how much I loved him and always will.

Now I will force myself to remember the best times of his life the time when we laughed until our stomach hurt. The birthday candles that lit up his face as he blew them out. The movies we watched together, and the meals we shared.

I will remember the first time he got on the school bus and waved goodbye and the clothes that I lovingly sewed for him each year. I will recall the serious and funny talks we would have and the joy of putting him to bed at night. These are the memories I will keep in my heart, now and for always.

Being a parent I have experienced the greatest amazement in his birth and the greatest despair at his loss. But in between these two extremes are the many moments of learning, joy, anticipation, pride, sorrow, sadness, and above all unconditional love.

It is not easy, but necessary to know that no one wants to face an accident, illness, loss or violence because few get through safe and sound. But the odds are not in our favor to not have this happen. At least 75% of us will experience a traumatic event in our lifetime and these episodes will cause great suffering. But they can also be a powerful force for positive change.

Trauma will change your life. Some people will have negative effects, but the majority can have positive changes. Those who survive the trauma say it has given them greater inner strength and they learned to live their lives in positive ways and just like me, they can recall so much detail of the period before and after the event.

I have written most of the experience down while it happens, but some things I did not. As I understand, it has something to do with how our mind claims memories.

Each year approximately 15,000 men, women, and children are victims of criminal homicide in the United States. As staggering as that figure is, it does not begin to indicate the toll of suffering that homicide causes because the survivors of a homicide can be conservatively estimated at approximately a half million wounded and scarred Americans, all victims of the murders of just the past decade.

That is why it is important to learn how to cope with murder. I know that learning of a loved one's murder is intense, sudden, and virtually impossible to understand and this is why most survivors face a long period of emotional struggle to reconstruct their lives.

It is normal, in the case of murder, the survivor becomes involved with the criminal justice system. Most survivors turn to the criminal justice system for a special kind of emotional support, as well as practical support in their passion to see the assailant apprehended, prosecuted, convicted, and punished. When this happens, as it did in my case, the journey to acceptance is much easier to tread.

There will always be the guilt from knowing that in the natural order of things, parents almost always die before their children. Hence the shock of death of one's child, compounded by murder is exacerbated.

Parents assume a natural role of protectors of their offspring. We need protect them from illnesses or natural disasters, so it seems logical we could have, and therefore should have, been able to protect our son or daughter from the murderer. This sense of protectiveness increases parental guilt and self-blame. It takes me some time to realize that Erik was grown with more control over his life than I could claim. If I can accept that it was not Erik's fault that this happened, then I must accept it was not mine.

I was able to raise Erik during a time when being black was looked down upon and being a dwarf caused even more of a stir. Yet somehow I found ways to protect and help him grow and except just who he was. That was quite a feat in itself and that makes me proud.

Murder is unquestionably the worst thing that one person can do to another. For its survivors, murder is a terrible tragedy. It shatters much of what was joyous and valuable in our lives. There is no cure for the aftermath of murder, but survivors can find help, can find understanding, and can construct a new life with a renewed sense of purpose. They can survive.

There are two important factors that I dwell on today. The first is that during a time when the police and courts are looked upon with disfavor, my experience was totally different. In Erik's case the police worked diligently and put in long hours to apprehend the murderer and prove her guilt. There was no evidence of the police looking at Erik as a black person and a dwarf and thus not proceeding conscientiously to capture his murderer, even after it was learned the guilty party was a white female. I know this to be true as each person involved in the case not only kept in touch with me, but after the case was over, willingly gave me all the information that they had accrued during and after the case concluded.

The interviews, the witnesses, and the steps involved in good police work were what kept the time schedule below that of the norm and with the awareness I applaud the police and the justice system in Oklahoma City, Oklahoma.

Just as important is the reality that I have accepted. The "anniversary date" of the murder is always a painful reminder of the death, but I know the date will not be distressing forever because my memories of the good times will overcome the bad. Holidays, birthdays, and other formerly-happy events will not be marred by his death, because I can conjure up the fond memories of yesteryear that will make the dates bittersweet.

I will probably never know what really happened that fateful day, September, 15, 2010. I have written a letter to Clara Blocker at the prison and previously tried to get her to tell me why she murdered my son, but she does not respond, so I have tried to put it all together and come up with what happened that day.

###

Clara Blocker was feeling the first signs of withdrawal and needed money. She searched her backpack for money, but doesn't have anything left. She needed to get some real drugs if she was going to make it through the day. In her bag she shuffled through her meds and may have thought about taking some of them to give her a buzz, but no matter how many of these she takes, whether it is the antidepressants, the bipolar medication, or the psychotics she knows they will not produce a "high" All they can do is help her to function normally and her normal is not something she wants to deal with. Besides taking them will interfere with the high she can get if she can reach her supplier.

It's too early to try and reach her supplier so she goes into the bedroom and wakes up Erik. It doesn't bother her that though she has been staying with him for less than a month, he is scared of her. It could play to her advantage.

Erik gets up, takes a shower, brushes his teeth and gets dress. He goes into the kitchen and takes his pills and then asks Clara if she has taken her meds.

Clara ignores him and Erik knows that she is quite antsy and short tempered lately so stays quiet. When he enters the living room, Clara tells him she's going out for a bit. She leaves the apartment.

Erik has seen Clara this way before. Their mutual acquaintance, David Elkin asks if Clara could stay with him while he takes care of some business out of town. Erik tells David it is fine with him, even after David lets him know that Clara has just been released recently from prison for selling and using drugs. Erik believes everyone deserves second chance. After all he has had to face being a little person and being partially paralyzed, he knows how hard it is to get accepted.

Clara is out most of the day and when she returns it is late afternoon. Erik goes about his day, leaving the apartment at one point and when he returns Clara is waiting for him. He opens the door and once inside, Clara goes over to lay on the mat of blankets that she has made for sleeping. She tries to sleep. She hasn't slept in three days and the mental distress is getting worse. She lays awake now with that nagging anxiety... exhausted but every time she feels close to falling asleep she gets excited and sleep continues to evade her. Her nose starts running and she has to get up and get a Kleenex.

Clara makes a call and reaches Chase who she talks into coming over and bringing some alcohol with him. Erik doesn't have anything hard to drink in the apartment. When Chase arrives he has a fifth of Tvarscki Vodka and Clara starts drinking immediately, trying to stop the stomach pains that are getting worst by the minute.

The friend leaves once the bottle is empty and Clara and Erik are alone.

Clara asks Erik if he has any money and he says he doesn't. Clara doesn't believe him and heads into his bedroom to check for herself. Erik enters the bedroom and though he is almost half her height, tells her to stop.

Clara is sweating, yawning, eye watering, and the stomach pains are unbearable. She is extremely agitated and out of control as she picks up the lava lamp on the bedroom table. She hits Erik on the back of his head, causing him to fall. Erik gets up and leaves the bedroom, making it across the living room when he hears Clara behind him and turns around to face her. Clara is beyond control as she asks him to tell her where his money is but Erik does not tell her.

Clara looks around and grabs the CD player off the stand and comes toward Erik who is still not fully recovered from the blow on the back of his head. Clara smashes the CD player into Erik's face. He falls on the floor in front of the sofa and doesn't get up.

Clara has only one focus and that is to find his money. She checks his pockets and finds his wallet. Inside she finds several hundred dollars and she takes it. Looking down she sees that there is blood on her shirt so she goes into the bathroom and takes the shirt off and tries to wash the stain in the sink. She goes to her backpack and gets out a fresh shirt.

Clara sees the letter in her backpack from her girlfriend, Teresa Stanfield and that makes her anger grow. This was her girlfriend and she wants to be with her but she is in jail. Not only that, but she is pregnant. She has been cheating on her.

Clara tries calling her supplier, but gets no answer. She goes outside and tries again, getting anxious by the minute. She needs to get a hold of him and soon. She notices that her phone is about to run out of minutes so she calls her friend David and reaches him. She asks if he can take her to get some minutes on her phone and he says that he will and asks if she has the money. She assures him that she does. He comes and picks her up and takes her to the store. On the way back she tells him she doesn't know if Erik will let her in and David assures her that Erik is a good guy and he will let her in. David explains that he will be able to take her back to his place in a few days, but can't right now.

Clara's day is going from bad to worse. She can't reach her supplier, is stuck here at Erik's apartment since David can't let her stay with him right now and she is going through the pains of withdrawal.

Clara gets out of his car and goes to the apartment door. She knocks on the door, but Erik doesn't answer. She keeps trying, banging loudly and drawing attention to herself until finally she stops and tries her supplier. As she talks on the phone, two women go by and she makes lewd comments at them, and then turns back to the phone.

Her dealer is asking what she wants and she tells him. She tells him she has two hundred dollars and after a few minutes hangs up the phone.

Her dealer tells her where to meet him, only she doesn't have a way to get there. It's too far to walk and David ha said he was on his way out of town when he dropped her off. Her day has just gotten worse.

Clara bangs loudly on the door, yelling at Erik to open up and finally, either because he doesn't want to disturb the neighbors; Erik relents and opens the door. Even in her condition, she can tell that Erik is in bad shape, but that's not her problem. Clara gives in now to taking her meds as she knows she won't be getting a fix tonight. The pain is tremendous now and she falls down on the mat of blankets, curls up in a ball and drifts off to sleep, waking back up as soon as she finally thinks she will get some sleep.

Morning comes quickly and Clara gets up. She looks over and sees that Erik is still lying on the floor in front of the couch where he fell the night before. She walks past him and goes into the bathroom to clean up and work out how she will be able to get a fix. When she comes out, she sees Erik is still laying there and she panics. She goes over to him. He is barely breathing and doesn't respond as she calls his name.

Like a caged animal she paces back and forth trying to decide what to do. Erik needs help. If he should die she would be in more trouble than she has been before.

Back and forth she walks until finally deciding she must call for help. She dial's 911.

www.ingramcontent.com/pod-product-compliance
Lightning Source LLC
Chambersburg PA
CBHW020331270326
41926CB00007B/128